AQA

PE

①

Symond Burrows
Ross Howitt
Sue Young

Editor: Mike Murray

AQA

PE

1

Carl Atherton
Symond Burrows
Ross Howitt
Sue Young

Editor: Mike Murray

Approval message from AQA

This textbook has been approved by AQA for use with our qualification. This means that we have checked that it broadly covers the specification and we are satisfied with the overall quality. Full details of our approval process can be found on our website.

We approve textbooks because we know how important it is for teachers and students to have the right resources to support their teaching and learning. However, the publisher is ultimately responsible for the editorial control and quality of this book.

Please note that when teaching the **AQA PE** course, you must refer to AQA's specification as your definitive source of information. While this book has been written to match the specification, it cannot provide complete coverage of every aspect of the course.

A wide range of other useful resources can be found on the relevant subject pages of our website: www.aqa.org.uk.

DYNAMIC LEARNING

HODDER EDUCATION
AN HACHETTE UK COMPANY

The Publishers would like to thank the following for permission to reproduce copyright material.

Photo credits

p.1 © Blend Images/Alamy Stock Photo; **p.18** © AlexBrylov – Thinkstock/iStock/Getty Images; **p.29** © Stefan Schurr – Fotolia; **p.30** *t* © shironosov – iStockphoto via Thinkstock/Getty Images, *b* © berc – Fotolia; **p.37** © Claus AndersenAagard – Fotolia; **p.41** © Blend Images/Alamy Stock Photo; **p.42** *tl* © matthewennisphotography – iStockphoto via Thinkstock/Getty Images, *tr* © Patrick Khachfe/JMP/REX/Shutterstock, *b* © Giuseppe Bellini/Getty Images; **p.44** © Martin Rose/Bongarts/Getty Images; **p.45** © Digital Vision. – Photodisc via Thinkstock/Getty Images; **p.47** *t* © Bojan656 – iStockphoto via Thinkstock/Getty Images, *bl & br* © Antonio_Diaz – iStockphoto via Thinkstock/Getty Images; **p.48** © stefanschurr – Thinkstock/iStock/Getty Images; **p.49** © Vladimirs Koskins – Fotolia; **p.50** *tl* © Jupiterimages – Pixland via Thinkstock/Getty Images, *ct* Courtesy of the US Federal government via Wikipedia (Public Domain), *cb* © emanelda – Fotolia, *bl* © Boris Ryaposov – Fotolia, *bc* © fotokostic – iStockphoto via Thinkstock/Getty Images, *br* © Netfalls – Fotolia; **p.51** *l* © Stefan Schurr – Fotolia, *c* © Friday – Fotolia, *r* © Carlos Santa Maria – Fotolia; **p.52** *tl* © yanlev – Fotolia, *tr* © Aflo Co., Ltd./Alamy Stock Photo, *bl* © alan poulson – 123RF, *br* © frank trautvetter – Fotolia; **p.53** *t* © Comstock – Stockbyte via Thinkstock/Getty Images, *b* © yanlev – Fotolia; **p.54** *l* Johnny Lye – Fotolia, *r* © Jupiterimages – Pixland via Thinkstock/Getty Images; **p.55** *tl* © Lucy Clark - Hemera via Thinkstock/Getty Images, *tr* © Kzenon – Fotolia, *bl* © Stefan Schurr – Fotolia, *bc* © Greg Epperson – Fotolia, *br* © Fredrick Kippe/Alamy Stock Photo; **p.57** *t* © Imagestate Media (John Foxx)/Vol 08 Modern Lifestyles, *b* © Fuse/Getty Images; **p.58** © .shock – Fotolia; **p.60** © Fuse/Getty Images; **p.65** © PCN Photography/Alamy Stock Photo; **p.66** *t* © beardean – iStock via Thinkstock/Getty Images, *b* © Mike Ehrmann/Getty Images; **p.67** © Monkey Business – Fotolia; **p.72** *t* © XiXinXing – iStock via Thinkstock/Getty Images, *b* © Blend Images/Alamy Stock Photo; **p.73** © Brian McEntire – iStock via Thinkstock/Getty Images; **p.74** © Stockbyte via Thinkstock/Getty Images; **p.75** © CARL DE SOUZA/AFP/Getty Images; **p.76** *l* © imageBROKER/Alamy Stock Photo, *r* © nojustice – iStock via Thinkstock/Getty Images, *bl* © Fuse/Getty Images; **p.77** © Imagestate Media (John Foxx) Leisure Time V3072; **p.79** © Fuse/Getty Images; **p.80** © ViktorCap – iStock via Thinkstock/Getty Images; **p.82** © Roger Sedres/Alamy Stock Photo; **p.84** © Wikipedia (http://creativecommons.org/licenses/by-sa/3.0/); **p.101** *l* © 2003 Topham Picturepoint, *r* © Topfoto; **p.103** © courtesy of the AAA; **p.110** © Dan Mullan/Getty Images; **p.133** © VeselovaElena – Thinkstock/iStock/Getty Images; **p.134** © ranplett/ iStockphoto; **p.135** *t* © tinalarsson – iStock via Thinkstock/Getty Images, *b* © Africa Studio – Fotolia; **p.136** © Serghei Velusceac – Fotolia; **p.137** *t* © Radu Sebastian – iStock via Thinkstock/Getty Images, *b* © Nic_Ol – iStock via Thinkstock/Getty Images; **p.139** © Charlie Crowhurst/Getty Images; **p.142** © Mark Nolan/Getty Images; **p.145** © Andres Rodriguez – Fotolia; **p.151** © LUNAMARINA – iStock via Thinkstock/Getty Images; **p.153** © Stockbyte/Thinkstock/Getty Images; **p.155** © Zoonar GmbH/Alamy Stock Photo; **p.158** © Jupiterimages – Pixland via Thinkstock/Getty Images; **p.162** © shironosov – Thinkstock /iStock/Getty Images; **p.164** *t* © Alison Bowden – Fotolia, *b* © emanelda – Fotolia; **p.165** © Mike Watson Images – Moodboard via Thinkstock/Getty Images, *b* © Fuse/Getty Images; **p.166** *t* © Deklofenak – Fotolia, *b* © Maridav – Fotolia; **p.167** *t* © definitely_a_fan – iStock via Thinkstock/Getty Images, *b* © fulvio eterno – Fotolia; **p.170** © The World of Sports SC/REX/Shutterstock; **p.171** *t* © Comstock - Stockbyte via Thinkstock/Getty Images, *b* © ArtmannWitte – Fotolia; **p.172** © 36clicks – iStock via Thinkstock/Getty Images; **p.173** © PCN Photography/Alamy Stock Photo; **p.174** © Ben Queenborough/BPI/REX/Shutterstock; **p.176** *l* © shironosov – Thinkstock/iStock/Getty Images, *r* © Design Pics via Thinkstock/Getty Images; **p.177** *t* © epa european pressphoto agency b.v./Alamy Stock Photo, *b* © Oscar Gonzalez/NurPhoto/REX/Shutterstock; **p.181** *t* © James Marsh/BPI/REX/Shutterstock, *b* © Cultura Creative (RF)/Alamy Stock Photo; **p.182** *r* © REX/Shutterstock, *l* © Vasily Smirnov – Fotolia; **p.184** *t* © Image Source Plus/Alamy Stock Photo, *b* © Aaron Lupton/ProSports/REX/Shutterstock; **p.185** © imageBROKER/REX/Shutterstock; **p.187** *l* © HelloWorld Images Premium/Alamy Stock Photo, *r* © Greg Epperson – Fotolia; **p.189** © Fuse – Getty Images; **p.190** *t* © Christina Bollen/Alamy Stock Photo, *c* © REX/Shutterstock, *b* © Milenko Bokan – iStock via Thinkstock/Getty Images; **p.191** *l* © Simon Balson/Alamy Stock Photo, *r* © pam burley – 123RF; **p.193** © rbouwman – iStock via Thinkstock/Getty Images; **p.194** *t* © Monkey Business – Fotolia, *b* © BPI/BPI/REX/Shutterstock; **p.195** © Matt West/BPI/REX/Shutterstock; **p.196** *r* © Alex Livesey/Getty Images, *b* © Stu Forster/Getty Images; **p.197** *l* © V.RUMI – Fotolia, *r* © Cultura RM/Alamy Stock Photo; **p.199** © Paul Grover/REX/Shutterstock; **p.200** © AMA/Corbis via Getty Images; **p.201** © Wavebreak Media Ltd – 123RF; **p.203** © Sipa Press/REX/Shutterstock; **p.204** © Sasha Samardzija/Alamy Stock Photo; **p.205** *t* © massimhokuto – Fotolia, *b* © PCN Photography/Alamy Stock Photo; **p.207** © Magi Haroun/REX/Shutterstock; **p.208** © BSIP, LAURENT/B. HOP AME/SCIENCE PHOTO LIBRARY; **p.210** © GUSTOIMAGES/SCIENCE PHOTO LIBRARY; **p.213** https://commons.wikimedia.org/wiki/File:Ergospirometry_laboratory.jpg - https://creativecommons.org/licenses/by-sa/3.0/deed.en; **p.214** © Iain Masterton/Alamy Stock Photo; **p.216** © Pete Saloutos/Getty Images; **p.222** © Cultura RM/Alamy Stock Photo; **p.223** © xalanx – 123RF; **p.224** *t* © Jasper Juinen/Getty Images, *c* © PHILIPPE HUGUEN/AFP/Getty Images, *b* © IAN KINGTON/AFP/Getty Images; **p.225** © Cathy Yeulet – 123RF; **p.226** *l & r* © Cathy Yeulet – 123RF; **p.230** © Blend Images/Alamy Stock Photo; **p.231** © David Rogers/Getty Images; **p.243** *tl* © matthewennisphotography – iStockphoto via Thinkstock/Getty Images, *tr* © Patrick Khachfe/JMP/REX/Shutterstock, *b* © Giuseppe Bellini/Getty Images.

Acknowledgements

Every effort has been made to trace all copyright holders, but if any have been inadvertently overlooked, the Publishers will be pleased to make the necessary arrangements at the first opportunity. Although every effort has been made to ensure that website addresses are correct at time of going to press, Hodder Education cannot be held responsible for the content of any website mentioned in this book. It is sometimes possible to find a relocated web page by typing in the address of the home page for a website in the URL window of your browser.

Hachette UK's policy is to use papers that are natural, renewable and recyclable products and made from wood grown in sustainable forests. The logging and manufacturing processes are expected to conform to the environmental regulations of the country of origin.

Orders: please contact Bookpoint Ltd, 130 Park Drive, Milton Park, Abingdon, Oxon OX14 4SE.

Telephone: (44) 01235 827720. Fax: (44) 01235 400454. Email education@bookpoint.co.uk Lines are open from 9 a.m. to 5 p.m., Monday to Saturday, with a 24-hour message answering service. You can also order through our website: www.hoddereducation.co.uk

ISBN: 978 1 4718 5956 4

© Carl Atherton, Symond Burrows, Ross Howitt, Sue Young 2016

This edition published in 2016 by

Hodder Education,

An Hachette UK Company

Carmelite House

50 Victoria Embankment

London EC4Y 0DZ

www.hoddereducation.co.uk

Impression number 10 9 8 7 6 5 4

Year 2020 2019 2018

Cover photo © Zena Holloway/Stone/Getty Images

Illustrations by Integra Software Services Pvt Ltd., Pondicherry, India

Typeset in 11/13pt ITC Berkeley Oldstyle Std Book by Integra Software Services Pvt. Ltd., Pondicherry, India

Printed in Italy

A catalogue record for this title is available from the British Library.

Contents

Introduction

This book has been written and designed specifically for the new AQA Physical Education specifications introduced for first teaching in September 2016.

AQA A-level Physical Education 1 covers the content required for AQA AS Physical Education (7581) for first examination in 2017 and **year 1** of AQA A-level Physical Education (7582) for first examination in 2018.

A separate book – **AQA A-level Physical Education 2** – covers the additional content required for AQA A-level Physical Education (7582).

To view the full specifications, and examples of assessment material, for AQA AS or AQA A-level Physical Education, please visit AQA's website: www.aqa.org.uk. The content of this book, as well as AQA A-level Physical Education 2, covers all topic options in the new specification.

How to use this book

Each chapter has a range of features that have been designed to present the course content in a clear and accessible way, to give you confidence and to support you in your revision and assessment preparation.

Chapter objectives
- Each chapter starts with a clear list of what is to be studied.

CHECK YOUR UNDERSTANDING
These questions have been designed specifically to help check that you have understood different topics.

STUDY HINTS
These are suggestions to help clarify what you should aim to learn.

ACTIVITIES
Activities appear throughout the book and have been designed to help you develop your understanding of various topics.

KEY TERMS
Key terms, in bold in the text, are defined.

PRACTICE QUESTIONS
These are questions to help you get used to the type of questions you may encounter in the exam.

SUMMARY
- These boxes contain summaries of what you have learned in each section.

Book coverage of specification content

AS content		A-level content		Covered in
	3.1.1 Applied anatomy and physiology		**3.1.1 Applied anatomy and physiology**	
3.1.1.2	Cardiovascular system	3.1.1.2	Cardiovascular system	Book 1, chapter 1.1
3.1.1.3	Respiratory system	3.1.1.3	Respiratory system	Book 1, chapter 1.2
3.1.1.4	Neuromuscular system	3.1.1.4	Neuromuscular system	Book 1, chapter 1.3
3.1.1.5	The musculoskeletal system and analysis of movement in physical activities	3.1.1.5	The musculoskeletal system and analysis of movement in physical activities	Book 1, chapter 1.4
		3.1.1.6	Energy systems	Book 2, chapter 1.1
	3.1.2 Skill acquisition		**2.1.2 Skill acquisition**	
3.1.2.1	Skill, skill continuums and transfer of skills	3.1.2.1	Skill, skill continuums and transfer of skills	Book 1, chapter 2.1
3.1.2.2	Impact of skill classification on structure of practice for learning	3.1.2.2	Impact of skill classification on structure of practice for learning	Book 1, chapter 2.1
3.1.2.3	Principles and theories of learning and performance	3.1.2.3	Principles and theories of learning and performance	Book 1, chapter 2.2
3.1.2.4	Use of guidance and feedback	3.1.2.4	Use of guidance and feedback	Book 1, chapter 2.2
		3.1.2.5.1	General information processing model	Book 2, chapter 2.1
		3.1.2.5.2	Efficiency of information processing	Book 2, chapter 2.1
	3.1.3 Sport and society		**3.1.3 Sport and society**	
3.1.3.1.1	Pre-industrial (pre-1780)	3.1.3.1.1	Pre-industrial (pre-1780)	Book 1, chapter 3.1
3.1.3.1.2	Industrial and post-industrial (1780–1900)	3.1.3.1.2	Industrial and post-industrial (1780–1900)	Book 1, chapter 3.1
3.1.3.1.3	Post World War II (1950 to present)	3.1.3.1.3	Post World War II (1950 to present)	Book 1, chapter 3.1
3.1.3.2.1	Sociological theory applied to equal opportunities	3.1.3.2.1	Sociological theory applied to equal opportunities	Book 1, chapter 3.2
	3.1.4 Exercise physiology		**3.2.1 Exercise physiology**	
3.1.4.1	Diet and nutrition and their effect on physical activity and performance	3.2.1.1	Diet and nutrition and their effect on physical activity and performance	Book 1, chapter 4.1
3.1.4.2	Preparation and training methods in relation to maintaining physical activity and performance	3.2.1.2	Preparation and training methods in relation to maintaining physical activity and performance	Book 1, chapter 4.2
		3.2.1.3	Injury prevention and the rehabilitation of injury	Book 2, chapter 3.1

	AS content		A-level content	Covered in
	3.1.5 Biomechanical movement		**3.2.2 Biomechanical movement**	
3.1.5.1	Biomechanical principles	3.2.2.1	Biomechanical principles	Book 1, chapter 5
3.1.5.2	Levers	3.2.2.2	Levers	Book 1, chapter 5
		3.2.2.3	Linear motion	Book 2, chapter 4.1
		3.2.2.4	Angular motion	Book 2, chapter 4.2
		3.2.2.5	Projectile motion	Book 2, chapter 4.3
		3.2.2.6	Fluid mechanics	Book 2, chapter 4.4
	3.1.6 Sport psychology		**3.2.3 Sport psychology**	
3.1.6.1.1	Aspects of personality	3.2.3.1.1	Aspects of personality	Book 1, chapter 6.1
3.1.6.1.2	Attitudes	3.2.3.1.2	Attitudes	Book 1, chapter 6.1
3.1.6.1.3	Arousal	3.2.3.1.3	Arousal	Book 1, chapter 6.1
3.1.6.1.4	Anxiety	3.2.3.1.4	Anxiety	Book 1, chapter 6.2
3.1.6.1.5	Aggression	3.2.3.1.5	Aggression	Book 1, chapter 6.2
3.1.6.1.6	Motivation	3.2.3.1.6	Motivation	Book 1, chapter 6.2
		3.2.3.1.7	Achievement motivation theory	Book 2, chapter 5.1
3.1.6.1.7	Social facilitation	3.2.3.1.8	Social facilitation	Book 1, chapter 6.3
3.1.6.1.8	Group dynamics	3.2.3.1.9	Group dynamics	Book 1, chapter 6.3
3.1.6.1.9	Importance of goal setting	3.2.3.1.10	Importance of goal setting	Book 1, chapter 6.3
		3.2.3.1.11	Attribution theory	Book 2, chapter 5.1
		3.2.3.1.12	Self-efficacy and confidence	Book 2, chapter 5.1
		3.2.3.1.13	Leadership	Book 2, chapter 5.1
		3.2.3.1.14	Stress management	Book 2, chapter 5.1
	3.1.7 Sport and society and the role of technology in physical activity and sport		**3.2.4 Sport and society and the role of technology in physical activity and sport**	
		3.2.4.1	Concepts of physical activity and sport	Book 2, chapter 7.1
		3.2.4.2	Development of elite performers in sport	Book 2, chapter 7.2
		3.2.4.3	Ethics in sport	Book 2, chapter 7.3
		3.2.4.4	Violence in sport	Book 2, chapter 7.4
		3.2.4.5	Drugs in sport	Book 2, chapter 7.5
		3.2.4.6	Sport and the law	Book 2, chapter 7.6
		3.2.4.7	Impact of commercialisation on physical activity and sport and the relationship between sport and the media	Book 2, chapter 7.7
3.1.7.1	The role of technology in physical activity and sport	3.2.4.8	The role of technology in physical activity and sport	Book 1, chapter 7 Book 2, chapter 7.8

Chapter 1.1
The cardiovascular system

During exercise there is an increased demand for oxygen to produce energy for the muscles to contract. The heart, lungs and blood all have to work together to supply the muscles with the oxygen and remove any waste products such as carbon dioxide and lactic acid that have been produced. You need to be able to understand how the cardiovascular (heart and blood) and respiratory (lungs) systems work together and how changes within these systems prior to exercise, during exercise of differing intensities, and during recovery, allow the body to meet the demands of exercise.

Chapter objectives

After reading this chapter you should be able to:

- Describe the cardiac conduction system.
- Explain the hormonal, neural and chemical regulation of responses during physical activity and sport.
- Describe the role of chemoreceptors, baroreceptors and proprioceptors in the regulation of responses during physical activity.
- Understand the impact of physical activity and sport on cardiac output, stroke volume and heart rate and explain the relationship between them in trained/untrained individuals and maximal/sub-maximal exercise.
- Understand Starling's law of the heart.
- Understand the impact of physical activity and sport on an individual's health.
- Identify how physical activity can affect heart disease, high blood pressure, cholesterol levels and strokes.
- Explain cardiovascular drift.
- Explain blood pressure using the terms systolic and diastolic and identify the relationship that venous return has with blood pressure.
- Understand the venous return mechanisms.
- Describe the transportation of oxygen and be able to explain the roles of haemoglobin and myoglobin.
- Understand the oxyhaemoglobin dissociation curve.
- Explain the Bohr shift.
- Explain how blood is redistributed during exercise through vasoconstriction and vasodilation.
- Explain arterio-venous oxygen difference (A-VO$_2$ diff).

The cardiovascular system

The heart

The cardiovascular system is the body's transport system. It includes the heart and the blood vessels. During exercise, an efficient cardiovascular system is extremely important as the heart works to pump blood through the various blood vessels to deliver oxygen to the working muscles and gather waste products. It is also responsible for transporting heat (which is a by-product of exercise) to the skin so a performer can cool down. This chapter will give a brief overview of structure and investigate how the cardiovascular system responds to the increased demand placed on it by exercise.

The structure of the heart

Chambers of the heart

The heart is divided into two parts by a muscular wall called the septum and each part contains two chambers – an atrium and a ventricle. The atria are smaller than the ventricles as all they do is push the blood down into the ventricles. This does not require much force so they have thinner muscular walls. The ventricles have much thicker muscular walls as they need to contract with greater force in order to push blood out of the heart. The left side of the heart is larger as it needs to pump blood all around the body, whereas the right side pumps deoxygenated blood to the lungs which are in close proximity to the heart.

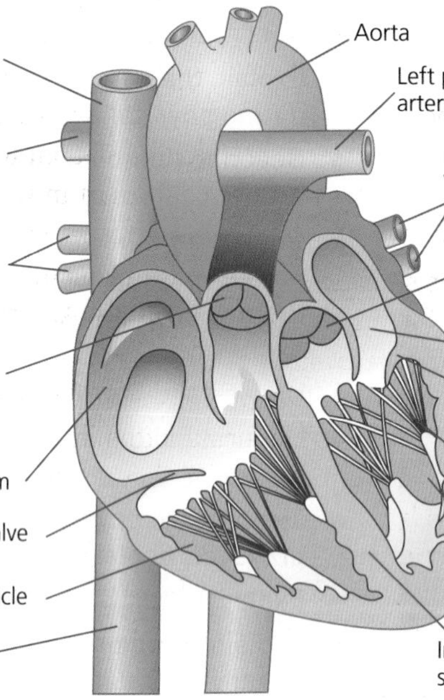

Figure 1 Diagram of the heart

Labels: Superior vena cava, Right pulmonary artery, Right pulmonary veins, Pulmonary semilunar valve, Right atrium, Tricuspid valve, Right ventricle, Inferior vena cava, Aorta, Left pulmonary artery, Left pulmonar veins, Aortic semilunar valve, Left atrium, Bicuspid valve, Chordae tendineae, Left ventricle, Interventricular septum

Blood vessels of the heart

Several blood vessels are attached to the heart. The vena cava brings deoxygenated blood back to the right atrium and the pulmonary vein delivers oxygenated blood to the left atrium. The pulmonary artery leaves the right ventricle with deoxygenated blood to go to the lungs and the aorta leaves the left ventricle with oxygenated blood leading to the body.

Valves of the heart

There are four main valves in the heart that regulate blood flow by ensuring it moves in only one direction. They open to allow blood to pass through and then close to prevent back flow. The tricuspid valve is located between the right atrium and right ventricle and the bicuspid valve between the left atrium and left ventricle. The semi-lunar valves can be found between the right and left ventricles and the pulmonary artery and aorta.

ACTIVITIES

Try to answer the following questions to check that you understand how the heart functions as this will help your understanding for the rest of this chapter.

1 Name the four chambers of the heart.

2 Which chambers are larger? Explain why.

3 Which side of the heart is larger? Explain why.

4 Name the main blood vessels that enter and leave the heart.

5 What are the names of the valves in the heart and where are they located?

6 What is the main function of valves?

7 Starting at the venae cavae, place the following structures in the correct order that a red blood cell would pass on its journey through the heart.

Aorta	Left ventricle	Lungs	Pulmonary artery
Bicuspid valve	Right ventricle	Left atrium	Tricuspid valve
Pulmonary vein	Right atrium		

Cardiac conduction system

The cardiac conduction system is a group of specialised cells located in the wall of the heart which send electrical impulses to the cardiac muscle, causing it to contract. When the heart beats, the blood needs to flow through it in a controlled manner, in through the atria and out through the ventricles. Heart muscle is described as being **myogenic** as the beat starts in the heart muscle itself with an electrical signal in the **sinoatrial node (SAN)**. This electrical impulse then spreads through the heart in what is often described as a wave of excitation (similar to a Mexican wave).

From the SAN the electrical impulse spreads through the walls of the atria, causing them to contract and forcing blood into the ventricles. The impulse then passes through the **atrioventricular node (AVN)** found in the atrioventricular septum. The AVN delays the transmission of the cardiac impulse for approximately 0.1 seconds to enable the atria to fully contract before ventricular **systole** begins. The electrical impulse then passes down through some specialised fibres which form the **bundle of His**. This is located in the septum separating the two ventricles. The bundle of His branches out into two bundle branches and then moves into smaller bundles called **purkinje fibres** which spread throughout the ventricles causing them to contract.

KEY TERMS

Myogenic: The capacity of the heart to generate its own impulses.

Sinoatrial node (SAN or SA node): A small mass of cardiac muscle found in the wall of the right atrium that generates the heartbeat. It is more commonly called the pacemaker.

Atrioventricular node (AVN or AV node): This node relays the impulse between the upper and lower sections of the heart.

Systole: When the heart contracts.

Bundle of His: A collection of heart muscle cells that transmit electrical impulses from the AVN via the bundle branches to the ventricles.

Purkinje fibres: Muscle fibres that conduct impulses in the walls of the ventricles.

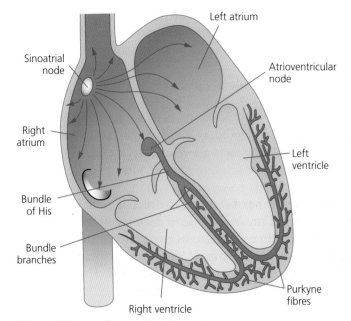

Figure 2 The cardiac conduction system

ACTIVITY

Rearrange these words so they show the correct order that the impulse travels in:

AVN	ventricular
bundle	systole
branches	bundle of His
purkinje fibres	atrial systole
SAN	

Memory tools

Remember the following mnemonic, **S A A B P V: S**ally **a**lways **a**ims **b**alls **p**ast **V**icky, to summarise the conduction system as five main points:

- **S**AN
- **A**trial systole
- **A**VN
- **B**undle of His
- **P**urkinje fibres
- **V**entricular systole

Or create your own!

Factors affecting the change in rate of the conduction system

The conduction system ensures that heart rate increases during exercise to allow the working muscles to receive more oxygen. As discussed earlier, the heart generates its own impulses from the SAN but the rate at which these cardiac impulses are fired can be controlled by three main mechanisms:

Neural control mechanism

This involves the **sympathetic nervous system** which stimulates the heart to beat faster, and the **parasympathetic system** which returns the heart to its resting level.

The nervous system is made up of two parts: the central nervous system (CNS), which consists of the brain and the spinal cord, and the peripheral nervous system, which consists of nerve cells that transmit information to and from the CNS.

These two systems are co-ordinated by the cardiac control centre located in the **medulla oblongata** of the brain. Sympathetic nervous impulses are sent to the SAN and there is a decrease in parasympathetic nerve impulses so that heart rate increases. The cardiac control centre is stimulated by chemoreceptors, baroreceptors and proprioceptors

Chemoreceptors

These are found in the carotid arteries and the aortic arch and they sense chemical changes. During exercise, **chemoreceptors** detect an increase in carbon dioxide. The role of blood carbon dioxide is important in controlling heart rate. An increased concentration of carbon dioxide in the blood will have the effect of stimulating the sympathetic nervous system, which means the heart will beat faster.

Baroreceptors

Baroreceptors contain nerve endings that respond to the stretching of the arterial wall caused by changes in blood pressure. Baroreceptors establish a set point for blood pressure. An increase above or decrease below this set point results in the baroreceptors sending signals to the medulla in the brain. An increase in arterial pressure causes an increase in the stretch of the baroreceptor sensors and results in a decrease in heart rate. Conversely, a decrease in arterial pressure causes a decrease in the stretch of the baroreceptors and results in an increase in heart rate. At the start of exercise the baroreceptor set point increases, which is important as the body does not want heart rate to slow down as this would negatively affect performance, as less oxygen would be delivered to the working muscles.

Proprioceptors

Proprioceptors are sensory nerve endings located in muscles, tendons and joints that provide information about movement and body position. At the start of exercise, they detect an increase in muscle movement. These receptors then send an impulse to the medulla, which then sends an impulse through the sympathetic nervous system to the SAN to increase heart rate. When the parasympathetic system stimulates the SAN, heart rate decreases.

Memory tools

Chemoreceptors → increase in CO_2 → increase in heart rate

Baroreceptors → increase in blood pressure → decrease in heart rate

Proprioceptors → increase in muscle movement → increase in heart rate

Hormonal control mechanism

Hormones can also have an effect on heart rate. The release of adrenaline during exercise is known as hormonal control. **Adrenaline** is a stress hormone that is released by the sympathetic nerves and cardiac nerve during exercise. It stimulates the SAN (pacemaker) which results in an increase in both the speed and force of contraction, thereby increasing cardiac output. This results in more blood being pumped to the working muscles so they can receive more oxygen for the energy they need.

The impact of physical activity on stroke volume, heart rate and cardiac output

During exercise, the need to transport more oxygen to the working muscles means the heart has to work harder. This means that more blood is pumped around the body and faster. Measurements such as **stroke volume**, heart rate and cardiac output all have to change as a result.

Stroke volume

This is the volume of blood pumped out by the heart ventricles in each contraction. On average, the resting stroke volume is approximately 70ml.

Stroke volume depends upon the following:

● Venous return: this is the volume of blood returning to the heart via the veins. If venous return increases, then stroke volume will also increase. (If more blood enters the heart, then more blood goes out!)

● The elasticity of cardiac fibres: this is concerned with the degree of stretch of cardiac tissue during the **diastole phase** of the cardiac cycle. The more the cardiac fibres can stretch, the greater the force of contraction will be. A greater force of contraction can increase the **ejection fraction**. This is called Starling's Law.

Memory tools

Starling's Law

Increased venous return → Greater diastolic filling of the heart → Cardiac muscle stretched → More force of contraction → Increased ejection fraction

KEY TERM

Proprioceptors: Sensory nerve endings in the muscles, tendons and joints that detect changes in muscle movement.

CHECK YOUR UNDERSTANDING
As an individual runs on a treadmill, his or her chemoreceptors will detect an increase in carbon dioxide levels and blood acidity. Name the other receptors, explain what they detect and describe the effect this has on heart rate.

KEY TERMS

Adrenaline: A stress hormone that is released by the sympathetic nerves and cardiac nerve during exercise which causes an increase in heart rate.

Stroke volume: The volume of blood pumped out by the heart ventricles in each contraction.

Diastole phase: When the heart relaxes to fill with blood.

Ejection fraction: The percentage of blood pumped out by the left ventricle per beat.

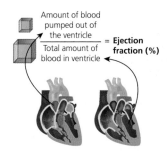

Ejection fraction = $\dfrac{\text{stroke volume}}{\substack{\text{end diastolic volume} \\ \text{(volume of blood in} \\ \text{the ventricles at rest)}}}$

Amount of blood pumped out of the ventricle / Total amount of blood in ventricle = Ejection fraction (%)

Figure 3 The ejection fraction

- The contractility of cardiac tissue (myocardium): the greater the contractility of cardiac tissue, the greater the force of contraction. This results in an increase in stroke volume. It is also highlighted by an increase in the ejection fraction. This refers to the percentage of blood pumped out by the left ventricle per beat. An average value is 60 per cent, but it can increase by up to 85 per cent following a period of training.

Heart rate

This is the number of times the heart beats per minute. On average, the resting heart rate is approximately 72 beats per minute.

Cardiac output

Cardiac output is the volume of blood pumped out by the heart ventricles per minute. It is equal to stroke volume multiplied by heart rate.

Cardiac output (Q) = Stroke volume (SV) × Heart rate (HR)

Q = 70 ml (see page 5) × 72

Q = 5040 ml (5.04 litres)

It can be seen from this calculation that if heart rate or stroke volume increase, then cardiac output will also increase.

Heart rate range in response to exercise

Heart rate increases with exercise but how much it increases is dependent on the intensity of the exercise. Heart rate will increase in direct proportion to exercise intensity – the higher the intensity, the higher the heart rate. Heart rate does eventually reach a maximum. Maximum heart rate can be calculated by subtracting your age from 220. An 18 year old will have a maximum heart rate of 202 beats per minute.

220 – 18 = 202

A trained performer has a greater heart rate range because their resting heart rate is lower and their maximum heart rate increases. Think of Sir Bradley Wiggins, who has a resting heart rate of 35 bpm, and Mo Farah with 33 bpm. These two performers will also have a higher maximum heart rate. Compare this to a 40-year-old untrained individual whose resting heart rate is 72 and their maximum heart rate is simply linked to their age, so it is 180. Their heart rate range is much lower!

The graphs opposite illustrate what happens to heart rate during maximal exercise such as sprinting and sub-maximal exercise such as jogging.

KEY TERM

Cardiac output: The volume of blood pumped out by the heart ventricles per minute.

Maximal exercise

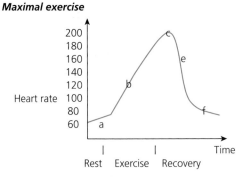

a = *Anticipatory rise* due to hormonal action of adrenaline which causes the SA node to increase heart rate

b = *Sharp rise in* heart rate due mainly to anaerobic work

c = Heart rate contiunes to rise due to maximal workloads stressing the anaerobic systems

d = *Steady state* as the athlete is able to meet the oxygen demand with the oxygen supply

Submaximal exercise

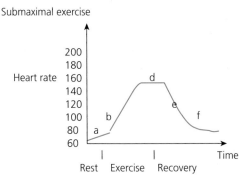

e = *Rapid decline* in heart rate as soon as the exercise stops

f = *Slower recovery* as body systems return to resting levels. Heart rate needs to remain elevated to rid the body if waste products, for example, lactic acid

Figure 4 Heart rate responses to high intensity and submaximal exercise

Regular aerobic training will result in more cardiac muscle. When the cardiac muscle becomes bigger and stronger, this is known as **cardiac hypertrophy**. This will have an important effect on stroke volume, heart rate and therefore cardiac output. A bigger, stronger heart will enable more blood to be pumped out per beat (i.e. stroke volume). In more complex language, the end diastolic volume of the ventricle increases. If the ventricle can contract with more force and thus push out more blood, the heart does not have to beat as often, so resting heart rate will decrease. This is known as **bradycardia** and when this occurs, oxygen delivery to the muscles improves as there is less oxygen needed for contractions of the heart.

Cardiac output in response to exercise

During exercise there is a large increase in cardiac output due to an increase in heart rate and an increase in stroke volume. Cardiac output will increase as the intensity of exercise increases until maximum intensity is reached and then it plateaus (evens out) (see Figure 5).

Table 1 shows the differences in cardiac output in a trained and an untrained individual, both at rest and during exercise. The individuals in this example are aged 18 so their maximum heart rate will be 202 beats per minute.

Table 1 Cardiac output in a trained and untrained individual, both at rest and during exercise

	Stroke volume × Heart rate = Cardiac output SV × HR = Q
During exercise: Untrained person	120ml × 202 = 24.24 litres
During exercise: Trained person	170ml × 202 = 34.34 litres
At rest: Untrained person	70ml × 72 = 5.04 litres
At rest: Trained person	84ml × 60 = 5.04 litres

KEY TERMS

Cardiac hypertrophy: The thickening of the muscular wall of the heart so it becomes bigger and stronger; also can mean a larger ventricular cavity.

Bradycardia: A decrease in resting heart rate to below 60 beats per minute.

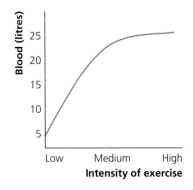

Figure 5 Graph to show cardiac output response to exercise

ACTIVITY

Look at Table 1 and comment on the difference between cardiac output at rest and during exercise for both the trained and untrained performer.

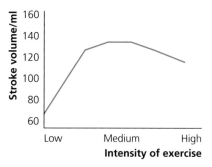

Figure 6 Graph to show stroke volume response to exercise

CHECK YOUR UNDERSTANDING

1 Define the terms cardiac output and stroke volume and explain the relationship between them.
2 What are the effects of a period of training on resting stroke volume and cardiac output?

KEY TERMS

Atherosclerosis occurs when arteries harden and narrow as they become clogged up by fatty deposits.

Atheroma: A fatty deposit found in the inner lining of an artery.

Angina: Chest pain that occurs when the blood supply through the coronary arteries to the muscles of the heart is restricted.

Memory tools

Maximum heart rate is calculated as 220 minus your age.

At rest, cardiac output for both the trained and untrained performer stays the same. It is maximum cardiac output that changes. During exercise, the increase in maximum cardiac output will have huge benefits for the trained performer as they will be able to transport more blood to the working muscles and therefore more oxygen. In addition, when the body starts to exercise, the distribution of blood flow changes. This means that a much higher proportion of blood passes to the working muscles and less passes to organs such as the intestine where it is less in demand. The amount of blood passing to the kidneys and brain remains unaltered.

Stroke volume in response to exercise

Stroke volume increases as exercise intensity increases. However this is only the case up to 40–60 per cent of maximum effort. Once a performer reaches this point, stroke volume plateaus (as shown in Figure 6). One explanation for this is that the increased heart rate near maximum effort results in a shorter diastolic phase. Quite simply, the ventricles do not have as much time to fill up with blood, so they cannot pump as much out!

The impact of physical activity and sport on the health of the individual

Heart disease

Heart disease is more commonly referred to as coronary heart disease or CHD and is the leading cause of deaths both in the UK and around the world. Coronary heart disease occurs when your coronary arteries, which supply the heart muscle with oxygenated blood, become blocked or start to narrow by a gradual build-up of fatty deposits. This process is called **atherosclerosis** and the fatty deposits are called **atheroma**. High blood pressure, high levels of cholesterol, lack of exercise and smoking can all cause atherosclerosis.

As the coronary arteries become narrow they are unable to deliver enough oxygen to the heart and pain and discomfort occurs. This pain and discomfort is called **angina**. If a piece of fatty deposit (atheroma) breaks off in the coronary artery it can cause a blood clot which results in a blockage forming. This can cut off the supply of oxygenated blood to the heart muscle resulting in a heart attack.

As the heart is a muscle, exercise helps it to stay in shape! Regular exercise keeps the heart healthy and more efficient. It can pump more blood around the body as exercise makes the heart bigger and stronger resulting in an increase in stroke volume. In addition, regular exercise can also maintain the flexibility of blood vessels, ensuring good blood flow, normal blood pressure and low cholesterol levels. The American Heart Association recommends at least 150 minutes per week of moderate exercise, like brisk walking.

High blood pressure

Blood pressure is mentioned in more detail later in this chapter. It is the force exerted by the blood against the blood vessel wall. This pressure comes from the heart as it pumps the blood around the body. High blood pressure puts extra strain on the arteries and heart and if left untreated increases the risk of heart attack, heart failure, kidney disease, stroke or dementia. Regular aerobic exercise can reduce blood pressure. It lowers both systolic and diastolic pressure by up to 5-10 mmHg which reduces the risk of a heart attack by up to 20 per cent.

Cholesterol levels

Cholesterol is discussed in more detail in Chapter 4.1. There are two types of cholesterol:

- LDL (low density lipoproteins) that transport cholesterol in the blood to the tissues and are classed as 'bad' cholesterol since they are linked to an increased risk of heart disease
- HDL (high density lipoproteins) that transport excess cholesterol in the blood back to the liver where it is broken down. These are classed as 'good' cholesterol since they lower the risk of developing heart disease.

Regular physical activity lowers bad LDL cholesterol levels. At the same time it significantly increases good HDL cholesterol levels.

Stroke

The brain needs a constant supply of oxygenated blood and nutrients to maintain its function. The energy to work all the time is provided by oxygen delivered to the brain in the blood. A **stroke** occurs when the blood supply to part of the brain is cut off causing damage to brain cells so they start to die. This can lead to brain injury, disability and sometimes death. There are two main types of stroke:

- Ischaemic strokes are the most common form and occur when a blood clot stops the blood supply.
- Haemorrhagic strokes occur when a weakened blood vessel supplying the brain bursts.

Research has shown that regular exercise can help to lower your blood pressure and help you maintain a healthy weight, which can reduce your risk of stroke by 27 per cent.

What is cardiovascular drift?

What should happen during **steady state** is that heart rate remains the same. However, new research has shown that if you monitor heart rate more closely, it does not remain the same but, instead, slowly climbs. This is cardiovascular drift (as seen in Figure 7). In more detail, cardiovascular drift is characterised by a progressive decrease in stroke volume and arterial blood pressure, together with a progressive rise in heart rate. It occurs during prolonged exercise (after 10 minutes) in a warm environment, despite the intensity of the exercise remaining the same. Suggestions as to why this occurs are that when we sweat, a portion of this lost fluid volume comes from the plasma volume. This decrease in plasma volume will reduce venous return and stroke volume (remember Starling's Law). Heart rate again increases to compensate and maintain a higher cardiac output in an attempt to create more energy to cool the body down. To minimise this cardiovascular drift, it is important to maintain high fluid consumption before and during exercise.

KEY TERMS

Stroke: A stroke occurs when the blood supply to the brain is cut off.

Steady state: Where the athlete is able to meet the oxygen demand with the oxygen supply.

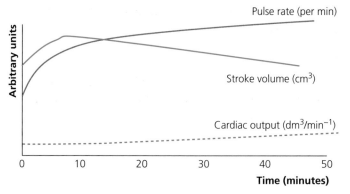

Figure 7 Graph to show cardiovascular drift

Memory tools

Cardiovascular drift occurs after a period of exercise → heart rate increases → stroke volume decreases → because fluid lost as sweat → resulting in a reduced plasma volume → reduced venous return → cardiac output also increases due to more energy needed to cool body/sweat.

The vascular system

The vascular system is made up of blood vessels that carry blood through the body. These blood vessels deliver oxygen and nutrients to the body tissues and take away waste products such as carbon dioxide. Together with the heart and lungs, the blood vessels ensure that muscles have an adequate supply of oxygen during exercise in order to cope with the increased demand for energy.

There are two types of circulation:

1 **Pulmonary** – deoxygenated blood from the heart to the lungs and oxygenated blood back to the heart.

2 **Systemic** – oxygenated blood to the body from the heart and then the return of deoxygenated blood from the body to the heart.

Review of the vascular system

Blood vessels

The vascular system consists of five different blood vessels that carry the blood from the heart, distribute it round the body and then return it to the heart.

Heart → Arteries → Arterioles → Capillaries → Venules → Veins → Heart

Each blood vessel is slightly different in structure. Veins have thinner muscle/elastic tissue layers. Blood is at low pressure and they have valves and a wider lumen, whereas arteries have the highest pressure (and consequently have more of an elastic outer layer to cope with these fluctuations in pressure), a smaller lumen and a smooth inner layer. Capillaries are only wide enough to allow one red blood cell to pass through at a given time. This slows down blood flow and allows the exchange of nutrients with the tissues to take place by diffusion.

Blood pressure

During exercise, it is important to increase blood flow through the circulatory system so the muscles receive the oxygen they require. An increase in blood pressure can achieve this.

Blood pressure is the force exerted by the blood against the blood vessel wall and is often referred to as:

blood flow × resistance

When the heart contracts, it forces blood out under high pressure. This is the called the **systolic pressure** or pressure of contraction. The lower pressure as the ventricles relax is called the **diastolic pressure**.

Blood pressure is measured at the brachial artery in the upper arm. A typical reading at rest is:

$\frac{120}{80}$ mmHg (millimetres of mercury)

Blood pressure is different in the various blood vessels and is largely dependent on the distance of the blood vessel from the heart. The low pressure of blood in the veins means that mechanisms are needed to pump the blood back to the heart.

KEY TERMS

Blood pressure: The force exerted by the blood against the blood vessel wall.

Systolic pressure: The pressure in the arteries when the ventricles are contracting.

Diastolic pressure: The pressure in the arteries when the ventricles are relaxing.

ACTIVITY

Copy and complete Table 2, then, using Figure 8, identify the pressure of blood in each of the blood vessels.

Table 2

BLOOD PRESSURE			
Artery	Arteriole	Capillary	Vein

ACTIVITY

Look at the graph and give three key points about blood pressure.

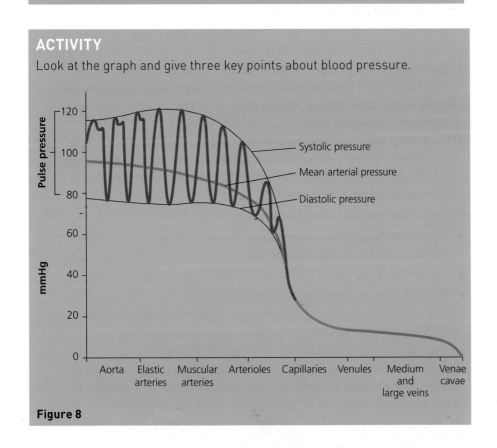

Figure 8

Venous return

Venous return is the return of blood to the right side of the heart via the vena cava. Up to 70 per cent of the total volume of blood is contained in the veins at rest. This means that a large amount of blood can be returned to the heart when needed. During exercise, the amount of blood returning to the heart (venous return) increases. This means that if more blood is being pumped back to the heart, then more blood has to be pumped out, so stroke volume will increase – this is Starling's Law.

Venous return mechanisms

However, the pressure of the blood in the large veins is very low and this makes it difficult to return blood to the heart. In addition, the large lumen of the vein offers little resistance to blood flow. This means that active mechanisms are needed to help venous return.

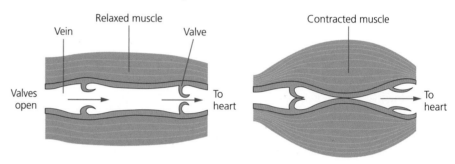

Figure 9 The skeletal muscle pump

1 **The skeletal muscle pump** (as shown in Figure 9) – when muscles contract and relax they change shape. This change in shape means that the muscles press on the nearby veins and cause a pumping effect and squeeze the blood towards the heart.

2 **The respiratory pump** – when muscles contract and relax during breathing in and breathing out, pressure changes occur in the thoracic (chest) and abdominal (stomach) cavities. These changes in pressure compress the nearby veins and assist blood return to the heart.

3 **Pocket valves** – it is important that blood in the veins only flows in one direction. The presence of valves ensures that this happens. This is because once the blood has passed through the valves, they close to prevent the blood flowing back.

Other factors that aid venous return are:

● A very thin layer of *smooth muscle* in the walls of the veins. This helps squeeze blood back towards the heart.

● *Gravity* helps the blood return to the heart from the upper body.

● The *suction pump action* of the heart.

It is important to maintain venous return during exercise to ensure the skeletal muscles are receiving enough oxygen to meet the demands of the activity. At rest, valves and the smooth muscle found in veins are sufficient enough to maintain venous return. However, this is not the case during exercise. The demand for oxygen is greater and the heart is beating faster, so the vascular system has to help out too. Now the skeletal muscle pump and the respiratory pump are needed to ensure venous return is maintained. During exercise, this is possible because our skeletal muscles are constantly contracting and our breathing is elevated. Immediately after exercise, we still need to maintain these mechanisms. Performing an active cool-down will keep the skeletal muscle pump and respiratory pump working, therefore preventing blood pooling (blood collecting in the veins).

The impact of blood pressure on venous return

Blood pressure has already been discussed earlier in this chapter. Remember, systolic pressure is the pressure in the blood vessels when the ventricles are contracting and diastolic pressure is the pressure in the blood vessels when the ventricles are relaxing. When systolic blood pressure increases, there is also an increase in venous return, and when systolic pressure decreases, there is a decrease in venous return.

The impact of a pressure gradient between the right atrium and the vena cava on venous return

As we have already mentioned, venous return (VR) is the flow of blood back to the heart in the veins, and under normal circumstances venous return is the same as stroke volume (i.e. what goes in comes out). Remember Starling's Law; if venous return increases, the heart contracts with more force, which will increase the ejection fraction and therefore the stroke volume. Venous return is determined by a pressure gradient. The pressure gradient is the mean systemic pressure minus the right atrial pressure, and resistance is the total peripheral vascular resistance.

$$\frac{\text{venous pressure } (P_V) \text{ - right atrial pressure } (P_{RA})}{\text{venous vascular resistance } (R_V)}$$

An increase in venous pressure (PV) or a decrease in right atrial pressure (PRA), or a decrease in venous resistance (RV), leads to an increase in venous return, whereas increasing right atrial pressure decreases venous return.

The blood pressure in both the right atrium (PRA) and the peripheral veins (PV) is normally very low, so that the pressure gradient driving venous return from the peripheral veins to the heart is also relatively low. Because of this, just small changes of blood pressure in either the right atrium or the peripheral veins can cause a large change in the pressure gradient, and therefore can significantly affect the return of blood to the right atrium. For example, during inspiration, the small changes in blood pressure between the atria and the abdominal cavity causes a large increase in the pressure gradient driving venous return from the peripheral circulation to the right atrium.

The transportation of oxygen

Oxygen plays a major role in energy production and a reduction in the amount of oxygen in the body will have a detrimental impact on performance. During exercise, when oxygen diffuses into the capillaries supplying the skeletal muscles, 3 per cent dissolves into **plasma** and 97 per cent combines with **haemoglobin** to form oxyhaemoglobin. When fully saturated, haemoglobin will carry four oxygen molecules. This occurs when the partial pressure of oxygen in the blood is high; for example in the alveolar capillaries of the lungs.

At the tissues, oxygen is released from oxyhaemoglobin due to the lower pressure of oxygen that exists there. The release of oxygen from oxyhaemoglobin to the tissues is referred to as oxyhaemoglobin dissociation. In the muscle, oxygen is stored by **myoglobin**. This has a higher affinity for oxygen and will store the oxygen for the **mitochondria** until it is used by the muscles. The mitochondria are the centres in the muscle where aerobic respiration takes place.

> **STUDY HINT**
>
> Increasing right atrial pressure decreases venous return; decreasing right atrial pressure increases venous return.

KEY TERMS

Plasma: The fluid part of blood (mainly water) that surrounds blood cells and transports them.

Haemoglobin: An iron-containing pigment found in red blood cells, which combines with oxygen to form oxyhaemoglobin.

Myoglobin: Often called 'muscle haemoglobin'. It is an iron-containing muscle pigment in slow-twitch muscle fibres which has a higher affinity for oxygen than haemoglobin. It stores the oxygen in the muscle fibres which can be used quickly when exercise begins.

Mitochondria: Often referred to as the 'powerhouse' of the cell as respiration and energy production occur there.

The oxyhaemoglobin dissociation curve

The oxyhaemoglobin dissociation curve helps us to understand how haemoglobin in our blood transports and releases oxygen. The curve represents the relationship between oxygen and haemoglobin, as shown in Figure 10.

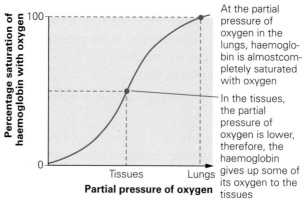

At the partial pressure of oxygen in the lungs, haemoglobin is almostcompletely saturated with oxygen

In the tissues, the partial pressure of oxygen is lower, therefore, the haemoglobin gives up some of its oxygen to the tissues

Figure 10 The oxyhaemoglobin dissociation curve

Think about a bucket. In the lungs, haemoglobin is saturated with oxygen so the bucket will be virtually full but at the tissues where haemoglobin releases some oxygen the bucket becomes partially empty.

From this curve, you can see that in the lungs there is almost full saturation (concentration) of haemoglobin but at the tissues the partial pressure of oxygen is lower. Haemoglobin gives up 23 per cent of its oxygen to the muscles and is therefore no longer fully saturated. This is fine at rest when the demand for oxygen by the muscles is not high, but during exercise this needs to increase and occur faster, so a bigger percentage of oxygen is released from the haemoglobin.

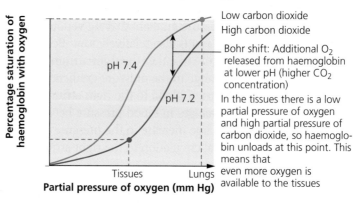

Low carbon dioxide
High carbon dioxide

Bohr shift: Additional O_2 released from haemoglobin at lower pH (higher CO_2 concentration)

In the tissues there is a low partial pressure of oxygen and high partial pressure of carbon dioxide, so haemoglobin unloads at this point. This means that even more oxygen is available to the tissues

Figure 11 The effect of changing acidity on the oxyhaemoglobin dissociation curve.

During exercise, this S-shaped curve shifts to the right because when muscles require more oxygen, the dissociation of oxygen from haemoglobin in the blood capillaries to the muscle tissue occurs more readily. This shift to the right is known as the **Bohr shift**.

Three factors are responsible for this increase in the dissociation of oxygen from haemoglobin which results in more oxygen being available for use by the working muscles:

- **Increase in blood temperature** – when blood and muscle temperature increases during exercise, oxygen will dissociate from haemoglobin more readily.

- **Partial pressure of carbon dioxide increases** – as the level of blood carbon dioxide rises during exercise, oxygen will dissociate faster from haemoglobin.

- **pH** – more carbon dioxide will lower the pH in the blood. A drop in blood pH will cause oxygen to dissociate from haemoglobin more quickly (Bohr shift).

KEY TERMS

Bohr shift: When an increase in blood carbon dioxide and a decrease in pH results in a reduction of the affinity of haemoglobin for oxygen.

pH: A measure of acidity. The range goes from 1 to14 and anything less than 7 indicates acidity.

CHECK YOUR UNDERSTANDING

During a 400-metre hurdle race, the oxyhaemoglobin curve shifts to the right. Explain the causes of this change to the curve *and* the effect that this change has on oxygen delivery to the muscles.

Redistribution of blood

The distribution of blood flow is different at rest compared to during exercise. During exercise, the skeletal muscles require more oxygen so more blood needs to be redirected to them in order to meet this increase in oxygen demand. The redirecting of blood flow to the areas where it is most needed is known as shunting or the **vascular shunt mechanism**. This redistribution of blood can be seen in Figure 12.

KEY TERM

Vascular shunt mechanism: The redistribution of cardiac output.

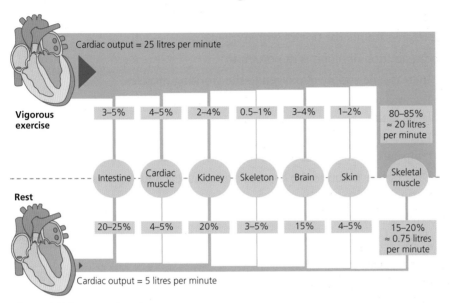

	Intestine	Cardiac muscle	Kidney	Skeleton	Brain	Skin	Skeletal muscle
Vigorous exercise (Cardiac output = 25 litres per minute)	3–5%	4–5%	2–4%	0.5–1%	3–4%	1–2%	80–85% ≈ 20 litres per minute
Rest (Cardiac output = 5 litres per minute)	20–25%	4–5%	20%	3–5%	15%	4–5%	15–20% ≈ 0.75 litres per minute

Figure 12 The vascular shunt

ACTIVITY

Look at Figure 12 and give reasons for the percentage change in cardiac output during exercise.

This redirection of blood flow to the working muscles means that sports performers should ensure they do not eat less than an hour before competition. A full gut would result in more blood being directed to the stomach instead of the working muscles and this would have a detrimental effect on performance, as less oxygen is being made available. Blood flow to the brain must remain constant to ensure brain function is maintained as the brain needs oxygen for energy. In addition, more blood needs to go to the heart because the heart muscle needs oxygen for energy to beat faster and more blood goes to the skin because energy is needed to cool the body down.

The control of blood flow

Both blood pressure and blood flow are controlled by the vasomotor centre, located in the medulla oblongata of the brain. During exercise, chemical changes, such as increases in carbon dioxide and lactic acid, are detected by chemoreceptors. (Remember we discussed the role of chemoreceptors on the heart.) These receptors will stimulate the vasomotor centre which will redistribute blood flow through **vasodilation** and **vasoconstriction**. Vasodilation is when the blood vessel widens to increase blood flow into the capillaries and vasoconstriction is when the blood vessel narrows to decrease blood flow. During exercise, more oxygen is needed at the working muscles so vasodilation will occur in the arterioles supplying these muscles, increasing blood flow and bringing in the much-needed oxygen, whereas vasoconstriction will occur in the arterioles supplying non-essential organs such as the intestines and liver.

Redirection of blood flow also occurs through stimulation of the sympathetic nerves located in the walls of the blood vessel. When sympathetic stimulation increases, vasoconstriction occurs and blood flow reduces

KEY TERMS

Vasodilation: The widening of the blood vessels to increase the flow of blood into the capillaries.

Vasoconstriction: The narrowing of the blood vessels to reduce blood flow into the capillaries.

STUDY HINT

During exercise the muscles require more oxygen so we have to direct more blood to them.

so it can be redistributed to other parts of the body such as the muscles during exercise. When stimulation by the sympathetic nerves decreases, vasodilation occurs and increases blood flow to that body part. (See Chapter 1.3 for an explanation of the sympathetic nervous system.)

Pre-capillary sphincters also aid blood redistribution. These are tiny rings of muscle located at the opening of capillaries. When they contract, blood flow is restricted through the capillary and when they relax, blood flow is increased. During exercise, the capillary networks supplying skeletal muscle will have relaxed pre-capillary sphincters to increase blood flow and therefore saturate the tissues with oxygen.

Redistribution of blood is important to:

- Increase the supply of oxygen to the working muscles.
- Remove waste products from the muscles, such as carbon dioxide and lactic acid.
- Ensure more blood goes to the skin during exercise to regulate body temperature and get rid of heat through radiation, evaporation and sweating.
- Direct more blood to the heart as it is a muscle and requires extra oxygen during exercise.

Memory tools

- More blood goes to the heart because the heart muscle needs oxygen to beat faster.
- More blood goes to the muscles as they need more oxygen for energy.
- More blood goes to the skin because energy is needed to cool the body down.
- Blood flow to the brain remains constant as it needs oxygen for energy to maintain function.

ACTIVITY

Copy out Table 3 and construct sentences to connect the key words in the spaces below.

Table 3

1	brain			blood flow
2	eat	competition		gut
3	vasomotor centre	chemoreceptors		medulla oblongata
4	vasoconstriction	vasodilation	arterioles	blood flow

KEY TERM

Arterio-venous difference: The difference between the oxygen content of the arterial blood arriving at the muscles and the venous blood leaving the muscles.

CHECK YOUR UNDERSTANDING

During a game of football, a player's arterio-venous oxygen difference (A-VO$_2$ diff) will increase. What is the significance of this increase in A-VO$_2$ diff to the player?

Arterio-venous difference (A-VO$_2$ diff)

This is the difference between the oxygen content of the arterial blood arriving at the muscles and the venous blood leaving the muscles. At rest, the **arterio-venous difference** is low as not much oxygen is required by the muscles. But during exercise, much more oxygen is needed from the blood for the muscles so the arterio-venous difference is high. This increase will affect gaseous exchange at the alveoli so more oxygen is taken in and more carbon dioxide is removed. Training also increases the arterio-venous difference as trained performers can extract a greater amount of oxygen from the blood.

SUMMARY

You need to remember the order in which the electrical impulses travel through the cardiac conduction system. The sympathetic system speeds up heart rate and the parasympathetic slows it down. Heart rate is controlled by the brain, which receives information from chemoreceptors, baroreceptors and proprioceptors. Hormonal control involves adrenaline, which causes an increase in heart rate. You need to be able to define stroke volume, cardiac output and heart rate and give the effects of exercise on these. Make sure you can define Starling's Law and cardiovascular drift.

Blood pressure is the force exerted by the blood against the blood vessel wall and it increases during exercise – make sure you know why. Learn the venous return mechanisms. Haemoglobin transports oxygen in the blood. In the muscle, oxygen is stored by myoglobin. This has a higher affinity for oxygen and will store the oxygen for the mitochondria until it is used by the muscles. The Bohr shift is when an increase in blood carbon dioxide and a decrease in pH results in a reduction of the affinity of haemoglobin for oxygen. Redirecting blood flow to the areas where it is most needed is known as shunting or the vascular shunt mechanism and is achieved through vasodilation. Vasoconstriction is the narrowing of the blood vessels to reduce blood flow into the capillaries. Arterio-venous difference is the difference between the oxygen content of the arterial blood arriving at the muscles and the venous blood leaving the muscles.

Regular physical activity has a positive effect on heart disease. It can lower blood pressure and bad LDL cholesterol levels and reduce the risk of a stroke.

PRACTICE QUESTIONS

1 Why does blood flow to the brain remain the same at rest and during exercise? (2 marks)

2 Why should an athlete not eat at least one hour before competition? (3 marks)

3 How is oxygen transported in the blood? (2 marks)

4 Explain how blood is redistributed to the working muscles. (3 marks)

5 During exercise, heart rate will increase to meet the extra oxygen demand required by the muscles. Explain how the increasing level of carbon dioxide in the blood raises heart rate. (3 marks)

6 Just before the start of an 800 m race, the athlete will experience a change in heart rate. What change occurs in the athlete's heart rate and why does this happen? (2 marks)

7 Explain what is meant by the term 'cardiovascular drift'. (2 marks)

8 Gymnastic performance will demand an increase in blood supply to the active muscles. The table below shows how various measurements concerned with the heart vary during rest and activity. Using the information in Table 4, calculate the cardiac output at rest. (2 marks)

Table 4 Difference in heart rate, stroke volume and systolic blood pressure at rest and during exercise

Measurement	At rest	During activity
Heart rate (bpm)	70	150
Stroke volume (mls)	70	90
Systolic pressure (mm Hg)	115	140

9 What do you understand by the term 'Starling's law' of the heart? (2 marks)

Chapter 1.2
The respiratory system

Chapter objectives

After reading this chapter you should be able to:

- Understand the following lung volumes: residual volume, expiratory reserve volume, inspiratory reserve volume, tidal volume and minute ventilation.
- Understand the impact of physical activity and sport on these lung volumes.
- Explain gas exchange of oxygen and carbon dioxide at alveoli and muscles, through the principles of diffusion and partial pressures.
- Understand the hormonal, neural and chemical regulation of pulmonary ventilation during physical activity.
- Explain the role of chemoreceptors, proprioceptors and baroreceptors in the regulation of pulmonary ventilation during exercise.
- Understand the effect of poor lifestyle choices on the respiratory system.

The body needs a continuous supply of oxygen to produce energy. When we use oxygen to break down food to release energy, carbon dioxide is produced as a waste product and the body must remove this. Respiration, therefore, is the taking in of oxygen and the removal of carbon dioxide. It includes:

- ventilation – getting air into and out of the lungs
- external respiration – gaseous exchange between the lungs and blood
- transport of gases
- internal respiration – exchange of gases between the blood in the capillaries and the body cells
- cellular respiration – the metabolic reactions and processes that take place in a cell to obtain energy from fuels such as glucose (this is covered in the second year of A-level).

Review of the structure of the lungs

> **STUDY HINT**
>
> A knowledge of the structure of the lungs and the respiratory airways will help in your understanding of the respiratory system.

Air is a mixture of gases and is drawn into the body through the *nose*. It passes through the pharynx and onto the larynx (voice box) then down the trachea (windpipe) and into the right and left bronchus. Air moves through each bronchus and they subdivide into secondary bronchi. These then get progressively thinner and branch into bronchioles and then respiratory bronchioles, which lead into the *alveoli* (as shown in Figure 1).

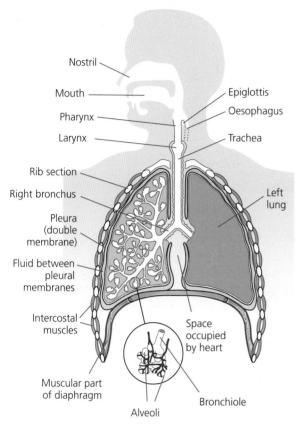

Figure 1 The structure of the respiratory system

Labels on figure:
Nostril
Mouth
Pharynx
Larynx
Rib section
Right bronchus
Pleura (double membrane)
Fluid between pleural membranes
Intercostal muscles
Muscular part of diaphragm
Alveoli
Epiglottis
Oesophagus
Trachea
Left lung
Space occupied by heart
Bronchiole

ACTIVITY

Rearrange the following words to show the correct passage of air:

larynx   nose   trachea   pharynx   alveoli   bronchioles   bronchi

Memory tools

Make up a mnemonic to try to remember the correct passage of air – such as 'nearly lobbed the ball brilliantly again' – **n**ose, **l**arynx, **t**rachea, **b**ronchi, **b**ronchioles, **a**lveoli.

The alveoli are responsible for the exchange of gases between the lungs and the blood. This occurs via **diffusion** which is the movement of gas molecules from an area of high partial pressure (high concentration) to an area of low partial pressure (low concentration).

The structure of alveoli is designed to help **gaseous exchange**. Their walls are very thin (only one cell thick) which means there is a short diffusion pathway. This is because there are only two layers of cells from the air in the alveoli to the blood. An extensive capillary network surrounds the alveoli so they have an excellent blood supply. They have a huge surface area because there are millions of alveoli in each lung, which allows for a greater uptake of oxygen.

Memory tools

Remember the diffusion of gases at the alveoli is helped enormously by their structure. Memorise **BOG** where **B** stands for **b**ig surface area, **O** for **o**ne cell thick and **G** for **g**ood blood supply.

KEY TERMS

Diffusion: The movement of gas molecules from an area of high concentration or partial pressure to an area of low concentration or partial pressure.

Gaseous exchange: The movement of oxygen from the air into the blood, and carbon dioxide from the blood into the air.

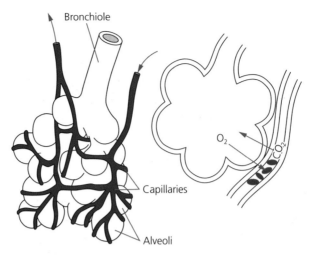

Figure 2 The alveoli

The mechanics of breathing

It is important to remember that air will always move from an area of high pressure to an area of low pressure via diffusion (explained earlier). The greater the difference in pressure, the faster air will flow. This means that in order to get air into the lungs (inspiration), the pressure needs to be lower here than in the atmosphere. To get air out (expiration), air pressure needs to be higher in the lungs than the atmosphere. Increasing the volume of the thoracic cavity (chest cavity) will reduce the pressure of air in the lungs. Decreasing the volume of the thoracic cavity will increase the pressure of air in the lungs, forcing the air out.

The contraction of muscles causes these pressure changes.

Table 1 The muscles used for inspiration and expiration at rest and during exercise

Ventilation phase	Muscles used during breathing at rest	Muscles used during exercise
Inspiration	Diaphragm External intercostals	Diaphragm External intercostals Sternocleidomastoid Scalenes Pectoralis minor
Expiration	Passive: diaphragm and external intercostals just relax	Internal intercostals Abdominals

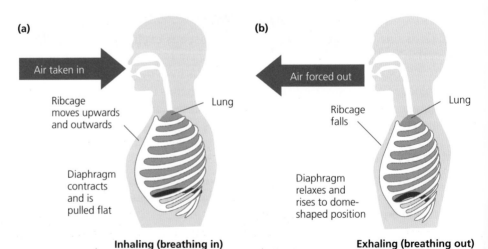

Figure 3 The mechanics of breathing

Lung volumes

This is the movement of air into and out of the lungs. Taking air into the lungs is inspiration and moving air out is expiration. At rest we inspire and expire approximately 0.5 litres of air. The volume of air inspired or expired per breath is referred to as the **tidal volume**. The volume of air inspired or expired per minute is referred to as minute ventilation and can be calculated by multiplying the number of breaths taken per minute (approximately 12) by the tidal volume:

Number of breaths (per min) × tidal volume = minute ventilation

12 × 0.5 = 6 litres/min

At rest, we still have the ability to breathe in and breathe out more air than just the tidal volume. This extra amount of air inspired is the **inspiratory reserve volume (IRV)** and the amount expired is the **expiratory reserve volume (ERV)**. Exercise will have an effect on these lung volumes. More oxygen is required so our depth of breathing increases. This means tidal volume increases because we are using more of our inspiratory reserve volume and expiratory reserve volume.

KEY TERMS

Tidal volume: Volume of air breathed in or out per breath.

Inspiratory reserve volume (IRV): Volume of air that can be forcibly inspired after a normal breath.

Expiratory reserve volume (ERV): Volume of air that can be forcibly expired after a normal breath.

STUDY HINTS

Do not use abbreviations in the exam.

ACTIVITIES

1 To help you understand inspiratory reserve volume, try the following:
   - Take a normal breath in (tidal volume) and hold it.
   - Now take an additional breath in until your lungs feel full. This is your inspiratory reserve volume.
2 To help you understand expiratory reserve volume, try the following:
   - Breathe out normally (tidal volume) and hold it.
   - Now breathe out further as much as you can. This is your expiratory reserve volume.
3 Work out what happens to these volumes during exercise. This time the initial breath in and out needs to be much deeper as breathing is both quicker and deeper during exercise.

When we breathe out as hard as we can, there is still some air left in the lungs; this is called the **residual volume**. Some air remains in the lungs after breathing because we can never totally empty our lungs even when we have exhaled as much as possible. This is because there will still be some air in the alveoli, bronchi and trachea as these are held open permanently by rings of cartilage.

Table 2 identifies the different parts of our total lung volume.

KEY TERM

Residual volume: The amount of air that remains in the lungs after maximal expiration.

Table 2 The different parts of an individual's total lung volume and the changes that take place in these volumes during exercise

Lung volume or capacity	Definition	Changes during exercise
Tidal volume	Volume of air breathed in **or** out per breath	Increase
Inspiratory reserve volume	Volume of air that can be forcibly inspired after a normal breath	Decrease
Expiratory reserve volume	Volume of air that can be forcibly expired after a normal breath	Slight decrease
Residual volume	Volume of air that remains in the lungs after maximum expiration	Remains the same
Minute ventilation	Volume of air breathed in or out per minute	Big increase

STUDY HINTS

You may be asked for a definition of a certain lung volume and an explanation of how these change during exercise.

21

KEY TERM

Spirometer: A device that is used to measure the volume of air inspired and expired by the lungs.

The volume of air we breathe in and out can be measured using a **spirometer**. Here, an individual breathes in and out of a sealed chamber through a mouthpiece. This makes the chamber inflate and deflate and as this happens, a pen recorder traces the breathing movements onto a chart. The machine is calibrated so that breathing volumes can be calculated. An example of a spirometer trace can be seen in Figure 4.

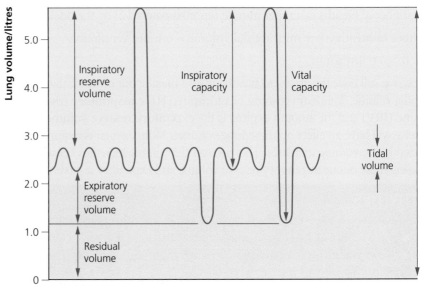

Figure 4 Spirometer trace of respiratory air

During exercise, the spirometer trace changes (Figure 5):

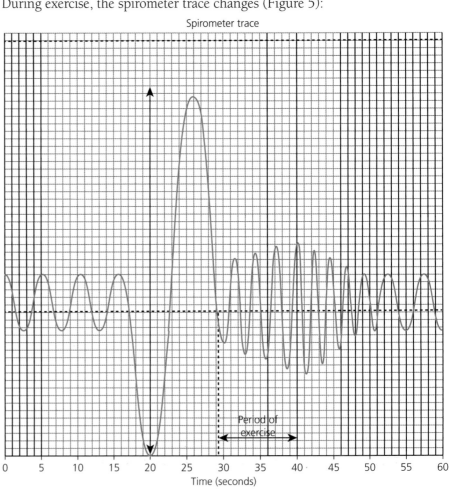

Figure 5 Graphical representation of tidal volume

Graphical representation of tidal volume is different. The lines are now longer and much closer together, which shows deeper and quicker breathing. As you'll see from Figure 5, the longer peaks and troughs for tidal volume mean that inspiratory reserve volume and expiratory reserve volumes are reduced.

CHECK YOUR UNDERSTANDING

Figure 6 shows the spirometer trace of a badminton player.

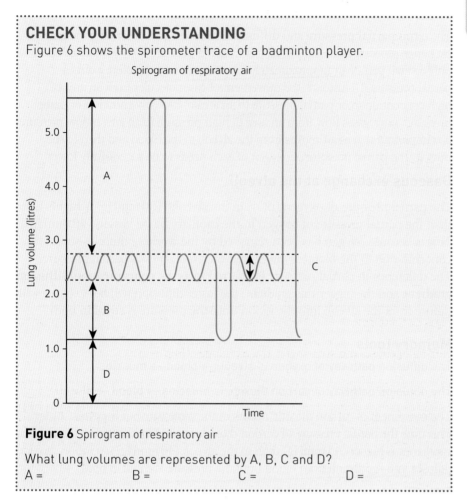

Figure 6 Spirogram of respiratory air

What lung volumes are represented by A, B, C and D?

A =   B =   C =   D =

Minute ventilation

Minute ventilation is the volume of air inhaled or exhaled from the lungs per minute. Changes in minute ventilation occur during different types of exercise. As you would expect, the more demanding the physical activity is, the more breathing increases to meet the extra oxygen demand. This is illustrated in Figure 7:

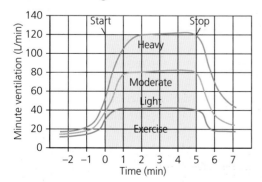

Figure 7 The respiratory response to various intensities of exercise

Gaseous exchange

Gaseous exchange is concerned with:

- Getting oxygen in air into the lungs so that it can diffuse into the blood and be transported to the cells of the body.
- The removal of carbon dioxide from the blood.

The terms **partial pressure** and **diffusion** are used when describing the gaseous exchange process. Quite simply, all gases exert a pressure. Oxygen makes up only a small part of air (approximately 21 per cent) so it therefore exerts a partial pressure. Diffusion is the movement of gas molecules from an area of high concentration or partial pressure to an area of low concentration or partial pressure. Since gases flow from an area of high pressure to an area of low pressure, it is important that as air moves from the alveoli to the blood and then to the muscle, the partial pressure of oxygen of each needs to be successively lower.

Gaseous exchange at the alveoli

The partial pressure of oxygen (pO_2) in the alveoli (100 mmHg) is higher than the partial pressure of oxygen in the capillary blood vessels (40 mmHg). This is because oxygen has been removed by the working muscles so its concentration in the blood is lower, and therefore so is its partial pressure. The difference in partial pressure is referred to as the **concentration/diffusion gradient** and the bigger this gradient, the faster diffusion will be. Oxygen will diffuse from the alveoli into the blood until the pressure is equal in both.

Memory tools

The diffusion pathway of oxygen is alveoli → blood → muscles

The diffusion pathway of carbon dioxide is muscles → blood → alveoli

The movement of carbon dioxide occurs in the same way but in reverse order. This time the partial pressure of carbon dioxide in the blood entering the alveolar capillaries is higher (45 mmHg) than in the alveoli (40 mmHg) so carbon dioxide diffuses into the alveoli from blood until the pressure is equal in both.

Table 3 Percentages of gases and water content in inspired and expired air

Percentages of gases and water content in inspired and expired air			
	Inspired air at rest (% gases)	**Expired air at rest (% gases)**	**Expired air during exercise (% gases)**
Oxygen	21	16.4	14
Carbon dioxide	0.03	4.0	6
Nitrogen	79	79.6	79
Water vapour	Varied	Saturated	Saturated

Gaseous exchange at the muscles

The partial pressure of oxygen has to be lower at the tissues than in the blood for diffusion to occur. As such, in the capillary membranes surrounding the muscle the partial pressure of oxygen is 40 mmHg and it is 100 mmHg in the blood. This lower partial pressure allows oxygen to diffuse from the blood into the muscle until equilibrium is reached. Conversely, the partial pressure of carbon dioxide in the blood (40 mmHg) is lower than in the tissues (46 mmHg) so again, diffusion occurs and carbon dioxide moves into the blood to be transported to the lungs.

Figure 8 highlights the differences in the partial pressure of oxygen and carbon dioxide in the alveoli, blood and muscle cell.

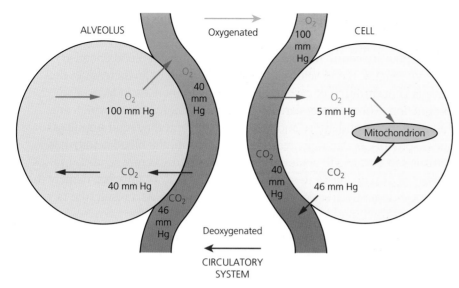

Figure 8 Movement of O$_2$ and CO$_2$ in the body due to partial pressures

Regulation of pulmonary ventilation during exercise

There are three factors involved in the regulation of pulmonary ventilation during exercise:

● neural control   ● chemical control   ● hormonal control.

Memory tools

Pulmonary ventilation simply means breathing!

Neural and chemical regulation of pulmonary ventilation

In simple terms, neural control involves the brain and the nervous system and chemical control is concerned with blood acidity. Both of these work together as a team to regulate breathing. When blood acidity is high, the brain is informed and it sends impulses through the nervous system to increase breathing!

Pulmonary ventilation is breathing and the nervous system controls this automatically through two systems: the sympathetic and parasympathetic.

Memory tools

Remember neural and chemical control were both discussed in Chapter 1.1 and are also important in the respiratory system.

Both of these cause opposite effects because their activating chemicals are different. The sympathetic nervous system prepares your body for exercise so it will increase breathing rate (how fast you breathe), whereas the parasympathetic nervous system will do the opposite and lower breathing rate. The respiratory centre located in the medulla oblongata of the brain controls the rate and depth of breathing and uses both neural and chemical control.

An increased concentration of carbon dioxide in the blood stimulates the respiratory centre to increase respiratory rate. The respiratory centre has two main areas. The inspiratory centre is responsible for inspiration and expiration. The expiratory centre stimulates the expiratory muscles during exercise.

The inspiratory centre sends out nerve impulses via the phrenic nerve to the inspiratory muscles (diaphragm and external intercostals) to cause them to contract. This stimulation acts for approximately two seconds and then

CHECK YOUR UNDERSTANDING

In order to make use of their stamina, footballers need to take in oxygen. Figure 9 shows values for the partial pressure of oxygen and carbon dioxide at two different locations in one gas exchange system.

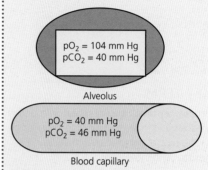

Figure 9 The differences in partial pressure of oxygen and carbon dioxide in the alveolus and blood capillary

ACTIVITY

Use the information from Figure 8 to explain how oxygen and carbon dioxide move between the two locations.

STUDY HINT

Exercise always involves the sympathetic system.

the impulses stop and passive expiration occurs due to the elastic recoil of the lungs.

The respiratory centre responds mainly to changes in blood chemistry. During exercise, blood acidity increases as a result of an increase in the plasma concentration of carbon dioxide and an increase in lactic acid production. These changes are detected by chemoreceptors, which are found in the carotid artery and the aortic arch and they send impulses to the inspiratory centre to increase ventilation until the blood acidity has returned to normal. To achieve this, the respiratory centre sends impulses down the phrenic nerve to stimulate more inspiratory muscles: namely the sternocleidomastoid, scalenes and pectoralis minor. As a result, the rate, depth and rhythm of breathing increase.

Other factors affecting neural control of breathing

- Mechanical factors – **proprioceptors** are sensory receptors located in the joints and muscles that provide feedback to the respiratory centre to increase breathing during exercise.
- Baroreceptors – a decrease in blood pressure detected by baroreceptors in the aorta and carotid arteries results in an increase in breathing rate.
- Stretch receptors – during exercise the lungs are also stretched more. Stretch receptors prevent over-inflation of the lungs by sending impulses to the expiratory centre and then down the intercostal nerve to the expiratory muscles (abdominals and internal intercostals) so that expiration occurs. This process is summarised in Figure 10:

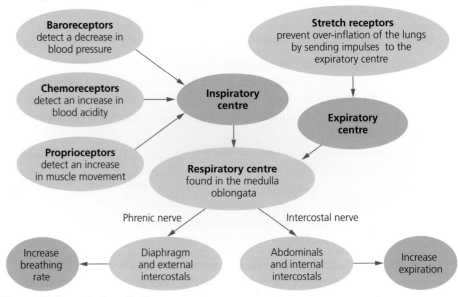

Figure 10 Control of ventilation

Memory tools

The order of neural/chemical control for inspiration is:

Receptors → medulla → phrenic nerve → diaphragm and external intercostals

The order of neural/chemical control for expiration is:

Receptors → medulla → intercostal nerve → abdominals and internal intercostals

Hormonal regulation of pulmonary ventilation during exercise

Adrenaline is a natural stimulant made in the adrenal gland of the kidney. It is transported in the blood and affects the nervous system. Adrenaline is often referred to as the body's activator and is released in response to exercise. Just before we start exercise, the brain sends impulses to the renal glands which respond and pump adrenaline into the blood in anticipation of the increased need for oxygen and carbon dioxide exchange. As a result, breathing rate increases in preparation for exercise and the demand to take in more oxygen and remove more carbon dioxide.

Memory tools

Adrenaline is the hormone that increases breathing rate in preparation for exercise.

Impact of poor lifestyle choices on the respiratory system

There are many lifestyle choices we make, such as what we eat, how much we exercise, how much alcohol we drink, or whether we choose to smoke. These can all have an impact on our health.

Smoking

Smoking has a huge effect on the respiratory system. It can cause irritation of the trachea and bronchi. It reduces lung function and increases breathlessness caused by the swelling and narrowing of the lungs' airways. Cigarette smoke damages the cells lining the trachea, bronchi and bronchioles. These tiny cells have microscopic hair-like cilia on their surface, which help to push mucus out of the lungs. When they are damaged, excess mucus builds up in the lung passages, which leads to a smoker's cough to try to get rid of the mucus.

Smoking can damage the alveoli as their walls break down and join together forming larger air spaces than normal. This reduces the efficiency of gaseous exchange, which also increases the risk of **COPD** (chronic obstructive pulmonary disease). Smoking also affects oxygen transport as the carbon monoxide from cigarettes combines with haemoglobin in red blood cells much more readily than oxygen. This reduces the oxygen-carrying capacity of the blood, which increases breathlessness during exercise.

KEY TERMS

Cilia: Cilia are microscopic hair-like projections that help to sweep away fluids and particles.

COPD is a chronic and debilitating disease and is the name for a collection of diseases such as emphysema. The main cause of emphysema is smoking. It is a long-term, progressive disease of the lungs that causes shortness of breath.

SUMMARY

- You need to be able to define tidal volume (volume of air breathed in **or** out per breath), inspiratory reserve volume (volume of air that can be forcibly inspired after a normal breath), expiratory reserve volume (volume of air that can be forcibly expired after a normal breath) and residual volume (volume of air that remains in the lungs after maximum expiration).
- Minute ventilation is the volume of air breathed in or out per minute.
- Learn to label tidal volume, inspiratory reserve volume, expiratory reserve volume and residual volume on a spirometer trace.
- Gaseous exchange is the taking in of oxygen and the removal of carbon dioxide.

- Partial pressure is a term used for the pressure exerted by an individual gas when it exists within a mixture of gases.
- Oxygen and carbon dioxide are exchanged via diffusion, which is the movement of gas molecules from an area of high concentration or partial pressure to an area of low concentration or partial pressure.
- Remember the diffusion pathway of oxygen is: alveoli → blood → muscles; and of carbon dioxide it is: muscles → blood → alveoli.
- Diffusion gradient is often referred to as the concentration gradient. It explains how gases flow from an area of high concentration to an area of low concentration. The steeper this gradient, the faster diffusion occurs.
- The sympathetic nervous system prepares your body for exercise so that it will increase breathing rate.
- The parasympathetic nervous system lowers breathing rate.
- Chemoreceptors detect increases in blood carbon dioxide and they send impulses to the inspiratory centre to increase ventilation until blood acidity has returned to normal.
- A decrease in blood pressure detected by baroreceptors in the aorta and carotid arteries results in an increase in breathing rate.
- When describing neural and chemical control of breathing, make sure you know the correct order for inspiration (receptors → medulla → phrenic nerve → diaphragm and external intercostals) and expiration (receptors → medulla → intercostal nerve → abdominals and internal intercostals).
- Adrenaline is the hormone that increases breathing rate.

PRACTICE QUESTIONS

1 Which of the following statements is correct?   (1 mark)

   a) Tidal volume is the amount of air breathed in after a normal breath.

   b) Expiratory reserve volume is the amount of air that can be breathed out.

   c) Minute ventilation is inspiratory reserve volume + expiratory reserve volume.

   d) Inspiratory reserve volume is the amount of air that can be forcibly inspired after a normal breath.

2 During exercise, the demand for oxygen by the muscles increases. How does an increase in blood carbon dioxide change breathing rate?   (4 marks)

3 Gas exchange and oxygen delivery influence performance in sporting activities. Explain how oxygen diffuses from the lungs into the blood and how it is transported to the tissues.   (4 marks)

4 Define tidal volume and identify what happens to this respiratory volume during exercise.   (2 marks)

Chapter 1.3
The neuromuscular system

Chapter objectives

After reading this chapter you should be able to:

- Identify the characteristics and functions of the three fibre types: slow twitch (type 1), fast oxidative glycolytic (type IIa) and fast glycolytic (type IIb) for a variety of sporting activities.
- Learn more about the role of the sympathetic and parasympathetic nervous system.
- Explain the recruitment of muscle fibres through an explanation of motor units.
- Explain the role of the two proprioceptor muscle spindles and golgi tendon organs in PNF.
- Understand the terms spatial summation, wave summation, all or none law and tetanic contraction.

This chapter will develop your understanding of the relationship between the nervous and muscular systems so you can see what goes on 'behind the scenes' neurologically. It details why and when the body recruits different muscle fibre types, how it adjusts the strength of contraction and explains how sensory organs can allow a muscle to stretch further in PNF.

The autonomic nervous system and neuromuscular system

The autonomic nervous system regulates the function of our internal organs such as the heart and also controls some of our skeletal muscles within the body. It works involuntarily, which means that things take place which we do not notice. For example, while playing football, we don't tell our muscles: 'OK, now we need a bigger contraction to jump high to head the ball!' The nervous system will do this automatically for us.

The movement of muscles during exercise is controlled by the brain via nerves. The neuromuscular system is where the nervous system and the muscles work together to allow movement. Changes in the neuromuscular system take place before, during and after exercise. These changes prepare the body for exercise and allow for the changing demands of different intensities of exercise. The sympathetic and parasympathetic systems are part of the peripheral nervous system and their role is to transmit information from the brain to the parts of the body that need to adjust what they are doing to prepare for exercise.

- The sympathetic nervous system prepares the body for exercise and is often referred to as the 'fight or flight response'.
- The parasympathetic nervous system has the opposite effect of the sympathetic system and relaxes the body and slows down many high energy functions. It is often explained by the phrase 'rest and relax'.

Figure 1 An endurance runner

STUDY HINT

Slow twitch fibres contract more slowly and do not fatigue quickly so they tend to be used by endurance runners who use the aerobic system to supply the majority of their energy.

KEY TERMS

Aerobic: Literally means 'with oxygen' so it refers to exercise that is low to medium intensity where the oxygen demand of the muscles can be met.

Anaerobic: Means 'without oxygen' and refers to exercise at high intensity such as sprinting, where the demand for oxygen by the muscles is so high that it cannot be met.

Figure 2 A sprinter

STUDY HINT

Fast twitch fibres contract quickly and generate a lot of force so they are used by power athletes.

Memory tools

Sympathetic system is fight or flight – it fires up the body for exercise!

Parasympathetic system is 'rest and relax' – it slows everything down!

Types of muscle fibre

Three main types of muscle fibre can be identified:

● slow oxidative (type I) (also known as slow twitch)
● fast oxidative glycolytic (type IIa)
● fast glycolytic (type IIb).

Our skeletal muscles contain a mixture of all three types of fibre but not in equal proportions. This mix is mainly genetically determined.

The relative proportion of each fibre type varies in the same muscles of different people. For example, in an elite endurance athlete there will be a greater proportion of slow twitch fibres in the leg muscles, and in the elite sprinter a greater proportion of fast twitch fibres in the leg muscles. Also, postural muscles tend to have a greater proportion of slow twitch fibres as they are involved in maintaining body position over a long period of time.

Slow twitch fibres (type 1)

These fibres have a slower contraction speed than fast twitch fibres and are better adapted to lower intensity exercise such as long-distance running. They produce most of their energy **aerobically** (using oxygen) and therefore have specific characteristics that allow them to use oxygen more effectively.

Fast twitch fibres (type II)

These fibres have a much faster contraction speed and can generate a greater force of contraction. However, they also fatigue very quickly and are used for short, intense bursts of effort. They produce most of their energy **anaerobically** (without oxygen). There are two types of fast twitch fibre:

● Type IIa fast oxidative glycolytic – these fibres are more resistant to fatigue and are used for events such as the 1500m in athletics where a longer burst of energy is needed.
● Type IIb fast glycolytic – these fibres fatigue much quicker than type IIa and are used for highly explosive events such as the 100m in athletics where a quick, short burst of energy is needed.

ACTIVITY

Copy and complete Table 1. Can you think of three sporting examples for each category where this type of muscle fibre provides the majority of energy?

Table 1

SLOW TWITCH (TYPE 1)	FAST TWITCH (IIa)	FAST TWITCH (IIb)
1 2 3	1 2 3	1 2 3

Characteristics of slow and fast twitch muscle fibres

All three fibre types have specific characteristics that allow them to perform their role successfully. These can be found in Table 2:

Table 2 Characteristics of slow and fast twitch muscle fibres

Characteristic	Type I	Type IIa	Type IIb
Contraction speed (metres per second)	Slow (110)	Fast (50)	Fast (50)
Motor neurone size	Small	Large	Large
Motor neurone conduction capacity	Slow	Fast	Fast
Force produced	Low	High	High
Fatigability	Low	Medium	High
Mitochondrial density	High	Medium	Low
Myoglobin content	High	Medium	Low
Capillary density	High	Medium	Low
Aerobic capacity	Very high	Medium	Low
Anaerobic capacity	Low	High	Very high
Myosin ATPase/glycolytic enzyme activity	Low	High	Very high

STUDY HINT

Remember to learn the characteristics of the fibre types, but also make sure you can explain how these characteristics are suited to producing ATP aerobically and anaerobically.

ACTIVITY

Each of the characteristics you have just learned can be divided into two groups. They can either be a functional characteristic or a structural characteristic. A functional characteristic is what the fibre does and a structural characteristic is the make-up of the fibre. Copy and complete Table 3 and place each of the characteristics from Table 2 into the relevant category.

Table 3 Functional and structural characteristics of muscle fibres

FUNCTIONAL CHARACTERISTIC	STRUCTURAL CHARACTERISTIC

CHECK YOUR UNDERSTANDING

A basketball player will use type IIb fibres to jump as high as possible to win a rebound. Can you give two characteristics of this fibre type?

The effect of training on fibre type

Fibre type appears to be genetically determined. However, it is possible to increase the size of muscle fibres through training. This increase in size is called **hypertrophy**, which results in a greater strength in the muscle.

KEY TERM

Hypertrophy: Where the muscle has become bigger and stronger.

The motor unit

Muscle fibres are grouped into motor units. A **motor unit** consists of a **motor neurone** and its muscle fibres. Only one type of muscle fibre can be found in one particular motor unit. Muscle fibres work with the nervous system so that a contraction can occur. The motor neurone transmits the nerve impulse to the muscle fibre. Each motor neurone has branches that end in the **neuromuscular junction** on the muscle fibre.

Memory tools

Motor = movement.

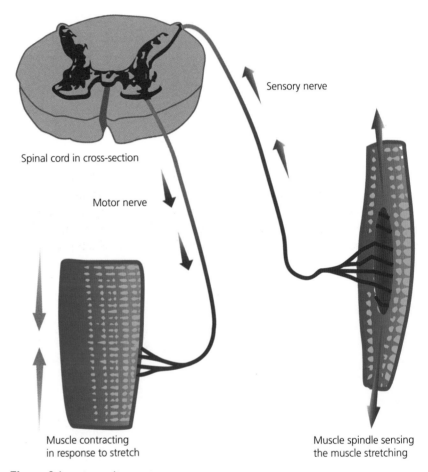

Spinal cord in cross-section

Sensory nerve

Motor nerve

Muscle contracting in response to stretch

Muscle spindle sensing the muscle stretching

Figure 3 A motor unit

Each muscle is made up of many motor units and they vary in size. A small muscle that is used for fine motor control, for example the muscles controlling eye movements, will have motor units that have only a few fibres per motor neurone. However, a large muscle used for gross motor control, such as the quadriceps when the leg is extended, will have motor units with a motor neurone feeding hundreds of fibres. (See Chapter 2.1 for a definition of fine and gross skills.)

The all or none law

Once the motor neurone stimulates the muscle fibres, either all of them contract or none of them contract. It is not possible for a motor unit to partially contract. This is called the **all or none law**. Here, a

KEY TERMS

Motor unit: A motor neurone and its muscle fibres.

Motor neurones: Nerve cells which transmit the brain's instructions as electrical impulses to the muscles.

Neuromuscular junction: Where the motor neurone and the muscle fibre meet.

minimum amount of stimulation called the 'threshold' is required to start a contraction. If the sequence of impulses is equal to or more than the threshold, all the muscle fibres in a motor unit will contract. However, if the sequence of impulses is less than the threshold, then no muscle action will occur.

Slow twitch and fast twitch motor units

Motor units contain the same type of muscle fibre so they are either slow twitch or fast twitch motor units. The brain will recruit slow twitch motor units for low intensity activity such as jogging or long-distance swimming. If a greater force of contraction is needed, the brain will recruit fast twitch motor units for activities such as sprinting or power lifting.

How to increase the strength of contraction

A basketball player jumping up for a rebound needs to exert as much force as possible to gain the height needed to win the rebound. In order to increase the strength or force exerted by her quadriceps muscle to extend her knee as she jumps, the following needs to take place:

- **Wave summation.** The greater the frequency of stimuli, the greater the tension developed by the muscle. This is referred to as wave summation where repeated activation of a motor neurone stimulating a given muscle fibre results in a greater force of contraction. Each time the nerve impulse reaches the muscle cell, calcium is released. In simple terms, calcium needs to be present for a muscle to contract. If there are repeated nerve impulses with no time to relax, calcium will build up in the muscle cell. This produces a forceful, sustained, smooth contraction which is referred to as a **tetanic contraction**.

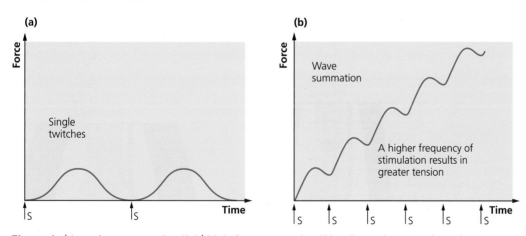

Figure 4 a) Low-frequency stimuli; b) high-frequency stimuli leading to increased tension

- **Spatial summation.** This occurs when impulses are received at the same time at different places on the neurone which add up to fire the neurone. It is the recruitment of additional and bigger motor units within a muscle to develop more force. This means the basketball player will use lots of large, fast twitch motor units in her quadriceps muscles to try to achieve as much height as possible as she jumps for the rebound.

STUDY HINT
Questions on motor units often ask how they can be used to produce muscle contractions of varying strength.

KEY TERMS

Muscle spindles: These detect how far and how fast a muscle is being stretched and produce the stretch reflex.

Golgi tendon organs: These are activated when there is tension in a muscle.

PNF (proprioceptive neuromuscular facilitation)

Proprioceptive neuromuscular facilitation is an advanced stretching technique. It is also considered to be one of the most effective forms of flexibility training for increasing range of motion. There are a few different PNF techniques but the most practical is the CRAC technique (contract–relax–antagonist–contract).

The role of muscle spindles and golgi tendon organs in PNF

In PNF, muscle action has to be controlled in order for movement to be effective. There are several internal regulatory mechanisms that make this possible.

Proprioceptors

Remember from the previous chapters that these are sensory organs in the muscles, tendons and joints that inform the body of the extent of movement that has taken place. **Muscle spindles** and **golgi tendon organs** are types of proprioceptors.

Muscle spindles

These are very sensitive proprioceptors that lie between skeletal muscle fibres. They are often called stretch receptors as they provide information (excitory signals) to the central nervous system about how fast and how far a muscle is being stretched. The central nervous system then sends an impulse back to the muscle telling it to contract, which triggers the stretch reflex. This reflex action that causes the muscle to contract to prevent over-stretching reduces the risk of injury.

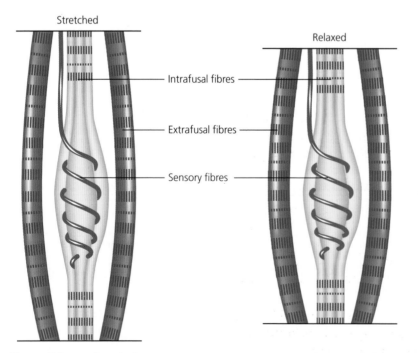
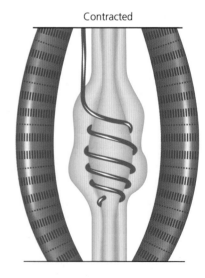

Stretched
Relaxed
Contracted

Intrafusal fibres

Extrafusal fibres

Sensory fibres

Figure 5 A muscle spindle

Golgi tendon organs

These are found between the muscle fibre and tendon. They detect levels of tension in a muscle. When the muscle is contracted **isometrically** in PNF, they sense the increase in muscle tension and send inhibitory signals to the brain which allows the antagonist muscle to relax and lengthen. This is known as **autogenic inhibition**.

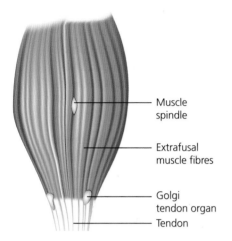

Figure 6 Location of golgi tendon organ and muscle spindle

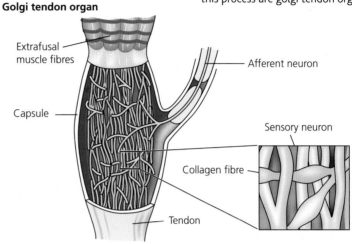

Figure 7 Golgi tendon organ

PNF in practice

(a)   (b)   (c)

Figure 8 PNF in practice

a) Here, the individual performs a passive stretch with the help of a partner and extends the leg until tension is felt. This stretch is detected by the muscle spindles. If the muscle is being stretched too far, then a stretch reflex should occur.

b) The individual then isometrically *contracts* the muscle for at least ten seconds by pushing their leg against their partner who supplies just enough resistance to hold the leg in a stationary position. Remember, golgi tendon organs are sensitive to tension developed in a muscle, and during an isometric contraction they are activated and the inhibitory signals they send override the excitory signals from the muscle spindles, therefore delaying the stretch reflex.

c) As the leg is lifted again, the golgi tendon organs are responsible for the antagonist muscle relaxing, which means the leg stretches further. This process can be repeated until no more gains are possible.

SUMMARY

In the central nervous system, the sympathetic system fires up the body for exercise and the parasympathetic system slows everything down. Slow twitch fibres are designed to use oxygen and so are used for endurance-based sports, while fast twitch fibres fatigue much faster because they work without oxygen, so they are used by power athletes for short bursts of high intensity exercise.

A motor unit is the motor neurone and muscle fibres and contains only one type of muscle fibre. The strength of a contraction can be altered through spatial summation and wave summation and the 'all or none' law. Make sure you can explain these terms. A tetanic contraction is a sustained muscle contraction caused by a series of fast repeating stimuli.

PNF is an advanced stretching technique and you need to be able to explain the physiology behind it using muscle spindles, which detect how far and how fast a muscle is being stretched and golgi tendon organs, which are activated when there is tension in a muscle to relax the antagonist muscle during the stretch.

PRACTICE QUESTIONS

1   The training that elite performers undertake may include proprioceptive neuromuscular facilitation (PNF) stretching. Explain the role of the muscle spindles and golgi tendon organs in PNF stretching.   (3 marks)

2   Contraction of different types of muscle fibres involves the use of motor units. What do you understand by the term 'motor unit'?   (2 marks)

3   How are motor units involved in the process of spatial summation?   (2 marks)

4   Describe the characteristics of the main muscle fibre type used by marathon runners.   (4 marks)

Chapter 1.4
The musculoskeletal system and analysis of movement in physical activities

Chapter objectives

After reading this chapter you should be able to:

● Identify the type of joint and articulating bones for the ankle, knee, hip, elbow and shoulder.

● Recognise the actions in these joints that occur in a sagittal plane/ transverse axis as flexion, extension, hyper-extension, plantar-flexion and dorsi-flexion.

● Identify the actions that occur in these joints in a frontal plane/sagittal axis as abduction and adduction.

● Recognise the actions in these joints that occur in a transverse plane/ longitudinal axis as horizontal abduction and horizontal adduction.

● State the main agonists and antagonists for the actions occurring at these joints.

● Explain the types of muscle contraction: isotonic (concentric, eccentric) and isometric.

In this chapter you will analyse five joints (ankle, knee, hip, elbow and shoulder). You will learn to identify the joint actions that occur in a range of physical activities and name the agonists and antagonists for these actions, explaining the type of contraction that is taking place as either isotonic or isometric.

Types of joints

The skeleton is a framework joined together by joints. Joints are necessary for muscles to lever bones, thus creating movement. A joint is formed where any two or more bones meet. Joints are classified by how much movement they allow. There are three types: fibrous or fixed joints; cartilaginous or slightly moveable joints; and synovial or freely moveable joints. You should aim to study two types of synovial joints including the hip, shoulder, elbow, knee and ankle, the ball and socket joint and the hinge joint (see Figures 2, 3).

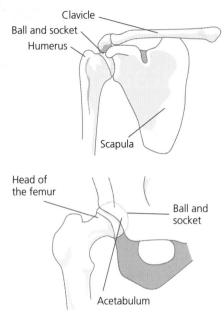

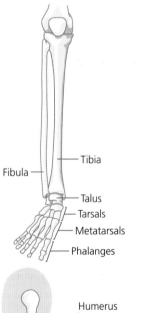

Figure 2 The hip joint and the shoulder joint

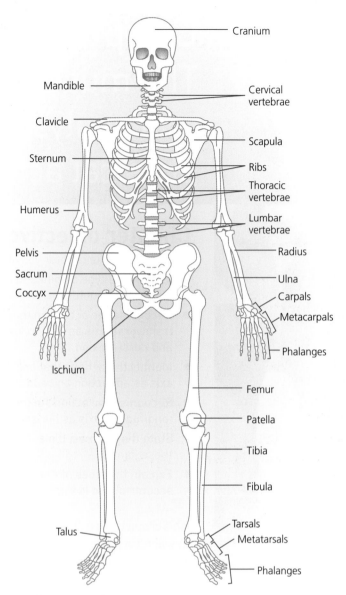

Figure 1 The human skeleton

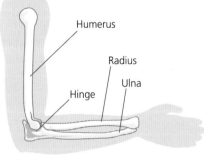

Figure 3 The elbow, ankle and knee joints

KEY TERM

Articulating: This refers to the bones that meet and move at the joint.

Ball and socket joint

This joint allows movement in every direction. It is formed by the round head of one bone fitting into the cup-shaped capsule of the connecting bone. The hip and the shoulder are ball and socket joints. The **articulating** bones of the hip are the femur and pelvis and the humerus and scapula articulate at the shoulder (see Figure 2).

Hinge joint

This joint allows movement in only one direction, due to the shape of the bones making up the joint. The ankle, knee and elbow are hinge joints. The articulating bones of the ankle are the talus, tibia and fibula. The femur and tibia articulate at the knee and the humerus, radius and ulna at the elbow (see Figure 3.)

STUDY HINT

You may not need to label a skeleton but you should remember the names of the bones that articulate at the ankle, knee, hip, shoulder and elbow.

Planes and axes

To help explain joint action, it is possible to view the body as having a series of imaginary lines running through it. These are referred to as planes of movement and divide the body up in three ways:

- The **sagittal plane:** this is a vertical plane, which divides the body into right and left halves.
- The **frontal plane:** this is also a vertical plane that divides the body into front and back halves.
- The **transverse plane:** this divides the body into upper and lower halves.

The three planes of movement are shown in Figure 4.

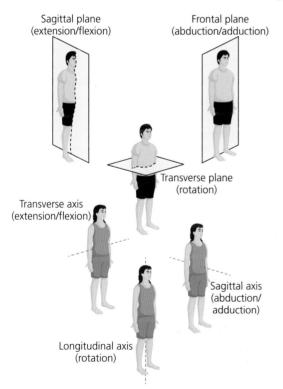

Sagittal plane (extension/flexion)

Frontal plane (abduction/adduction)

Transverse plane (rotation)

Transverse axis (extension/flexion)

Sagittal axis (abduction/ adduction)

Longitudinal axis (rotation)

Figure 4 Planes of movement

When performing an activity, a body or body parts will move in one of these planes or in all three of them, depending on the action being performed. In a full twisting somersault, for example, the gymnast will move in all three planes.

KEY TERMS

Transverse axis: Runs from side to side across the body.

Sagittal axis: Runs from front to back.

Longitudinal axis: Runs from top to bottom.

ACTIVITY

Try to think of your own mnemonic to remember which plane and axis the joint actions take place in the following:
- Abduction and adduction occur in a frontal plane about a sagittal axis.
- Horizontal abduction and horizontal adduction occur in a transverse plane about a longitudinal axis.

KEY TERMS

Flexion: Decreasing the angle between the bones of a joint.

Extension: Increasing the angle between the bones of a joint.

Plantar-flexion: Pointing the toes/pushing up on to your toes.

Dorsi-flexion: Pulling the toes up to the shin.

Hyper-extension: Increasing the angle beyond 180° between the bones of a joint.

There are three axes of movement about which rotation occurs:

- **Transverse axis** that runs from side to side across the body.
- **Sagittal axis** which runs from front to back.
- **Longitudinal axis** that runs from top to bottom.

The joint action taking place (which we will look at next) can be related to both planes and axes. You should remember:

- **Flexion, extension, plantar-flexion, dorsi-flexion** and **hyper-extension** occur in a sagittal plane about a transverse axis.
- Abduction and adduction occur in a frontal plane about a sagittal axis.
- Horizontal abduction and horizontal adduction occur in a transverse plane about a longitudinal axis.

Memory tools

Flexion, **e**xtension, **p**lantar-flexion, **d**orsi-flexion and **h**yper-extension occur in a **s**agittal plane about a **t**ransverse axis.

Try to remember this with the mnemonic:

Fast **E**ffective **P**ressure **D**enies **H**arry **S**ome **T**ime

Joint actions in the sagittal plane about a transverse axis

The joint actions that take place in the sagittal plane and transverse axis are flexion, extension and hyper-extension. All five of the joints in the syllabus flex and extend, but in the ankle joint the action is called plantar-flexion and dorsi-flexion.

Flexion occurs when there is a decrease in the angle around a joint. When there is an increase in the angle that occurs around a joint, extension occurs. If the angle increases by more than 180 degrees, then hyper-extension takes place.

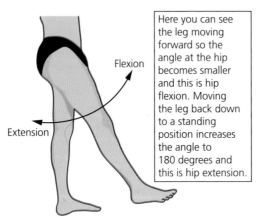

Here you can see the leg moving forward so the angle at the hip becomes smaller and this is hip flexion. Moving the leg back down to a standing position increases the angle to 180 degrees and this is hip extension.

Figure 5 Hip flexion and extension

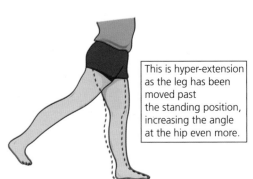

This is hyper-extension as the leg has been moved past the standing position, increasing the angle at the hip even more.

Figure 6 Hip hyper-extension

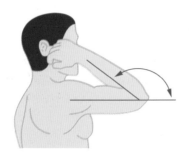

Figure 7 Elbow flexion and extension

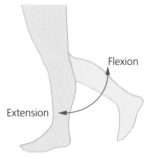

Figure 8 Knee flexion and extension

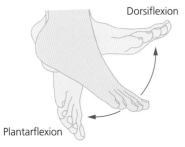

Figure 9 Ankle plantar-flexion and dorsi-flexion

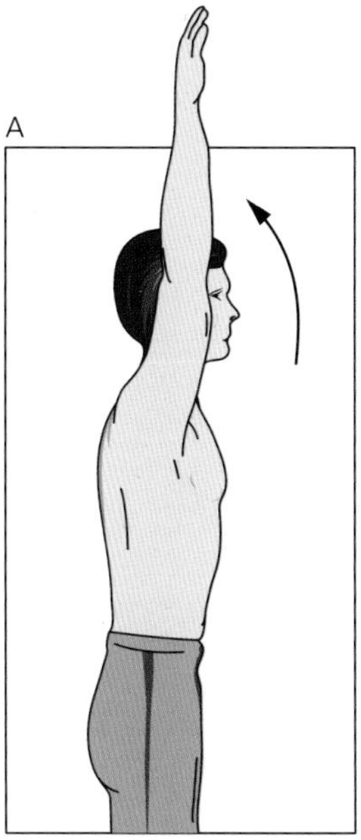

However, shoulder flexion and extension are an exception to the angle rule. It is easier to remember instead that with the arms by the side of the body, raising the arms forward is flexion and lowering the arm down and backwards is extension.

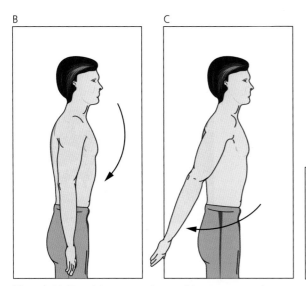

Figure 11 Shoulder extension and hyper-extension

When the arm goes forward it is flexion (A) and the angle is 180 degrees. When the arm moves backwards to the side of the body it is extension and the angle is 0 degrees (B). Moving the arm back further is hyper-extension (C).

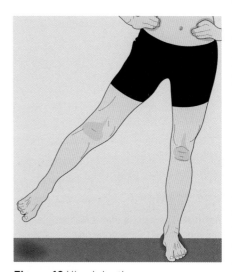

Figure 10 Shoulder flexion

Figure 12 Flexion, extension, hyper-extension and plantar-flexion in action! Can you identify the joint actions occurring at the ankles, knees, hips, elbows and shoulders?

Joint actions in the frontal plane about a sagittal axis

Abduction is movement away from the midline of the body, for example, raising your arms and legs out to the side away from your body. Adduction is movement towards the midline of the body, for example, lowering the arms and leg back to the sides of the body.

Joint actions in the transverse plane about a longitudinal axis

Horizontal adduction is movement of the arm forward across the body at 90 degrees to shoulder abduction. For example, raise your arm out to the side until it is parallel to the floor (abduction of the shoulder) and then move it across the body. Horizontal abduction is movement of the arm backwards across the body to shoulder abduction. For example, raise your arm and hold it at 90 degrees (flexion of the shoulder), then move it away from the body.

Figure 13 Hip abduction

Memory tools

If something is abducted it is taken away. Look at the word **add**uction – think of adding the arm or leg back to the body.

> ### ACTIVITY
> Copy and complete Table 2 to show the joint actions.
>
> **Table 2**
>
> | JOINT | JOINT ACTIONS |
> |---|---|
> | Shoulder | |
> | Elbow | |
> | Hip | |
> | Knee | |
> | Ankle | |

CHECK YOUR UNDERSTANDING

1 Label the joint actions in the elbow and shoulder for Figures 14 and 15.

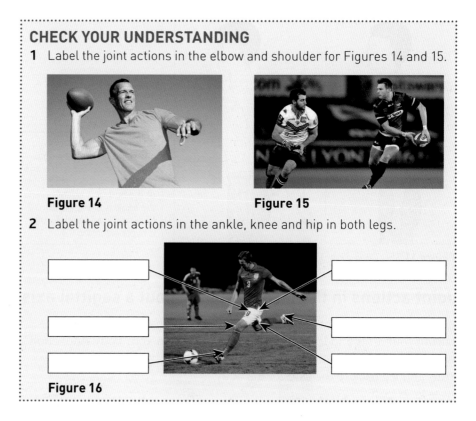

Figure 14   **Figure 15**

2 Label the joint actions in the ankle, knee and hip in both legs.

Figure 16

Agonists and antagonists

A joint cannot move by itself, it needs muscles to move bones into position. When a muscle contracts, one end is anchored in place and the other end pulls the bone, causing movement. If we use the biceps as an example, the anchor point is on the scapula (shoulder) and the other end of the muscle attaches on the radius (forearm). The bicep is responsible for flexion of the elbow and when the muscle contracts, the radius moves upwards towards the shoulder.

KEY TERMS

Agonist: The muscle that is responsible for the movement that is occurring.

Antagonist: The muscle that works in opposition to the agonist (to help produce a co-ordinated movement).

When the biceps contracts, it is responsible for the movement that is occurring and is said to be acting as an **agonist**. There can be more than one agonist acting at a joint although this does depend on the type of movement that is being performed. An **antagonist** muscle is one that works in opposition to the agonist, so when the biceps is contracting, the triceps is lengthening and acting as the antagonist.

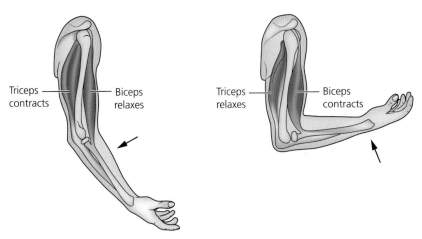

Triceps contracts   Biceps relaxes

Triceps relaxes   Biceps contracts

Figure 17 Agonist and antagonist muscles in the arm

When one muscle is acting as an agonist and the other is acting as the antagonist, the muscles are said to be working together as a pair to produce the required movement. This arrangement is commonly referred to as antagonistic muscle action. If we look at flexion of the knee, the hamstrings are the agonist muscles and the quadriceps are the antagonist muscles.

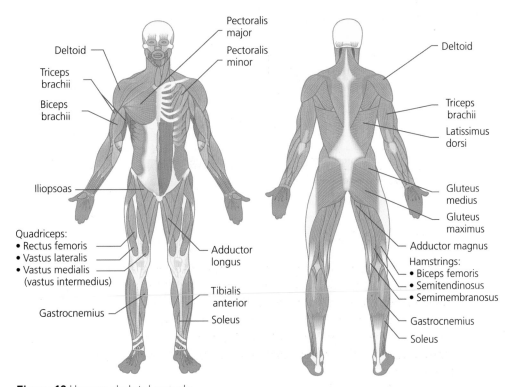

Deltoid
Triceps brachii
Biceps brachii
Iliopsoas
Quadriceps:
• Rectus femoris
• Vastus lateralis
• Vastus medialis
  (vastus intermedius)
Gastrocnemius

Pectoralis major
Pectoralis minor

Adductor longus
Tibialis anterior
Soleus

Deltoid
Triceps brachii
Latissimus dorsi
Gluteus medius
Gluteus maximus
Adductor magnus
Hamstrings:
• Biceps femoris
• Semitendinosus
• Semimembranosus
Gastrocnemius
Soleus

Figure 18 Human skeletal muscle

Table 3 The main agonist and antagonist for each of the joint actions

Joint action	Agonist	Antagonist
Elbow flexion	Biceps	Triceps
Elbow extension	Triceps	Biceps
Ankle plantar-flexion	Gastrocnemius	Tibialis anterior
Ankle dorsi-flexion	Tibialis anterior	Gastrocnemius
Knee flexion	Hamstrings	Quadriceps
Knee extension	Quadriceps	Hamstrings
Hip flexion	Iliopsoas/hip flexors	Gluteals
Hip extension/hyper-extension	Gluteals	Hip flexors
Hip adduction	Adductors (adductor brevis/longus/magnus)	Tensor fascia latae and gluteus medius/minimus
Hip abduction	Tensor fascia latae and gluteus medius/minimus	Adductors (adductor brevis/longus/magnus)
Hip horizontal adduction	Adductors	Tensor fascia latae and gluteus medius/minimus
Hip horizontal abduction	Tensor fascia latae and gluteus medius/minimus	Adductors
Shoulder flexion	Anterior deltoid	Latissimus dorsi
Shoulder extension/hyper-extension	Latissimus dorsi	Anterior deltoid
Shoulder horizontal abduction	Latissimus dorsi	Pectorals
Shoulder horizontal adduction	Pectorals	Latissimus dorsi
Shoulder adduction	Posterior deltoid/latissimus dorsi	Middle deltoid/supraspinatus
Shoulder abduction	Middle deltoid/supraspinatus	Posterior deltoid/latissimus dorsi

CHECK YOUR UNDERSTANDING

Figure 19 shows a javelin thrower just prior to delivering his throw. As the thrower *prepares* to throw the javelin, identify the *joint action* and *main agonist* occurring at the elbow and shoulder joints during this movement.

Figure 19 A javelin throw

Types of muscular contraction

When a muscle works, it contracts. A muscle can contract in different ways, depending on the muscle action that is required. An isotonic contraction is when a muscle contracts to create movement. There are two types of isotonic contraction. When the muscle shortens as the fibres contract, a **concentric contraction** is taking place and when the fibres contract as the muscle lengthens, an **eccentric contraction** occurs. An **isometric contraction** takes place when the muscle is contracting but there is no movement occurring.

Isotonic

A muscle causes movement in an isotonic contraction and there are two types:

Concentric contraction

This is when a muscle shortens under tension, e.g., during the upward phase of an arm curl, the biceps performs a concentric contraction as it shortens to produce flexion of the elbow.

Eccentric contraction

This is when the muscle lengthens under tension (and does not relax). When a muscle contracts eccentrically, it is acting as a brake in helping to control the movement of a body part during negative work. An example could be in landing from a standing jump. Here, the quadriceps are performing negative work as they are supporting the weight of the body during landing. The knee joint is in the flexed position but the quadriceps are unable to relax as the weight of the body ensures that they lengthen under tension.

Isometric contraction

This is when a muscle can contract without actually lengthening or shortening and the result is that no movement occurs. An isometric contraction occurs when a muscle is acting as a fixator or acting against a resistance. A good example is the crucifix position in gymnastics (see Figure 20).

To explain the different types of muscle contraction further. If we use the bicep curl (Figure 21) as an example:

a) During the upward phase, the bicep brachii contracts to produce flexion of the elbow joint. In this situation it is performing a *concentric contraction*.

b) During the downward phase, if you put your hand on a partner's bicep brachii you will still feel tension. This means the muscle is not relaxing but performing an *eccentric contraction* where it lengthens under tension.

c) If the weight is held still at a 90-degree angle, the bicep brachii is under tension even though we do not see any movement. This is an *isometric contraction*.

KEY TERMS

Concentric contraction: When a muscle shortens under tension.

Eccentric contraction: When a muscle lengthens under tension or performs negative work and acts like a brake.

Isometric contraction: When a muscle is under tension but there is no visible movement.

STUDY HINT

Eccentric is the type of contraction most misunderstood. Remember it is a contraction so the muscle cannot be relaxing, it is lengthening under tension.

STUDY HINT

When asked to identify the type of contraction, if the answer is isometric then expect to see the words 'still', 'stationary' or 'held', or their equivalent, in the wording of the question.

Figure 20 The crucifix position in gymnastics is a good example of an isometric contraction.

STUDY HINTS

Be careful: sometimes the agonist does not automatically become the antagonist when the movement changes, for example, flexion to extension. In the downward phase of the biceps curl, most students think that the bicep is now the antagonist as elbow extension takes place. However, the bicep is still the agonist as it is lengthening under tension, which means it is contracting to control the lowering of the forearm while it supports the weight.

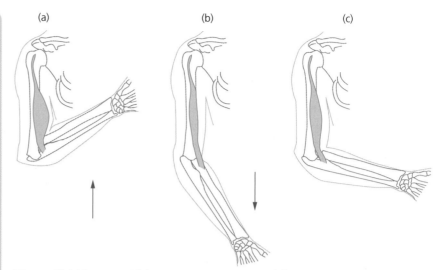

(a)   (b)   (c)

Figure 21 A biceps curl (a) concentric contraction (b) eccentric contraction (c) isometric contraction

ACTIVITIES

Answer the following questions for the movements involved in a press-up.
1 Perform the downward phase of a press-up.
  ● What is happening at the elbow joint?
  ● Which muscle is contracting?
  ● What type of contraction is it performing?
2 Now perform the upward phase of a press-up.
  ● What is happening at the elbow joint?
  ● Which muscle is contracting?
  ● What type of contraction is it performing?
3 Try to hold the press-up in the downward phase.
  ● Which muscle feels as if it is contracting?
  ● What type of contraction is it performing?

ACTIVITIES

Answer the following questions for the movements involved in a squat.
1 Perform the downward phase of a squat.
  ● What is happening at the knee joint?
  ● Which muscle is contracting?
  ● What type of contraction is it performing?
2 Now perform the upward phase of a squat.
  ● What is happening at the knee joint?
  ● Which muscle is contracting?
  ● What type of contraction is it performing?
3 Try to hold the squat in the downward phase.
  ● Which muscle feels as if it is contracting?
  ● What type of contraction is it performing?

SUMMARY

It is important to be able to analyse five joints and be able to apply your knowledge to include the type of joint, the bones that articulate, the joint action each joint can perform, together with the plane and axis that these joint actions occur in. In addition, you need to be able to identify an agonist for each of these joint actions and name the type of contractions these agonists are performing as concentric, eccentric or isometric.

PRACTICE QUESTIONS

1 Which of the following statements is correct? (1 mark)

a) Flexion, extension and hyper-extension occur in a sagittal plane about a transverse axis.

b) Flexion, extension and hyper-extension occur in a transverse plane about a longitudinal axis.

c) Flexion, extension and hyper-extension occur in a frontal plane about a sagittal axis.

d) Flexion, extension and hyper-extension occur in a transverse plane about a sagittal axis.

2 Figure 22 shows a weightlifter performing a squat. Using the picture, identify the joint action, main agonist and the type of muscle contraction occurring at the hip and ankle joints as the weightlifter performs the downward phase. (6 marks)

Figure 22 A weightlifter performing a squat

3 Figures 23 and 24 show a press-up being performed during a fitness session:

Figure 23 A gymnast performing a press-up, part A

Figure 24 A gymnast performing a press-up, part B

a) Using Figures 23 and 24, name the main agonist and antagonist acting on the elbow as the gymnast moves from position A to position B. (2 marks)

Agonist =

Antagonist =

b) Name the type of muscle contraction that occurs in the main agonist:

At position A while the gymnast is stationary.

As the gymnast moves from position A down to position B. (2 marks)

Chapter 2.1
Skill characteristics and their impact on transfer and practice

Chapter objectives

After reading this chapter you should be able to:

- Gain insight into the characteristics of skilled performance, so that you can understand what makes actions skilful.
- Help identify the different types of skills.
- Give practical examples to explain how skills can be transferred from one type to another, including positive, negative, zero and bilateral transfer.
- Understand how the features and characteristics of skill impact on the way practice is organised and presented.
- Understand how skill continua and the graphical illustration of those continua can be interpreted by players and coaches so that appropriate types of practice are chosen.

This section introduces the concept of skill, a term closely associated with sports performance, and provides an in-depth look into what constitutes skilful performance. What types of skill are there? A look at how that skilful performance can be refined via practice will be examined by linking the types of skill to method of practice or presentation.

Characteristics of skill

A classic definition of the term **skill** was given by the sports psychologist Barbara Knapp (in 1963) who described skill as 'a learned ability to bring about pre-determined results with the minimum outlay of time, energy or both'. This classic definition incorporates the fact that skill is learned from natural abilities and suggests that there is more to the concept of skill than you might think.

Skill has essential characteristics. When watching a really good performance, such as that of an Olympic gymnast performing a floor routine, you might begin to imagine the qualities that would make that performance really good to watch. Those qualities are discussed here.

Such a gymnastic performance does not happen by chance: some work must have gone into it and therefore this leads us to be able to state the first quality of a skill – it is **learned.** The essential characteristic which separates skill from ability is that, while abilities are natural, skill has to be developed, usually by periods of hard practice!

Skill is also **consistent**. A penalty taker in a team game or a basketball player taking a free throw would be described as skilful if they could achieve a high percentage rate of success over a number of games. In these two examples, another quality that defines skill is **accuracy**; the penalty taker needs to hit the target in a precise spot to score.

Skilled performance is **controlled**. The diver executing a high dive from the ten-metre board must control their mid-air movements to ensure that when they hit the water, the entry causes minimal splash. Skill is **goal directed** in the sense that it has an aim: the athlete in a hurdles race has the aim of clearing the hurdles and hitting the finish line in the fastest possible time.

Skill is **aesthetically pleasing**, which means that it looks good. Imagine the grace and elegance with which an ice skater performs an ice dance routine to music to illustrate the point. Skill is also **fluent**, **economical**, **smooth** and **efficient**. These four terms imply that a skilled performer, as indicated in Knapp's definition, can execute the task with minimal use of energy while achieving a high level of success. A climber would hope to complete the first phase or pitch of a route without wasting too much energy so that there is enough energy in the tank for the next pitch to be attempted and more chance of a successful conclusion.

Figure 1 A gymnastic performance shows some of the characteristics of skill

Memory tools

To help you remember the characteristics of skill, the following rhyme or acronym may help you.

The characteristics of skill can be related to the terms **ACE FACE**!

- **A** = aesthetically pleasing
- **C** = consistent
- **E** = efficient
- **F** = fluent
- **A** = accurate
- **C** = controlled
- **E** = economical

Skill classification: the use of continua

It has already been indicated that skill is developed through practice. In order to make that practice relevant, skill can be classified into various groups so that the correct form of practice can be chosen. The grouping or classifications of skill are based on clearly defined criteria and those criteria are included in a continua which shows the extent to which a skill matches the set criteria. Those criteria are discussed below. It is important to have knowledge of such skill criteria because the coach or player can then realise by how much a skill fits the criteria and so practice can be adjusted. A coach in a team game might deduce that a pass is very open and therefore introduce variety in training to create that unpredictable environment.

Open and closed skills: environmental influence

The first criterion is based on the influence of the environment.

An **open skill** is performed when the sporting environment is unpredictable and changes frequently. An unpredictable environment simply means all the things that the performer has to think about when playing sport – such as the pitch, the opposition and the position of team mates. This means that the performer must make decisions as the skill is in progress

STUDY HINTS

The last four characteristics of skill have similar meaning. Remember, when you are describing the characteristics of skill, try to make sure that you give four characteristics that differ in their description.

CHECK YOUR UNDERSTANDING

Skills are learned and efficient. State another three characteristics of skill.

KEY TERM

Skill: The learned ability to bring about predetermined results with the minimum outlay of time, energy or both

KEY TERM

Open skill: A skill performed in an unpredictable environment.

Figure 2 A pass in a team game is an example of an open skill

Figure 3 Shot putt – a closed skill

Figure 4 Tackle – a gross skill

Figure 5 Table tennis – a fine skill

and such a skill might best be practised with variety. An unpredictable environment does not necessarily refer to the weather but can include the changing positions of players on the pitch and the unexpected bounce of a ball.

The opposite of an open skill is a **closed skill** which is performed in a predictable environment when, rather than having to adapt actions during the execution of the skill, the performer can repeat the actions consistently and there are fewer decisions to make. Performing a shot putt is a repeated uniform action in which the regulations and conditions of the throwing action are unlikely to change. Such a skill may best be performed by repetition of the same action.

Gross and fine skills: extent of muscles used

The next set of criteria is based on the extent of the muscle groups used in the action.

A **gross skill** is one which is performed using large muscle groups such as the shoulder muscles used to initiate a rugby tackle, together with the leg muscles used to drive the opponent to the ground. The large muscles of the quadriceps used in the tackle will have a large number of fibres.

A **fine skill** is one that uses the smaller, more intricate muscle groups such as the control needed to return a shot in table tennis or even the steady hand needed when attempting to fire a shot in pistol shooting. Small muscles can be used for fine motor control such as the muscles used to control movements of the eyes and of the fingers.

Self-paced and externally paced skills: control and rate of execution

The next set of criteria are concerned with the amount of control the performer has over the rate of execution of the skill and the speed with which the skill is performed.

During a **self-paced skill**, the performer controls the speed at which the skill is performed and often has some control over when to start it. When taking a penalty, the player will decide before the penalty is taken how hard to strike the ball and when to commence the run up (albeit after the referee has indicated that the penalty can commence).

In an **externally paced skill**, the performer has no control over when to start the skill or how fast it might be performed. In a regatta, the sailor must react to the speed of the wind and the flow of the current

Figure 6 Penalty – self-paced skill

Figure 7 Sailing – externally paced skill

when performing a manoeuvre, and has to start the race on the sound of the horn.

Discrete, continuous and serial skills: continuity

The next set of criteria are based upon the continuity of the task.

A **discrete skill** has a clear beginning and end and is one short sharp action. An example is a tennis serve – a fast action, after which the player either stops and repeats if the serve does not go 'in' or, on completion of a successful serve, will then move into position to deal with a possible return. Either way, the service action is clearly identified.

A **continuous skill** has no clear beginning and end and often the end of one part or sub-routine of the skill is the start of the next part. A sub-routine is an action that is part of the whole skill movement. Cycling is an example – when the actions of pedalling can be repeated continuously until the task is completed, or in a non-competitive situation can be stopped when the cyclist feels that they need a rest!

There is a third type of skill based on the criteria of this category that uses discrete skills linked together to form a more continuous movement. A **serial skill** is defined as one in which several discrete skills are linked together in a specific order to form a completed task.

Examples of such skills include gymnastic, dance or trampoline routines during which distinct discrete skills such as the seat drop, pike and somersault on the trampoline can be practised individually and then put together to form the completed movement. Each skill is a discrete movement – put it together and you have a serial skill. Another classic example is the triple jump in athletics when the hop, step and jump, discrete skills in their own right, are combined to make up the movement.

High and low skills: organisation

Skills can be classified according to how easily they can be broken down into parts, or sub-routines.

A skill that is easily broken down into its sub-routines is called a **low organised skill**. An example is a swimming stroke because the arm action, leg action and body positioning can be easily identified and practised separately if needed.

Figure 10 Tennis serve – discrete skill

Figure 8 Cycling – continuous skill

Figure 9 Gymnastics – serial skill

KEY TERM

High organised skill: A skill that is not easily broken into parts.

A **highly organised skill** is not easily broken down into parts. In the case of a volley in football, the action is very quick and the sub-routines merge quickly as the skill is performed.

Figure 11 Swimming stroke – low organised skill

Figure 12 Volley – high organised skill

Simple and complex skills: degree of difficulty

The final criterion on which skills are classified is the degree of difficulty the skills possess in terms of the amount of information needed to complete the skill.

A **simple skill** needs limited decisions to be processed during its execution and there is not a lot for the performer to think about as the skill is being completed. A forward roll in gymnastics is an example.

KEY TERMS

Simple skill: A skill that requires few decisions when being performed.

Complex skill: A skill that requires decision making using lots of information when performed.

A **complex skill** is one in which there may be many decisions to make and an amount of information needed before the performer can attempt the skill. A dribble in hockey is an example since the player has to take into account the position of other players, attackers and defenders, as well as concentrating on the ball and the control of the stick! The player has to think about the cognitive parts of the skill such as the position of opponents, as well as the psychomotor parts – the stick action.

Figure 13 Forward roll – simple skill

Figure 14 Hockey dribble – complex skill

Justification of skill placement on each of the continua

Now that the types of skill have been discussed, there is another aspect to the understanding of skill classification – skills can change! A skill classified as one thing can change in different situations and, as the game or performance develops, skills can be classified in different ways.

For example, in an isolated practice situation, a basketball dribble, when the players are lined up and practising in turn without opposition, can be classed as a closed skill since the environment is predictable. However, in a practice situation of three vs two or during a game, the same skill now becomes open since the environment is changing and unpredictable.

At the start of a swimming race the swimming start may be classed as a discrete skill since it has a clearly defined beginning and end. However, as the actual race gets underway, the swimming stroke can be classed as continuous since it is unclear when one arm action, for example, ends and another arm action begins.

Figure 15 Swimming start – discrete

Figure 16 Swimming race – continuous

KEY TERMS

Transfer: The effect of the learning and performance of one skill on the learning and performance of another.

Positive transfer: When the learning of one skill helps the learning of another.

STUDY HINTS

Remember if you are defining or explaining the different types of transfer, you should try to use different words from those already contained in the term. In other words, do not explain the term 'positive transfer' by stating that it is when there is a positive effect between skills.

KEY TERM

Negative transfer: When the learning of one skill hinders the learning of another.

Transfer of learning

An essential feature of a skill is that it is learned. In this section, we are going to look at how such learned skills can be transferred from one sporting situation to another. The theory of **transfer** is defined as the effect of the learning and performance of one skill on the learning and performance of another, and this transfer effect can happen in a number of ways.

Types of transfer

Positive transfer

The first type of transfer is called **positive transfer** and this is defined as when the learning of one skill helps or aids the learning of another.

Positive transfer tends to happen when two skills have a similar shape and form – the actions of the two skills are similar so that the movements of one skill help the action of the other.

Examples would include the similar arm actions of the overarm volleyball serve and the tennis serve or the similar actions of a basketball pass and a netball pass.

Figure 17 The netball pass has a similar action to the basketball pass

Figure 18 Basketball pass

Negative transfer

The second type of transfer is not as helpful and is called **negative transfer**. This happens when the action of one skill hinders the learning of another.

Negative transfer happens when there might be some familiarity with the environment in which the two skills are performed and this familiarity may cause confusion when the actions of the two skills are not the same. Badminton and tennis are games played on a court divided by a net, but the action of the tennis serve uses the arm; the wrist action of the badminton serve is different, hence negative transfer.

Figures 19 & 20 The tennis serve may have a negative effect on the badminton serve

> **STUDY HINT**
> Negative transfer is sometimes confused with zero transfer – an effect that is really not transfer at all because nothing happens – not positive, not negative, nothing!

Zero transfer

Zero transfer is when the learning of one skill has no effect on another since the two skills in question have no similarities and no aspect of confusion. The swimming arm action and the foot placement in rock climbing having nothing in common and therefore there is no transfer affect between them.

KEY TERM

Zero transfer: When the learning of one skill has no impact on the learning of another.

Figure 21 The swimming stroke and climbing have no transfer effect

Figure 22 Rock climbing

Figure 23 The actions of a shot in football can be transferred from right foot to left foot

Bilateral transfer

Another form of transfer happens, as the name suggests, from one limb to another. **Bilateral transfer** happens when the learning of one skill is transferred across the body, in the way that a right-footed footballer would be encouraged to use the left foot when required, so that the impact of a shot from the left foot becomes equal to the impact of a shot with the right foot.

KEY TERM

Bilateral transfer: When the learning of one skill is passed across the body from limb to limb.

Ensuring positive transfer

As far as a coach is concerned, it is the useful effect of positive transfer that is required since this may help players to acquire a greater range of skills. Positive transfer can be encouraged by making sure that training is realistic, so that the use of cones or rugby tackle bags are replaced by real people in small sided games – a more relevant representation of the game!

CHECK YOUR UNDERSTANDING

1 Explain what you understand by the term positive transfer and give an example of two skills that might promote positive transfer when performed in practice.

2 Consider the skills of a throw in the game of rounders and a javelin throw. What type of transfer do you think could take place between these two skills? Can you explain your choice?

KEY TERM

Whole practice: Practising the skill in its entirety.

The coach should make sure that one skill is well learned before moving on to a more advanced skill so that the players experience slow, planned progression and during such progress, the coach could reward and reinforce the players for the correct adaptation of positive transfer by praising players for using skills with similar actions.

The impact of skills classification on the structure of practice for learning

Having discussed the different types of skills and classified those skills according to various criteria, it is also important to discuss how knowledge of skill type can help both coach and player pick the right form of practice so that the most beneficial effect can be found when skills are used in the game or event.

When criteria are used to define an open skill such as a pass, the environment is unpredictable and changing. Therefore practice should be varied to account for the changes the player might encounter in the game. Skill classification should determine the best type of practice to use and the coach should consider the type of skill before deciding how to practise it. The types of practice and the ways to present the skill to the learner are discussed below.

Methods of presenting practice

Skills can be presented as a whole or by breaking them down into sub-routines. The decision on which type of practice to use depends on the type of skill, the performer and the advantages that can be gained.

Whole practice

Whole-practice methods involve performing the skill in its entirety without breaking it into sub-routines. This is the ideal way to teach a skill because it promotes understanding, establishes the links between sub-routines and creates fluency. The coach might decide to use whole practice when:

- The skill is fast, ballistic and discrete such as the sharp action of a tennis serve.
- The skill is highly organised and cannot easily be broken down into sub-routines.
- The skill is simple and does not require much thought so that fewer demands are placed on the performer.
- The feel (**kinaesthesis**) of the whole task is required as the learner develops and is ready to perform the whole task.
- The performer is advanced in the autonomous stage of learning, when movement is detailed and precise, and able to cope with the demands of the whole task.
- The links between sub-routines need to be maintained or the skill needs to be performed in a specific order, such as in a trampoline routine.

Examples of the use of whole practice therefore include a golf swing performed by an experienced player because it is discrete, fast and quick and hard to break down into its parts. The coach would especially use whole practice with an expert since they can cope with the demands of the task and may just need fine tuning!

Advantages of whole practice

The advantages of using whole practice are that it gives a feel for the whole skill and the links between each sub-routine are maintained, as in the golf example when the hip movements lead to a controlled arm action. The performance may therefore be more fluent, and by using whole practice, it may take only a short amount of time to perfect the performance.

- Whole practice helps to create specific images that can be stored as a plan called a motor programme which is stored in the long-term memory and contains a mental image of all the parts of the skill. This is useful when the skill needs to be recalled from memory and performed.
- Whole practice is more realistic than part practice so it helps to produce the effect of positive transfer between skills learned in training and those same skills performed on the pitch.
- Whole practice helps to make the skill consistent – a major characteristic of skilled performance – and it will help the performer to keep good habits and be able to perform skills almost automatically.

Disadvantages of whole practice

Whole practice can, however, have some disadvantages. It may place unnecessary demands on the performer who may not be able to cope with all the aspects of the skill at once, especially if they are a beginner. There could be a possibility of fatigue if the performer tries to do the whole task without a break and there may be too much information for the performer to process.

There is a solution to the problems associated with whole practice when the coach or player may have a specific weakness to work on or the task might be difficult to break down and is being attempted by a novice. The coach may attempt **whole-part-whole practice**.

Whole-part-whole practice

With **whole-part-whole practice** the performer has an attempt at the whole skill to get an initial feel for the movement. Then each part of the task is practised individually or specific weaknesses are highlighted, practised separately and then put back into the whole skill. An example is a fairly experienced volleyball player who has a problem with the spike: the whole action can be looked at and then a specific issue with the arm action is identified and corrected.

The whole-part-whole method is used when a beginner is doing a complex task and may need to concentrate on one part of the skill to get this part right before making progress. This is important when the skill is hard to break down or it has high organisation so that the coach concentrates on one aspect of the skill at a time. Since the skill is not broken up, then the links between the sub-routines are maintained. The coach could even highlight a specific weakness, isolate this weakness and then correct it.

Advantages of whole-part-whole practice

The advantages of whole-part-whole practice are that it can provide motivation when success is achieved when a long-standing weakness is corrected; it provides immediate feedback (see section on feedback in Chapter 2.2); and therefore corrects errors and allows the selected part

Figure 24 A golf swing is a ballistic skill that is best practised using the whole method

KEY TERM

Whole-part-whole practice: Assessing the skill, identifying a weakness to practise, then putting the skill back together.

Figure 25 When practising a volleyball smash, a weakness could be rectified by whole-part-whole practice

to be integrated successfully into the whole action, therefore improving performance and correcting errors. Fluency and integration of the sub-routines can be maintained while errors are corrected – a double bonus! This method maintains the feel for the whole skill and the transition between each part of it.

Disadvantages of whole-part-whole practice

The problem with whole-part-whole practice is that it may produce negative transfer effects unless the coach integrates the part back into the whole during the same training session. Once the part is isolated, the coach should link it back into the whole action as soon as the part has been rectified so that the correct whole action can be learned when the corrections are fresh in the mind. The process of whole-part-whole practice is more time consuming than just doing the whole thing.

Sometimes it is necessary to break the task down into parts as you practise. Although practising each component of the task is a longer process, it can be worth the patience and perseverance.

One method of breaking the skill into parts is called **progressive part practice**.

Progressive part practice

Progressive part practice is sometimes called **chaining**. The first part of the skill is taught and then the rest of the parts are added in sequence. This method of practice is used for serial skills when the order is important and when the links between sub-routines need to be made. It might also be used for dangerous skills such as learning a routine on a trampoline.

For example, a dance routine could be developed by teaching each part of the sequence in order. The first part of the routine is taught first and the second part is added on, and so on, until the sequence is complete.

Figure 26 A dance routine can be broken down into a sequence and can be practised in progressive parts

The progressive part methods of practice are useful when the skill is low-organised and can be broken down so that each part is clear. Progressive part practice can be used when the skill is serial so chaining can occur and each part can be gradually added until the skill is complete. A complex skill could benefit from the use of part practice since one complex feature of the skill can be isolated, taking pressure off the performer.

CHECK YOUR UNDERSTANDING
What are the advantages of using the whole-part-whole method of practice?

KEY TERMS

Progressive part practice: Practising the first part of the skill then adding parts gradually. Sometimes called chaining.

Chaining: Linking the sub-routines, or parts of a task, together in order when practising. The first two parts are learned, then the third part is added; that part is learned and added to the first two, and so on.

Advantages of progressive part practice

The advantages of part practice are that the learner is allowed to focus on one aspect of the task and can potentially correct specific weaknesses. The learner can rest so fatigue is reduced. If the performer is low on motivation, each part brings success in stages so that the motivation levels are restored.

Progressive practice builds an initial understanding and it may improve the confidence of the performer as success is gradually achieved. Progressive practice allows both coach and player to focus on specific issues or key aspects of the task.

Disadvantages of progressive part practice

The disadvantages of part practice are that it can be time-consuming, it might neglect the feel of the whole task and it might ignore the links between sub-routines. As with whole-part-whole practice, there could be a danger of negative transfer between each sequence of the skill so the coach should ensure that the first part of the task is learned well before attempting to make further progress.

In the discussion above of whole and part practice, it was suggested that the performer may need a break when trying to practise a continuous skill. Indeed the coach may take into account the needs of the performer and the type of skill being practised to decide whether to complete the session without a break or to give the players a rest.

Types of practice

Massed practice

Massed practice is continuous, with no rest between sessions. It is used when the skill is discrete, simple and the environment is closed. This means that there are unlikely to be many changes needed to the skill and numerous repetitions can be undertaken.

Advantages of massed practice

The advantages of using massed practice are that it promotes fitness so that the performer can cope with the extended demands of the task. Practising without a break makes the skill become almost automatic so fixed responses become habitual and the player can repeat the skill consistently. Motor programmes – those images stored in the memory – can be stored more easily so that they can be recalled in the future. Massed practice is an efficient use of coach and player time – it gets the job done quickly!

Disadvantages of massed practice

The disadvantages of massed practice are that it can produce fatigue, especially if the performer lacks fitness, and again there is a danger of negative transfer unless the coach makes the practice conditions similar to the real game. The demands on the player are high in this form of practice so the coach should make sure the practice is kept simple and the player has the motivation to keep repeating the drills!

Distributed practice

Distributed practice involves rest intervals between sessions. It should be used when the skill is continuous and the performer may need a break. It could be used when the skill practice is changed because the skill is open and unpredictable and the break is used to explain the changes or additions to the

> **CHECK YOUR UNDERSTANDING**
> When would you use progressive part practice?

> **KEY TERM**
> **Massed practice:** No rest intervals.

> **KEY TERM**
> **Distributed practice:** Rest intervals.

practice drill. During practice of a complex or externally paced skill, the coach might use a break to relieve the pressure and intensity from the players.

The advantages of using distributed practice are that it takes the pressure off the performer and allows some recuperation after a tough session of practice and the possible onset of fatigue.

Distributed practice is good for beginners since it allows controlled progress to be made at the pace of the performer and feedback or coaching advice can be offered to the performer during the rest interval. The performer could use **mental practice** during the break in practice. Mental practice is when the player goes through the key points of the skill in their mind without actual movement.

Distributed practice may offer some motivation to the performer when praise is given by the coach during the rest interval and success in a part of the skill provides intrinsic motivation. Distributed practice offers a safe way of practising more dangerous activities, when clear guidelines can be given to avoid the dangerous aspects of the task.

Disadvantages of distributed practice

The disadvantages of distributed practice are that it is time consuming and should not be used when the training session is tight and requires fast progress. It may not, therefore, be useful for expert players who wish to over-learn their skills. Again, there is a danger of negative transfer that could happen after the rest interval if the coach fails to integrate the practice session.

Distributed practice may be used when the players are offered a break as the type and content of the training session is changed. Indeed, changing the skills and drills and changing the type of practice used is known as **varied practice**.

Varied practice

It is often appropriate during training for team sports to change the drills and the type of practice so that the players learn to adapt to changes in the environment. For instance, the coach may use massed practice with a fixed drill to practise shooting without opposition; the coach may then switch to more progressive practice and use some 3 vs 2 drills.

Varied practice should be used when the skill is open and the environment is unpredictable. This means that there are likely to be changes in the sporting environment when the skill is performed, so the practice session should replicate these conditions. An externally paced skill may mean that the performer has to adapt to changes in the environment, so again varied practice should be used to practise such skills. During a continuous skill, the player may need a little variety to maintain motivation.

Advantages of varied practice

The advantages of varied practice are that it allows the players to adapt their skills to changing environments and is very appropriate for open skills. The variety of practice prevents the players from becoming stale and may add a little fun and games to the practice session, increasing the motivation of the players. Varied practice helps to build the sub-routines or parts of the skill and it also helps to develop a method of adapting existing skills from the memory store, called a 'schema'.

Mental practice: Going over the skill in the mind without movement.

What is the difference between massed practice and distributed practice?

Varied practice: Changing the practice type and the practice drills.

Figure 27 A team training drill uses the principles of varied practice

Disadvantages of varied practice

The disadvantages of varied practice are the familiar ones of it being more time consuming and it increasing the risk of negative transfer unless the changing drills are integrated into the aims of the practice session. An additional problem of varied practice is that it might place unnecessary demands on the players if they are given too many things to focus on and there is also therefore a danger of fatigue.

Mental practice

The process of **mental practice** is an increasingly popular technique which is used in addition to physical practice to aid performance. The athlete goes through the performance in the mind without movement, either just before a major event or as part of a training programme between periods of practice. Mental practice has the greatest results when it is combined with physical practice. Players may use mental practice as part of the warm-up to provide preparation for the task ahead. A games player may mentally rehearse a move or a set play before the kick off.

The benefits of mental practice

The benefits of mental practice are that it improves confidence and lowers anxiety. There is evidence to suggest that mental practice actually stimulates the muscle receptors so that the player is better prepared and reaction times are increased. Mental practice develops cognitive ability and improves the decision making and thinking of the player. A real bonus of mental practice is that it can be done when the player is injured, helping to maintain the memory of the skill.

Mental practice can be external or internal. External mental practice involves forming an image of yourself performing the skill, as if you were on television, i.e. looking at yourself from the outside. Internal mental practice looks at performance from within, i.e. imagining what it feels like to perform the skill and looking at how your anxieties and mental control of the skill can be improved.

Coaching mental practice

Mental practice is so useful that many sports coaches include it in their training. Approaches depend on the degree of experience of the performers.

For beginners, coaches might include mental practice in the training programme as part of distributed practice. They would concentrate on the basics of the skill and introduce more advanced topics by making sure the first part is learned mentally before they progress. For example, they would go over the grip of the ball mentally with the players before they progress to the actual pass.

- For beginners, the mental practice should be short and the key parts of the task should be emphasised. The particular benefits of mental practice should be to lower arousal and anxiety, to build confidence, to provide a basic picture of the requirements of the skill, to reduce errors and to provide motivation.

- With expert performers, the techniques of mental practice should be established so that coaches can devote a whole session to preparing for a major game. Specific tactics or strategies could be highlighted, perhaps focusing on an opponent's weakness, and the performers could then be allowed to control the session.

> **CHECK YOUR UNDERSTANDING**
> For what type of skills would you use varied practice?

- For advanced performers, it is important to develop mental practice because it can give that extra edge by improving reaction time, activating the muscles, helping the performer to focus, and making sure the performer remains in the autonomous phase of learning, with automatic responses.

When mental practice is being undertaken, coaches should try to ensure that it gives maximum benefit to the performer by making sure it is done in a relaxed environment and that successful results are always the ones that are rehearsed. Mental practice can be done in conjunction with physical practice and this combination usually gives the best results.

CHECK YOUR UNDERSTANDING
What are the advantages of using mental practice?

ACTIVITY

Having discussed the different types of practice, pick a skill from a sport of your choice and attempt to classify that skill according to the criteria highlighted earlier in this chapter. Having classified your skill, now suggest the types of practice you might use to learn your chosen skill. Give reasons for your choices.

STUDY HINTS

The key to answering a question that asks you to link a type of practice to a skill classification is to classify the skill first and then explain why a particular type of practice should be used to learn it.

To help you, Table 1 below shows the methods of presentation and the types of skills they should be used for, while Table 2 shows the methods of practice and the types of skills they should be used for.

Table 1 Table to summarise types of presentation

Type of presentation	When to use	Advantages	Disadvantages	Example
Whole Skill in its entirety, sub-routines intact	**When skill is:** Fast Closed Discrete Self-paced Simple High organised	Fluency – feel of the skill Develops kinaesthesis or understanding Keeps links between sub-routines	Too much information Beyond the capabilities of performer Not for beginners	Tennis serve
Whole-part-whole Do whole task Isolate weakness Work on it, put it back into whole task	**When skill is:** Complex Fast/ballistic Difficult to isolate parts of skill yet performer has a specific weakness	Shows weakness Corrects it	Time consuming Some skills cannot be broken down	Golf swing when the performer has a poor grip
Progressive parts Each part of the skill is added, gradually 'chaining'	**When skill is:** Complex Serial Externally paced Low organised	Keeps links between parts Stages of success gives motivation, reduces danger, reduces fatigue, reduces demands Focus on weaknesses	Time consuming If the first part is incorrect, all is lost Negative transfer	A dance routine

Table 2 Table to summarise types of practice

Type of practice	When to use	Advantages	Disadvantages	Example
Massed practice No rest intervals	**When skill is:** Discrete Simple Closed Highly organised Self-paced	Forms motor programmes Increases fitness Enhances over learning Good for habitual responses Efficient	No time for feedback Fatigue Too demanding	Basketball player practising a free throw
Distributed practice Rest intervals between sessions	**When skill is:** Continuous Complex Low organised, can break it down Serial Externally paced	Allows recovery Less mental pressure Allows, mental rehearsal/feedback Reduces danger	Time consuming Negative transfer	A swimmer practising stroke technique in training
Varied practice Changing the skills and drills Changing the type of practice	**When skill is:** Complex, easy part at first then add Open Externally paced	Builds a schema Gives motivation Allows adaptation	Time consuming Possibility of a negative transfer Fatigue Too demanding	Players practising a football pass
Mental practice Go over it in the mind without movement	**When skill is:** Serial, complex Used by both novice and expert: *Novice:* basics in parts, usually during rest in distributed practice *Expert:* whole task, do it for real Two ways: *Internal:* emotions *External:* mental picture of environment	Improves reaction time Builds motor programmes Builds confidence Controls anxiety	Must be correct! Environment must be calm	A performer on the trampoline going over the routine before competition

SUMMARY

In this chapter, the way sports skills can be classified according to various criteria have been studied and the link between the type of skill and the best method of presentation and practice to use has been established. These criteria include the influence of the environment, the use of muscles, pacing, continuity, degree of difficulty and the organisation of the task.

The methods of presentation and practice from which to choose were discussed as follows.

Methods of presentation

- Whole practice: when the skill is performed in its entirety.
- Whole-part-whole practice: when the complete task is performed and then one aspect is isolated and practised so that it can be returned into the whole task with better technique.
- Progressive part practice: when the skill is broken down into its sub-routines and practised in sequence. →

Types of practice

- Massed practice: when the skill is undertaken without a break.
- Distributed practice: when a rest interval is taken during the practice session.
- Varied practice: when different types of practice and different drills are used.
- Mental practice: when the performer goes through the performance in the mind without movement.

The influence of skills transfer, when the learning of one skill affects the learning of another, was discussed in terms of how transfer affects performance in a positive, negative, bilateral way or not at all, if the transfer is zero.

The type of transfer useful to a coach is positive transfer and this can be achieved by making training realistic, pointing out the transfer possibilities, giving praise for successful transfer and making slow, planned progress. Examples of the links a coach may make between the skill classification and the best type of presentation or practice to use are:

- When the skill is simple and discrete, the skill might be practised as a whole without too much demand on the performer; or the coach might use massed practice to groove the performance, such as the cricketer practising a cover drive.
- A complex skill or a skill performed as part of a routine might be coached using progressive part practice, such as in a gymnastics routine.
- If the coach spots a specific weakness such as the incorrect grip on a tennis racket, the coach might use whole-part-whole practice.
- When the skill is continuous, the coach might allow a break in practice to aid recovery.
- When the skill is open, the coach may create an unpredictable environment using varied practice.
- Mental practice can be used before a major competition to calm any nerves.

PRACTICE QUESTIONS

1 The skill of a free throw in basketball is an example of a skill that can be classified as: (1 mark)

 a) open, externally paced and discrete

 b) closed, self-paced and discrete

 c) open, self-paced and discrete

 d) closed, externally paced and continuous.

2 What do you understand by the term 'transfer of learning'? Explain the forms that transfer can take. (3 marks)

3 The sport of athletics is a major feature of the Olympic Games. State a skill in athletics that you think is closed, a skill that you think is serial and a skill that you think is gross. Give reasons for your choices. (3 marks)

4 Swimming may be taught using either the whole method or part method. What are the advantages of using the whole method and the part method? (5 marks)

Chapter 2.2
Principles and theories of learning and performance

Chapter objectives

After reading this chapter you should be able to:

- Describe the stages of learning that a performer goes through as skills are learned, and account for the different types of feedback that are needed at each stage.
- Explain how sports skills can be learned using psychological theories, including operant conditioning, observational learning, insight and social development theories.
- Discuss the role of feedback and guidance on helping to improve performance.

To benefit the performer, skills need to be learned. Some of the theories that can be applied to help the learning of skills are discussed in this chapter. With reference to skill acquisition, the term **learning** is defined as a permanent change in behaviour that occurs as a result of practice. Yet just because skills are learned does not mean that they will always be performed to the best effect. There are many influences on the performer such as an increase in anxiety that can make even elite performers in sport make mistakes. **Performance** is described as a more temporary occurrence influenced by other factors such as anxiety and the nerves that may be felt by a player just before a major game.

The stages of learning

As skills are learned, a sports performer must pass through a transition that moves them from the beginner level to the expert level of performance. This transition can occur in three stages and you should be able to identify the main features of each stage.

> ### STUDY HINT
>
> It is a good idea to ensure that you can show how performance improves as the stages are reached and be prepared to describe the obvious! Those obvious features for each stage are given below.

Stage 1: The cognitive stage

The word cognitive, as used in the previous section with reference to a cognitive skill, means thinking and working out. In terms of the **cognitive stage of learning**, the performer has to think carefully about their actions and try to understand how to copy the demonstrations and instructions

Learning: A permanent change in behaviour as a result of practice.

Performance: A temporary occurrence that can change from time to time because of many external and internal influences.

Cognitive stage of learning: The first stage of learning used by a novice. Understanding and sub-routines are explored by trial and error.

Associative stage of learning: The second stage of learning as motor programmes are developed and performance is smoother.

Autonomous stage of learning: The final stage of learning used by an expert when movement is detailed and specific.

Figure 1 A young hockey player doing a pass – the cognitive stage of learning

Figure 2 An experienced adult hockey player doing a pass – the autonomous stage of learning

they may have seen from a coach. The performer may use extrinsic feedback to help them and such feedback has to be carefully considered; hence movements are often slow and uncoordinated as the performer thinks before taking action. Motor programmes – the components of the skill that can be stored in the memory – are not yet developed and the performer may use trial and error in their approach to the task: having a go at the skill, thinking and adapting their actions, then having another attempt to see if any improvements are being made.

An example of the cognitive stage is a novice hockey player working out the actions of a pass.

Stage 2: The associative stage

The **associative stage** is one of longer duration than the cognitive stage, when the performer moves from being a competent beginner to an accomplished performer. To make progress during this stage, the performer has to practise, and then practise some more. The trial and error process may still be used to perfect the action and the performer may still use feedback, which can now become more internal (see further on). The performer may compare their current level of performance to that of a top-class performer (a process called modelling), and then try to adjust practice to reach that top level. Movements become smoother and more coordinated throughout this stage as the final stage of learning is almost reached.

Stage 3: The autonomous stage

This final, **autonomous stage of learning** is reached after effective practice, and such practice must continue if the performer is to remain in this high level stage, when actions are fluent, efficient and automatically undertaken. The performer can concentrate on fine details of the task since the basics of the skill are performed almost without thinking. The motor programme is fully developed now and can help in the fine control of the action. In this stage, the performer is classed as an expert such as the elite hockey player pictured in Figure 2, picking out the perfect pass to a team mate with precision and accuracy.

ACTIVITY

Learn a new skill!
Try a skill that is new to you such as throwing a quoit in the air and trying to 'thread' it with a relay baton or throwing a bean bag into a target. See how many attempts out of ten are successful at first and then see if your success rate improves as you go through the stages of learning.

STUDY HINTS

A theme throughout the phases of learning is the use of motor programmes. To help your understanding, consider a motor programme to be an image that contains all the parts of a skill – those parts that you may be given from the coach such as the grip on the ball or the placement of the feet. In the cognitive stage, that image is yet to be developed; it forms in the associative stage and is used as an aid in the autonomous stage.

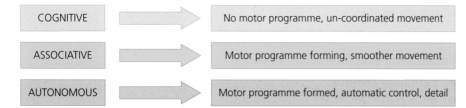

COGNITIVE	→	No motor programme, un-coordinated movement
ASSOCIATIVE	→	Motor programme forming, smoother movement
AUTONOMOUS	→	Motor programme formed, automatic control, detail

Figure 3 The stages of learning and motor programmes

Purposes and types of feedback

One way of improving performance is to use **feedback**, a concept defined as information received to amend performance and make improvement. There are various forms of feedback that are available for use in sport and the correct use of feedback is an essential tool needed to help players improve. The first form of feedback is called **positive feedback** and this entails information about what was good; it tells the player what is going well and offers motivation to maintain effort. Positive feedback may often be combined with praise to give that extra feel-good factor to the player. **Negative feedback**, although equally important, is not as pleasant and the intention here is to give the performer information as what is going wrong so that errors can be corrected and bad habits eliminated. As players gain more experience, negative feedback can be appreciated since it gives clarity on which aspects of the task need to be improved.

Extrinsic feedback is derived from an outside source such as the coach so that the performer gains a view of what they need to improve on or which aspects of the task they need to maintain. Advice on the types of practice and methods needed to improve may be given. As the player gains experience, the feedback used may come from within and is called **intrinsic feedback**. The performer may have developed a feel for the task using the sense of kinaesthesis and can use this internal feel to know when they have hit a bad shot, for example.

Feedback which gives an initial outcome of the attempted skill is called **knowledge of results**. This form of feedback gives an indication of whether or not the skill has been successful. Did the pass reach its intended target? Did the netball shot score? Successful outcomes need to be maintained and unsuccessful ones need to be eliminated, so knowledge of results forms an early basis for improvement. Knowledge of the initial result can be expanded with a more detailed analysis of the action called **knowledge of performance**. This gives reasons why the shot went in or not and is concerned with technique and how that technique can be developed to produce a better performance than the last attempt.

The types of feedback discussed are not exclusive in the sense that a player, for example, may receive praise from the coach at the end of the game, so the player gets both positive and extrinsic feedback. Regardless of the type of feedback used, the coach should make the feedback effective by trying to make it both understandable and relevant to the performer in the sense that it relates only to the player in question and is given in simple, direct terms. To maintain motivation, some positives should always be included. It is essential that the feedback used is appropriate to the performance level.

Figure 4 A coach giving advice is extrinsic feedback

Memory tools

To help you recall the types of feedback use the following mnemonic:

Perhaps Not Every Person Is Realistic:

- **P**erhaps = Positive
- **N**ot = Negative
- **E**very = Extrinsic
- **P**erson = Performance (knowledge of)
- **I**s = Intrinsic
- **R**ealistic = Results (knowledge of)

Stages of learning and type of feedback

To make feedback effective, the coach should consider the stage of learning the performer receiving the feedback is in. In the early or cognitive stage of learning, a novice will benefit from encouragement and external advice. They need advice because they have little existing knowledge of the skill and positive encouragement would motivate the performer to continue learning the task. As a starting point, the initial outcome of early attempts at the task should be noted.

In the autonomous stage of learning, the performer requires detailed feedback on how to control their performance. They can benefit from error correction and they would use their existing knowledge of the task to make internal adjustments.

The middle stage of learning, the associative stage, can be a long phase in which the performer makes steady progress. Early in this phase, external information would be used to refine the movements and as this stage develops, the use of more intrinsic feedback is used to control the performance.

ACTIVITY

Study the text on the stages of learning earlier in this section. Then look at the types of feedback discussed above and see if you can suggest the types of feedback that are appropriate for each stage of learning. Can you suggest reasons for your choices? Record your answers in a table like the one below that you can use as a learning tool. Complete your table now before you look at the one at the back of the book (answers section) and then compare your answers.

STAGE OF LEARNING	TYPES OF FEEDBACK

CHECK YOUR UNDERSTANDING

1 What type of feedback would you use for a performer in the associative stage of learning?
2 How could a coach make sure that the feedback given to players has the best results?

KEY TERM

Plateau: A period of no improvement in performance.

Learning plateaus

A learning **plateau** is a period during performance when there are no signs of improvement; the performer does not appear to be getting any better at doing the task. This lack of improvement can be illustrated by a graph called a learning curve (see Figure 5).

A learning curve is a visual representation of what happens when a closed skill is performed repeatedly over a period of time by a novice. The skill in question might be a new or novel task and the performer learns the skill from scratch – learn as you go, if you like!

STUDY HINT

You should be able to interpret the significant points of a typical learning curve and to give reasons why performance may reach a plateau, a period when no improvement is made, along with strategies that could be used to overcome that lack of improvement.

ACTIVITY

Learning curve

Set up a novel skill in an appropriate small space. An example might be throwing a tennis ball into a target hoop from a set distance or even aiming to throw a bean bag into a bucket. Allow a set time of 20 minutes to have as many attempts as you can, but block each attempt into sets of 10 and count how many successful attempts are achieved out of ten. Record your score and continue with sets of 10 for the full 20 minutes. Then plot your results as a graph, with the time on the horizontal axis and the score out of 10 for each set on the vertical axis. Study the shape of your graph and see if it looks like the typical learning curve as depicted in Figure 5. A period of no improvement in performance is called a plateau and this concept could be demonstrated by producing a learning curve of your own.

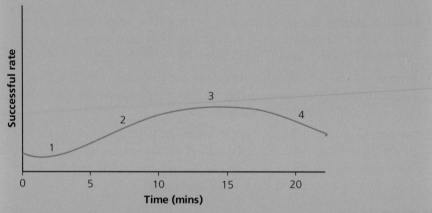

Figure 5 A typical learning curve showing the rate of improvement shown when attempting a closed skill over a 20-minute period

Explaining the graph

A learning curve is a graphic illustration that shows how the rate of learning of a performer doing a closed skill over a period of time can vary. A typical learning curve looks like the one shown above and it can be divided into four stages. These stages are:

1 **Stage 1** where the rate of learning is slow and performance level is poor because the performer is new to the task and is in the cognitive stage of learning, working out the required sub-routines of the task and possibly using trial and error learning.

2 At **Stage 2** there is a rapid acceleration in the rate of learning because the performer has begun to master the task and gain some success, providing reinforcement and motivation.

3 At **Stage 3** there is no improvement in the rate of learning and the performance has reached a 'plateau'. The performance maintains the same level.

4 **Stage 4** is a period towards the end of the task when, perhaps due to fatigue, the performance may actually deteriorate.

There is a drop in the rate of improvement and the performance may actually start to get worse, a concept called drive reduction. **Drive reduction** occurs because the performer has gained success on the task and the initial drive to succeed has been lost; the challenge of mastering the task has been overcome and a new challenge or extension to the task is needed to maintain motivation.

Causes of the plateau

The plateau effect can be caused by a number of reasons, including the following:

1 **Lack of motivation.** The lack of incentives or extrinsic rewards may cause the performer to lose drive and energy for the task.

2 **Boredom.** The repetitive nature of a closed skill may cause boredom.

3 **Coaching.** The coach may issue incorrect instructions or use incorrect practice methods (see previous section) so that the skill is not done correctly.

4 **Limit of ability.** The performer may not improve simply because they have reached the full extent of their ability. They can't improve because they don't have the underlying skill level.

5 **Targets set too low.** Perhaps the task is one that does not allow the learner to use the full range of their skills – they can't improve because the limits of the task do not allow them to!

6 **Fatigue.** Continuous action over an extended period of time would inevitably result in tiredness, especially if the same muscles are being used repeatedly. See also the section on DOMS (see page 146), the delayed onset of muscle fatigue in the Physiology section.

Memory tools

To help you remember the causes of a plateau, use the following mnemonic:

'Many Bees Can Look Towards Flowers'

- **M**: **M**otivation
- **B**: **B**oredom
- **C**: **C**oach
- **L**: **L**imit of ability
- **T**: **T**argets too low
- **F**: **F**atigue

Solutions to the plateau effect

To overcome the plateau effect, the performer could consider solutions to the causes listed above. Some solutions to the plateau effect are given below.

1 The task could be extended so that a new challenge to test the performer is given and new targets or goals could be set to see if such task extensions are met.

2 The player could find a new coach to raise performance levels.

3 Perhaps this coach could offer more praise and positive reinforcement to provide motivation.

4 A rest could be taken to avoid fatigue.

5 More variety could be added to the task so boredom might be avoided.

6 The concept of the plateau could be explained to the performer so that they do not take personal responsibility for their lack of improvement.

7 The player could get some feedback to help improve performance and motivation.

ACTIVITY

Copy and complete Table 2 about the causes of and cures for learning plateaus.
Fill in the blanks!

Table 2 The causes of and cures for learning plateaus

CAUSE	CURE
Lack of motivation	
	Rest
Poor coaching	
	Different practices
Targets too low	
	Explain the plateau concept

CHECK YOUR UNDERSTANDING

After practising the same closed skill for a period of time, a performer may reach a period when the performance does not improve, which is called a plateau. What could the performer do to overcome the plateau?

Methods of guidance

Often used in addition to feedback, methods of guidance are a set of four techniques that may be used by a coach to enhance learning and offer assistance to the performer. In the main, the methods of guidance are used for beginners but even experts may benefit from some technical advice. The four methods of guidance are detailed here.

1 Visual guidance

Visual guidance is a demonstration of the required task. The intention is to create a mental image for a beginner that can be used as a reference point for future practice. As the name implies, this visual image can be given by the coach or another player in the form of a demonstration, or it could be given using media formats such as social media sites, books, charts or video. The coach and player should ensure that if the demonstration is given by a fellow player or peer, then it should be seen as within the capabilities of the player attempting to copy the demonstration, so that it is performed by a player of equal ability to maintain motivation and confidence. The coach and player should also follow the guidelines discussed in the section on observational learning (see page 77) – the coach should repeat the demonstration and allow the performer time to practise it. The demonstration should be shown from different angles and mental rehearsal, when the player goes over the movements of the skill in the mind without movement, may be used to complement the learning. The key points of the skill should be highlighted and reinforcement should be used to encourage retention of the skill in the memory.

KEY TERM

Visual guidance: Guidance that can be seen, a demonstration.

Table 3 Advantages and disadvantages of visual guidance

Advantages of visual guidance	Disadvantages of visual guidance
Visual guidance can be used to highlight a specific weakness. For example, during indoor climbing, the coach may point out to the performer the exact point or hold on which to place the foot. Visual guidance tries to show what the skill should look like as a result of practice. It creates a mental image. It is nearly always used in conjunction with verbal guidance.	The problems with visual guidance are that the demonstration must be completely accurate, otherwise it may be copied incorrectly and the performer may not have the ability to perform the demonstration if the coach does not ensure success. Indeed, if too much information is given, the performer may become confused. Steady and slow are the keys to visual guidance!

Figure 6 Coach may use visual guidance to show the climber where to place their foot

2 Verbal guidance

Verbal guidance is an explanation of the task. It is nearly always used in conjunction with visual guidance, when the coach speaks to the performer during the demonstration to highlight the points being made. This helps to build the correct mental image in the memory. However, verbal guidance can also be used by a more experienced player, when technical and detailed advice is given to complement the actions in practice, or tactical advice is given during performance, e.g. when a basketball player is told to stay close and follow the movements of their nominated opponent when defending. In this example, the coach uses the verbal guidance as a key or prompt to ensure the correct actions are displayed. Verbal guidance can be used by coaches to explain aspects of conditioning or fitness, perhaps when a more physical type of session is planned and the coach may only need to describe and explain the content of the session without, in this case, the need for a visual demonstration.

Figure 7 A basketball player given advice during play – an example of verbal guidance

The problems and considerations when using verbal guidance are as follows:

● If too much information is given to the performer, then it may cause confusion and place too much demand on the memory system.

● The performer may lose concentration unless the coach makes the verbal information brief, relevant and meaningful.

● The language used by the coach should be understandable, in the sense that a beginner may not recognise technical terms that would be understood by an expert.

● Verbal guidance is a means of giving feedback so the coach should ensure that the correct type of feedback is used for the performer: perhaps positive for a novice and detailed and negative for an expert.

The next two types of guidance are more hands-on and physical and are used to help beginners learn new skills.

3 Manual guidance

Manual guidance involves physical support, such as holding a gymnast on a vault or during a headstand. It can involve a type of forced response, for example, when the coach holds the arm of a tennis player to help her learn the movement of a forehand stroke.

Table 4 Advantages and disadvantages of manual guidance

Advantages of manual guidance	Disadvantages of manual guidance
● Manual guidance has the very important advantage of helping to eliminate danger. For example, support for the gymnast would prevent a fall.	● The problem with manual guidance is that it can have a detrimental effect on performance if it is over-used.
● It helps to build the confidence of the performer who might not be able to gain the feel of the whole task without help and support from manual guidance.	● Once the initial feel of the task is established, too much reliance on physical support could begin to interfere with the feel of the task as done in the real environment, causing the performer to develop bad habits.
● Fear and anxiety associated with dangerous or difficult tasks may be reduced if the support is on hand to help the performer; when the task is more complex, it could be broken down into stages with the help of physical support. For example, when the gymnast attempts a part of a floor routine, it may be that they are temporarily held in a specific position to gain the feel of the point at which they should release the hands.	● The performer may also begin to depend on the support too much, not feeling able to do the task without the physical help, in a sense losing confidence rather than gaining it!
	● So the coach should restrict and control the use of this type of guidance to avoid over-usage, remembering that this form of guidance can result in the coach being up close and personal to the performer, and such close proximity may be off-putting.

4 Mechanical guidance

Mechanical guidance is a device used to help performance, such as an armband in swimming or a harness on the trampoline. It has similar advantages and disadvantages to manual guidance since it also incorporates a form of physical support. The advantages of mechanical guidance are:

● It builds confidence – the successful completion of the task, even though assistance was given, gives the performer the sense that they can do it!

CHECK YOUR UNDERSTANDING
Explain what you understand by visual guidance. What are the advantages and disadvantages of using this method?

KEY TERM

Manual guidance: Physical support.

Figure 8 Gymnast being supported physically uses manual guidance

KEY TERM

Mechanical guidance: An artificial aid.

- It eliminates danger – a harness on the trampoline, an armband in swimming both help to prevent injury.
- It gives an early feel for the whole skill. This helps promote learning by alerting the senses to the movements of the task.
- Mechanical guidance has the distinct advantage that it can be used with disabled athletes or those recovering from injury, allowing a feel and completion of the task that can then be developed further.

Figure 9 Using a swimming armband is an example of mechanical guidance

The problems associated with mechanical guidance are similar to manual guidance:

- If used for too much time, mechanical guidance can interfere with the feel of the task.
- The performer might depend on it too much, so a sense that the task can't be completed without the artificial help could promote a loss of confidence.
- Motivation could be lost if the performer thinks the skill is not being performed independently, and incorrect intrinsic feedback could encourage bad habits if feedback is not given in addition to the mechanical support.

> **CHECK YOUR UNDERSTANDING**
> What is mechanical guidance? What are the advantages and disadvantages of using this method?

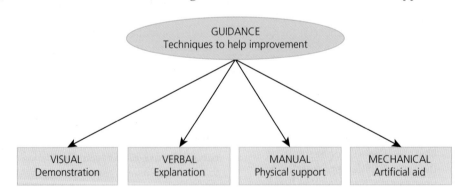

Figure 10 Types of guidance

The theories of learning

In addition to the application of some hard practice, there are some strategies that both coach and player can employ to enhance the learning of skills. These strategies are outlined within some theoretical concepts and the principles of each of these theories of learning are now discussed.

Operant conditioning

> **KEY TERM**
>
> **Operant conditioning:** The use of reinforcement to ensure that correct responses are repeated.

In this theory, the coach uses a manipulative approach to ensure that skills are learned, using the principle that actions for which the athlete is rewarded are more likely to be repeated. If you feel you have done something well, you are more likely to remember it! Operant conditioning is the use of **reinforcement** to link correct responses to a stimulus. It is therefore known as a **behaviourist theory**, since it connects the stimulus to the response.

Operant conditioning is based on the pioneering work of the psychologist Skinner (1948) who observed rats in a cage called the 'Skinner box'. The cage was fitted with a mechanism that delivered food to the rats every time it was touched. At first, the rats hit the mechanism by accident but quickly learned to hit the mechanism to gain their reward.

Operant conditioning is characterised by the following three key features:

● It is based on trial-and-error learning.
● The coach might manipulate the environment when using operant conditioning.
● It shapes behaviour by using reinforcement.

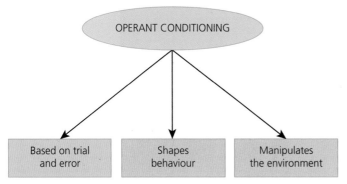

Figure 11 Operant conditioning

Operant conditioning works on the principle that reinforced actions are strengthened and that incorrect actions can be weakened. It is based on the idea that success acts as a **satisfier** to strengthen correct actions. During trial-and-error learning, if the successful responses are rewarded, then they are likely to be repeated. If unsuccessful responses are ignored or given an **annoyer**, such as criticism, then they may be avoided.

The stimulus–response bond

Operant conditioning works by strengthening the link between the stimulus and the response. This is known as the stimulus-response (S–R) bond. A simple example of the S-R bond can come from the game of badminton. If a shuttlecock is returned high in the air and mid-court, the best response would be to do a smash shot. By linking this appropriate response to the stimulus, then actions can be learned. The ways that coaches could link the stimulus to the response using the principle of operant conditioning involves positive reinforcement, negative reinforcement and punishment. These forms of reinforcement help to shape behaviour.

Positive reinforcement is when a pleasant stimulus is given to increase the likelihood of a correct response occurring again in the future. The coach who offers praise to the swimmer for a correct leg action or the reward of a certificate for achieving 25 metres in the pool as a young swimmer will offer motivation to continue repeating such successes.

KEY TERM

Behaviourist theory: This attempts to explain how actions can be linked to stimuli.

STUDY HINT

If you are explaining the principles of operant conditioning, always refer to the three aspects of trial and error, manipulating the environment and shaping behaviour.

Figure 12 During a badminton smash, the player links the stimulus of the flight of the shuttlecock to the action of the smash

KEY TERMS

Satisfier: An action that promotes a pleasant feeling so that responses are repeated.

Annoyer: An action that creates unease to promote the avoidance of incorrect responses.

Positive reinforcement: A pleasant stimulus after the correct response.

Negative reinforcement: Taking away an unpleasant stimulus after the correct response.

Punishment: An unpleasant stimulus to prevent incorrect actions recurring.

Figure 13 A certificate is a form of positive reinforcement

Figure 15 A red card player being sent off

STUDY HINTS

Negative reinforcement is often mistaken for punishment. Students seem to think that criticism or a coach shouting at a player is negative reinforcement – it's not! It is the withdrawal of such criticism that is the negative effect. Think of negative reinforcement as a minus sign in maths, it's negative: –ve! Punishment means giving the player something unpleasant so that they do not repeat incorrect actions, therefore punishment is adding something, albeit something not nice!

Negative reinforcement promotes correct actions occurring to a stimulus by taking away an unpleasant stimulus when the performer does it right. Negative criticism is withdrawn when the performer does well. A coach who has given a negative comment to a player who has used the incorrect technique would stop the negative feedback when the technique improves.

If a coach who is repeatedly telling a performer that they are doing badly or performing the skill incorrectly suddenly becomes quiet, then the learner knows that they have begun to perform the skill correctly – this is negative reinforcement.

It is reinforcement because it increases the likelihood of the correct response being repeated.

Figure 14 The coach should stop shouting when the correct action happens to ensure negative reinforcement

Punishment is when a coach gives an unpleasant stimulus to prevent incorrect actions from happening again. The player who is punished with a red card in football for committing a bad foul would hopefully learn not to repeat the offence!

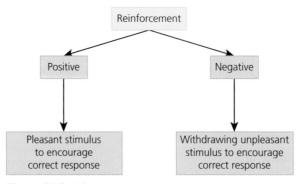

Figure 16 Reinforcement

When using the process of operant conditioning the coach may also use whole or whole-part-whole practice to isolate the key aspects of the task, another means of manipulating the environment. Mental practice can also be used to go over the correct aspects of the task in the mind to help shape behaviour.

Observational learning (Bandura)

This theory was researched by the psychologist Albert Bandura in 1977. It suggests that both acceptable and unacceptable behaviour can be learned by watching and then copying other people. Young football players may often be seen copying the goal celebrations of their professional counterparts. A coach can use this ability to copy behaviour to their advantage by using strategies to ensure that the demonstrations and role models used to show skills during practice are successfully copied by the players.

Bandura suggested that a performer is more likely to copy a model demonstration if the coach uses four processes.

1 Attention

Making sure the performer takes note of the relevant cues. The more attractive the 'demo' is to the player, the more likely it is to be copied.

Grab the **attention** of the learner by selling your demonstration. Point out its function or the reason why you are asking them to learn it – hopefully to gain an advantage during play. For example, tell a tennis player that the reason you are demonstrating a sliced serve is to drag the opponent off court to open up the court for a winning shot. Make the model stand out by making it loud, bright or attractive and therefore more memorable to the learner. Make sure any information you give is loud and clear! The demonstration should be accurate and always correct.

Figure 17 In tennis, pointing out the reason for a particular shot is an effective tactic and can make it seem more attractive and memorable to the learner

2 Retention

Retention is the ability to remember important information and recall it from the memory system. Make sure the learner is able to recall the demonstration in the memory by breaking any information given into

KEY TERM

Attention: Making the demonstration attractive to the performer.

KEY TERM

Retention: Remembering the demonstration and being able to recall it.

'chunks' and by repeating it. Make sure the demonstration is accurate and clear. The use of a role model or an expert player in the group may ensure an accurate demonstration is given. The learner should attempt the skill as soon as it has been seen, so that the demo is fresh in the mind! Hence the need to practise as soon as possible after the demonstration so the performer can still remember how to do it.

3 Motor production

Motor production is making sure the player is capable of physically copying the demonstration, i.e. giving a task that is set at the same level of ability as the performer and making sure that the task can be understood. In the early stages of practice, success should be ensured by setting easy tasks and then making progress as the task becomes more complex. The player should be given time to practise and learn well before moving on to the next part of the task.

4 Motivation

Motivation is the drive needed to copy the demonstration. Motivate the learner by giving praise and rewards or offering positive feedback and positive reinforcement.

A summary of the observational (Bandura) model of observational learning is shown in Figure 18.

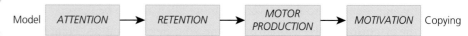

Figure 18 Observational learning

Model demonstrations and behaviours are more likely to be copied if:

- They are close to appropriate social norms, in other words, they are performed by a player of similar ability.
- They are reinforced.
- They are powerful, visually and physically.
- They are consistent.
- They are relevant.

Social development theory: Vygotsky

Vygotsky (1978) looked at the development of young children and decided that interaction with others plays a vital role in learning. Interaction with others can produce learning by social development. In sport, skills can be learned from others such as coaches and teachers, and these influential others are known as a 'more knowledgeable other' or an MKO.

The coach or MKO not only gives direct examples and advice but may also influence the learner by demonstrating values and actions such as a high degree of effort, a healthy lifestyle and clear communication that can be adopted by the learner.

During development, the skills are learned from the coach by a process that Vygotsky called **inter-psychological learning**, when the learner uses the MKO to get advice, feedback and tactical knowledge.

Once external advice has been absorbed, learning can then take place within the learner who will use cognitive aspects of skill acquisition to internally

KEY TERMS

Motor production: Having the mental and physical ability to do the task.

Motivation: Having the drive to do the task.

STUDY HINTS

Attention should not be described as paying attention; retention should not be described as retaining information; motivation is not being motivated. Use alternative words to those in Bandura's model.

CHECK YOUR UNDERSTANDING

During learning, the coach may use a demonstration to show key points of a skill. From your understanding of the process of observational learning, what can the coach do to make sure such demonstrations are more likely to be copied and understood?

KEY TERMS

Social development: Learning by association with others.

Inter-psychological learning: Learning from others externally.

analyse, think about and construct actions based on what they have learned externally. This learning from within takes place after the inter-psychological stage and is called **intra-psychological learning**.

Vygotsky also suggested that learning can be constructed in stages. As the skills are learned, the learner will use three parameters on which to build or construct their learning.

Constructivism: Vygotsky

To construct means to build and that is what this theory suggests – you build on what you know! Working with others helps to develop skills since you can learn from the actions of those who are more experienced and add their actions to the ones you already know, thereby building up your skills. During the process of intra-psychological learning (see above), the learner will assess what level of performance they are currently working at and therefore what they need to do to learn more and move to the next level. The MKO, or coach, may help to give more advice as the skill is advanced.

Vygotsky suggested that the learner will use three levels of performance to assess what they need to do to improve. He suggested that the learner uses **zone of proximal development** – an assessment of what they need to do next to learn the skill. The three stages of proximal development are:

1 What can I do alone?

2 What can I do with help?

3 What can I not do yet?

In sport, the learner will therefore build up learning through each stage, e.g. in hockey, a player may be able to hold the stick and roll the ball with it along the ground and they can do this by themselves. They may, however, not be able to keep the ball close to the stick when running with it without the help of the coach or other players, and they can't yet do a complete dribble with the ball in practice against other players. To help them learn this skill, they need to observe and copy others and take advice. Learning and copying from others is called social learning. The actual actions that are needed to take the performer to the next stage are up to the learner and will be decided based on the learner's experience and expectations.

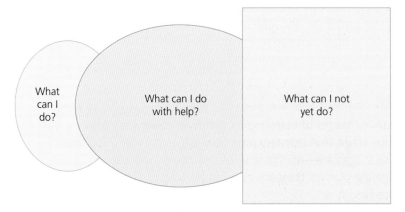

Figure 20 Vygotsky constructivism: The stages of proximal development

KEY TERMS

Intra-psychological learning: Learning from within after gaining external knowledge from others.

Constructivism: Building up learning in stages, based on the current level of performance.

Zone of proximal development: the next stage of learning based on the performer's needs, expectations and current level of performance.

Figure 19 A hockey dribble can be learned from others and built up in stages

STUDY HINT

Proximal means WHAT NEXT!

ACTIVITY

Can you think of any reasons why Vygotsky's theory may not be applicable to the learning of sports skills?

CHECK YOUR UNDERSTANDING

1 What is the zone of proximal development?

2 What are the three stages of Vygotsky's constructive learning theory?

Figure 21 An athlete in a 3000m race may have worked out their tactics for the whole race using insight theory

Insight learning (Gestaltist theories)

This theory of **insight learning** was suggested by a group of German psychologists called the '*Gestalts*', a term that means concentrating on the whole rather than the parts.

This theory, as the term 'insight' suggests, says that the performer uses existing knowledge to form an idea of how to deal with problematic sporting situations because they might have an idea from their general sporting knowledge which they can put into practice. When a player is presented with a problem, sporting knowledge is used to work out a solution to that problem and that idea is then tried. For example, in a 3000m athletics race, the athlete may be aware that some of the runners in that race have a fast finish over the last 400 metres. The athlete works out that it would be a good tactic to set off at a fast pace and maintain this pace throughout the race; the idea is that the fast finish is negated by the effort of keeping up with the pace so the problem is reduced. If this tactic works, then it will be used again in similar situations in the future. The athlete has learned to change their behaviour – the very definition of learning given at the start of this chapter!

The features of insight theory are that it concentrates on the whole task, therefore this theory is good for use in realistic situations that are closely linked to the game or event. Since the solution or tactic has been worked out by the athlete, it may provide a sense of self-satisfaction and give intrinsic motivation to the performer. If the tactic has worked, the athlete will feel pretty good with themselves!

The insight approach poses questions to the performer but it is not trial and error! It encourages the performer to think for themselves and develops the cognitive process. In this sense, insight theory may work better than simply being told by the coach and it should generate more understanding of the actions required to perform the skill in different situations. In dance, for example, it may be that the dancer has been struggling to generate enough rotation to complete a turn. The dancer then works out that if they open up the foot a little more and aim to place the hips just outside the line of the foot, then more speed and rotation are generated. Problem solved!

The insight theory may also generate a specific role for the performer. In our 3000-metre race example, the role of the athlete was to be a front runner. By working out problems, the athlete learns to use the cognitive process, thinking is encouraged and the performer may begin to think about the use of their skills in competitive situations in the future.

SUMMARY

There are three stages of learning: a cognitive, associative and autonomous stage that learners pass through as they develop their skills. These stages are important since the coach needs to recognise which stage the players they are coaching are at, so that they can give appropriate feedback.

A plateau is a period of time during the performance of a skill when the performer seems to make little or no progress. The coach must recognise the plateau and offer solutions to reduce its effects.

The theories of learning are based on the work of eminent sports psychologists whose influence on the understanding of how we learn new skills is of extreme importance. These theories include:

- The work of Skinner (1948), based on the Skinner box experiments, suggested that reinforced actions can be made stronger and therefore learned.
- Bandura (1977) suggested that learning can take place by observation when four important principles are followed.
- Vygotsky (1978) promoted another way of learning from others when interaction leads to social development and constructive learning.
- Then the work of the German group of psychologists called the *Gestalts* gave us the concept of learning by using experiences from the whole task.

These theories are important so that sports coaches can understand how learning takes place and those same coaches may use feedback and guidance to offer further help to the players and athletes in their charge. There are other psychological aspects that can influence learning and performance in sport and these are studied in Chapter 6.1.

PRACTICE QUESTIONS

1 A coach giving a player a fine for being late for training is an example of: (1 mark)

   a) negative reinforcement

   b) positive reinforcement

   c) punishment

   d) manipulating the environment.

2 Describe the theory of operant conditioning and show how a coach might use it to improve performance. (4 marks)

3 Name the three stages of learning that a sports performer experiences while developing their skills and describe the characteristics of the level of performance associated with each stage. (4 marks)

4 Bandura's model of observational learning uses four principles to help sports performers learn skills by copying demonstrations. Explain how the terms attention, retention, motor production and motivation help the process of learning. (4 marks)

5 When a sports performer continually practises a closed skill for a period of 20 minutes, they may reach a stage when there is no improvement in their performance, called a plateau. Suggest reasons why this plateau effect may have occurred. How could the plateau effect be overcome? (4 marks)

6 Explain the term insight learning and show how this approach can have a positive effect on performance. (3 marks)

Chapter 3.1
Emergence of the globalisation of sport in the twenty-first century

Chapter objectives

After reading this chapter you should be able to:

- Understand sporting recreation in the pre-industrial society (pre-1780); its characteristics (e.g. rural, local, two-tier class system) and its impact on sporting recreation, particularly in relation to mob football, real tennis and athletics.

- Understand sport and industrial and post-industrial society (1780–1900); its characteristics and impact on sporting recreation (i.e. rational recreation), particularly in relation to association football, lawn tennis, and track and field athletics, as seen at the Wenlock Olympian Games.

- Understand the impact on sport of the following socio-cultural factors in industrial and post-industrial Britain: the Industrial Revolution; urbanisation; transport and communication; the British Empire; provision through factories; churches; local authorities; the three-tier class system (and the emphasis on the middle class and their impact on working-class sporting opportunities); the development of National Governing Bodies; the status of amateur and professional performers from the late eighteenth century through to present day; a consideration of the changing role of women in sport.

- Understand the characteristics and impact of sport on post-World War II society through to the present day, particularly in relation to association football, tennis and athletics (e.g. via a consideration of the 'golden triangle' and factors affecting the emergence of elite female performers in football (players and officials), tennis and athletics in the late twentieth century to the early twenty-first century).

Pre-industrial Britain: Popular recreation (pre-1780)

Sport is often said to reflect the society of the time. The purpose of this first section linked to the historical development of sport is to try to show how sport was indeed a reflection of features of society in pre-industrial Britain.

Life in pre-industrial Britain

Pre-industrial society (i.e. pre-1780) had a number of features/characteristics (sometimes referred to as 'socio-cultural' factors) including the following:

- Communications and transport were limited.
- There was widespread illiteracy: the lower classes were uneducated, with little ability to read or write.

- Cruel or violent existences were the norm for the lower class; the upper class lived in comfort and luxury.
- There was very limited free time as work was based on the land; free time was dictated by the agricultural calendar/seasons; the lower class worked very long hours.
- Class divisions clearly existed; there was a two-tier clearly divided society in existence (upper class and lower class) based on a **feudal system**.
- People lived in the countryside/rural areas.

Characteristics of popular recreation

There are a number of characteristics of **popular recreation** which can be identified during pre-industrial times. Long hours of work for the lower class meant popular recreation activities were occasional and therefore restricted to annual events when breaks in the agricultural calendar allowed their participation (e.g. on Festival or Holy Days). With limited transport available, popular recreation activities were local and specific to each community and the area they lived in the countryside. Activities used the natural resources available to them, e.g. open land for mob games. Literacy was very low among the lower classes in society so any rules were very basic and applied to a particular community, i.e. locally set and applied (unlimited number of players, no time limits and no officials were the 'norm' in mob games). Activities were aggressive and male dominated, reflecting a harsh society – lots of damage to property and injuries to the participants themselves were evident when participation in mob games occurred. Wagers were placed by the upper classes as part of sporting contests. On occasions, the activities participated in by the lower class were 'functional' as they were linked to their work requirements. (e.g. when employed as footmen which led to race walking as an athletic activity).

ACTIVITY

The characteristics of pre-industrial Britain were very much reflected in most of the popular recreational activities participated in by the lower class in particular (e.g. mob games). Complete Table 1 to illustrate your understanding of the linkage between socio-cultural factors in pre-industrial Britain and popular recreation activities of the time.

Table 1

SOCIO-CULTURAL FACTOR IN PRE-INDUSTRIAL BRITAIN	POPULAR RECREATION CHARACTERISTIC TO REFLECT THIS
Limited transport/communications	
Illiteracy/uneducated	
Harsh society	
Seasonal time/long working hours	
Pre-industrial/pre-urban revolutions	
Two-tier society/feudal system	

Having identified the general features of pre-industrial Britain and how popular recreation activities of the time reflected such features, the next section will cover in more detail how pre-industrial society influenced certain popular sporting pastimes of the time.

KEY TERMS

Feudal system: Broadly defined, it was a way of structuring society around a relationship derived from the holding of land in exchange for service or labour.
Popular recreation: The sport and pastimes of people in pre-industrial Britain.

STUDY HINT

You can remember lots of key characteristics of pre-industrial Britain via the letter 'C' (i.e. **c**ruel; **c**lear **c**lass divisions; **c**ountryside living was the norm).

ACTIVITY

Research the early mob football game of Haxey Hood (e.g. via watching it on *YouTube*) and identify three ways in which it reflects the characteristics of pre-industrial Britain. For example, who participated? The vigorous young men of the village. When? 'Old' Christmas Day, 6 January. Where? Haxey, North Lincolnshire.

Mob football is an example of an activity played in pre-industrial Britain which very much reflected the characteristics of popular recreation and socio-cultural factors evident at the time. It was played by the lower class in society, reflecting the clear division of society into two tiers, with certain sports for the lower classes, e.g. mob football.

Mob football was a localised form of activity, e.g. Ashbourne mob football, due to limited transport being available, as well as very little development in the way of communications such as newspapers. It was very rural in nature as the population of the time was spread out in the countryside and lived in small villages. Society was very simple and mob games made use of what was readily available. Mob football was therefore played by the lower class in the fields using natural resources available to them (e.g. a pig's bladder instead of a leather football!). Long working hours meant that the lower class only played mob football occasionally, e.g. on Holy Days such as Shrove Tuesday. Mob football was male dominated and highly violent and often unruly in nature, which very much reflected living conditions in the society of the time. Illiteracy was widespread among the lower class in society so there was very little in the way of rules and regulations in the mob football they played.

Popular recreation activities such as mob football became increasingly unpopular with the local authorities as the nineteenth century progressed and were eventually banned for a variety of different reasons including the following:

● They were violent or unruly in nature.
● They led to injury or death in extreme cases.
● They led to damage of property.
● They involved gambling/wagering.
● They were linked to alcohol consumption/drunken behaviour.

Figure 1 A real tennis court.

Real tennis (also called 'Royal Tennis' or 'the sport of kings') was another activity played in pre-industrial Britain, but it did not reflect the typical popular recreation characteristics of many activities at the time.

Real tennis was an exclusive activity, courtly and royal in nature, played by the upper class males of society. For example, Henry VIII had a real tennis court at Hampton Court. The upper classes were educated and highly literate so complex rules could be written down for the sport as they could readily understand and apply them. The upper class played real tennis to a high moral code so it lacked violence and was instead played in a civilised manner, with opponents mutually respectful of one another. With plenty of leisure time, the upper class were able to play real tennis on a regular basis in expensive, purpose-built facilities using expensive specialist equipment,

STUDY HINT
You should think about direct links between socio-cultural factors and characteristics of an activity, e.g. mob football. For example, you could say that mob football was violent and reflected a harsh and cruel society where violence was common.

e.g. racquets. The upper class also had the ability to travel to play real tennis so it was non-local in nature. Real tennis was a skilful game with difficult technical demands, which enabled the upper class to show their 'superiority' over the lower class.

Athletics as a popular recreation activity in pre-industrial Britain

Athletics in pre-industrial Britain took the form of an activity known as **foot racing**/'pedestrianism' which basically consisted of footmen (i.e. hired servants) competing as messengers by the upper class/gentry for their speed of movement across open land. The foot racers/pedestrians were allowed to compete against one another, with the gentry wagering on how many miles they could cover in a specified time period. Racing developed with running/walking allowed and some 'challenge rules' introduced. Success in athletics meant increased social status for a 'gentleman' so the upper class were happy to act as **patrons** to the working-class performers. The gentry acted as 'patrons' of the lower-class runners by setting up races and providing prize money for success.

Early athletics in pre-industrial Britain also took the form of a 'festival occasion', with individuals organising rural, community festivals containing 'athletic events', including running, hurdles and football. Prizes were awarded by upper-class patrons for successful participants who were mainly from the lower class.

Characteristics of popular recreation linked to pre-1780 festivals included:

- Rules were simple/unwritten.
- Events were local with people from neighbouring villages joining in with the festivities and competitions which occurred annually, i.e. once a year!
- It was set in a rural location.
- Betting occurred, with wagers placed on the outcomes of races, etc.

Industrial and post-industrial development of sport (1780–1900)

In this next section linked to the historical development of sport, the main focus will be on how sport reflected a rapidly changing society as it moved from being an agriculturally/rurally based society to one which was very much dominated by factory life in a machine-based/urban environment.

The development of rational recreation

In pre-industrial Britain, the sports pastimes for the masses (i.e. lower class) were termed as 'popular recreation' activities, some of which have been described in the previous section of this chapter (e.g. mob football). As Britain changed into an industrially based society, sports and pastimes developed in a number of different ways, reflecting such societal changes. The activities participated in were termed as '**rational recreation**'. Rational suggests that a level of order, logic and structure began to be applied to sports such as football, reflecting a more ordered industrially based society. The purpose of this next section is therefore to identify and explain a number of the socio-cultural factors which led to 'mass sport' in such a society.

CHECK YOUR UNDERSTANDING

In what ways was real tennis different from most other popular recreation activities, e.g. mob football?

KEY TERMS

Foot racing: A form of competitive running/walking in the seventeenth and eighteenth centuries involving feats of endurance. As time progressed, it evolved into pedestrianism/race walking.

Patron: A member of the gentry who looked after a lower-class performer, e.g. by arranging competitions for them to participate in, putting up prize money and generally looking after the welfare of the performer.

KEY TERM

Rational recreation: In the nineteenth century, these were sports pastimes for the lower classes which were designed by the middle classes to be well ordered, organised and controlled.

The Wenlock Olympian Games

In 1850, the Wenlock Agricultural Reading Society (WARS) resolved to form a class called the Olympian Class which was set up to promote moral, physical and intellectual improvements, especially in the lower-class people of Wenlock. Participation in outdoor recreation challenges was an important means of promoting such improvement, with prizes offered for successful participants to encourage taking part.

In 1860 the Olympian Class became known as the Wenlock Olympian Society. The driving force behind the Wenlock Olympian Games was **Dr William Penny Brookes**, who was inspired to create such an event because of his work as a doctor and surgeon in the borough town of Much Wenlock in Shropshire.

The first Wenlock Olympian Games were held in October 1850 and were a forerunner to the modern Olympic Games. There was a mixture of athletics and traditional country sports including quoits, football, cricket, running and hurdles. Rules were written and they drew athletes from all over the country. In the early games, there were also some fun events, including the blindfolded wheelbarrow race and an 'Old woman's race', with a pound of tea for the winner! Pageantry and celebration were important parts of the Games from the start. For example, a band led the procession of flag bearers, officials and competitors as they marched to the event. Olympic hymns were sung and a crown of laurel leaves was placed on the head of the winner at a medal ceremony.

As well as holding annual Wenlock Olympian Games, Dr William Penny Brookes and the Wenlock Olympian Society campaigned for physical education to be on the school curriculum and promoted the benefits of sport and exercise nationally. For example, Brookes founded with others the National Olympian Association who held their first Festival in 1866 at the Crystal Palace, attracting 10,000 spectators.

Baron Pierre de Coubertin visited the Olympian Society in 1890, which held a special festival in his honour. De Coubertin was inspired by Dr Brookes and went on to establish the International Olympic Committee (IOC) and reform the modern Olympic Games in Athens (1896).

Social and cultural influences on the development of rational recreation

The Industrial Revolution

The **Industrial Revolution** was a key period in British history which witnessed massive changes in the way people lived their lives. For example, it led to more of the population being concentrated in towns and cities working in factories, as opposed to living in the countryside and working off the land.

The influence of the Industrial Revolution on the development of rationalised sports and pastimes changed over the nineteenth century. During the first half of the nineteenth century, the initial effects were often negative, as outlined below:

- **Migration of the lower classes into urban areas** looking for work in the new factories being built – led to a loss of space to play traditional mob games and overcrowding; no room for traditional mob games.
- **Lack of leisure time** – the shift from 'seasonal' to 'machine' time, leading to long 12-hour working days, six days a week; the Sabbath (i.e. Sunday) was a religious observance 'day of rest'.

KEY TERM

Dr William Penny Brookes: The founder of the Wenlock Olympian Games in 1850.

ACTIVITY

The Wenlock Olympian Games are still held annually in July at the Gaskell Recreation Ground. Visit **www.wenlock-olympian-society.org.uk/** to research how the early forms of activities participated in at the Games reflected society of the time.

KEY TERM

Industrial Revolution: Deemed to have occurred during the mid-eighteenth to the mid-nineteenth centuries. This period marked a change in Britain from a feudal, rural society into an industrialised, machine-based, capitalist society, controlled by a powerful urban middle class.

- **Lack of income** – low wages and poverty were evident, with little spare income for leisure pursuits.
- **Poor health** – along with poor working and living conditions that led to pollution, and a lack of hygiene, also meant little energy to play sport.
- **Loss of rights** – restrictions were placed on mob games and blood sports by changes in criminal laws.
- **A lack of public provision** – no access to private facilities or no personal equipment for the lower classes.

Memory tools

You can remember the initial negative effects of industrialisation via the 'HITFOR' acronym!

- **H** = poor **health and hygiene**
- **I** = lack of **income**
- **T** = lack of **time**
- **F** = **facility** provision was lacking
- **O** = **overcrowding** and lack of space
- **R** = loss of **rights**

In the second half of the nineteenth century, some improvements had a positive effect, as outlined below:

- **Health and hygiene improved** as a result of gradual improvements in living conditions and local council provision of public baths to improve cleanliness and help stop the spread of disease, enabling more energy/willingness to participate in sport.
- There was a **gradual increase in wages and more time for sport** due to the Factory Acts and Saturday half-days being provided to the workers (i.e. a gradual decrease in working hours).
- Development of **the new middle class** (i.e. self-made men who took advantage of the new business opportunities available in the newly industrialised Britain). This changed ways of behaving and playing sport. It became more acceptable and respectable and was played to a high moral code; they developed strict rules, leagues and competitions; they provided facilities/public parks via their involvement in the local council; they gave more time off work, broken time payments, etc.
- The influence of **ex-public schoolboys** via industry, the Church, etc.
- **The values of athleticism** (i.e. physical endeavour with moral integrity, i.e. always trying hard and working to the best of your ability but taking part in the spirit of fair play) spread to the lower classes.
- **Industrial patronage** (i.e. kind factory owners becoming 'patrons of sport' for the working class by providing support for them to participate in various ways) led to provision for recreation and sport – factory teams were set up, sporting facilities were provided and excursions to the seaside were organised.
- Improvements in **transport and communications** via the development of roads and steam trains influenced the distances spectators and players could travel, and leagues were established. Fixtures and results could be published in the papers of the time.
- It **became cheaper to travel** so participation in sport and the spectating of sport became more accessible.

KEY TERM

Industrial patronage: Factory teams were set up by factory owners as a way of decreasing absenteeism and encouraging loyalty in the workforce.

CHECK YOUR UNDERSTANDING

Identify four ways in which the leisure opportunities for the working classes improved as a result of industrialisation.

KEY TERM

Urbanisation: Large numbers of people migrating/moving from rural areas into towns and cities, seeking regular work in the factories.

STUDY HINT

Make sure you can identify how the development in the railway system positively impacted on the development of structured/organised sport in late nineteenth-century Britain.

Many of the developments identified above (e.g. transport/communications) will be explored in greater detail later in the chapter as they played a crucial role in the move to structured/organised sport for the masses.

Urbanisation

Urbanisation in the industrial period had a huge impact on the development of many of the sports we play today. As many violent sports such as mob games were banned as society became more civilised, new forms of entertainment emerged. A large working class population created a demand for mass entertainment, while a lack of space created the need for the development of purpose-built facilities. Gradual improvements in working conditions through government legislation resulted in more free time for workers to spend engaged in entertainment, and as a consequence, attendance at football matches and other activities increased, as football grounds and other purpose-built facilities were constructed to meet the rising demand.

The following is a summary of the key features of urbanisation that contributed to the development of sport in this period.

- **Lack of space:** In cities, unlike the countryside, space was at a premium. This led to the development of purpose-built facilities (e.g. football grounds).

- **Large working-class populations:** Urbanisation meant a large working-class population that needed entertaining, resulting in mass spectator numbers at football and rugby matches for the first time.

- **Loss of traditional sports:** Many traditional working-class sports such as mob games were banned in a civilised urban society, so there was a need for new sports to emerge.

- **Change in working conditions:** Initially, the working classes worked long hours in the factories, and had limited free time, incomes or energy to devote to sport. As this situation improved, sports attendance and participation went up.

The transport revolution

The development of steam trains and railways increased spectator and participation opportunities and spread interest in sport. Faster trains enabled people to travel further and more easily, giving more time for sports matches. Spectators could follow their teams to away matches and regular national fixtures, leagues and cup competitions developed, creating a need for unified rules or codification. Field sports, climbing and walking all became more accessible via improved access into the countryside. Although trains were expensive and used mostly by the middle and upper classes, they gradually became more affordable. Excursions, often sponsored by employers, also allowed working people to travel to the countryside and seaside.

The following is a summary of the key ways in which the development of the railways contributed to the development of sport in this period.

- **Movement of teams/spectators**: The development of the railways and steam trains enabled faster and further travel, leading to nationwide fixtures developing on a regular basis.

- **Improved access to different parts of the country:** Nationwide train travel enabled sport to develop from local to regional to national, with leagues forming, involving clubs from across the country (e.g. Football League).

- **Cheaper train travel**: Train travel became relatively cheap and affordable which led to working classes following their teams and sporting heroes home and away.
- **Improved access to the countryside**: Activities such as rambling became popular as rural areas were reachable and affordable via train travel.

Communications

Urban industrial society was associated with a gradual improvement in educational provision for the working class in the second half of the nineteenth century, which led to improvements in their reading and writing abilities.

'Communications' (e.g. via newspapers) improved as society became more literate. Such developments in the printed media increased the knowledge and awareness of sport in a number of different ways (e.g. when fixtures were taking place involving their local team; increased knowledge of results of matches involving the team they supported).

It led to the emergence of sporting heroes and role models as people could read match reports and relate to their favourite players scoring goals and/or helping to win matches due to their high levels of skill.

The influence of the Church

Changing views of the Church during Victorian times (i.e. late nineteenth century) also helped to promote sport and recreation among their local communities.

Reasons why the Church promoted sport included the fact that it encouraged social control (i.e. improved behaviour) through 'civilised' activities diverting people away from 'less socially acceptable activities' such as drinking and gambling. Church facilities such as halls provided venues for 'improving the morality' of the working classes. Sport was viewed as a good way of promoting Christian values. The development of the YMCA promoted the healthy body/healthy mind link. The clergy viewed sport as a good way to increase church attendance and help swell their congregations!

In terms of how they helped provide more opportunities for sporting involvement, the approval and active involvement of the clergy gave encouragement for the working classes to participate in rationalised sporting activities such as association football. The Church organised teams, set up clubs and organised competitions. Many modern-day football clubs have their origins traceable to church organisations (e.g. Aston Villa via Villa Cross Methodist Church). The Church provided facilities to play sport in their church halls and on their playing fields. A number of church groups formed, with sporting involvement a key part of their programmes of activities, e.g. the Boys' Brigade, Scouts, the YMCA, etc.

The emergence of the middle classes in a three-tier society

The newly formed middle class emerged as a result of urbanisation and industrialisation and played a key role in sporting developments during the nineteenth century. Unlike their social superiors in the upper class, many of the middle class were self-made individuals who had some empathy and concern for the working classes. One way they could help improve the lives of the working classes was via an improvement in sporting provision.

CHECK YOUR UNDERSTANDING
Identify the impact of developments in transport on sporting opportunities for the working classes.

ACTIVITY
Identify three ways in which improved literacy positively influenced the development of rational recreation.

CHECK YOUR UNDERSTANDING
Identify how the Church encouraged the post-industrial game of football.

STUDY HINT

When questions are set on historical aspects of sport that use the command word 'Explain', you should use link words, e.g. 'led to'; 'via'.

The following is a summary of the key ways in which members of the middle class supported such developments.

- **Codification:** The development of strict rules as public school and university old boys played a key role in the formation of many national governing bodies (NGBs) of sport. They controlled sport and became key organisers via their administration experience which enabled them to form and run clubs and NGBs (e.g. the Football Association set up in 1863; the Rugby Football Union in 1871; the Lawn Tennis Association in 1888). The middle class took prominent leadership roles in such organisations.

- **Competitions:** The development of leagues and competitions via middle-class involvement in public schools/universities/clubs/NGBs/factory teams/church teams.

- **Public provision:** The development of public facilities (e.g. parks and public baths) via middle-class '**philanthropists**', factory owners, the Church, the passing of government Acts in their role as local politicians.

- **Increased leisure time:** As middle-class factory owners, they gradually gave their workers more leisure time (e.g. a Saturday half day) which allowed more time to watch sport or to participate in sport.

- **Move to 'professionalism':** The middle class helped in the development of early commercial/professional sport (e.g. acting as agents, promoters in athletics; as factory owners setting up factory teams and paying broken time payments in football).

ACTIVITY

Copy and complete Table 2 comparing pre-industrial socio-cultural factors relating to popular recreation with post-industrial factors relating to rational recreation.

Table 2

PRE-INDUSTRIAL FACTORS	POST-INDUSTRIAL FACTORS
Seasonal time/Agricultural time	
Limited transport/ communications	
	Increased literacy
	Civilised lifestyle; increased law and order
Feudal society; two-tier society	
	More advanced technology

The British Empire

English public schools played an important role in the export of the 'games ethic' around the globe.

Sport was seen as a very good and powerful way of instilling moral values into people across the world and of binding the various people of the Empire together. Young men educated to become leaders of the British Empire spread the playing of games in a number of different ways as identified below.

Development of sport in Britain and its spread through the British Empire

The ways in which nineteenth-century public school boys and university old boys influenced the development of sport in Britain and its spread through the British Empire are listed below:

- As **teachers:** They developed teams and taught traditional sporting values in schools throughout the Empire.
- As **industrialists/factory owners:** They set up teams and gave workers time off to play competitive sport nationally and internationally.
- As **clergy:** They developed church teams or became missionaries and took sport abroad (good for social control/morality, etc.).
- As **officers in the British army:** They used sport with the armed services and spread sport throughout the Empire.
- As **diplomats:** They travelled the world and took sport with them (e.g. rugby and cricket).
- They formed the **national governing bodies** of sport (e.g. RFU) which codified sports and established leagues and competitions which eventually spread internationally as well as nationally.

Public provision and its influence on the development and spread of rational recreation

The development of public baths in urban and industrial areas positively influenced the opportunities for working-class rational recreation. Poor living conditions, disease and pollution were the harsh side-effects of industrialisation. To try to combat this, and improve the health and hygiene of the working classes, local authorities felt a civic responsibility to apply for grants to provide public washing facilities and improve their status as a town (e.g. via the Wash Houses Act of 1846). Increased provision was made in the second half of the nineteenth century for public bath houses, with first- and second-class facilities to reflect the social class an individual came from. Plunge baths developed for swimming/recreational use. Such involvement in positive physical activity was seen as a means of social control of the working classes, keeping them away from drinking and violence as much as possible. It also helped improve productivity at work as workers became healthier and less prone to serious diseases and infection.

The development of national governing bodies (NGBs)

During the mid-to-late nineteenth century, lots of NGBs began to develop in England (e.g. the Football Association in 1863) for the following reasons:

- Sport was becoming increasingly popular with more widespread playing of sport.
- More teams and clubs were forming.
- More national and international fixtures were being organised.
- Leagues and competitions were required for these teams to compete in.
- Nationally agreed rules and codification for different sports were required (e.g. association football); a single set of rules to play to was required in order to enable 'fair competition'.
- Maintenance of the 'amateur ideal' to deal with professionalism and early commercialisation of sport and the desire to maintain control of sport

KEY TERM

Public provision: Local council provision of facilities (e.g. sport/recreational) for the masses to participate.

STUDY HINT

It is important to be aware of the Municipal Reform Act and government provision which provided funding for public facilities such as baths and parks and eventually led to swimming as a sport for the working classes.

CHECK YOUR UNDERSTANDING

Why did local authorities in the nineteenth century start to provide recreational and sporting activities for their local communities?

CHECK YOUR
UNDERSTANDING
Why did some NGBs try to
prevent professionals from
competing in their sport?

ACTIVITY
Ex-public-school and university
old boys saw the need for more
structure in sport and were very
important in the formation of
many NGBs in the late nineteenth
century. Research how the FA was
formed by visiting its website and
exploring its history and origins.

KEY TERM

Rational recreation: Involves the post-
industrial development of sport. It was
characterised by a number of features
including respectability, regularity, strict
administration and codification.

among the middle/upper classes, e.g. 'exclusivity' via occupation, where the
middle and upper classes were able to set rules of eligibility to effectively
exclude the working classes from joining in (and potentially beating them!).

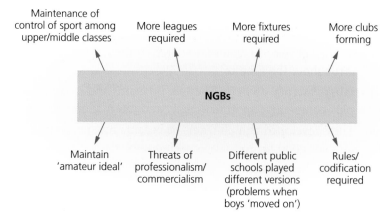

Figure 2 Factors affecting the formation of NGBs

Characteristics of rational recreation

Rational recreation involves the post-industrial development of sport for
the masses.

This was characterised by features such as:

- **Respectability:** It was non-violent in nature and the emphasis was on
  fair play.

- **Regionally/nationally/regularly played:** Competitions were played
  regionally, nationally and internationally. Watching Saturday-afternoon
  football for the masses was particularly popular in their time off work.

- **Stringent administration and codification:** Strict and complex written
  rules were set down by national governing bodies (NGBs) for the conduct
  of a sport.

- **Referees/officials:** They were present to enforce the newly developed
  rules in sporting contests.

- **Purpose-built facilities:** Sport took place in specially constructed
  grounds, pitches or tracks, often set around urban areas with large
  populations to draw on for spectators (as there was less space available in
  urban areas).

- **Skills/tactics based:** Players had positional roles they became 'specialist'
  in; performers trained to improve their techniques and fitness levels to
  increase their chances of winning.

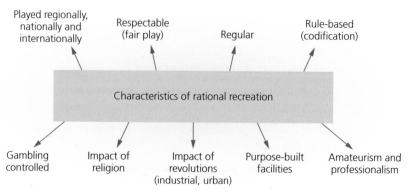

Figure 3 Characteristics of rational recreation

Memory tools

Many of the characteristics of rational recreation begin with the letter 'R' (e.g. **R**ules/codification; **R**egular; **R**egional; **R**eferees/officials; **R**espectable).

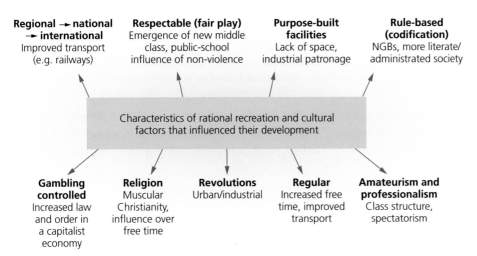

Figure 4 Characteristics of rational recreation and cultural factors that influenced their development

Amateurism and professionalism

Participation in sport over time has been viewed as being played according to two very different codes. Firstly, there is the **amateur** code which stresses sport purely for the sake of it; secondly, there is the **professional** code which places far more of an emphasis on winning.

Amateurism was associated with sport during the late nineteenth century. Its values included:

- 'Manliness', robustness, striving and physical endeavour.
- Appreciating the value of health and fitness.
- Appreciating the value of rule-regulated activity.
- High moral integrity.

The characteristics of a 'gentleman amateur' included:

- Being a respected member of society with a public school background; high status in sport reflected by high status in society.
- Belonging to the social elite, having wealth and plenty of free time for sport.
- Participation in sport was viewed as a character-building exercise; training was frowned upon as this would constitute professionalism.
- Playing a 'range of sports' using their natural talents.
- Playing sport to a high moral code, e.g. immediate acceptance of rules of the game/refereeing decisions; showed restraint in victory, good humour in defeat; indeed, a 'referee' was deemed as largely unnecessary to proceedings as amateurs believed they could govern themselves.

Positive impacts of amateurism

The positive impacts of a nineteenth-century 'gentleman amateur' (i.e. amateurism) included:

- Elite sport was run by and dominated by the upper and middle classes who had high status in sport as well as in society (i.e. **amateurs held a higher status than professionals** at the time!).

KEY TERMS

Amateur: A person who plays sport for the love of it and receives no financial gain.

Professional: a person who plays sport for financial gain.

STUDY HINT

The word 'amateur' comes from the Latin word, meaning 'for the love of'. Certainly the gentleman amateur in Victorian times played sport with an emphasis on taking part and enjoyment.

ACTIVITY

A prime example of the 'gentleman amateur' was found at the Corinthian Football Club (1882) which was formed to bring together England's best amateur footballers. Research the Corinthian Casual Football Club and see how its values adhere to the code of amateurism.

ACTIVITY

Read the following information about amateurism and professionalism in eighteenth- and nineteenth-century Britain and identify three key differences between the gentleman amateur and the professional.

'The gentleman amateur from the upper class was so wealthy that he could afford not to work and had the time to play sport whenever he wanted. He did not train and played sport for the love of it, with winning unimportant and sportsmanship part of a high moral code.

The professional was generally from a poor background and worked long hours for poor pay. When playing sport the need and desire to win was very important to live and survive so they trained hard to improve. The working-class professional was thought to be corruptible as he was controlled by money.'

- The **code of amateurism** was based on playing sport to clearly set rules which were put in place by the middle and upper classes that formed many NGBs, e.g. the FA in 1863.

- Amateurism adhered to a **code of ethics** (dominant at the time), playing sport to a high set of moral values (i.e. fair play and sportsmanship; immediate acceptance of the rules/refereeing decisions).

- **Belonging to the social elite**, i.e. having wealth and plenty of free time for sport, meant they could afford to play sport for the love of it rather than for monetary gain (it's not the winning but the taking part).

- **Participation in sport** was seen as more important than winning and taking part was viewed as a character-building exercise. They played according to their God-given abilities and training was frowned upon as this would constitute professionalism!

- The **all-rounder** was viewed with high regard by the amateurs, i.e. playing a variety of sports and developing competency in a number of them.

- Amateurs were the '**elite performers**' of the nineteenth century.

- The '**new middle classes**' admired the cultural values of the upper-class gentleman amateur. They played sport in their free time according to similar principles of amateurism.

As sports such as football became increasingly popular and the working classes had increased time and wages, the demand for spectator sports increased.

The working classes had low status and were the poorest members of society who had to make money from sport or they could not afford to play. The working-class professional came from a poor background and was perceived to be corruptible as he was controlled by money – for instance, he would take a bribe to 'throw' a fight or lose a game on purpose. Early professionals in walking and running races, for example, were paid according to results. Hence training was specialised and winning became the most important thing. Foul play and gamesmanship (i.e. stretching the rules to their absolute limit) were used to try to gain an advantage and increase the chances of winning. Challenges to refereeing decisions became increasingly common as 'professionalism' set in.

Table 3 uses Rugby Union and Rugby League to directly compare key features of the gentleman amateur with the working-class professional.

Table 3 Comparing key features of the gentleman amateur with the working-class professional

Gentleman amateur (e.g. Rugby Union)	Working-class professional (e.g. Rugby League)
Upper class/Middle class	Working class
Wealthy	Poor
Lots of free time	Very little free time due to long working hours
No desire to train to improve performance	Committed to train and perform as well as possible
High morality: emphasis on taking part/ fair play/sportsmanship	Low morality: winning was all important; open to bribes/would cheat to win

Positive impacts of nineteenth-century professionalism on sport development

As the poorest members of society, the working class had to be paid a wage for time off work when representing their factory team, i.e. broken time payments emerged, which meant working classes could eventually play sport and receive payments for doing so. Early professionals in walking and running races were paid according to results so standards of performance improved as a result of dedicated training. The working class played sport for financial gain (professional sports performers' wages were limited compared to today, but earnings were still greater than the normal working-class wage of the time).

Professionalism slowly developed at the end of the nineteenth century (e.g. employment in a factory was sometimes based on a talent to play a particular sport), with the full onset coinciding with the commercialisation and media coverage of sport in the late twentieth century. Earning money from sport was seen as an avenue of social mobility. This created a determination to succeed, i.e. high rewards at stake and the pressure to succeed to maintain a certain lifestyle.

Key features of early twentieth-century amateurs

At the start of the twentieth century, amateurs maintained their prominence in sport in a number of ways, including their positions at the top of national governing bodies, which influenced access to sports for the working classes into amateur sports such as Rugby Union. The amateurs were therefore still the best performers, playing with high morality, emphasising sportsmanship in their participation.

- **High status:** They held high status in sport and society.
- **Controllers of sport:** The middle and upper classes controlled sport, excluding (e.g. financially) working classes from 'amateur sports'.
- **Top performers**: It was more likely that top performers would come from middle or upper classes.
- **Highly moral:** They had sufficient income and leisure time to play sport for the love of it, receiving no payment. They emphasised fair play and sportsmanship.

Key features of modern-day 'amateurs'

As the twentieth century progressed, the amateurs began to lose some of their status and power in sport. Society slowly began to be based more on equality of opportunity, with achievements based more on merit and personal performance standards.

Modern-day 'amateurs' of the late twentieth/early twenty-first centuries:

- These tend to be of lower status (professionals now are of higher status).
- Some high-level performers are still not professional (e.g. gymnasts).
- There has been a blurring of amateur and professional distinctions, with less likelihood of exclusions as society has become more egalitarian, i.e. equal and achievement based on merit.
- Performance at the top level in most sports is now open to all.
- Some amateurs receive finance to pay for training expenses etc. (e.g. National Lottery/Sports Aid money). It could be argued that this enables them to train as full-time athletes in modern-day sport and they do not gain financially from Lottery funding. Does this mean they are still amateurs?

The 'positives' of modern-day 'amateurism'

The amateur code has still continued in British sport in a number of ways such as:

- Codes of amateurism are still evident in British sport, e.g. via fair play and sportsmanship.
- It is still viewed positively and promoted in a number of ways, e.g. Fair Play awards in football; shaking of hands prior to and at the end of sporting contests; through the Olympics with the Olympic Ideal based on principles of amateurism.
- Sports like Rugby Union maintained their amateurism until late into the twentieth century and still have codes of conduct based on such principles, e.g. calling the referee 'Sir'.

Modern-day professionalism

Many factors are responsible for the growth of professional sport and the increased status of professional performers from the twentieth century through to the modern day, such as:

- All classes can compete; social class is no longer a barrier to participation. Social mobility is far more possible now than it was in nineteenth-century Britain. Social class is no longer a barrier to success.
- People are now respected for their talents and efforts in reaching the top.
- There are high rewards for professionals through media and sponsorship (e.g. footballers, tennis players).
- Professionals have more time to train (i.e. many are full-time sports professionals), leading to higher standards of performance than amateurs in the same sport.
- Celebrity status, more media coverage and investment in sport have all led to vast increases in financial rewards available for sportsmen and women as large numbers of sports have become able to support professional performers, e.g. in golf, tennis and football. Many professionals are very wealthy and are able to afford big houses, expensive cars, etc. Such materialism is highly valued by many in modern-day society.
- Positive role models act as motivators for others to achieve in professional sport.
- Money invested into sports enables events and the sports themselves to operate and survive commercially; there has been a general increase in commercial sport and the sponsorship of sport.
- More spectators attend matches, with easier, more affordable travel enabling increased spectator numbers at professional sport events.

The rationalisation and modern-day development of Association Football

A variety of reasons can be given to explain the growth and development of Association Football, from the mid-nineteenth century through to the present day. In terms of industrialisation and post-industrialisation there was:

- **Urbanisation:** Large numbers of people living in one place gave a large captive audience for football. The lack of space in urban areas led to purpose-built, specialist facilities for playing football, with terraces to house the high spectator demand.

- **More free time/increased leisure time**: As workers spent less time in the factories, more time was available to them to watch and play sport. Saturday afternoon at 3pm became the traditional time for Association Football matches.

- **More disposable income:** Improved standards of living via higher wages gave the 'working class' enough money to pay entrance/gate money and pay for transport to matches, as national fixtures began and spread football nationwide.

- **Improved transport:** The development of trains, in particular, enabled fans to travel to watch 'away' fixtures and increased the regularity of matches, with the resultant need for organised leagues/cup competitions to be set up. The FA Cup was first played for in the 1871–72 season.

- **Increased professionalism:** The opportunities to play football professionally as a job gradually increased, e.g. via broken time payments which enabled workers to get time off work to play football but still be paid their wage. Professional football, first recognised by the FA in 1885, was looked upon as a 'good job' as it was a chance for some to escape the factory system of work and urban deprivation that accompanied it.

- **Social class links:** Middle-class influence and approval gave Association Football more 'respectability', with its emphasis on high morality and sporting etiquette. This was challenged relatively quickly by the working class who made it 'the people's game', with larger numbers both playing and watching Association Football, as the Football League commenced from 1888 onwards.

- **Increased organisation:** Football quickly became highly structured and standardised when in 1863 ex-public schoolboys set up the FA. National rules and codification meant the game was far more controlled with less violence, which reflected an increasingly civilised society. Referees controlled the games to further improve the behaviour of the players. Football quickly expanded, with lots of teams being set up via factories and churches.

> **ACTIVITY**
> Consider how 'improved transport' aided the development of Association Football as a 'rational game' from the mid-nineteenth century onwards.

In the first half of the twentieth century, sport alongside the radio and the cinema became part of a commercialised mass entertainment industry. For example, the BBC began its live coverage of sports events in 1927. Football became Britain's major sporting activity as the twentieth century progressed, with attendances and gate receipts soaring. However, the wages of the players did not reflect this increased income until later in the second half of the twentieth century, due to the setting of a 'maximum wage' which constrained earnings. In 1900 the maximum wage was set at £4 a week but it was slow to increase as illustrated by the timeline in footballer's wages shown in Figure 5 (see page 98).

The key time period for professional footballers was the mid-twentieth century when the maximum wage was abolished as a result of threatened strike action by the Professional Footballers' Association (PFA).

More recently in the late twentieth and twenty-first centuries, football has undergone a massive increase in commercialisation linked to far more media coverage, e.g. via TV and the internet. Top players such as Messi and Ronaldo are known the world over with pop star/role model status. Their salary scales have massively increased, with the **Bosman Ruling** giving 'freedom of contract' to players and massive transfer fees being paid, particularly to a player who is 'out of contract'.

Transport has continued to develop, meaning international travel is far quicker and more available to all than it was in the past.

KEY TERM

Bosman Ruling: A European Court of Justice decision made on 15 December 1995 concerning freedom of movement for workers. An important decision as it allowed the free movement of labour in the European Union. It effectively allowed footballers within the EU to move at the end of their contract to another club without a transfer fee being paid.

Technologically there is more use of additional officials linked to referees, as well as innovations such as Hawkeye and the Goal Decision System (GDS) to help ensure the decisions reached are the correct ones.

---

10 key stages in a footballer's wages!

Football's finances have certainly changed in the 130 years or so since 'professionalism' was legalised on 8 December 1895.

Ten important landmarks can be identified in the rise of a professional footballer's wages as illustrated by the timeline below.

1901
A £4 a week wage limit is introduced

1922
The wage cap increases to £8 a week.
(£6 in the summer/off-season)

1947
Jimmy Guthrie becomes the Players' Union Chairman and achieves an increase in maximum wage to £12 a week (£10 in the summer/off-season}

1961
PFA chairman Jimmy Hill won the abolition of the maximum wage with Johnny Haynes becoming the first £100 a week footballer

1994
Chris Sutton became the first £10,000 a week footballer when he moved from Norwich City to Blackburn Rovers

1995
The 'Bosman Ruling' allowed out of contract players free transfers and therefore the potential to negotiate far higher wages with their new clubs

2000
Roy Keane became the first £50,000 a week footballer when he signed for Manchester United

2001
Sol Campbell became the first £100,000 a week player following his Bosman 'free transfer' from Tottenham to Arsenal

2010
Carlos Tevez earns a reported £286,000 a week which equates to over a million pounds a month

CURRENT FA PREMIER LEAGUE
Wayne Rooney takes home over £300,000 a week at Manchester United

Figure 5 Timeline of a professional footballer's wages

The emergence of elite female footballers in modern-day sport

In the UK, football has become increasingly available to women. A number of socio-cultural factors can be identified which have led to an increase in opportunities for women to participate and progress through to elite level in activities such as football in modern-day society. These include:

- **Equal opportunities:** More sports are generally available and socially acceptable, including football. Legally, the Sex Discrimination Act has been passed, leading to less sexual discrimination in sport on the basis of gender. The War effort from women also led to the breaking down of myths and stereotypes about the physical capabilities of women.

- **Increased media coverage of women's football:** BT Sport provides live coverage of the Women's Super League (WSL); women's football is part of EA Sports FIFA 16 Game.

- **More female roles models in football:** as performers, coaches and officials.

- **More provision via school PE programmes:** in National Curriculum PE lessons as well as via extra-curricular opportunities.

- **Increased approval/encouragement via the FA:** e.g. the women's national team are fully supported by the FA; the FA Cup Final was held at Wembley for the first time in 2015.

- **More clubs are forming:** at local, as well as 'professional' levels.
- **Increased participation via more funding into the game:** at grass roots level as well as elite level.
- **More free time:** as the traditional domestic responsibility role has decreased.

As the twenty-first century has progressed, women's football has become increasingly prominent across the world. UEFA have set up competitions such as the Women's EURO and the UEFA Champions League, which have gained in media exposure. Top women footballers have emerged as personalities and role models for young girls to admire and aspire to. Some statistics to illustrate the growth in women's football within Europe were published by UEFA for the 2014–15 season and included the following key facts:

- Total number of registered female players: 1,208,550.
- Total number of European countries with a women's national football league: 51.

ACTIVITY

Visit **www.uefa.org/football-development/womens-football** or look at Figure 6 and identify three other statistical facts about the women's game from UEFA's infographics for 2014–15.

WOMEN'S FOOTBALL IN EUROPE STATISTICS

There are 1,208,558 registered players, or 0.3% of the female population

There are 7,641 qualified females referees and 21,164 qualified female coaches

Between 1985 and 2014 the number of female players grew five times

51 countries in Europe have a women's national league

53 associations have a national team

The following countries have more than 60,000 female players:

NORWAY	ENGLAND
SWEDEN	FRANCE
DENMARK	GERMANY
NETHERLANDS	

Figure 6 UEFA women's football infographics

Source: UEFA document: Women's Football in Europe

In England, women's football enjoyed a post-World Cup boom following the success of the team in finishing third overall in Canada. The 2015 World Cup itself was an expanded tournament with 24 teams competing and all of England's matches televised live on the BBC. The success can be traced in part to the setting up of the 'Women's Super League' which has provided women with more opportunities to play professionally and earn up to £50,000 a year when combining club wages with FA central contracts of £23,000 at this time.

Elite female officials in football

The story of the emergence of elite female officials in football is not quite so encouraging. At the end of the twentieth century, a very limited number of female officials were progressing through to the Football League. The first female ever to officiate in the Football League and then Premier League, both as an assistant referee, was Wendy Toms. Progress following on from this breakthrough has been slow. In more recent years, a lot has been done to

CHECK YOUR UNDERSTANDING

Suggest three reasons why women's participation in football has increased during the twentieth century through to the current day.

develop opportunities for female referees in England. For example, the creation of the 'Women's Referee Development Pathway' has been viewed as a significant step forward in creating a more focused and professional organisational structure for female referees to progress through.

FIFA		Women's FIFA Referee or Assistant Referee
3	1	Referee – Women's Super League and Premier League
4	2	Referee – Combination League Assistant Referee – Women's Premier League and Women's Super League
5	3	Referee – Regional Premier League Assistant Referee – Combination League
6	4	Referee – Regional League Assistant Referee – Regional Premier League
7	5	Referee – County women's Leagues Assistant referee – Regional League
8	6	Youth (U16)
9	7	Trainee

Figure 7 Women's Referee Development Pathway (levels 7–1) and their male equivalents.

Source: The Football Association

In terms of female officials at Levels 1–8 currently operating in England, the FA put the number at over 850 and climbing. While relatively small in number in relation to their male counterparts, the fact that the FA reports an increasing number of female referees at different levels of the game provides optimism, with ambassadors and elite role models in refereeing for young girls to aspire to.

The rationalisation and modern-day development of lawn tennis

Lawn tennis was a middle-class invention as the middle classes aspired to be like the upper classes in society but were excluded from or could not play real tennis. Hence, with the help of Major Walter Clopton Wingfield who patented his game of tennis on 23 February in 1874, they devised their own form of tennis which suited their middle-class suburban housing with lawned gardens as appropriate venues for tennis courts. Walls and hedges ensured privacy from the lower classes who were initially excluded from participation.

The middle classes established 'private' tennis clubs where gardens were deemed unsuitable to house a tennis court.

Figure 8 Lawn tennis and emancipation of women – picture of lawn tennis court, 1876

Figure 9 Miss Maud Watson, first female Wimbledon champion in 1884

By 1877, the All England Croquet Club had been renamed the All England Croquet and Lawn Tennis Club. As a rational sporting activity mainly for the middle class, lawn tennis was first introduced at Wimbledon in 1877, joining croquet as another sport.

It was viewed as an important activity in the emancipation of women, with female participation first allowed in 1884, helping to overcome suppression and negative stereotypes. Positive female role models inspired participation e.g. Lottie Dodd who won five ladies singles titles in the late nineteenth century and was an outstanding all-round sportswoman. The first female winner of Wimbledon was Miss Maud Watson. The game of lawn tennis aided women as it was a game which could be played in the seclusion and privacy of their own gardens. Women could play the game as a 'minimum exercise activity' dressed in a modest and reserved way, with their bodies fully covered by high-necked, long-sleeved dresses. As lawn tennis was 'not too vigorous', women were not expected to sweat which was seen as unladylike. They could play the game with both males and females as part of social gatherings, improving their health at the same time.

The following is a summary of the key features of lawn tennis as it developed in the industrial/post-industrial era.

- **Middle-class invention:** It was a middle-class development/invention as an affordable alternative to real tennis, which set the middle class apart from the working class and led to private clubs developing for participation.
- **Played by the middle class:** It was played in middle-class suburban gardens on lawns big enough to house private tennis courts.

- **Organised by the middle class:** The middle class had the organisational experience necessary to form their own private clubs.
- **Use of specialist equipment:** The middle class had sufficient finance to purchase their own equipment. (Wingfield sold a 'kit' as a portable product necessary to play the game of tennis. It cost five guineas (21 shillings or £1.05) and included the net, balls, racquets and poles for the net.)
- **Use of standardised rules:** Wingfield's 'kit' also contained a rulebook which helped standardise the game, with lawn tennis played to the same rules no matter where it was played.
- **Played by males and females**: Tennis allowed respectable social and gender mixing; it was a good, civilised, 'social game' which both sexes could play.
- **Public provision**: It eventually spread to the working class via public parks.

Modern-day tennis spread around the world, with tournaments in the USA, France and Australia taking place alongside Wimbledon as the four 'majors'. Players soon realised they could earn considerable amounts of money from their tennis skills and professional tours and tournaments were established as early as the 1920s to enable them to do so. However, the rest of tennis, including the four 'Majors' remained strictly amateur, with professionals excluded from participation.

It was not until beyond the mid-twentieth century (in 1968) that commercial pressures and rumours of some amateurs taking money illegally (colloquially known as 'shamateurism') led to the abandonment of the distinction between amateur and professional, inaugurating the 'open era' in which all players could compete in all tournaments.

With the beginning of the **'open era'**, the establishment of an international professional tennis circuit and revenues from the sale of TV rights, the popularity of the game has spread worldwide and the sport has tried to shed its English middle-class image. Tennis in the UK is still perceived by many to be a middle-class preserve. This may be because it developed later than other sports or it may be due to the fact that joining a tennis club has always appeared unduly difficult or off-putting, with the requirement to stick to rigid dress codes. The image of the sport as a means to gather socially rather than as a competitive opportunity has been hard to shed.

The open era witnessed distinct inequalities in the amount of prize money offered to men and women. The 1968 Wimbledon Championship awarded £2000 to Rod Laver, the men's singles winner, with only £750 given to Billie Jean King, the women's champion. Representatives from the Women's Tennis Association (WTA), including Billie Jean King, fought for equal recognition and prize money, with equality achieved in 2007 at Wimbledon when both winners earned £700,000. By 2015 it had risen to £1,760,000 each for the respective men's and ladies' singles champions.

The emergence of elite female tennis players in modern-day sport

The work of the WTA (which is now a global leader in women's professional sport) illustrates how tennis can be viewed as one of a few sports in which female professional performers played a significant part. As part of the battle fighting pay differentials in tennis tournaments such as Wimbledon, a number of women decided to create their own tour away from the men's. The WTA therefore developed their own professional circuit in the late twentieth century, which provided ground-breaking opportunities for

---

CHECK YOUR UNDERSTANDING
State three characteristics of lawn tennis as a 'rational recreation' activity.

KEY TERM

Open era: When professional tennis players were allowed to compete alongside amateurs and earn money.

women to play at the top level, eventually earning millions of pounds through tournament earnings and sponsorship deals. Billie Jean King became the first female athlete to earn £100,000 in a single year, with Chris Evert generating over $1,000,000 in career earnings by the mid-1970s. The WTA also stated that in 2015, more than 2500 elite players competed for $129 million in prize money at the 55 WTA events and four Grand Slams available in tennis. Lots of potential role models for girls, as well as large sponsorship deals, continue in the early twenty-first century via worldwide media coverage of women's elite tennis tournaments.

The rationalisation and modern-day development of track and field athletics

The industrialisation of society led to rural fairs being replaced by urban fairs, as people migrated in large numbers to towns and cities looking for work. Athletics events became popular in such towns and cities, with purpose-built tracks and facilities in most major cities by the mid-nineteenth century. Walking and running races took place over set distances on race courses. Large numbers of people attended athletics events, with up to 25,000 spectators at meetings as the nineteenth century progressed. Wagering was still common in athletics. Class divisions were also still evident as it became a 'rationalised' activity. Upper- and middle-class amateurs ran for enjoyment or to test themselves, while the lower classes ran to make money and were deemed 'professionals'.

An 'exclusion clause' (excluding the working class/manual workers) attempted to separate modern athletics from the old professional/corrupt form. In 1866, the Amateur Athletic Club (AAC) was formed by public school and ex-university men who were gentleman amateurs and did not allow mechanics, artisans or labourers to join (i.e. they excluded the working classes, or those earning money from running, from membership of the AAC). They brought respectability to athletics, emphasising endeavour, fair play, courage and no wagering.

The Amateur Athletic Association (AAA), established on 24 April 1880, withdrew the exclusion clause and 'opened up' the sport to everyone. A professional became somebody who ran for money as opposed to someone from the working class. Track and field athletics was not deemed to be an acceptable activity for women as it was thought unladylike and unable to follow an appropriate dress code. The Women's AAA was not founded until 1922 with female participants not allowed into the Olympics until Amsterdam 1928. Even then, women were not allowed to race in events above 800m as they were seen as 'too strenuous'.

As the twentieth century progressed, in the immediate post-Second World War period, interest in athletics was stimulated when the Olympics took place in London in 1948. However, while the rest of the world found ways to get round the strict amateur rules of international athletics, Britain left its athletes to manage as best they could. 'Trust funds' were eventually established which enabled athletes to safeguard their eligibility to take part in amateur competitions, but still allowed them to receive financial rewards as an athlete. The governing body for athletics kept control of the sport by insisting that all payments should be channelled or authorised by them. Payments from the fund for day-to-day living expenses were allowed and the balance became available to the athlete on retirement.

Amateur Athletic Association

Figure 10 The badge of the Amateur Athletic Association

Such arrangements enabled a group of male and female athletes to go around the world and compete in a programme of championships and grand prix events, with both appearance money as well as prize money for winning. Today, there are no trust funds as payments can be made directly to athletes and/or their agents within rules which were laid down by the International Amateur Athletics Association (IAAA), which is now called the International Association of Athletics Federations (IAAF).

At the end of the twentieth century into the early twenty-first century, the IAAF established and organised a number of major international athletics competitions for male as well as female athletes to compete in and earn considerable amounts of money. For example, in 2010, a new global one-day competition structure headed by the IAAF Diamond League was unveiled. It involves 14 invitational track and field meetings in Asia, Europe, the Middle East and Asia. Large spectator numbers, both live and via global media coverage, ensure athletes can generate healthy incomes via prize money and sponsorship deals with large multinationals such as Nike and Adidas.

The emergence of elite female athletes in modern-day sport

Treatment of women in athletics remained 'indifferent' at best through to the late twentieth century. Even at this relatively late stage in the century, women were still excluded from a number of events in the Olympics. The marathon was not open to women until the Los Angeles Olympics in 1984. The triple jump and hammer were only introduced for women in Atlanta 1996 and Sydney 2000 respectively. Fortunately the negative myths and stereotypes about the capabilities of elite level female athletes are being challenged and competitions such as the Diamond League enable female as well as male athletes to earn millions as a result of their talents.

The 'golden triangle'

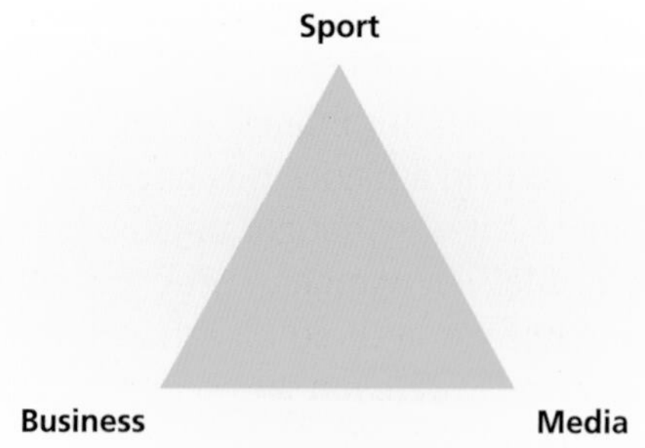

Figure 11 The 'golden triangle'

Sport, the **media**, business and sponsorship are all strongly inter-linked and mutually dependent – the **'golden triangle'**. Each element of the 'triangle' relies on the others. For instance, without media coverage, sports are less attractive to sponsors who want their business or product to be publicised to as many people as possible. The media uses sport to gain viewers, listeners and readers. In turn, businesses and sponsors use the media to advertise their products and services: organisations often pay substantial sums to sport and the media for advertisements.

ACTIVITY

Think of three different ways in which the 'golden triangle' can lead to disadvantages for sport.

KEY TERMS

Media: An organised means of communication by which large numbers of different people can be reached quickly.

Golden triangle: The golden triangle refers to the relationship between sport, business and media.

Commercialism, media and sponsorship

There is massive media interest in certain 'high-profile' sports – television companies pay huge amounts of money for the right to show a sporting event, e.g. football on Sky Sports and BT Sport – as sport has a positive image. **Sponsorship** deals result from television exposure. **Merchandising** too relates to media exposure – clothing and equipment companies such as Nike and Adidas have become strong rivals in sponsoring teams and individuals to aid their merchandising. Governing bodies and other organisations have become multinational companies. For example, the US National Basketball Association (NBA) and National Football League (NFL) have spread their influence and products around the world in 'demonstration' games.

Characteristics of commercial sport

Commercial sport has close links with:

- **professional sport** – it is high quality; has high skill levels
- **sponsorship and business** – they go hand-in-hand
- **entertainment** – watching sport is part of a mass-entertainment industry; viewing needs to fit into a relatively short time scale
- **contracts** – e.g. involving sales of merchandise and bidding for television rights
- **athletes as commodities** – e.g. as an asset to companies through product endorsement, which brings increased sales/profits; athletes become well-known role models
- **wide media coverage** – and interest in high-profile sports that are visually appealing and have high skill levels, well-matched competition and simple/understandable rules.

Effects of commercialisation on professional performers

As a result of commercialisation, professional sportsmen and sportswomen:

- Receive high incomes for sports participation and commercial activities promoting products, which gives financial security and allows full-time training and competition.
- Are paid for successful results, which makes winning important.
- Can be put under pressure to perform when injured.
- Must specialise in a sport in order to compete, which requires serious training, dedication and self-sacrifice.
- Are effectively entertainers who become household names, e.g. Messi and Ronaldo.
- Are controlled by the sponsor, become public commodities and suffer from a lack of privacy.

Effects of commercialisation on sport

Some sports have changed as a result of commercial and media interest, for instance:

- Rules and scoring systems have been changed or introduced to speed up the action and prevent spectator boredom – e.g. the multi-ball system at football matches cuts down on time-wasting; badminton scores on every point.
- Breaks are provided in play so that sponsors can advertise their products and services.

KEY TERMS

Commercialism: The process of attempting to gain money from an activity e.g. sport.

Sponsorship: When a company pays for their products to be publicly displayed or advertised, usually as an attempt to increase the sales of their goods.

Merchandising: The practice in which the brand or image from one 'product' is used to sell another, e.g. professional sports teams/performers promote various products.

ACTIVITY

Identify three different types of media you might use to 'follow sport'.

CHECK YOUR UNDERSTANDING

Identify the characteristics of a sport which make it attractive for TV coverage.

- Competition formats have changed – e.g. Twenty20 cricket is a major revenue-earner due to spectator, television and commercial interests.
- Sports played by women receive less coverage, which can negatively affect participation and funding – there are fewer female role models and there is less money to reinvest into sport at grassroots and professional levels.
- The increased use of technology through the media has led to a more personal experience for the viewer (e.g. the stump cam in cricket).

Reasons why companies invest large amounts of money into sport e.g. via sport sponsorship

- increased sales/commercial benefits/increased profit/increased publicity
- increases brand awareness/adds value to a brand e.g. Nike golf and Rory McIlroy
- creates an association with excellence at the highest levels of sport
- creates an association with the healthy image of sport
- gives an opportunity to link to corporate hospitality
- sponsorship can decrease the amount of tax paid by a company; tax relief
- improve company morale/employees feel linked to the success of sport.

The media

There are a number of different types of media involved in covering sport. These include newspapers, radio, the internet and social media. TV can be viewed as the most powerful aspect of the media – the buying and selling of TV broadcasting rights is a very important part of twenty-first century sport as it has 'gone global'!

Globalisation in sport is seen via:

- The sponsorship of events (e.g. Coca-Cola as a 'universal sponsor).
- The way players are recruited to play for teams in countries other than their own.
- The spreading of different sports to 'new nations' e.g. the 1994 soccer World Cup which was successfully hosted in the USA.
- Increasing pressure on athletes to perform to their best; this may lead some to use illegal substances to maintain high performance levels and the accompanying rewards that success brings in a number of high-profile sports.

English football on TV

Following the BBC starting its TV services in 1936, English football has been broadcast since 1937. The very first televised game of football was a specially arranged friendly between Arsenal and Arsenal Reserves at Highbury. This was followed by the first international match between England and Scotland on 9 April 1938. October 1946 saw the first live televised match between Barnet and Wealdstone, but in general, there was very little football coverage on TV in the mid-twentieth century apart from the FA Cup Final and the odd England vs Scotland match.

In 1964, BBC introduced *Match of the Day* with the intention of training cameramen for the forthcoming World Cup.

The rise of intercontinental communications satellites, as well as advances in videotape, led to the first widespread international coverage of the 1966 World Cup held in England. As history shows, England won the World Cup

KEY TERM

Globalisation: The process whereby nations are increasingly being linked together and people are becoming more interdependent via improvements in communication and travel.

that year, which increased the popularity of the sport and led to more and more football viewers for *Match of the Day* as well as on ITV.

In the late twentieth century and into the early twenty-first century, the relationship between sport and the media has moved to a new era. This can be linked to technological advances which produced developments such as the satellite. This has enabled the spectator to watch sports live from anywhere in the world. The increased money involved in the media rights to events has meant that the media may well be able to exercise control over the events they have effectively 'bought'. For example, in 1992 satellite station BSkyB paid £304 million for a five-year contract to cover the English Premier Football League. This amount has been vastly increased in recent years with a surge in the value of the Premier League TV contract from 2016–19 which went for a staggering £5.136 billion. Kit sponsorship deals of top Premier League clubs have also increased and give clubs an annual income of many millions of pounds, e.g. Manchester United has signed an annual deal worth £30 million through to 2025 with Adidas.

The impact of social media on sport

In the last few years, **social media** has changed the behaviour at all levels of both sports performers and fans in the sports world. The younger generation, which grew up with social media as a major means of communication, will naturally use social media in more and more ways in terms of their sporting interests/involvement. These days, more and more fans prefer getting their sports news from Twitter and Facebook rather than from TV or national news websites. Top sports performers are 'all' involved in social media in a big way and they have created lots of excitement via their social media communications as opposed to other media channels such as newspapers. Soccer has a worldwide fan base which (in 2015) boasted two of the most followed athletes on Twitter, i.e. Kaka (with 9,862,492 followers) and Ronaldo (8,491,741). In 2015 Ronaldo passed 50 million 'Likes' on his Facebook fan page and he was the first athlete on social media to do so.

Ronaldo uses social media to improve his connection with his fans while at the same time promote his personal branding (see http://socialmediacoachforathletes.com/top-athletes-and-social-media/ and https://twitter.com/Cristiano).

The English Premier League dominates when it comes to love for individual teams. Manchester United is the number one, with nearly 27 million fans on Facebook. Chelsea and Arsenal both boast more than 11 million fans.

There are a number of big players in the world of social media including Twitter, Facebook, Instagram, BlogSpot and WordPress. In addition, YouTube is increasingly being used by many athletes to help them achieve their goals (e.g. posting videos of edited highlights to attract university scholarships/coaches).

The power and reach provided by social media to sports performers has changed sport at all levels. It has enabled top-level sports performers to build up very large and engaged fan bases in a very short space of time. Social media has empowered athletes at every level to engage with a much wider audience than was possible a few years ago. However, while this has a number of positives, a number of elite performers have got into trouble for their postings on social media. For example, regular tweeter Rio Ferdinand was suspended for three matches and fined £25,000 by the FA in October 2014 over his Twitter comments linked to a 'promiscuous girl/woman'. Lots of performers are not

ACTIVITY

Think about and list four positive effects the media can have on a sport.

KEY TERM

Social media: Online apps and websites which allow users to interact by sharing content and taking part in social networking.

trained to understand the responsibilities and liability that go with such 'global communication'. Specialist organisations are being set up to provide social media training at a variety of levels (e.g. Social Media Coach for Athletes).

In 2009 the Football League launched social media accounts on Twitter to engage directly with fans. The WTA also use a variety of social media to promote women's tennis, for example, via:

- Facebook.com/WTA
- Twitter.com/WTA
- www.youtube.com/user/wta

England Athletics view social media as a great potential way for athletics clubs to share information with their members, as well as with other individuals interested in athletics. They have produced information to help clubs understand the basics of social media and hopefully avoid any embarrassing situations through its inappropriate usage!

SUMMARY

In summary, as a result of studying this section you should be able to understand a variety of historical influences on the development of sporting activities, from pre-industrial times through to the modern-day contemporary scene. The content included in this chapter will help you to:

- Identify the characteristics of pre-industrial Britain and how these influenced popular recreation activities of the time (e.g. via mob football, real tennis and athletics).
- Identify the characteristics of industrial and post-industrial Britain and how these influenced the development of sporting activities such as association football, lawn tennis and track and field athletics through to the late nineteenth century.
- Understand and explain a range of socio-cultural factors in industrial and post-industrial Britain which impacted on the development of sport, e.g. the industrial, urban and transport/communications revolutions; the role of the middle classes, factory owners, Church and local authorities in supporting sporting developments at home and abroad.
- Understand the reasons for the development of national governing bodies of sport in the nineteenth century.
- Understand the changing status of the amateur and the professional sports performer from the late eighteenth century through to the modern day.
- Consider the changing role of women in sport and factors affecting their emergence in modern-day elite sport via a consideration of their involvement in football, tennis and athletics.
- Understand how the 'golden triangle' influences the development of sport in modern-day society.

PRACTICE QUESTIONS

1 Which of the following is a characteristic of popular recreation? (1 mark)

   a) Regularly played

   b) Officials present

   c) Highly violent

   d) Highly structured

2 State the characteristics of popular recreation. (4 marks)

3 Identify key characteristics of **rational recreation**. (4 marks)

4 List and explain the different **socio-cultural factors** which influenced the development of rationalised sport in late nineteenth-century Britain. (6 marks)

5 Discuss the effects of **industrialisation** on sporting opportunities for the working classes. (4 marks)

6 'Victorian vicars made super sports.' During the late nineteenth century, the Church set up organisations, formed sports teams and provided facilities for sports participation among the working classes. Why did it do this? (2 marks)

7 Outline reasons why opportunities to reach elite level sport were restricted for the working class in the late nineteenth century. (4 marks)

8 What factors led to an increase in the status of **professional** sports performers in twentieth-century Britain? (4 marks)

Chapter 3.2
The impact of sport on society and of society on sport

Chapter objectives

After reading this chapter you should be able to:

- Understand the following key terms in relation to their study of sport and their impact on equal opportunities in sport and society: society; equal opportunities; discrimination; stereotypes; prejudice.
- Understand the following key terms in relation to their study of sport and their impact on equal opportunities in sport and society: socialisation (primary and secondary); social processes (social control and social change); social issues (causes and consequences of inequality); social structures/stratification, e.g. schools/sports clubs.
- Understand social action theory in relation to social issues in physical activity and sport.
- Understand the barriers to participation in sport and physical activity and possible solutions to overcome them for under-represented groups in sport.
- Understand the benefits of raising participation.
- Understand the inter-relationship between Sport England, local and national partners to increase participation at grassroots level and under-represented groups in sport.

The sociology of sport

This section of the textbook will introduce and explain how the 'science' of sociology helps us to understand equality of opportunity in sport and society in general.

Sociology can be viewed as having two main concerns:

1 Examining interactions and interdependence, i.e. the way people live in groups within society and therefore interact with others throughout their everyday lives.

2 Examining how human behaviour becomes controlled, e.g. via family members, friends, schools, etc.

The sociology of sport is an applied sub-discipline of sociology which considers the relationship between sport and **society**. When analysing such a relationship, it also considers social processes occurring within sport (e.g. socialisation) and considers how inequalities in sport can be overcome for groups in society such as women, individuals with a disability and ethnic minority groups.

Key terms defined and related to equality of opportunity in sport

These terms will be explained and applied as appropriate at various stages during this chapter.

Society

A human society is a group of people involved in persistent interpersonal relationships, often a large social grouping sharing the same geographical territory, typically subject to the same political authority and dominant cultural expectations.

A society can therefore be viewed as the sum total of all the relationships in a given space (e.g. within a specific country or nation state). Success in sport on a global scale is often viewed as an important measure of the relative status of a society or nation in the world. For example, national identity and national pride are often achieved as a result of success at events such as the Olympics (e.g. in Britain through Team GB's third position on the medal table at London 2012). Other examples of where sporting success particularly impacts on society include:

- the Ashes: England playing Australia at cricket is particularly important, with Australia being a former colony looking to get one over their 'mother country'!
- USA vs Russia: The competition at the Olympics has been described as a 'war without weapons' and a throwback to the old 'Cold War', using sport as a means of proving political supremacy (i.e. the USA's success as a reflection of capitalist society being superior; while Russian success is used as a reflection of socialist society being superior).

Socialisation

Socialisation is a lifelong process where members of a society learn its norms, values, ideas, practices and roles in order to take their place in that society.

It can be divided into two main parts: primary and secondary socialisation.

Primary socialisation

This refers to socialisation during the early years of childhood which takes place mainly within the immediate family (i.e. the mother, father, brothers and sisters). A key process involved at this stage is the **internalisation** of a society's culture where individuals absorb and accept its shared norms and values. The nature of living in a society is such that people are constantly communicating within a social group among family and close friends. Much of the early basic socialisation occurs as a young child when families and early friends teach basic values and accepted behaviour patterns. Play is a good way to learn how to share, interact and practise becoming an adult. For many families, physical exercise provides a time when they come together, whether it be a shared involvement in an activity such as cycling, or a family commitment to one (or more) member of the family who has devoted themselves to regular involvement in sporting competition.

Secondary socialisation

This occurs during the later years (e.g. as teenagers and adults) when the family is less involved and other 'agencies' are deliberately set up for the socialisation process and begin to exert more and more influence (e.g. peer groups, friends, schools). School is an important part of social development.

STUDY HINT

It is important that you are able to define and apply to equality of sporting opportunities a range of sociological terms contained in the syllabus such as society, socialisation and social stratification.

KEY TERM

Society: An organised group of people associated for some specific purpose or with a shared common interest.

KEY TERMS

Socialisation: A lifelong process where members of a society learn its norms, values, ideas, practices and roles in order to take their place in that society.

Internalisation: The learning of values or attitudes that are incorporated within yourself.

ACTIVITY

Think about and write down the various purposes of play during the primary socialisation process. What skills/values do children develop as a result of informal play with their friends and family?

CHECK YOUR UNDERSTANDING

Define the terms primary socialisation and secondary socialisation.

KEY TERMS

Gender socialisation: The act of learning to conform to culturally defined gender roles through socialisation.

Social control: A concept that refers to the way in which people's thoughts, feelings, appearance and behaviour are regulated in social systems.

Institution: An established organisation founded for a religious, educational, professional or social purpose.

CHECK YOUR UNDERSTANDING
Identify different reasons why aerobics is a popular pastime among women compared to a sport such as rugby.

KEY TERM

Social change: An alteration in the social order of a society.

For example, it can help with the socialisation process by teaching important moral skills such as co-operation, teamwork and learning to take responsibility for one's own actions.

Gender socialisation involves the learning of behaviour and attitudes historically considered appropriate for a given sex. 'Boys learn to be boys' and 'girls learn to be girls' via the many different 'agents of socialisation', including family, friends, school, college and the mass media. This has a major impact on participation in sport, as we will discuss later!

Social processes – social control and social change

Social control

Social control is a concept that refers to the way in which people's thoughts, feelings, appearance and behaviour are regulated in social systems.

Society is made up of various **institutions**, with the family viewed as the most basic unit. These institutions work together for the benefit of society, undertaking a variety of 'social processes' to ensure socialisation into society, maintaining order and social control.

However, in society there are various social processes at work which act as constraints and potentially limit the opportunities to become involved in sport. Historically, our society has been male dominated, with restrictions placed on women engaging in sport. Nowadays, the constraints are less pronounced, however milder forms of social control exist in the form of what is deemed to be gender appropriate behaviour. For example, mild disapproval from their husband or male partner might persuade women to limit their physical activity to what they view as 'respectable' and therefore 'socially acceptable'. So they might choose badminton over rugby or aerobics over boxing if under the influence of social control. Social control from peers or the media to 'look feminine' and maintain a slim appearance could also rule out certain sports requiring muscular development which is seen as 'unfeminine', e.g. weightlifting, boxing and rugby.

Social pressures mean that sometimes women are made to feel guilty about leaving a young baby and therefore tend to give up previous active leisure pursuits once their child has been born. A lack of free time compared to men and lower disposable income can also act as agents of social control and decrease the opportunities for women to involve themselves in regular healthy sporting activity, as illustrated by the following data on sport's participation. Sport England's Active People survey (8Q3–9Q2) discovered that 40.6 per cent of men compared to 30.7 per cent of women took part in sport at least once a week.

Social change

The statistics above confirm the sports participation inequalities existing when comparing women to men. It is very difficult for any social group to bring about change without having strong influence in the decision-making groups (e.g. local councils; national governing bodies, etc.). **Social change** occurs when institutions re-adjust to meet 'new needs' of groups in society such as women. For example, social changes offered by leisure providers such as local councils via more crèche facilities to minimise/lessen the negative effects of traditional childcare responsibilities and/or feelings of guilt at leaving young children while mothers participate in sporting activity.

In addition to gender inequalities, certain ethnic groups such as Indians and Pakistanis have faced constraints on their participation in sport. Some of these have been viewed as emerging from within the family unit itself (e.g. via cultural norms valuing educational achievement over sporting participation, as well as restricting women's participation due to clothing restrictions).

'Social change' can therefore be viewed as an alteration in the social order of a society. Sporting activities can be used in specialist programmes to try to bring about social change in a positive way.

In terms of gender, the 'This Girl Can' campaign has been launched by Sport England as a high-profile scheme to try to bring about social changes in the way women's participation in sport and physical activity is viewed.

'Cricket for Change' is a UK charity established in 1981 impacting on the lives of disadvantaged children. The aim of this scheme via its programmes such as 'Street Chance' is to increase aspiration, promote mutual respect and enhance relationships within the wider community by providing free structured community cricket coaching and competitive opportunities for young people (i.e. 8–15 year olds from areas of social deprivation, high youth crime and antisocial behaviour.) West Indies international cricketer Chris Gayle has set up an academy as part of the scheme and he states:

> *'Cricket is indeed a powerful sport. It has certainly changed my life. I was given the tools and support to succeed and I want to share this with the academy. I have a simple approach and I want these young people to see that simple can help you achieve great things.'*

Social issues – causes and consequences of inequality

Many people dream of a society where all members are equal and there is no ranking of people in terms of prestige, power, wealth, etc. It is obvious to us all that such a society remains a dream rather than a reality and all human societies have some form of social inequality, with power, prestige and wealth unequally divided.

Social **inequality** occurs when resources in a society are unevenly distributed among socially defined categories of people. There is a range of different social inequality categories of people who are identifiable via socially defined characteristics such as ethnic or racial and gender identities. Related to this is economic inequality on the basis of unequal distribution of income or wealth and is a frequently studied type of social inequality, with major implications for all aspects of life, including participation in sport.

Sex and gender-based prejudice and discrimination (i.e. sexism) are major contributory factors to social inequality as they give rise to different role divisions, which ultimately lead to fewer women in positions of power and decision making, whether this be in the world of sport or more generally in political activities within society. Women's participation in work has been increasing globally (e.g. in professional sport) but women still face wage differences compared to men's earnings, as well as differences in terms of political influence and their role in most major religions.

If we focus on participation in sport, there are a number of possible causes of inequality. These include:

● lack of money/costs of participating
● lack of confidence/self-esteem
● lack of role models to aspire to as participants/coaches/leaders of sports organisations in positions of responsibility
● myths or stereotypes in some sections of society about the capabilities of women, ethnic minorities and disabled people.

ACTIVITY
Visit **www.cricketforchange.org. uk/cricket-for-change/the-chris-gayle-academy/** and note down three key points about Cricket for Change as a scheme designed to help bring about social change.

KEY TERMS
Social issues: Problems that affect many people within a society.
Inequality: The unfair situation where resources or opportunities are distributed unevenly within a society.

ACTIVITY
Identify any myths about women which may negatively affect their participation in sport or physical activity.

113

Memory tools

You can remember key causes of inequality via **MR MC**!

- **M** = **M**oney
- **R** = **R**ole models
- **M** = **M**yths
- **C** = **C**onfidence

As far as sport and physical activity are concerned, there are a number of negative consequences of such inequalities as they result in lower participation rates in sport among a number of groups/sections of society, including people with disabilities, women, those from ethnic minority groups, the unemployed and elderly people. (See statistics to illustrate this in other parts of this chapter linked to gender, ethnicity and disability in particular.)

Social structures and social stratification

A number of different social structures exist which have an impact (positively and negatively) on an individual and their overall life chances. When linked to participation in sport, the type of school you go to (e.g. state vs private) can affect the activities you get to try out, as well as the amount of time devoted to sport, and the quality of teaching/coaching received to develop your talents, and the quality of facilities you train in.

Social stratification is a type of social inequality and is the division of a society into different levels on the basis of a 'social characteristic', such as wealth or status. Social differences are divided into different layers in societies such as those like our own when the relative possession or non-possession of a social characteristic such as wealth or status becomes the distributing principle for individuals within a system of unequal rewards. Modern-day societies use individual wealth as a means of stratification. The importance of stratification is that those at the top of the system have greater access to resources than those at the bottom. (For example, in the feudal society of pre-industrial Britain, the upper class had greater access to equipment and facilities which meant they could participate in sports such as real tennis which used a specialist court and equipment: see Chapter 3.1.)

In some ways, participation in sport means participants can leave behind their 'normal lives' and adopt a 'new athletic identity' in a sporting context. This (temporarily) replaces the inequalities of everyday life with a situation where we are all equal!

However, the idea that sport provides equality of opportunity can be viewed as problematic as the very nature of sport emphasises competition and dominance. The realities of the 'real world' and people's relative position in the social class hierarchy do affect their involvement in sport. For example, disposable income can influence the type of activity participated in, the type of club joined, the equipment used and so on. For example, equestrian and other horse-related activities tend to be relatively expensive and require high income levels linked to the upper class in society.

The social stratification system continues to be visible in sport with a number of sections or groups of society identified by Sport England as under-represented in terms of sports involvement, e.g. ethnic minority groups, individuals with a disability, etc.

When looking at the organisation and structure of society, it is clear some individuals and groups have traditionally held the positions of power. In the

KEY TERM

Social stratification: A type of social inequality where society is divded into different levels on the basis of a social characteristic, such as wealth or status.

ACTIVITY

Identify a sporting activity linked to those from a middle- or upper middle-class group and give reasons why there is limited access to this activity for those in 'lower' social classes.

UK, those in such positions have tended to be white males from the middle classes. This leads to the social stratification of society being reflected in sport, with a hierarchy evident, giving power and influence to those at the top.

For many years, **social class** variations in sports participation have been highlighted by research and data produced by Sport England.

Social class/stratification and schools

While National Curriculum PE aims to offer all young people a broad and balanced programme, it is evident some young people may be disadvantaged as a result of social inequality.

Children from low-income families tend to have poorer health than other children. Such poor levels of health may undermine their physical abilities and/or skill levels. Children from low-income families also have less money to spend on sports equipment, additional specialist coaching, etc. Schools themselves may magnify the social class differences (e.g. public schools and state schools situated in more affluent areas often have better sports facilities than schools located in working-class areas).

Social class and sports clubs

Involvement in extra-curricular activities may be negatively affected by working-class expectations on children to carry out domestic responsibilities (e.g. looking after younger children in the family, doing household chores, etc.). Economic inequalities are also likely to impact on membership of sports clubs, increasing the likelihood of more middle- and upper-class children joining clubs compared to working-class children.

This can be illustrated via the Sport England Active People Survey data on tennis participation among the 16+ age group (see below), which for many occurs within tennis clubs. In terms of social class, the data below illustrates the fact that there are higher rates of participation in tennis among the highest socio-economic groups. While 202,500 adults from National Statistics Socio-economic Classifications (NS-SEC) levels 1–4 (managerial/ skilled professions) participated in tennis at least once a week, only 64,100 adults from NS-SEC levels 5–8 (non-skilled/manual professions) did so.

ACTIVITY

Compare the possible differences between sports facilities at a state school with those of a private school in the area you live in.

ACTIVITY

Look at the data in Figure 1 from 2011–12 which illustrates the Sport England Active People results on sports participation linked to socio-economic groups (i.e. social class). What does the data illustrate to you about social class and its impact on participation in sport?

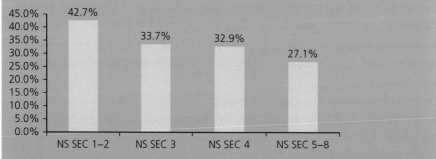

Figure 1 Participation in sport at least once a week by socio-economic group
Source: StreetGames Briefing Paper: Tennis participation and social class

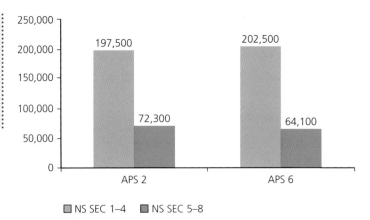

Figure 2 Tennis participation at least once a week by socio-economic group

Source: StreetGames Briefing Paper: Tennis participation and social class

> **CHECK YOUR UNDERSTANDING**
> How can participation in sport and other physical activity be increased among individuals in the working class?

KEY TERMS

Social action theory: A way of viewing socialisation, emphasising social action.

Progression: The process of gradually developing towards a more advanced state.

Interactionist approach: The study of how individuals behave within a society.

Social action theory and its influence on physical activity and sport

Social action theory accepts that sport is produced and developed at a particular time through the relationships and social networks of people who share similar views. The links between these people and their social interdependence are the key ideas of such a theory.

Sports involvement and **progression** are therefore determined by the relationships between people based on the different amounts of power they have in society. The way these relationships are built up and why they change is an open-ended process.

Sport has therefore developed in a complex way alongside aspects of society such as class structure, education and family. Social action theory stresses the fact that people can intervene in social processes and change them.

The interactionist approach

In sociology, the **interactionist approach** is the study of how individuals behave within a society. It is a theoretical perspective that stems from social processes, for example co-operation and conflict, which occur when humans interact.

Interactionism works from the individual towards society and stresses the fact that it is people who actually create society. The ways we communicate and interact (e.g. via language/gesture) are emphasised. Although it is accepted that society does control individuals, there is always the opportunity for some creative action. Through the use of language, people negotiate the various social roles they are expected to play.

For interactionists, social institutions such as the sports club are seen not as separate from people, but as the product of the interaction of various people involved.

In explaining sport, the theory is mainly concerned with the experiences of sports people and how they interact with each other in social groups and in turn how they affect external social factors. Interactionist theory is helpful in understanding how to:

● Change sports to match the perspectives and identities of those playing them.

● Make sport organisations more democratic and less hierarchically organised (e.g. via giving all members equal voting rights when making decisions related to the running of a sports club).

> **STUDY HINTS**
> Key parts of interactionist theory:
> ● Society is created and maintained through social interaction.
> ● Sports are studied in terms of how they are created and given meaning by people.

Key terms for the study of equality in sport

There are a number of key terms you need to understand when studying **equal opportunities** in sport and physical activity.

Embedded in British law, equal opportunities is a term used in our society to emphasise the importance of treating all people the same, unhampered by artificial barriers, discrimination, prejudices or preferences.

The explanation of equal opportunities given above identifies **discrimination** and **prejudice** as important factors which can determine whether equality of opportunity is present within a society or not. In addition, negative **stereotypes** can also adversely affect an individual's chances of taking part in sport.

Sport's interpretation of equal opportunities can be explained via reference to Sport England's equality and diversity policy which is as follows:

We believe sporting opportunities should be open to all and we are committed to:

- *Developing a culture that enables and values everyone's full involvement.*
- *Creating an environment in which everyone has opportunities to play, compete, officiate, coach, volunteer and run community sport.*
- *Overcoming potential barriers for those wishing to play sport, particularly if they are from groups who are currently under-represented in sport.*

Discrimination can be divided into two types, namely:

- **overt discrimination**: visible/obvious (e.g. verbal racist abuse of a player)
- **covert discrimination**: hidden/less obvious (e.g. non-selection of an individual as captain because of their race).

Benefits of raising participation

It has been well publicised that the UK Government has been encouraging its population to become more active for a variety of different reasons. Regular physical activity can improve health and fitness by helping people achieve a healthy body weight, reduce their blood pressure, lower their feelings of stress, anxiety and depression and so on. By helping to reduce the risk of a range of physical problems, strain on the NHS is reduced and the obesity problem society continues to face is challenged.

In addition to improving physical fitness and mental health, regular exercise also provides a range of social benefits to the individual and society. Meeting new people and making new friends can result in a sense of community integration. Higher levels of self-confidence for individuals result as they improve and develop their physique and skill levels.

Participation in sport/physical activity is a positive use of free time which can help keep individuals out of trouble and reduce the crime figures in society.

Economically, regular participation can help individuals perform better at work due to their improved mental and physical ability. They are also less likely to contribute to annual sickness absence costs. Spending money on equipment and/or the use of facilities also provides people with jobs and benefits the country financially.

KEY TERMS

Equal opportunities: The right to access the same opportunities, regardless of factors such as race, age, sex, mental or physical capability.

Prejudice: To form an unfavourable opinion of an individual, often based on inadequate facts (e.g. lack of tolerance, dislike of people from a specific race, religion or culture which can negatively affect a coach's treatment of a performer from an ethnic minority group).

Discrimination: The unfair treatment of a person or, minority group; to make a distinction and act on a prejudice.

Stereotyping: A standardised image; making simple generalisations about all members of a group which allows others to categorise and treat them accordingly (e.g. negative stereotypes about women which negatively impact on their participation in sport/physical activity).

CHECK YOUR UNDERSTANDING
The participation of ethnic minorities in sport can be negatively affected by discrimination. Explain what is meant by the term 'discrimination'.

STUDY HINT
It is important that you can define and explain equality of opportunity in relation to key influences such as discrimination, stereotyping and prejudice.

CHECK YOUR UNDERSTANDING
Explain the benefits to society of increasing participation rates in sport and physical activity.

STUDY HINTS
The use of the command term 'Explain' requires you to develop your answers. For example, in the check your understanding question on the right, by identifying a benefit of increasing participation and linking it to how it positively impacts on society.

Table 1 A summary of the benefits to individuals and society of raising participation in sport/physical activity

Benefit	Individual benefits	Benefits to society
Health (physical and mental)	Increased health and fitness; lower body weight; lower blood pressure/stress levels; raised self-esteem	Less strain on the NHS; lower obesity levels
Social	Improved social skills; improved ability to develop friendships	Increased community integration; improved community morale
Crime	More positive use of free time	Lower crime statistics
Employment	Increased productivity at work; lower absenteeism	Workplace/employer benefits as less time off work/higher productivity rates
Economic	Increased spending on healthy pursuits	More money is put into the economy via increased 'leisure-spend'

Sport England's data on sports participation has shown some improvements since it started its regular bi-annual Active People surveys in 2005–6. In the figures released in June 2015, adult numbers taking part had risen by 1.4 million compared to 2005–6, but most adults were still reported as not taking part in sport (i.e. 58 per cent). The fact that just over half of all adults in England play no sport at all is a very worrying statistic for those engaged in trying to encourage such participation.

It is still therefore important to be able to identify various barriers to participation for various sections of society under-represented in sport, as well as seeking to provide solutions to try to overcome these barriers.

Organisations such as Sport England and the Centers for Disease Control and Prevention in the USA have identified a number of barriers to physical activity and suggested a range of solutions to help raise participation levels (see www.cdc.gov/physicalactivity/everyone/getactive/barriers.html.)

Table 2 Barriers to participation and possible solutions

Barriers	Solutions
Lack of time	Add physical activity to a daily routine e.g. walk or ride to work/school
Negative social influences; poor PE experiences	Invite family and friends to exercise with you; join a group where physical activity plays an important part, e.g. a youth club offering activities such as Duke of Edinburgh Award
Lack of motivation	Invite a friend to exercise with you on a regular basis; join an exercise class
Lack of skill	Select activities requiring few or no skills e.g. walking/jogging
Lack of resources/costs of participation	Select activities which require few facilities/limited equipment, e.g. walking, jogging, skipping
Family obligations/domestic responsibilities	Exercise with the children – go for a walk or swim; play tig!

Memory tools

You can remember some of the main barriers to participation in sports via the acronym **TIME**:

- **T** = **T**ime
- **I** = **I**ncome
- **M** = **M**otivation
- **E** = **E**ducation

You will need to be aware of three main target groups, i.e. groups/sections of society specifically aimed at due to their relative lack of involvement in sport/physical activity. The groups we need to focus on in terms of barriers to participation along with various solutions to such barriers are people with disabilities, individuals from ethnic minorities and women/teenage girls.

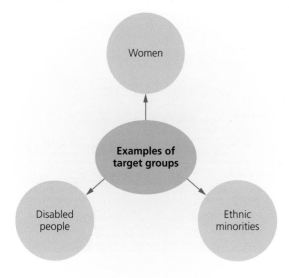

Figure 3 Examples of target groups

Barriers to participation in sport and possible solutions

Disability

Generally speaking, people with disabilities have a low level of participation in sport. This can be illustrated via Figures 4 and 5 from the Active People Survey.

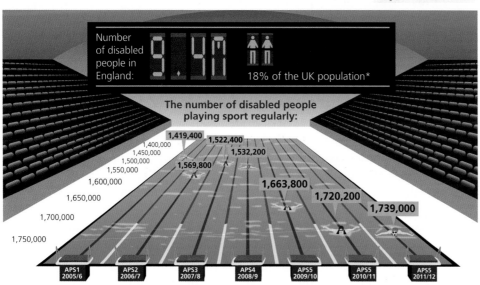

Figure 4 Number of disabled people in England vs the number of disabled people playing sport regularly from 2005–2011/12

Source: www.sportengland.org/our-work/disability/disability-infographics/

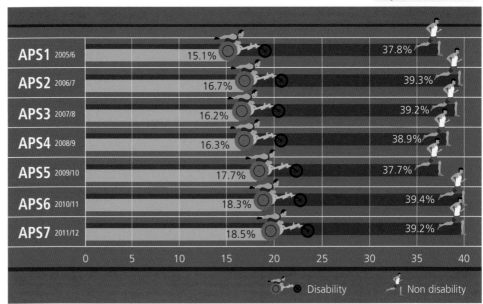

APS1 2005/6	15.1%		37.8%
APS2 2006/7	16.7%		39.3%
APS3 2007/8	16.2%		39.2%
APS4 2008/9	16.3%		38.9%
APS5 2009/10	17.7%		37.7%
APS6 2010/11	18.3%		39.4%
APS7 2011/12	18.5%		39.2%

Disability   Non disability

Figure 5 Percentage of non-disabled people in England playing sport regularly vs percentage of disabled people playing sport regularly

Source: www.sportengland.org/our-work/disability/disability-infographics/

The Sport England Active People Survey (APS) **infographics** from 2011–12 (APS7) illustrate that 1,739,000 people with a **disability** regularly played sport during this time period compared to 1,419,00 when it first started gathering data in 2005–6. While this is a welcomed improvement in disabled participation, it still only means 18.5 per cent (around 1 in 5) of people with a disability in England play sport regularly, compared to 39.2 per cent (around 1 in 2.5) of non-disabled people.

Disability may be physical, sensory or mental in nature, with all of these impairments potentially negatively affecting participation in sport in some way. Society continues to discriminate and impose barriers on disabled people's participation in physical activity as illustrated in Figures 4 and 5. Overt discrimination is highly visible and could occur when there is verbal abuse aimed at individuals with a disability participating in sport. Covert discrimination is harder to uncover and might occur when individuals at a sports club vote for their annual captain and their negative stereotypes influence them against voting for a disabled candidate, for example.

One high-profile example of discrimination against an elite disabled athlete occurred in December 2000 when the BBC had to apologise to Tanni Grey-Thompson when she was forced to receive her trophies at their Sports Personality of the Year awards in her audience seat as no ramp was provided to take her onto the stage. This highlighted problems with facility access at the turn of the century which negatively impacted on participation in sport among people with a disability and led to more awareness that such an issue needed addressing as we entered the twenty-first century.

Disability sport is sometimes participated in at the same time as able-bodied sport (i.e. it is **integrated**). Alternatively, disability sport can occur completely separately from able-bodied sport (i.e. it is **segregated**).

When analysing disability sports participation, **common barriers** which negatively affect them include the following:

● Negative self-image or lack of confidence.

● Relatively low income levels; costs of participation such as membership fees and transport costs, etc.

● Lack of access into and around facilities, e.g. facility front desk is too high for disabled individuals to communicate with; doorways are too narrow; ramps do not exist within areas of a facility, etc.

● Lack of organised programmes.

● Low levels of media coverage/few role models to aspire to; leads to a lack of information available.

● Lack of specialist coaches/specialist clubs/competitions to access; lack of adapted/accessible equipment.

● Myths/stereotypes about the capabilities of people with a disability; lower societal expectations; safety concerns – disability participation has traditionally been considered dangerous.

A range of **solutions** are being implemented to try to decrease the effects of such barriers for people with a disability, including the following:

● Providing more opportunities for success; helping talented athletes reach the highest levels possible, e.g. the Paralympics.

● Increased investment in disabled sport – subsidise it and make it more affordable.

● Providing transport to facilities; improved access into/around facilities, e.g. via local authority sport and leisure departments using specialist architects when planning facilities so that they meet the needs of disabled people.

● Improved technology, e.g. prosthetics/wheelchairs.

● Increased media coverage and promoting role models to relate and aspire to.

● Training of more specialist coaches; setting up more clubs for people with a disability to access.

● Educating people on the myths/stereotypes about the capabilities of the disabled and challenging inappropriate attitudes.

● Designing activities specifically for individuals with disabilities, e.g. goalball/boccia for the visually impaired, or modifying existing activities to enable involvement in them, e.g. wheelchair tennis and basketball, etc.

● Specialist organisations such as the English Federation for Disability Sport (EFDS) and Sport England working to support and co-ordinate the development of sporting opportunities for people with disabilities.

Ethnicity

Britain is a multi-cultural, multi-racial, egalitarian (i.e. equal) society. Equal opportunities to participate in sport should exist for all racial groups in society. Such equality is not yet a reality due to many factors including racism.

Racism

Racism is illegal but still exists in society (and therefore in sport, as a reflection of society) on the basis of someone's skin colour, language used or cultural observances. Racism stems from prejudice linked with the power of one racial group in society over another. This can lead to discrimination, i.e. unfair treatment/acting on a prejudice, e.g. exclusion of an individual from participation on the basis of their race/ethnicity.

STUDY HINT

When identifying barriers to participation in relation to disability, it is important to link coaching to a shortage of specially trained leaders/coaches, and to link activities to failure to modify/adapt them, i.e. link points being made to the specific target group in focus.

ACTIVITY

Research sports such as Boccia and Goalball (e.g. via YouTube) to try to find out how they have been designed to help individuals with visual impairments get involved in sporting activity. Write a few paragraphs stating how such sports can help overcome some of the barriers stated above.

KEY TERMS

Race: The physical characteristics of an individual.

Racism: A set of beliefs or ideas based on the assumption that races have distinct hereditary characteristics that give some races an intrinsic superiority over others; it may lead to physical or verbal abuse.

Ethnic groups: people who have racial, religious or linguistic traits in common.

KEY TERMS

Stacking: The disproportionate concentration of ethnic minorities in certain positions in a sports team, which tends to be based on the stereotype that they are more valuable for their physicality than their decision-making and communication qualities.

Channelling: Ethnic minorities may be pushed into certain sports and even certain positions within a team, based on assumptions about them.

Stacking is a term used as an illustration of possible racism in sport. It is used particularly in relation to explaining the lack of team captains from ethnic minorities as it is based on the stereotypical assumption which asserts that ethnic minority individuals are more valued for their athletic prowess compared to their decision-making or leadership capabilities. Ethnic minorities may also be **channelled** (i.e. pushed) away from certain sports into others, based on stereotypical assumptions about them (e.g. Asians channelled away from football into cricket).

As a society it is important that we encourage diversity in sport and physical activity as it encourages social inclusion and better health, as well as improving standards of performance within our country. However, there are still worrying statistics which illustrate the fact that **ethnic diversity in sport and physical activity is not necessarily being achieved**.

Research reported by Sporting Equals in 2015 suggests that more than 50 per cent of people from black and ethnic minority (BME) communities do not participate in sport or physical activity. According to Sport England (2005):

- Sports participation rates for BME populations is lower than the national average of 46 per cent:

Community	Average participation rate
Bangladeshi	30%
Pakistani	31%
Indian	39%
Black Caribbean	39%

- 74 per cent of south Asian women do not exercise regularly compared with 55 per cent of all women.
- Few people from BME communities hold official positions within sports organisations – 3 per cent in coaching, 3.6 per cent in volunteer management and 7 per cent in the professional workforce.

Possible causes of under-representation of ethnic groups in sport/physical activity include:

- Conflict with religious/cultural observances (e.g. a particular concern with Muslim women).
- A higher value placed on education as opposed to sporting participation; discouragement via family and friends.
- Fear of racism/racist abuse, prejudice, discrimination.
- Fewer role models to aspire to, particularly in coaching/managerial positions (e.g. in football there are very few black footballers who break into and maintain management positions at Premier League/Football League clubs).
- Fear of rejection/low levels of self-esteem.
- Stereotyping/attempts at channelling ethnic minorities into certain sports and away from others.
- Language barriers may exist for some ethnic minority groups.

(NB Not all ethnic groups are the same; and not all ethnic groups will face precisely the same forms of discrimination and challenges.)

Possible solutions to racial disadvantage in sport/physical activity include:

- Training more ethnic minority coaches, teachers and sports leaders and educating them on the effects of stereotyping.
- Ensuring there is single-sex provision, e.g. for Muslim women to overcome any cultural barriers which might negatively impact on participation.
- Publicising and punishing severely any racist abuse (e.g. as the FA have done when the then Liverpool player Suarez racially abused his Manchester United counterpart, Evra).
- Ensuring provision in PE programmes is appropriate for all ethnic preferences, e.g. ensuring kit rules and showering procedures are reflective of cultural norms.
- Organising campaigns against racism in sport.
- Kick it Out is football's equality and inclusion organisation which is working through the football, educational and community sectors to challenge discrimination and campaign for change.

In Association Football, players' representatives have long been campaigning for positive action to be taken when it comes to the recruitment of managers and coaches for the 'top jobs'. In October 2015 Wayne Allison was appointed as the first Black, Asian and Minority (BAM) project manager. One of his key roles for the FA is to try to convince Premier League and football league clubs to agree to a voluntary version of the 'Rooney Rule' which will require them to interview at least one non-white person for each coaching and managerial position. The **Rooney Rule**, established in the USA in 2003, and named after its instigator Dan Rooney, requires National Football teams in the USA to interview minority candidates for head coaching and senior football operation jobs. It has been viewed as successful in opening doors for minority head coaches in American football. For example, during the period 1992–2002 only 7 of 92 head coaching vacancies went to a minority (i.e. less than 10 per cent). In the decade following from 2003, minorities have filled 17 of the head coaching vacancies (i.e. around 20 per cent).

Gender: the under-representation of women in sport

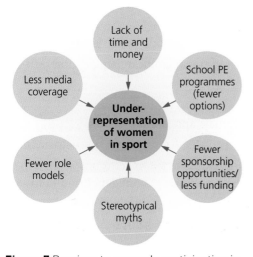

Figure 7 Barriers to women's participation in sport

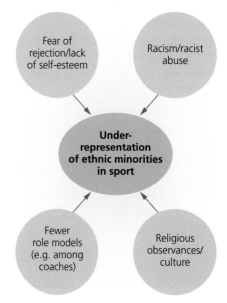

Figure 6 Barriers to participation for ethnic minority groups

CHECK YOUR UNDERSTANDING
Identify barriers to sports participation which still exist for ethnic minority groups in twenty-first century Britain.

KEY TERM

Rooney Rule: Requires National Football teams in the USA to interview minority candidates for head coaching and senior football operation jobs.

STUDY HINT

Equality of opportunity questions often use the command word 'Discuss'. Be prepared to provide arguments for and against equality of opportunity, particularly in relation to the target groups specified on the syllabus.

Gender: The biological aspect of a person, either a male or female.

Sexism: The belief that one sex is inferior to the other, usually women.

Suggest what sports or sports events women appear most frequently in on TV and/or in newspapers and what impact you think this might have on women's participation in sport.

Summarise the barriers to women's participation in sport and physical activity via the acronym **TRIPS**, where:

T = **T**ime
R = **R**ole models
I = **I**ncome/costs
P = **PE** programmes
S = **S**ponsorship

One of the key issues to consider in relation to women's participation in sport is whether negative factors such as discrimination and/or **gender** stereotyping deny women the freedom to choose the activities they wish to participate in, be this Zumba for some or rugby for others. Women should have the same opportunity as their male counterparts to participate and excel in their chosen sports. However, more men participate in sport than women. Sport England's June 2015 Active People data illustrate such a point: 40.6 per cent of men play sport at least once a week compared to 30.7 per cent of women. A variety of possible reasons (i.e. barriers) can be given to explain the continued under-representation of women in sport. They include the following:

- Stereotypical myths are still evident in society, e.g. the belief that women lack the aggression necessary for 'certain sports' where this is key, e.g. in rugby.
- There is still far less media coverage of women's sport compared to men's. In 2007, a Women's Sport and Fitness Foundation (WSFF) study stated that newspaper coverage of women's sport accounted for only five per cent of total coverage in 2006.
- There are fewer positive/attainable role models in sport for other women to aspire to, e.g. as performers, coaches, officials, or in positions of power, making decisions on national governing bodies. Women in Sport identify the pressure many women feel to be thin as opposed to being healthy; the media promote a thin, decorative and passive ideal of the female body. Such an image is at odds with an 'active' body.
- Fewer sponsorship opportunities/opportunities to become full-time sports performers.
- Negative impact of school PE programmes, e.g. rules on showering/kit; lack of appealing choice of activities. The Women's Sport and Fitness Foundation (WSFF, now called Women in Sport) published a report called *Changing the Game, for Girls* in May 2012 which stated that just over half of all girls (i.e. 51 per cent) were put off physical activity by their experiences of school sport and PE. Just 12 per cent of 14-year-old girls were reaching the recommended levels of physical activity – half the number of boys at the same age; of the least active, 46 per cent of girls said they didn't like the activities they got to do in PE, compared to 26 per cent of the most active. (See **www.womeninsport.org/resources/ changing-the-game-for-girls-policy-report/**.)
- Lack of fitness, low levels of self-confidence, body image issues.
- Lack of leisure time due to work, traditional childcare and/or domestic responsibilities.
- Lack of disposable income.
- Channelling women into certain 'female appropriate' sports.
- Fewer leagues/competitions/clubs available for women to participate in.

It is important that we continue our attempts to try to get more women to play sport as it enhances their well-being, increases confidence and helps to prevent ill health.

Possible solutions to gender inequality in sport

- Introduce/enforce laws which make sex discrimination unlawful in many spheres of life, e.g. the Sex Discrimination Act 1975.
- Encourage greater social acceptance of women having jobs/careers with more disposable income giving increased financial independence.

- Encourage shared domestic/childcare responsibilities, creating more leisure time for women to devote to sport; improved childcare provision has also helped try to overcome the 'time barrier'.

- Increased media coverage of women's sport; give women's international sport the recognition it deserves; provide more positive/attainable role models to aspire to.

- Increased sponsorship attracted to women's sport, e.g. via Women in Sport/WSFF and its work boosting investment in women's sport via its work in securing sponsors for the FA and England Hockey.

- Providing education to refute/reject the stereotypical myths; improved PE provision e.g. via the WSFF's 'Changing the Game for Girls'– a toolkit for schools to try to find ways to improve PE provision for girls.

- Providing more opportunities for women to join sports clubs/participate in the activities they enjoy.

- By making changing rooms/sports facilities as clean and attractive as possible.

- In modern-day society, the use of social networking methods to link women playing sport can be used to create friendships with like-minded individuals and hopefully increase motivation/interest to continue with it.

- Via the work of organisations such as Sport England, as well as specialist organisations such as Women in Sport (formerly the WSFF).

One of the most significant achievements identified in promoting women's sport by the WSFF was their ability to persuade the organisers of the Oxford and Cambridge Boat Race that the women's race should be held on the same day as the men's which happened for the first time in 2015. In addition, they have helped develop new requirements which mean that every publicly funded sport has to have at least 25 per cent of women on their board by 2017.

> ### STUDY HINTS
> You may need to demonstrate a knowledge of various causes of under-representation of women in sport along with suggested solutions to such barriers. For example, if a lack of time due to traditional childcare/domestic responsibilities is identified as a barrier to participation, a possible solution linked directly to this includes improved crèche provision at leisure centres.

Learning from the shopping experience – what would encourage more girls to take part in sport?
Top 5 answers for young women

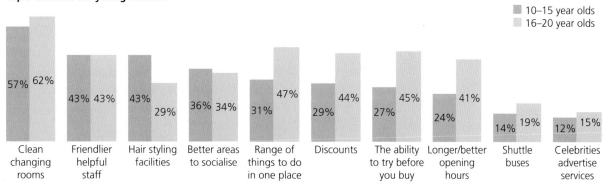

Figure 8 What would encourage more girls to take part in sport?

Source: Women's Sport and Fitness Foundation

As noted earlier in this chapter, certain sports are more popular for women than others. The Active People Survey 7 (APS7) identifies swimming, athletics and various fitness/gym-related activities as the most popular activities among women. Women's football is increasingly publicised as an important case study illustrating how a traditional 'male' sport is slowly becoming more open and accessible to girls and women at all levels of the game. It was identified in October 2012 (in a Football Factsheet produced by the WSFF) as the most popular participation team sport in the country among women. Based on the Active People Survey from April 2011–April 2012, women's participation in football at least once a week was found to be 252,000 as compared to 215,000 taking part in netball, its closest rival in the 'team sport' category. A number of socio-cultural reasons can be given to explain this, including:

- Increased opportunities in society in general.
- Increased media coverage of women's football, e.g. the World Cup in Canada, June 2015, giving more female role models to identify with and aspire to.
- More opportunities for girls to play football in school PE programmes.
- More football clubs to join in the area they live.
- The rejection of stereotypes affecting female participation in contact activities such as football.
- A general increase in leisure time and disposable income available to women.
- More opportunities to play the game professionally in England, e.g. via formation of the FA Women's Super League (WSL) as part of a five-year FA strategy 'Game Changer', which is building on the successes of the 2012 Olympics and 2015 World Cup to turn the sport into the second largest team sport in the country, behind only men's football, by 2018.

Active People is the largest survey of sport and active leisure ever carried out in Europe. It started in 2005–6 so the most recent figures can be compared to this benchmark time period as and when figures are released in June and December of each year. Active People provides information nationally in relation to who is taking part in sport and how they are participating, linked to age, gender and ethnicity. It also gives data on the local picture linking to local authorities and county sport partnerships. In 2014–15, sports 'on the rise' included running, following a popular trend towards informal running like parkrun and Colour Run, and basketball, with upward trends particularly among young people in school and further education.

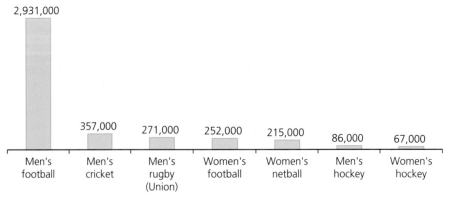

Figure 9 Number of men and women participating in top team sports at least once a month

Source: WSFF Football Factsheet October 2012

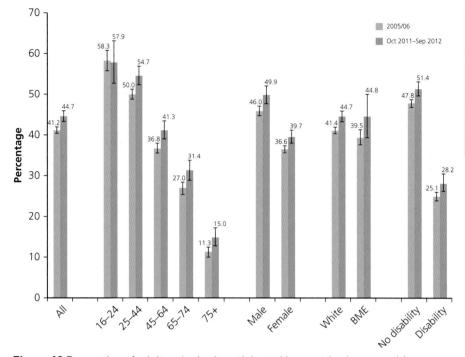

Figure 10 Proportion of adults who had participated in sport by demographics, 2005/06 to October 2011–September 2012 (at least one session of 30 minutes of moderate intensity sport in the last week)

Source: DCMS report Taking Part 2012/13 Quarter 2

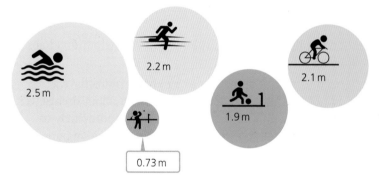

Figure 11 Top five sports: number of adults taking part in sport at least once a week by sport

Source: Active People Survey 8Q3–9Q2 (Sport England 2014–15)

Benefits of raising participation

Participation in physical activity and/or sport is an important part of a healthy lifestyle. Those who lead an active lifestyle are more likely to live longer and are less likely to develop serious diseases such as coronary heart disease.

Health benefits

Regular participation in physical activity and/or sport can help protect individuals from a range of health problems and can therefore be viewed as beneficial in the following ways:

● decreased risk of heart disease/stroke

● avoidance of high/low blood pressure

● decreased risk of type 2 diabetes

● maintaining a healthy weight/decreased risk of obesity

- strengthening of bones and muscles/decreased risk of osteoporosis and back pain
- improved mental health and stress management; decreased risk of conditions such as anxiety/depression
- decreased risk of some cancers (e.g. colon cancer and breast cancer).

Fitness benefits

Increased physical activity leads to an increased ability to carry out daily tasks as a result of improvements to various aspects of fitness, depending on the type of activity undertaken (e.g. continuous activities such as long-distance cycling and running lead to improved stamina/endurance). Regular participation in physical activity and/or sport can help improve an individual's level of fitness and therefore may be viewed as beneficial in the following ways:

- improved posture
- improved body shape/body tone as a result of weight loss; improved body composition
- improved cardiovascular fitness
- improved muscular strength/muscular endurance
- improved flexibility
- improved agility/balance/co-ordination
- improved speed/power
- improved reaction time.

Social benefits

Regular participation in physical activity and/or sport can help individuals socially in the following ways:

- Raised levels of chemicals such as serotonin and endorphins have a calming effect and help an person to feel happier/better about themselves. When individuals feel better about themselves they are more likely to benefit emotionally and socially as well, e.g. via a more positive outlook on life.
- Improved sleep patterns result from participation in regular exercise, which can enhance a person's mood and their relationships.
- The boost in a person's mood can also help improve skills of concentration, which allow a clearer focus on social relationships.
- As an individual's social and emotional health improves, confidence/ self-esteem is likely to increase, and involvement in sport/exercise classes becomes increasingly likely.
- Sport/physical activity introduces us to new people who share a common interest and helps develop new friendships/relationships.

Sport England's and local/national partners' aim to increase participation of under-represented groups

Sport England has an overall mission to 'Create a sporting habit for life'. It works with a range of partners locally and nationally to try to achieve its mission.

Local partners

Sport England works with a range of local partners to try to ensure sport is accessible across every region in the country. They invest in/fund 49 **county sport partnerships (CSPs)** spread across the country so that programmes can be delivered regionally/locally to meet specific local needs where these exist.

CSPs work with a number of sport/physical activity providers including local authorities, health organisations, national governing bodies, sports clubs and schools/education providers – all with a commitment to increasing participation across 'their network'. One example is Oxfordshire's CSP which calls itself 'Oxfordshire Sport and Physical Activity' and has set itself the target to make Oxfordshire the most physically active county in England by 2017.

Sport England also offers help and expertise to local authorities to help them develop sport in their area, designing and implementing schemes and initiatives specific to their needs and requirements.

Sport England's local outreach teams work across the different regions offering support and advice as and when necessary at a local level.

Sport England is committed to providing sporting opportunities for all and putting in place schemes and initiatives which attempt to overcome barriers for those wishing to play sport, particularly if they are from groups who are currently under-represented in sport. Sport England is an organisation focused on helping people and communities across the country create a 'sporting habit for life'. To help achieve their mission, between 2012 and 2017 Sport England committed themselves to over £1 billion of National Lottery and Exchequer funding in organisations and projects aiming to:

- help more people have a sporting habit for life
- create more opportunities for young people to play sport
- nurture and develop talent
- provide the right facilities in the right places
- support local authorities and unlock local funding
- ensure real opportunities for communities.

One of Sport England's key roles is to help its partners, such as governing bodies, to deliver sporting opportunities to as many people as possible and particularly to groups who experience specific issues that may prevent them participating regularly in sport.

National partners

Sport England works directly with a number of nationally funded partners, including those identified below:

- **English Federation of Disability Sport (EFDS)** – a national charity dedicated to increasing participation in sport and physical activity among disabled people.
- **Sporting Equals** – an organisation which exists to actively promote greater involvement by disadvantaged communities and particularly in the black and minority ethnic (BME) population.
- **Women in Sport** – the new name for the WSFF, which aims to make being active more attractive to women and teenage girls by trying to break down the barriers which exist and are putting women off.

KEY TERM

County sport partnerships (CSPs): National networks of local agencies working together to increase numbers in sport and physical activity.

ACTIVITY

Do some research to identify how the CSP in your area is working to increase participation (e.g. how it is delivering the Sportivate programme aimed at increasing participation in young people). What do you think the advantages and disadvantages are of a 'regional approach'?
See www.sportengland.org/our-work/local-work/county-sports-partnerships/.

- **StreetGames** – a national charity dedicated to developing sport with disadvantaged communities, making it accessible to all, regardless of social circumstances.

In terms of social class, StreetGames is working to create networks at national and local levels (e.g. nationally with NGBs, and locally with local authorities and local sports clubs) to strengthen the commitment to 'doorstep sport', i.e. providing access to sports in local communities where people live. To try to overcome some of the issues surrounding participation in terms of the lower socio-economic groups in society, StreetGames provides affordable, low-cost sessions within the neighbourhood of communities so travel is less of an issue. Sessions take place at times convenient to targeted participants in multi-sport sessions of an informal nature, designed to appeal and make participation more likely.

In terms of disability sport, Sport England is working with the EFDS to challenge and change low levels of disability participation in sport to enable disabled people to view taking part in sport as a viable lifestyle choice.

In 2015, out of the £150 million of Lottery funding from **'Places People Play'**, Sport England ring-fenced £10.2 million to improve the sport on offer for disabled people. 'Inclusive Sport' was another initiative designed to build on Sport England investments to improve the expertise offered by the disability sport sector to other organisations that want to get disabled people playing sport. The Inclusive Sport programme was aimed at increasing the number of disabled young people (14+) and adults regularly playing sport as part of Sport England's wider commitment to increasing regular sport participation by disabled people. **'Get Equipped'** is a funding scheme aimed at providing disabled performers with the specialist equipment required to engage in sporting activity.

Participation by disabled people is a key strategic outcome for Sport England's work with NGBs. They work closely with a number of sports' governing bodies to support and provide advice in relation to disability provision.

Sport England committed itself to investing in specialist disability sport organisations such as the EFDS to help increase the speed of implementing their strategy to increase sports participation among this target group. Other disability sports organisations they have funded so they can advise, support and guide other sports governing bodies to create opportunities for participation include British Blind Sport, British Wheelchair Sport (Wheelpower) and Mencap Sport/Special Olympics GB.

Local partners working to increase disability sports participation include CSPs. The EFDS works with nine focus CSPs via dedicated engagement officers to give more concentrated support to increase disability sport participation (e.g. Active Essex).

The Sport England Active People Survey infographics included earlier in this chapter (Figures 4 and 5) illustrate that the work of such organisations has gone some way to increasing participation in sport among disabled individuals but there is still a long way to go.

Women

Sport England is working hard with local and national partners including CSPs, NGBs and Women in Sport to get more women playing more sport. Some of these initiatives include the following:

- Making women's sport a major priority financially across the board in the 46 core sport NGBs in which they are investing millions of pounds.

- In 2015 they invested £2.3 million into '**I Will If You Will**'– a year-long pioneering behavioural change pilot in the local authority of Bury to help understand how to get more women playing sport. If this pilot scheme (i.e. trial) is successful in achieving its aim of getting more women playing sport, it will help inform Sport England and local authorities of schemes and initiatives which work for women.

- They have also invested millions of pounds into 'Women in Sport' via the WSFF to help sports bodies attract more women and teenage girls to do sport more regularly.

- Millions more went into 20 **Active Women** projects across different local authorities to encourage women in disadvantaged communities and women with young children to be more physically active and tackle the gender gap in sport. Examples of such projects include:
  - **Breeze** – a large-scale programme designed to get more women into riding bikes for fun.
  - **Back to Netball** – a programme that helps women throughout England try out or re-engage with netball.
  - **Us Girls** – a programme which has worked in nearly 50 disadvantaged areas across England to get girls into sport.

- In 2015 they also introduced '**This Girl Can**' in a wave of media publicity. Essentially it is a scheme designed to help overcome barriers to increase participation in sports among women and girls.

See also www.sportengland.org/our-work/equality-diversity/women/.

Ethnic minorities

Sport England is committed to ensuring that everyone has access to sporting opportunities. In 2013, they invested £1 million into its national partner **Sporting Equals** to help more black and minority ethnic (BME) communities get into sport. Sporting Equals exists to promote ethnic diversity across sport and physical activity and is the only organisation in the UK to do so. Originally set up in 1998 by Sport England, in partnership with the Commission for Racial Equality, they are now a fully independent body with a clear mission to actively promote greater involvement in sport and physical activity by all communities that are disengaged (particularly among the BME population). Sport England and Sporting Equals work closely with a number of local and national providers of sporting opportunities such as NGBs and local authorities. Ultimately they all aim to make a sustainable difference to the inclusion of under-represented communities in sport and physical activity, so as to improve the long-term opportunities and health outcomes of those communities.

Investment in national governing bodies (NGBs)

National governing bodies submitted **Whole Sport Plans** to Sport England to operate from 2013–17, detailing how they would invest money to help them increase the number of young people playing their own sport once a week and how to nurture talent. For example, British Rowing identified a number of different programmes/approaches designed to get more people into their sport. For example:

- **Rowability**: rebranding of 'Adaptive Rowing' to develop partnerships with disability organisations and establish five new recognised delivery centres.

STUDY HINT

Be prepared to identify and briefly explain schemes and initiatives Sport England has put in place to increase participation and 'Create a sporting habit for life'.

KEY TERM

Whole Sport Plans: A business plan/document submitted to Sport England outlining each national governing body's strategies to grow participation and enhance talent over the four-year period the Whole Sports Plan is in operation.

- **Generating the Habit**: providing a framework to support the local delivery of rowing to young people, adults and volunteers across a variety of environments.
- **Indoor Rowing (young people)**: aiming to deliver participation at the local level through school games competition formats to ensure that young people have a positive first experience of indoor rowing and educate pupils and teachers about indoor rowing.

SUMMARY

As a result of studying this section, you should be able to clearly define and apply in relation to sport a number of sociological terms such as socialisation and social stratification which play a key role in influencing the activities we participate in as individuals and as a society.

You will also gain knowledge of and understand what is meant by equality of opportunity and the negative impact on participation of discrimination, stereotyping and prejudice.

After studying this section, you will be able to identify and explain a number of possible barriers to participation for ethnic minority groups, women and people with disabilities, as well as outline solutions to many of these barriers.

You will gain an understanding of the role of Sport England in working with its national partners (e.g. EFDS) and local partners (e.g. CSPs) to try to increase participation levels among under-represented groups in society.

Data and statistics will be used to illustrate historical and current patterns of participation among women, ethnic minorities, disabled and socially disadvantaged individuals to help improve your understanding of the issues facing such groups, as well as improve your skills of data analysis and interpretation.

PRACTICE QUESTIONS

1 Which of the following statements best define the term 'socialisation'? (1 mark)

    a) Social mixing at a party with friends and family.

    b) Early learning of how to behave in society.

    c) What you learn as a teenager in adult life.

    d) A lifelong process whereby members of society learn the values, ideas, practices and roles of that society.

2 Define the following terms: stereotyping and prejudice. (2 marks)

3 Identify the benefits to the individual of participating in club sport. (3 marks)

4 Give reasons why disabled sports participants have improved opportunities to take part in sport in the early twenty-first century compared to the late twentieth century. (4 marks)

5 Identify the economic barriers which may account for the lower rate of participation of women in sport and physical activity. (2 marks)

6 Identify schemes and initiatives Sport England has put in place to improve opportunities for women and young girls to participate in sport. (4 marks)

Chapter 4.1
Diet and nutrition and their effect on physical activity and performance

Chapter objectives

After reading this chapter you should be able to:

- Identify the seven classes of food as: carbohydrates, fats, proteins, vitamins, minerals, fibre and water.
- Identify the exercise-related function of each of these types of food.
- Identify the positive and negative effects of creatine, sodium bicarbonate, caffeine and glycogen loading on the performer.

Balanced diet

Nutrition and diet can contribute to a successful performance. A **balanced diet** is essential for optimum performance in all sporting activities. What you eat can have an effect on your health, your weight and your energy levels! Top performers place huge demands on their bodies during both training and competition. Their diet must meet those energy requirements, as well as provide nutrients for tissue growth and repair. There are seven classes of food that should be present in all sports performers' diets and these will be looked at throughout the course of this chapter:

- carbohydrates
- fats
- proteins
- vitamins
- minerals
- fibre
- water.

Carbohydrates

There are two types of carbohydrates.

- **Simple carbohydrates:** these are found in fruits and are easily digested by the body. They are also often found in processed foods and anything with refined sugar added.
- **Complex carbohydrates:** these are found in nearly all plant-based foods, and usually take longer for the body to digest. They are most commonly found in bread, pasta, rice and vegetables.

KEY TERMS

Balanced diet: A diet containing a variety of foods from each of the food groups so there is an adequate intake of nutrients.

Glucose: A simple sugar and the major source of energy for the body's cells.

Glycogen: The stored form of glucose found in the muscles and the liver.

Glycaemic index: This ranks carbohydrates according to their effect on our blood glucose levels.

Figure 1 Sources of carbohydrates

KEY TERMS

Cholesterol: A type of fat found in the blood.

LDL (low-density lipoproteins): They transport cholesterol in the blood to the tissues and are classed as 'bad' cholesterol since they are linked to an increased risk of heart disease.

HDL (high-density lipoproteins): They transport excess cholesterol in the blood back to the liver where it is broken down. HDLs are classed as 'good' cholesterol since they lower the risk of developing heart disease.

Carbohydrates are the principal source of energy used by the body. They are also the main fuel for high intensity or anaerobic work. Carbohydrate in food is digested and converted into **glucose** and enters the bloodstream. The glucose is stored in the muscles and liver as **glycogen** but these stores are limited so regular refuelling is necessary.

It is also important to consider the '**glycaemic index**' and release rate of different carbohydrates and the consequence this has on *when* they should be consumed in relation to training. Foods with a lower glycaemic index cause a slower, sustained release of glucose to the blood. This means that blood glucose levels are maintained for longer. Foods with a high glycaemic index cause a rapid, short rise in blood glucose but this will be short lived. Foods with a low glycaemic index should be eaten 3–4 hours before exercise, and include beans on toast, pasta or rice with a vegetable-based sauce, breakfast cereal with milk, crumpets with jam or honey. Foods with a high glycaemic index should be eaten 1–2 hours before exercise and include fruit smoothies, cereal bars, fruit-flavoured yoghurt and fruit. One hour before exercise, liquid consumption appears more important through sports drinks and cordials.

Memory tools

Carbohydrates are the principal source of energy used by the body at all levels of activity, from rest to intense activity.

Fats

There are different types of fats. Saturated fats can be found in both sweet and savoury foods but most come from animal sources. Too much saturated fat leads to excessive weight gain which will affect levels of stamina, limit flexibility and lead to health problems such as coronary heart disease, diabetes and high blood pressure. It also leads to high **cholesterol** levels. Cholesterol is made predominantly in the liver and is carried by the blood as **low-density lipoprotein (LDL)** and **high-density lipoprotein (HDL)**. Too much LDL can lead to fatty deposits developing in the arteries which can have a negative effect on blood flow. HDL, on the other hand, takes cholesterol away from the parts of the body where it has accumulated to the liver where it is disposed of.

Trans-fats are a type of unsaturated fats that can be found in meat and dairy products but most are made from an industrial process that adds hydrogen to liquid vegetable oils (hydrogenation), which causes the oil to become solid at room temperature. Using artificial trans-fats allows food to have a longer shelf life! Trans-fats can also lead to high levels of blood cholesterol and can be found in meat and dairy products. We should consume no more than five grams per day, but as they are found in hydrogenated vegetable oil and most supermarkets in the UK have removed hydrogenated vegetable oil from their own-brand products, it is saturated fats that we need to watch out for.

However, not all fats are bad. Replacing saturated and trans-fats with unsaturated fats is important as fat is a major source of energy in the body. They are used for low intensity, aerobic work such as jogging. Fats cannot be used for high intensity exercise where oxygen is in limited supply as they require oxygen to be broken down. Fats are also a carrier for the fat-soluble vitamins A, D, E and K.

Memory tools

Fats are an energy source for long duration, low-intensity exercise.

Proteins

These are a combination of many chemicals called **amino acids** and are important for muscle growth and repair and to make enzymes, hormones and haemoglobin. Proteins are a minor source of energy and tend to be used more by power athletes who have a greater need to repair and develop muscle tissue. Generally, proteins tend to provide more energy when glycogen and fat stores are low. Meat, fish, eggs and dairy products are good sources of protein.

Memory tools

Proteins are necessary for muscle growth and repair.

Figure 2 Examples of fats

KEY TERM

Amino acids: Used in all body cells to build proteins.

> **STUDY HINTS**
>
> Table 1 summarises the exercise-related role of carbohydrates, fats and proteins.
>
> **Table 1** The exercise-related role of carbohydrates, fats and proteins
>
> | FOOD CLASS | EXERCISE-RELATED FUNCTION |
> |---|---|
> | Carbohydrates | Principal source of energy for both low intensity (aerobic) and high intensity (anaerobic) exercise. They are the only food source that can be broken down anaerobically, e.g. the 200-metre race is an anaerobic event. |
> | Fats | Used for long duration, low intensity exercise such as marathons. |
> | Protein | Minor source of energy and tend to be used more by power athletes who have a greater need to repair and develop muscle tissue. |

CHECK YOUR UNDERSTANDING
Why should a games player have a diet rich in fat?

Vitamins

Vitamins are essential nutrients that your body needs in small amounts in order to work properly.

There are two types of vitamins:

- **Fat-soluble vitamins – A, D, E and K.**
  These vitamins are found predominantly in fatty foods and animal products such as milk, dairy foods, vegetable oils, eggs, liver and oily fish. The body stores fat-soluble vitamins in the liver and fatty tissues for use at a later date.

- **Water-soluble vitamins – the B vitamins and vitamin C.**
  These are found in a wide range of foods such as fruit, vegetables and dairy products. They are not stored in the body so they need to be taken daily. Excessive consumption will not have any beneficial effects as any additional amounts will be excreted through urine.

Figure 3 Examples of proteins

Figure 4 Examples of foods containing vitamin sources

Table 2 lists vitamins and summarises the exercise-related function of each.

Table 2 Vitamins and the exercise-related function of each

Vitamin	Source	Exercise-related function
C (ascorbic acid)	Green vegetables and fruit	• Protects cells and keeps them healthy. • Helps in the maintenance of bones, teeth, gums and connective tissue such as ligaments
D	Most vitamin D is made by our body under the skin when it is exposed to sunlight. To a lesser extent it can come from oily fish and dairy produce	• Has a role in the absorption of calcium, which keeps bones and teeth healthy
B1 (thiamin)	Yeast, egg, liver, wholegrain bread, nuts, red meat and cereals	• Works with other B group vitamins to help break down and release energy from food • Keeps the nervous system healthy
B2 (riboflavin)	Dairy products, liver, vegetables, eggs, cereals, fruit	• Works with other B group vitamins to help break down and release energy from food. • Keeps the skin, eyes and nervous system healthy
B6	Meat, fish, eggs, bread, vegetables, cereals	• Helps form haemoglobin • Helps the body to use and store energy from protein and carbohydrate in food
B12 (folate)	Red meat, dairy products and fish	• Makes red blood cells and keeps the nervous system healthy • Releases energy from food

STUDY HINT

You need to know about vitamins C, D and B complex (B1, B2, B6 and B12).

CHECK YOUR UNDERSTANDING

Give the exercise-related function of two vitamins.

KEY TERM

Electrolytes: Salts and minerals found in the blood that can conduct electrical impulses in the body.

Memory tools

Vitamins keep an individual healthy with a good immune system and this allows a performer to train maximally and recover quickly.

Minerals

Minerals assist in bodily functions; calcium, for example, is important for strong bones and teeth and iron helps form haemoglobin, which will enhance the transport of oxygen and therefore improve stamina levels. Minerals tend to be dissolved by the body as ions and are called **electrolytes**. Two of the functions they have are to facilitate the transmission of the nerve impulses and enable effective muscle contraction, both of which are important during exercise. Good sources of minerals are meat, fish, eggs, dairy products, cereals, vegetables, fruit and nuts.

Figure 5 Beef liver contains many minerals

Fibre

Good sources of fibre are wholemeal bread and pasta, potatoes, nuts, seeds, fruit, vegetables and pulses. Fibre is important during exercise as it can slow down the time it takes the body to break down food, which results in a slower, more sustained release of energy. Dietary fibre causes bulk in the small intestine, helping to prevent constipation and aiding digestion.

Water

Water is extremely important in the human body. It constitutes up to 60 per cent of a person's body weight and is essential for good health. It transports nutrients, hormones and waste products around the body. It is the main component of many cells and plays an important part in regulating body temperature. When you take part in exercise, energy is required and some of that energy is released as heat. Water will keep you from overheating. The evaporation of sweat helps to cool you down, but this means water is lost during this cooling-down process. Once the body starts to lose water during exercise, **dehydration** can happen. As a result of this, the following can happen:

- Blood viscosity increases, reducing blood flow to working muscles and the skin.
- Reduced sweating to prevent water loss, which results in an increase in core temperature.
- Muscle fatigue and headaches.
- Reduction in the exchange of waste products/transportation of nutrients.
- Increased heart rate resulting in a lower cardiac output.
- Decreased performance/decreased reaction time/decreased decision making.

It is therefore important when exercising to drink early and often to maintain optimal performance, so make sure you take on fluids regularly.

Figure 6 Examples of foods containing fibre

KEY TERM

Dehydration: Occurs when the body is losing more fluid than it is taking in.

Figure 7 Dehydration

CHECK YOUR UNDERSTANDING
What are the possible physiological effects of a lack of water on a performer?

Sports drinks such as Lucozade Sport and Gatorade can boost glucose levels before competition, while water will rehydrate during competition. Research suggests that for every kilogramme of body weight lost during exercise, the performer needs to drink 1.5 litres of fluid.

ACTIVITY

Copy and complete Table 4 to summarise the exercise-related role and source for each of the food groups listed.

Table 4 The exercise-related role and source for each of the major food groups

FOOD GROUP	EXERCISE-RELATED FUNCTION	SOURCE
Carbohydrates		
Fats		
Protein		
Vitamins		
Minerals		
Fibre		
Water		

Dietary supplements

Supplements are products used to enhance sporting performance. This chapter looks at the dietary supplements used by athletes that provide additional nutrients to improve health and well-being or to enhance sporting performance. Supplements can be legal or illegal.

Glycogen loading

The body's preferred fuel for any endurance sport is muscle glycogen. If muscle glycogen breakdown exceeds its replacement, then glycogen stores become depleted. This results in fatigue and the inability to maintain the duration and intensity of training. In order to replenish and maintain glycogen stores, an endurance athlete needs a diet rich in carbohydrates. Most research seems to suggest that endurance athletes need to consume at least 6 to 10 grams of carbohydrate per kilogram of their body weight.

Some endurance athletes manipulate their diet to maximise aerobic energy production. One method is **glycogen loading** (often called carbo-loading). Six days before an important competition, a performer eats a diet high in protein for three days and exercises at relatively high intensity to burn off any existing carbohydrate stores. This is followed by three days of a diet high in carbohydrates and some light training. The theory is that by totally depleting glycogen stores, they can then be increased by up to two times the original amount and can prevent a performer from 'hitting the wall'.

KEY TERM

Glycogen loading: A form of dietary manipulation to increase glycogen stores over and above that which can normally be stored. It is used by endurance performers.

Table 5 Table to summarise the advantages and disadvantages of glycogen loading

Positive effects	Negative effe`cts
• Increased glycogen storage • Increased glycogen stores in the muscle • Delays fatigue • Increases endurance capacity	During the carbo-loading phase: • Water retention, which results in bloating • Heavy legs • Affects digestion • Weight increase During the depletion phase: • Irritability • Can alter the training programme through a lack of energy

Figure 8 An endurance performer would benefit from glycogen loading

Newer research has shown that replenishing glycogen stores during the first 20-minute window after exercise can then enhance performance the next day. In the 20 minutes immediately after exercise, the body is most able to restore lost glycogen. Many elite performers drink chocolate milk within 20 minutes post-exercise to optimise recovery. This means they consume a 3:1 to 4:1 ratio of carbs-to-protein. This combination of carbohydrates to protein helps the body re-synthesise muscle glycogen more efficiently than carbohydrates alone. Also, a liquid can be absorbed much faster than a solid and the performer can also rehydrate at the same time.

Creatine monohydrate

Creatine monohydrate (more commonly referred to as '**creatine**') is a supplement used to increase the amount of phosphocreatine stored in the muscles. Phosphocreatine is used to fuel the **ATP–PC system** which provides energy. Increasing the amount of creatine in the muscles will allow this energy system to last longer. It can also help improve recovery times. Athletes in explosive events, such as the sprints, jumps and throws, are likely to experience the most benefits as they can perform at higher intensity for longer. Possible side-effects could include dehydration, bloating, muscle cramps and slight liver damage, although studies suggest that a daily intake of five grams or over usually ends up in urine rather than in the muscle!

Table 6 Table to summarise the advantages and disadvantages of creatine supplementation

Positive effects	Negative effects
• Aims to provide ATP (energy) • Replenishes phosphocreatine stores • Allows the ATP–PC system to last longer • Improves muscle mass	• Possible side-effects: muscle cramps, diarrhoea, water retention, bloating, vomiting • Hinders aerobic performance • Mixed evidence to show benefits

Sodium bicarbonate

Sodium bicarbonate is an antacid and can increase the **buffering** capacity of the blood so it can neutralise the negative effects of **lactic acid** and **hydrogen ions** that are produced in the muscles during high-intensity

KEY TERMS

Creatine: A compound the body can make naturally which supplies energy for muscular contraction; can also be used as a supplement to increase athletic performance.

The ATP–PC system: An energy system that provides quick bursts of energy and is used for high intensity exercise but it can only last for up to ten seconds.

ATP (adenosine tri-phosphate): Energy, quite simply!

KEY TERMS

Sodium bicarbonate (NaHCO3): A white soluble compound used as an antacid.

Buffering: The ability of the blood to compensate for the build-up of lactic acid or hydrogen ions to maintain the pH level.

Hydrogen ions: Responsible for the acidity of the blood.

Lactic acid: A by-product of anaerobic respiration; as it accumulates, it causes fatigue.

activity. The concept behind drinking a solution of sodium bicarbonate or 'soda loading' is that it reduces the acidity within the muscle cells, in order to delay fatigue, and allows the performer to continue exercise at a very high intensity for longer. However, it can also result in vomiting, pain, cramping, diarrhoea or a feeling of being bloated.

Athletes who use the lactic acid system in their events such as the 400 metres in athletics, rowing and 100- to 400-metre swim races, will produce a lot of acidity and can benefit from 'soda loading'. However, the negatives outweigh the positives as too often athletes choose not to 'soda load' because of the gastric disruption.

Table 7 summarises the advantages and disadvantages of taking sodium bicarbonate.

Table 7 The advantages and disadvantages of taking sodium bicarbonate

Positive effects	Negative effects
• Reduces acidity in the muscle cells • Delays fatigue • Increases the buffering capacity of the blood	• Possible side effects include vomiting, pain, cramping, diarrhoea, bloating

Caffeine

Caffeine is a stimulant so it can increase mental alertness and reduce fatigue. It is also thought to improve the mobilisation of fatty acids in the body, thereby sparing muscle glycogen stores. It is used by endurance performers who predominantly use the aerobic system since fats are the preferred fuel for low-intensity, long-durance exercise. Research suggests that quantities of 3 mg (micrograms) of caffeine per kilogram of body weight or more showed the biggest improvement in sport performance (100 mg of caffeine = three cans of cola drink). Caffeine can be found in coffee, tea, cola, chocolate, energy bars with caffeine and caffeinated gels. The drawbacks of caffeine are the increased risk of dehydration as it is a **diuretic**; irritability; insomnia and anxiety.

Table 8 summarises the advantages and disadvantages of taking caffeine.

Memory tools

You need to learn the positive and negative effects of glycogen loading, creatine, bicarbonate of soda and caffeine consumption.

Table 8 The advantages and disadvantages of taking caffeine

Positive effects	Negative effects
• Stimulant/increased mental alertness • Reduces effects of fatigue • Allows fats to be used as an energy source/delays use of glycogen stores • Improves decision making/improves reaction time • May benefit aerobic performance/endurance athletes	• Loss of fine control • Against rules of most sports in large quantities • Possible side-effects include: dehydration, insomnia, muscle cramps, stomach cramps, vomiting, irregular heartbeat, diarrhoea

KEY TERMS

Caffeine: A naturally occurring stimulant.

Diuretic: Increases the production of urine.

ACTIVITY

Create your own table and summarise the positive and negative effects of glycogen loading, creatine, bicarbonate of soda and caffeine consumption.

With a partner or in small groups, see if you can remember the positive and negative effects of glycogen loading, creatine, bicarbonate of soda and caffeine consumption.

SUMMARY

Carbohydrates are the principal source of energy for all types of exercise (see Methods of training on page 149). Fats are an energy source for long-duration, low-intensity exercise and proteins are necessary for muscle growth and repair. Make sure you know the importance of vitamins C, D and B complex (B1, B2, B6 and B12) and the minerals calcium, sodium and iron. Water transports nutrients, hormones and waste products around the body and plays an important part in regulating body temperature, while fibre slows down the time it takes the body to break down food, which results in a slower, more sustained release of energy. Some athletes choose to supplement their diet in an attempt to improve performance:

- Glycogen-loading increases glycogen stores and is used by endurance performers.
- Creatine is a supplement used by power athletes so they can work harder for longer and experience greater strength gains.
- Sodium bicarbonate lowers blood acidity.
- Caffeine is used by endurance performers as it helps to provide energy through the mobilisation of fatty acids.

PRACTICE QUESTIONS

1 Which of the following statements about Vitamin D is true? (1 mark)

   a) Helps absorb calcium, which keeps bones and teeth healthy.

   b) Helps form haemoglobin.

   c) Makes red blood cells and keeps the nervous system healthy.

   d) Keeps the skin, eyes and nervous system healthy.

2 Footballers need stamina to play the game effectively. State two classes of food that are most suitable for players who require stamina and explain why they are needed in their diet. (3 marks)

3 Which class of food is most important for a weightlifter? Give reasons for your answer. (2 marks)

4 Discuss the potential benefits and harmful effects to an athlete in taking caffeine supplements. (4 marks)

Chapter 4.2
Preparation and training methods in relation to maintaining physical activity and performance

Chapter objectives

After reading this chapter you should be able to:

- Understand the terms quantitative, qualitative, objective, subjective, validity and reliability for laboratory conditions and field tests.
- Explain the physiological benefits of a warm-up and cool-down.
- Explain the principles of training as SPORT and FITT.
- Understand and be able to apply the principles of periodisation.
- Explain how interval, continuous, fartlek, circuits, weights and PNF training can improve physical fitness.

Training planning

It is important to plan training effectively in order to improve performance. Elite athletes will plan their training year very carefully to optimise their performance, selecting the relevant method of training and testing procedure to monitor and evaluate whether their training programme is a success. Each individual training session needs to be well planned with a warm-up and cool-down, and the principles of training need to be applied so improvements can be made.

Key data terms for laboratory conditions and field tests

Quantitative and qualitative

Quantitative data contains factual information and numerical data. Most fitness tests use quantitative data. In Cooper's 12 minute test, for example, the distance covered in 12 minutes is measured in metres then results are compared to a standardised table. **Qualitative data** is subjective as it looks at feelings, opinions and emotions. The Borg scale is a qualitative method of **rating perceived exertion (RPE)** and is used to measure a performer's level of intensity during training. Perceived exertion is how hard you feel your body is working. During exercise, you use the Borg scale to assign numbers to how you feel. If you feel you are working too hard, you can then reduce the intensity. Similarly, if you feel it is too easy, then you can up the intensity. There are numerous RPE scales but the most common ones are the 15-point scale and the 9-point scale. The 15-point scale is illustrated below:

Table 1 The Borg rating of perceived exertion scale

Rating of perceived exertion	
6	No exertion
7	Extremely light (30% effort)
8	
9	Very light (50% effort)
10	
11	Fairly light (60% effort)
12	
13	Moderately hard (70% effort)
14	
15	Hard (80% effort)
16	
17	Very hard (90% effort)
18	
19	Extremely hard (100% effort)
20	Exhaustion

When drawing conclusions from fitness testing, the results can be analysed quantitatively and qualitatively. Quantitative analysis compares the scores to other people or standardised tables and qualitative analysis makes judgements on these scores.

Memory tools

A quantity is a number!

Objective data

Objective data is based upon facts and is measurable. In fitness testing, objective tests will involve a measurement. Maximal fitness tests are usually objective. These require the performer to work at maximum effort, usually to exhaustion. They are often very reliable, objective tests and involve a measurement of some sort. The Wingate test measures anaerobic power where a performer cycles as fast as possible for 30 seconds on a cycle ergometer (a bike that has resistance applied). A counter is used to measure how many times the flywheel completes one full turn in five-second intervals. This is an example of an objective measurement. The multi-stage fitness test (bleep test) measures stamina and is a progressive 20 metre-shuttle run test. Performers must reach the line at the end of each shuttle before the bleep. When they can no longer do this, the level achieved is recorded.

Subjective data

Subjective data is based upon personal opinions, assumptions, interpretations and beliefs.

Sub-maximal tests such as the **Harvard step test** are more subjective and usually rely on data that is predictive or estimated, which can result in problems with accuracy and objectivity.

KEY TERMS

Rating perceived exertion (RPE): Simply giving an opinion about how hard you feel your body is working during exercise.

Quantitative data: Can be written down or measured with numbers.

Qualitative data: Is descriptive and looks at the way people think or feel.

KEY TERM

Objective: Involves facts.

KEY TERMS

Subjective: Involves opinion.

Harvard step test: This involves stepping up and down on a bench to a set rhythm for five minutes. Recovery heart rates are then recorded.

Validity and reliability of testing

When testing a performer, it is important to ensure that the test is valid and it is set up in such a way as to produce reliable results.

Validity

To assess the **validity** of a fitness test, two questions are important:

- *Is the research method relevant and does it do exactly what it sets out to do?* For example, doing just the 'sit and reach' test to assess flexibility only covers the hamstrings and lower back. Therefore it is a valid test for the lower body but not for the upper body.
- *Is the test sport-specific?* It is important to conduct a test so that the sporting actions are the same and the muscles are also used in the same way as they are in the performer's activity. For example, the 'multi-stage fitness' test involves running so it is a valid test for a games player where a lot of running is involved, but less so for a cyclist or a swimmer where the movement patterns are different.

Reliability

A **reliable** test is one where the results are consistent and can be repeated with the same outcome. In order for the 'step test' to be reliable, it is important to ensure that the procedure is correctly maintained so that everyone who completes the test does so at the same rate, height and cadence and that there is full extension between steps. Competent, well-trained testers also need to be used to reduce errors. To ensure a test is reliable, the following needs to be taken into account:

- tester should be experienced
- equipment should be standardised
- sequencing of tests is important
- repetition of tests to avoid human error.

ACTIVITY

Copy and complete Table 2 and decide on the validity and reliability of the tests.

Table 2

TEST	VALIDITY	RELIABILITY
Multi-stage fitness test		
Vertical jump		
30-m sprint test		
Illinois agility run		

The importance of a warm-up and cool-down

Warm-up

The warm-up helps prepare the body for exercise and should always be carried out before the start of any training session. The first stage of any warm-up is to perform some kind of cardiovascular exercise such as jogging, gently increasing your heart rate. This will increase cardiac output and breathing rate and through the vascular shunt, more blood is directed to the working muscles. Together, these three factors will increase the amount of oxygen being delivered to the muscles.

The second stage is the performance of stretching/flexibility exercises, especially with those joints and muscles that will be most active during the training session. The type of stretching used will depend on the activity.

Static stretching is stretching while not moving and can be active or passive.

- **Active stretching** involves the performer working on one joint, pushing it beyond its point of resistance, lengthening the muscles and connective tissue surrounding it.
- **Passive stretching** is when a stretch occurs with the help of an external force, such as a partner or gravity or a wall.

Ballistic stretching involves performing a stretch with swinging or bouncing movements to push a body part even further. It is important that this type of stretching should only be performed by an individual who is extremely flexible, such as a gymnastic or a dancer who will try to push their body beyond the limits of their range of movement in comparison to a football player.

The third stage should involve the movement patterns that are to be carried out, for example, practising shooting in basketball or netball, or dribbling in hockey or football.

Physiological effects of a warm-up

A warm-up can have the following physiological effects:

- Reduces the possibility of injury by increasing the elasticity of muscle tissue.
- The release of adrenaline will increase heart rate and dilate capillaries. This allows more oxygen to be delivered to the skeletal muscles (see Chapter 1.1 on redistribution of blood flow).
- Muscle temperature increases and this will firstly enable oxygen to dissociate more easily from haemoglobin and secondly, allow for an increase in enzyme activity, making energy readily available through better chemical reactions.
- An increase in the speed of nerve impulse conduction allows us to be more alert, improving reaction time.
- Efficient movement at joints through an increased production of synovial fluid.
- Allows for rehearsal of movement so the performer is practising the same skills they use in their activity.
- Mental rehearsal, stress or anxiety reduction, psychological preparation.
- Supplies an adequate blood flow to the heart to increase its efficiency (see Chapter 1.1 on redistribution of blood flow).

Cool-down

A cool-down takes place at the end of exercise. It consists of some form of light exercise to keep the heart rate elevated. This keeps blood flow

Figure 1 A passive static stretch

high and allows oxygen to be flushed through the muscles, removing and oxidising any lactic acid that remains. Too much lactic acid will cause your performance to deteriorate. Performing light exercise also allows the skeletal muscle pump to keep working, which maintains venous return and prevents blood from pooling in the veins. Blood pooling can lead to fainting or dizziness and occasionally a loss of consciousness. A cool-down may also result in limiting the effect of DOMS (delayed onset of muscle soreness) which is characterised by tender and painful muscles, often experienced some 24 to 48 hours following heavy exercise. This muscle soreness occurs from the structural damage to muscle fibres and connective tissue surrounding the fibres. DOMS usually occurs following excessive eccentric contractions when muscle fibres are put under a lot of strain. This type of muscular contraction occurs mostly in weight training.

Principles of training

A good training session will be well planned with a thorough warm-up and a cool-down, and the activities in between should include the principles of training, so improvements can be made. You need to be able to identify the principles of training and also apply them.

Memory tools

Remember the acronym **SPORR**, where:

S = **s**pecificity, **P** = **p**rogression, **O** = **o**verload, **R** = **r**eversibility and **R** = **r**ecovery.

- *Specificity* is important to make sure the training you do is relevant for your chosen activity. You need to consider whether you are using the same energy system, muscle fibre type, skills and movements. The intensity and duration of the training should also be similar to your activity.

- *Progressive overload* is where the performer gradually trains harder throughout their training programme because their fitness improves. A performer who wishes to improve their power, for example, will be lifting heavier weights at the end of their training programme compared to the start. This is because every few weeks the amount of weight lifted will be increased. It is important not to overload too much too soon. Doing more gradually will reduce the risk of injury.

- *Reversibility* is often referred to as detraining. If training stops then the **adaptations** that have occurred as a result of the training programme deteriorate.

- *Recovery* is important. Rest days are needed to allow the body to recover from training. Research suggests that the 3:1 ratio should be used where the performer trains hard for three days and then rests for one.

Table 3 highlights a typical training week for an athlete. Some elite athletes prefer to have one day of rest per week and for it to be the same day each week.

Table 3 A typical training week for an athlete

Monday	Tuesday	Wednesday	Thursday	Friday	Saturday	Sunday	Monday
Train	Train	Train	Rest	Train	Train	Train	Rest

CHECK YOUR UNDERSTANDING
What are the benefits of performing a cool-down?

KEY TERM

Adaptation: A change that takes place in the body as a result of training.

CHECK YOUR UNDERSTANDING
Describe how a games player would apply the specificity principle to improve fitness.

FITT principles

In order to improve performance, it is important to apply the FITT principles:

- **F** stands for **frequency** so you need to train more often.
- **I** is **intensity** so to improve you must train harder.
- **T** is the **time** spent training so this needs to gradually increase.
- **T** stands for the **type** of exercise. Using different forms of exercise maintains motivation but the type chosen needs to be relevant to your chosen activity. For example, if an improvement in stamina is the aim of a training programme, there are a variety of different types of training that can be used to maintain motivation such as continuous training, circuit training and fartlek training. (See later in this chapter for a description of these.) However, if you are a games player, you need to make sure that these types of training involve running (as opposed to cycling), so you are exercising your muscles in a similar way in which you use them in the game.

Memory tools

Remember the acronym **FITT**, where:

F = **F**requency, **I** = **I**ntensity, **T** = **T**ime and **T** = **T**ype.

Periodisation

Elite performers need to programme their training year very carefully so they can improve performance but also reduce the risk of injury. **Periodisation** is a key word when planning a training programme. It involves dividing the year into blocks or sections where specific training occurs. These blocks of time are referred to as 'cycles' and periodisation divides training into three 'cycles': the macrocycle, mesocycle and microcycle.

KEY TERM

Periodisation: Dividing the training year into specific sections for a specific purpose.

Macrocycle

The **macrocycle** is the 'big' period which involves a long-term performance goal. In rugby, it may be the length of the season or for an athlete it could be four years as they build up to the next Olympics. A macrocycle is made up of three distinct periods:

- **The preparation period** involves general conditioning and the development of fitness levels.
- **The competition period** is where the performer refines skills and techniques, as well as maintaining fitness levels.
- **The transition period** is the rest and recovery stage. This phase allows the athlete to recharge physically and mentally and ensures an injury-free start to the forthcoming season.

Table 4 highlights a macrocycle for a football player:

KEY TERMS

Macrocycle: Period of training involving a long-term performance goal.

Preparation period: Similar to pre-season training where fitness is developed.

Competition period: The performance period where skills and techniques are refined.

Transition period: The end of the season where rest and recovery takes place.

Table 4 A macrocycle for a football player

Football season – Macrocycle		
Preparation – late June and July	Competition – early August to early May	Transition – mid-May to mid-June
This is pre-season where fitness takes place	Matches	This is post-season for rest and relaxation to allow the body to recover

Mesocycle

A mesocycle is usually a 4- to 12-week period of training with a particular focus. A performer may have a component of fitness as their focus, e.g. a sprinter will focus on power, reaction time and speed, whereas an endurance performer will focus more on strength endurance and cardio-respiratory endurance.

Microcycle

A microcycle is a description of one week or a few days of training that is repeated throughout the length of the mesocycle, for example, what a basketball player may do from Monday to Sunday including rest days. Table 5 shows the type of training an elite NBA star may undertake. On top of this, there will also be travel time to games and the games themselves.

Table 5 The type of training an elite NBA star may undertake

Monday	Tuesday	Wednesday	Thursday	Friday	Saturday	Sunday
Strength and conditioning	2-hour practice session Walk-through covering the tactics for the game Upper body weights	Rest	2-hour practice session Walk-through covering the tactics for the game Lower body weights	Strength and conditioning 2-hour practice session	2-hour practice session Upper body weights	Strength and conditioning 2-hour practice session Lower body weights

Tapering and peaking

Tapering is where there is a reduction in the volume of training prior to a major competition. This usually occurs a few days beforehand, but can depend on the event or type of competition. Planning and organising training in this way prepares the athlete both physically and mentally for the big event and allows **peaking** to occur. It is important for the coach to ensure that peak performance occurs in a certain timeframe so the performer can benefit from the removal of training-induced fatigue but reversibility has not yet come into effect.

Double periodisation

Some sports require an athlete to peak more than once in a season. A long-distance athlete, for example, may want to peak in winter during the cross-country season and then again in the summer on the track. An international footballer may want to peak for an important cup final for his club but also a cup competition later in the year for his country! If so, these performers have to follow a double periodised year.

ACTIVITY

Table 6 is an example of a periodised year for a rugby player. Label the different periods of the macrocycle and explain what the rugby player is going to do in each of these periods.

Table 6 Example of a periodised year for a rugby player

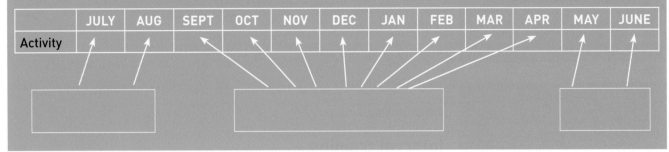

	JULY	AUG	SEPT	OCT	NOV	DEC	JAN	FEB	MAR	APR	MAY	JUNE
Activity												

Memory tools

Macro = big; **meso** = medium; and **micro** = small units of time.

Training methods

When planning a training programme, it is important to choose the relevant training method to improve physical fitness. There are several training methods which improve different aspects of fitness.

Continuous training

Continuous training works on developing **aerobic** power. It involves low-intensity exercise for long periods of time without rest intervals, such as jogging, swimming and cycling. This develops stamina (the ability to exercise the whole body for long periods of time) and places stress on the aerobic system. As a result, improvements in the cardiovascular and respiratory systems take place which increases the ability to take up, transport and use oxygen more effectively.

Fartlek training

The word 'fartlek' is Swedish and means speed-play. This is a slightly different method of continuous training where the pace of the run is varied to stress both the aerobic energy system due to its continuous nature and the **anaerobic** energy systems through the high intensity bursts of exercise. This is a much more demanding type of training and will improve an individual's stamina and recovery times. A typical session will last for approximately 40 minutes, with the intensity ranging from low to high. The individual can determine the intensity and duration of training. Fartlek training offers more variety through the use of aerobic and anaerobic work and is beneficial to games players where the demands of the game are constantly changing to involve aerobic and anaerobic respiration.

A typical fartlek session for a games player involves varying the pace of their run by integrating sprints into the workout and following these with recovery runs in the form of slow jogs. The route can also be varied to include both uphill and downhill work.

> **CHECK YOUR UNDERSTANDING**
> Explain the different stages in periodisation.

> **KEY TERM**
> **Aerobic:** Means with oxygen.

> **KEY TERM**
> **Anaerobic:** Means without oxygen.

Typical fartlek session:

10 minutes jogging

6 x (20 seconds fast running with 80 seconds slow jog recovery)

5 minutes walking

5 minutes jogging

Run uphill for one minute, jog down, repeat twice

3 minutes jogging

2 minutes walking

Interval training

Interval training is predominantly used by elite athletes to improve anaerobic power. It is a form of training in which periods or intervals of high-intensity work are followed with recovery periods. This method of training is very versatile as it can be adapted to suit a variety of anaerobic needs.

When planning an interval training session, it is important to take the following into account:

- duration of the work interval
- intensity or speed of the work interval
- duration of the recovery period
- number of work intervals and recovery periods.

Circuit training

In circuit training, the athlete performs a series of exercises at a set of 'stations'. Exercises to include are arm exercises (e.g. press-ups), leg exercises (e.g. single leg squats), trunk exercises (e.g. sit-ups) and cardiovascular exercise (e.g. running). When planning a circuit, it is important to decide on the number and variety of stations, the number of repetitions or time spent at each station and the length of the rest interval. In addition, you will also need to consider the number of participants, their level of fitness and the amount of time, space and equipment available. The resistance used is the athlete's body weight and the layout of each exercise should ensure that the same body part is not exercised continuously to allow for recovery. A circuit can be designed to cover any aspect of fitness but tends to be used for general body conditioning and is easily adapted to meet the needs of an activity.

The circuit in Figure 2 is done in pairs where one person (A) runs, while the other (B) completes the exercises. After two complete running circuits, the partners change over activity so that A now completes the exercises and B now runs. After two minutes, the whistle blows and whoever is completing the exercises moves on to the next one. The duration of the circuit is 20 minutes but can be adapted to use more time.

Weight training

Weight training can be used by everyone to develop muscular strength. It involves doing a series of resistance exercises through the use of free weights or fixed weight machines that tend to be described in terms of **sets** and **repetitions**. A repetition is the number of times you do a particular weight

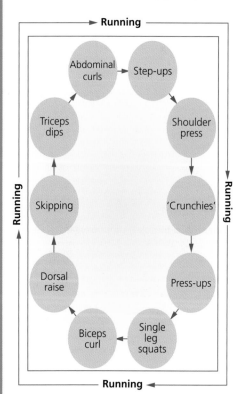

Figure 2 An example of a circuit

exercise and a set is the number of cycles of repetitions that you do; for example, a performer may squat ten times. This means they have done one set of ten repetitions. The number of sets and repetitions that are performed and the amount of weight lifted will depend on the type of strength being improved. Before a programme can be designed, it is important to determine the maximum amount of weight that a performer can lift with one repetition (**1 rep max/1RM**). Then if maximum strength is the goal, it will be necessary to lift high weights with low repetitions, for example, 4–5 sets of 2–6 repetitions at 80–100 per cent of 1 rep max. However, if muscular endurance is the goal, it will be necessary to perform more repetitions of lighter weights, for example, three sets of ten repetitions at approximately 50 per cent of 1 rep max.

The choice of exercise should relate to the muscle groups used in sport, both the agonists and antagonists (specificity). The exercises are usually classed into four groups:

- Shoulders and arms, e.g. bench press, curls, pull-downs
- Trunk and back, e.g., sit-ups, back hyper-extensions
- Legs, e g., squats, calf raise, leg press
- All body exercises, e.g., power clean, snatch, dead lift.

Figure 3 Weightlifting

(a)　(b)　(c)

Figure 4 PNF

KEY TERMS

Repetitions: The number of times you do an exercise, often referred to as reps.

Sets: The number of cycles of repetitions (reps).

1 rep max (1RM): The maximum amount a performer can lift in one repetition.

CHECK YOUR UNDERSTANDING
Which methods of training could be used to improve a) power and b) stamina?

Proprioceptive neuromuscular facilitation (PNF)

PNF stands for proprioceptive neuromuscular facilitation and is an advanced stretching technique. It is a form of passive stretching where the stretch position is held by something other than the agonist muscles, for example, a partner or a wall. PNF is considered to be one of the most effective forms of flexibility training for increasing range of movement. How it works is discussed in more detail in Chapter 1.3 on the neuromuscular system. To summarise, it is where the muscle is isometrically contracted for a period of at least ten seconds. It then relaxes and is stretched again, usually going further a second time.

Fitness testing can use quantitative data (measured with numbers) or qualitative data (descriptive/feelings). They also use objective data (facts) and subjective data (opinions).

When carrying out fitness tests, validity and reliability are important. Why do you think they are important?

The principles of training are specificity, progressive overload, reversibility and recovery and FITT stands for frequency, intensity, time and type. Make sure you can define and apply these.

Periodisation is dividing the training year into sections called macrocycle, mesocycle and microcycle and you need to be able to discuss what each of these mean and what they consist of.

Tapering is reducing the volume and/or intensity of training prior to competition and peaking is organising training so the performer is at their mental and physical best.

The examined training methods and the aspects of physical fitness they improve are:

- Interval training – anaerobic power
- Continuous and fartlek – aerobic power
- PNF – flexibility
- Weights – strength
- Circuits – muscular endurance.

PRACTICE QUESTIONS

1 Which of the following statements about data is true? (1 mark)

   a) Qualitative data can be written down or measured with numbers.

   b) Quantitative data is descriptive and looks at the way people think or feel.

   c) Reliability means the test can be repeated accurately.

   d) Subjective data is based upon facts and is measurable.

2 Describe how you would apply the 'FITT' principles to improve fitness. (4 marks)

3 What are the physiological benefits of performing a warm-up? (4 marks)

4 When planning a training programme for an elite athlete, tapering and peaking are crucial to the athlete's success. What do you understand by the terms 'tapering' and 'peaking'? (2 marks)

Chapter 5
Biomechanical principles and levers

Chapter objectives

After reading this chapter you should be able to:

● Identify Newton's three laws of linear motion applied to sporting movements.

● Define the scalars speed and distance, giving equations and units of measurement.

● Define centre of mass and identify the factors affecting stability.

● State the three classes of lever and give examples of their use in the body during physical activity and sport.

● Identify the mechanical advantage and disadvantage of each class of lever.

This chapter will develop your understanding of the mechanics of movement, looking at how motion (how we move) and forces (cause movement to change) can be applied to performance in physical activity and sport.

Newton's laws of linear motion

Linear motion is motion in a straight or curved line, with all body parts moving the same distance at the same speed in the same direction. A 100-metre athlete will travel with linear motion in a straight line during their race and a 200-metre athlete will travel with linear motion in a curved line when running the bend. Newton's laws are physical laws which you may have encountered in your study of Physics. They describe the relationship between a body and the forces acting upon it, and the body's motion in response to these forces to help us understand human movement.

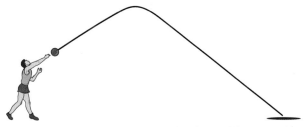

Figure 1 The flight path of a shot is a form of linear motion

KEY TERM

Linear motion: Motion in a straight or curved line, with all body parts moving the same distance at the same speed in the same direction.

KEY TERMS

Inertia: The resistance an object has to a change in its state of motion.

Newton's first law of inertia: A force is required to change the state of motion.

KEY TERM

Newton's second law of acceleration: The magnitude (size) and direction of the force determines the magnitude and direction of the acceleration.

ACTIVITY

When Usain Bolt ran his world record 100 metres, his acceleration out of the blocks was 9.5 m/s². Work out the force at work on Bolt who has a mass of 94 kg. Your answer will be in newtons.

KEY TERM

Newton's third law of motion: For every action [force] there is an equal and opposite reaction [force].

Newton's first law of motion (the law of inertia)

Inertia is the resistance an object has to a change in its state of motion. If an object is at rest, it will remain still. Similarly, if it is moving in one direction it will continue to do so at the same velocity until another force is exerted upon it. The bigger the mass, the larger the inertia of a body or object. This means that more force will be needed to change its state of motion. Consider two rugby league players running towards you. One is a prop weighing 100 kg and the other a winger weighing 75 kg, which one would you prefer to stop? The answer would be the winger as they will be easier to stop because they have less inertia. Only the very brave would attempt to stop the prop! Newton's first law states:

'Every body continues in its state of rest or motion in a straight line, unless compelled to change that state by external forces exerted upon it.'

In simple terms, a force is required to change the state of motion. If a body changes its state of motion, it starts, stops, accelerates, decelerates or changes direction. In the high jump, for example, the athlete runs horizontally towards the bar and then changes their state of motion at take-off when they travel vertically to try to clear the bar.

Newton's second law of motion (the law of acceleration)

*'The rate of momentum of a body (or the **acceleration** for a body of constant mass) is proportional to the force causing it and the change that takes place in the direction in which the force acts.'*

In simple terms, this law means that the magnitude (size) and direction of the force applied to a body determine the magnitude and direction of the acceleration given to a body. The rate of acceleration is directly proportional to the force causing the change and the following equation is often used to calculate the size of a force:

Force = mass × acceleration (F = ma)

This suggests that if the masses involved remain constant, then acceleration is equal to the size of the force causing it. To provide the acceleration at the start of a sprint race, an athlete will have to apply a large force internally with their gluteals, quadriceps and gastrocnemius as they drive forward. Similarly a tennis player will impart a large force on the ball so that it accelerates over the net in the direction in which the force has been applied.

Newton's third law of motion (the law of action/reaction)

'To every action [force], there is an equal and opposite reaction [force].'

Newton's third law of motion describes what happens when *two bodies* (or objects) exert forces on one another. Action and reaction are equal and opposite and always occur in pairs. *Action* acts on one of the bodies, and the *reaction* to this action acts on the other body. At a sprint start, the athlete *pushes back* on the blocks as hard as possible (this is the '*action*'), and the blocks *push forward* on the athlete (this push forward is the *reaction*) and provides forward acceleration on the athlete. Most questions on Newton's third law involve a **ground reaction force** (GRF). This is the force exerted on the ground by the body in contact with it. An individual standing still on the ground exerts a contact force (weight of the individual) and at the same time, an equal and opposite ground reaction force is exerted by the ground on the individual.

Figure 2 shows a swimmer pushing backwards on the water with their hands and feet (this is the force with the thick arrow – the *action*). At the same time, the water thrusts the swimmer forward (this is the force with the thin arrow – the *reaction*).

KEY TERM

Ground reaction force: The equal and opposite force exerted on a performer who applies a muscular force on the ground.

STUDY HINT

Questions on Newton's third law may involve a **ground reaction force**.

Figure 2 The law of action and reaction in swimming

STUDY HINT

Make sure you include the words 'equal and opposite' when you are defining the Newton's third law.

Table 1 applies these laws to football.

Table 1 Newton's laws, applied to football

Newton's laws	Application
Law of inertia	In a penalty, the ball (body) will remain on the spot (state of rest) unless it is kicked by the player (an external force is exerted upon it).
Law of acceleration	When the player kicks (force) the ball during the game, the acceleration of the ball (rate of change of momentum) is proportional to the size of the force. So, the harder the ball is kicked, the further and faster it will go in the direction in which the force has been applied.
Law of action/reaction	When a footballer jumps up (action) to win a header, a force is exerted on the ground in order to gain height. At the same time, the ground exerts an upward force (equal and opposite reaction) upon the player.

STUDY HINT

Make sure you know which law is which!

ACTIVITY

Now complete Table 2, giving an example of how each of the laws can be applied to a sport of your choice.

Table 2

NEWTON'S LAWS	APPLICATION
Law of inertia	
Law of acceleration	
Law of action/reaction	

CHECK YOUR UNDERSTANDING

Using your knowledge of Newton's Three Laws of Motion, try to explain how a high jumper takes off from the ground.

Measurements used in linear motion

There are lots of different measurements used in linear motion. A **scalar quantity** is when measurements are described in terms of just their size or magnitude. Direction is not taken into account. Speed, distance, mass and temperature are scalar quantities.

Speed

Speed can be defined as the rate of change of position and can be calculated as follows:

$$\text{Speed in metres per second (ms)} = \frac{\text{Distance covered in metres (m)}}{\text{Time taken in seconds (s)}}$$

Distance

Distance is the length of the path a body follows when moving from one position to another. For example, a 200-metre runner who has just completed a race has run a distance of 200 metres. Distance is also a scalar quantity because it just measures size.

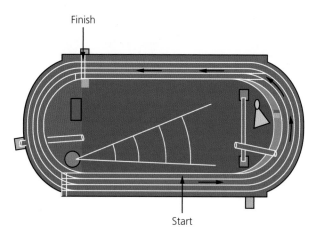

Figure 3 Picture showing distance

Memory tools

An easy way to calculate speed and distance is to use the triangle in Figure 4:

Distance = speed × time

Speed = distance/time

To calculate the speed of a sprinter running the 100 metres in 12 seconds:

Speed = distance/time

So 100/12 = 8.3m/s

When calculating speed and distance, it is important that the units used correspond with each other. If the question gives the distance in kilometres and the time in hours, then the measurement of speed should be calculated as km/h.

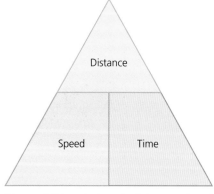

Figure 4 Triangle to calculate speed and distance

Consider an A-level PE student who runs for 30 minutes and covers 5.5 km. Calculate the speed the student ran:

The answer needs to be given in hours so 30 minutes equals 0.5 hours.

Speed = distance/time

So 5.5/0.5 = 11 km/hr^{-1}

ACTIVITY

Calculate the average speed for the three components of a triathlon in Table 3.

Table 3

DISTANCE	TIME	AVERAGE SPEED (M/S)
1.5-km swim	30 mins, 30 secs	
40-km cycle	90 mins	
10-km run	45 mins	

Speed and distance can also be used in graphs, along with time (see Figure 5).

The graph in Figure 5 shows that when a performer is stationary, the line on the graph is horizontal. Running at a steady speed in a straight line means the line on the graph remains straight but is now angled. The steeper the line is, the faster the speed of the performer. The runner represented by the blue line is running faster than the runner represented by the red line.

Centre of mass

The **centre of mass** is the point of concentration of mass, or more simply, the point of balance of a body. The human body is an irregular shape so the centre of mass cannot be identified easily. In addition, the body is constantly moving so the centre of mass will change as a result. For example, raising your arms in the air raises your centre of mass in order to keep the body balanced. In general, the centre of mass for someone adopting a standing position is in between the hip region and differs according to gender. Males have more weight concentrated in their shoulders and upper body so their centre of mass is slightly higher than in females, who have more body weight concentrated at their hips.

Factors affecting stability

All sports require good balance. Kicking a football, when you are not in a balanced position, results in an inaccurate pass. Similarly, an unbalanced position as a rugby player makes a tackle will result in the tackle being unsuccessful. To increase your stability, the following mechanical principles need to be considered:

- **The height of the centre of mass** – lowering the centre of mass will increase stability.
- **Position of the line of gravity** – should be central over the base of support to increase stability.

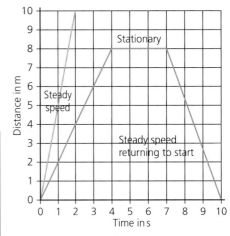

Figure 5 A distance/time graph

KEY TERMS

Centre of mass: This is the point of balance.

Line of gravity: This is the line extending vertically downwards from the centre of mass.

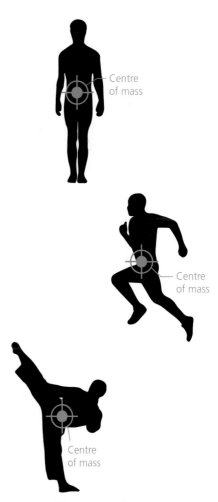

Figure 6 The centre of mass

KEY TERM

Area of support base: The larger the area, the greater the stability.

- **Area of the support base** – the more contact points, the larger the base of support becomes and the more stable they become. For example, a headstand has more contact points than a handstand so is a more balanced position.
- **Mass of the performer** – often the greater the mass, the more stability there is because of increased inertia.

If you lower your centre of mass, you will increase stability. A low stance in rugby, judo and wrestling, for example, makes it harder for an opponent to push you over. However, if your centre of mass starts to move near the edge of the base of support, you will start to over-balance. A sprinter in the 'set' position will have their centre of mass right at the edge of the area of support. As they move when they hear the starting pistol, they will lift their hands off the ground and become off-balanced. This will allow the athlete to fall forward and will create the momentum for the speed they require to leave the blocks as quickly as possible.

When performing the Fosbury flop in the high jump, the centre of mass of the performer passes under the bar while their body goes over. This technique is beneficial because the high jumper does not have to lift their centre of mass as great a distance to clear the bar as another high jumper who uses the scissor kick – their centre of mass will remain in the body and therefore has to be lifted over the bar.

ACTIVITY

Choose a sport and explain how one of the factors above can be used to increase stability.

CHECK YOUR UNDERSTANDING

Give two factors that can increase stability.

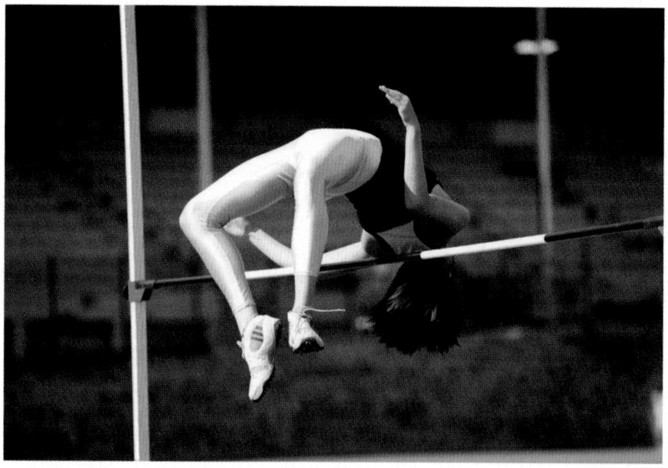

Figure 7 The Fosbury flop

Levers

KEY TERMS

Fulcrum: The point about which the lever rotates.

Resistance: The weight to be moved by the lever system.

Effort: the force applied by the user (muscle) of the lever system.

A lever consists of three main components, namely: a pivot (**fulcrum**); weight to be moved (**resistance**) and source of energy (**effort** or force). In the body, the skeleton forms a system of levers that allows us to move. The bones act as the levers, the joints are the fulcrums, the effort is provided by the muscle and the resistance is the weight of the body part that is being moved (often against the force of gravity).

Classification of levers

There are three types of lever: first, second and third and the classification of each depends on the position of the fulcrum, resistance and effort in relation to each other.

- In **first class levers**, the fulcrum is located between the effort and the resistance. There are two examples of this type of lever in the body. The movement of the head and neck during flexion and extension and extension of the elbow are both first order levers.

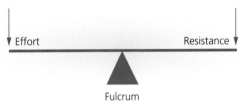

Figure 8 First class lever

- In **second class levers**, the resistance lies between the fulcrum and the effort. There is only one example of this lever in the body and that is plantarflexion of the ankle.

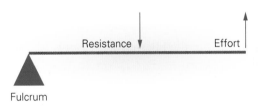

Figure 9 Second class lever

Third class levers can be found in all the other joints of the body. Here, the effort lies between the fulcrum and the resistance. Some examples are hip, knee and elbow flexion.

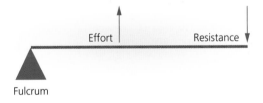

Figure 10 Third class lever

Memory tools

A useful rhyme is **FRE 123** where 1 2 3 is the type of lever and FRE refers to the word that is in the middle. For example, F for fulcrum is the first letter so when fulcrum is in the middle it is a first class lever.

KEY TERMS

First class lever: The fulcrum lies between the effort and resistance.

Second class lever: The resistance is between the fulcrum and effort.

Third class lever: The effort is between the fulcrum and the resistance.

STUDY HINT

If you are asked to classify and label a lever, make sure you do not abbreviate, for example use the label 'effort' not the letter 'E'.

STUDY HINT

Relating levers to the human body can be confusing. The 'effort' is labelled from the muscle's insertion (where it is attached on the bone), not from the muscle itself.

STUDY HINTS

You should aim to be able to analyse five joints. They are all third class levers except for the ankle, which is a second class lever and extension of the elbow joint, which is a first class lever (See Chapter 1.4 on the musculoskeletal system and analysis of movement in physical activities.)

ACTIVITY
Label the fulcrum, effort and resistance for flexion of the elbow on Figure 11 then do the same for extension of the elbow:

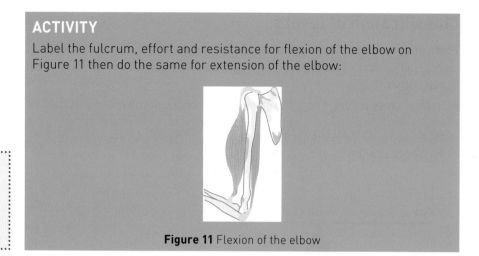

Figure 11 Flexion of the elbow

CHECK YOUR UNDERSTANDING
Name and sketch the lever system that operates during extension of the elbow.

KEY TERMS

Force arm: The length of the line between where the fulcrum and effort are labelled.

Resistance arm: The length of the line between where the fulcrum and the resistance are labelled.

Mechanical advantage and disadvantage

A lever can have a mechanical advantage or disadvantage and this all depends on the length of the **force arm** and the **resistance arm**. The force arm is the name given to the shortest perpendicular distance between the fulcrum and the application of force (effort). The resistance arm is the shortest perpendicular distance between the fulcrum and the resistance.

Perpendicular distance is simply the length of the line between either where the fulcrum and the resistance is labelled or the fulcrum and effort is labelled.

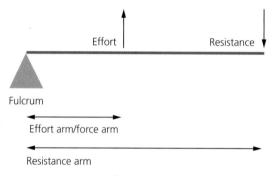

Figure 12 The effort/force arm and the resistance arm

KEY TERMS

Mechanical advantage: Where the force arm is longer than the resistance arm.

Mechanical disadvantage: Where the resistance arm is longer than the force arm.

Mechanical disadvantage is when the resistance arm is greater than the force arm. This means that the lever system cannot move as heavy a load but can do it faster. It also has a large range of movement. **Mechanical advantage** is when the force arm is longer than the resistance arm. This means that the lever system can move a large load over a short distance and requires little force. However, it has a small range of movement and it is difficult to generate speed and distance.

Table 4

Type of lever	Mechanical advantage	Mechanical disadvantage
Second class: Plantarflexion of the ankle	Can generate much larger forces Has to lift the whole body weight	Slow, with a limited range of movement
First class: Triceps in extension of the elbow **Third class:** Biceps in flexion of the arm	Large range of movement and any resistance can be moved quickly	Cannot apply much force to move an object

SUMMARY

You need to be able to define and apply all three of Newton's laws of motion and make sure you are aware that Newton's first law is inertia; the second law is acceleration; and the third law is reaction. You also need to know definitions, equations, formulae and units of measurement for speed and distance and demonstrate the ability to plot, label and interpret these on biomechanical graphs and diagrams. Remember that stability relies on the centre of mass and the factors that affect stability are height of the centre of mass, area of the support base, position of line of gravity and body mass. With levers, you need to identify the different class of lever, depending on the position of the fulcrum, resistance and effort and explain the terms mechanical advantage, where the force arm is longer than the resistance arm and mechanical disadvantage, where the resistance arm is longer than the force arm. You also need to give a mechanical advantage and disadvantage of each class of lever.

PRACTICE QUESTIONS

1   Which of the following statements is true?   (1 mark)

   a) A first order lever has the resistance in the middle.

   b) A first order lever has the effort in the middle.

   c) A second order lever has the fulcrum in the middle.

   d) A third order lever has the effort in the middle.

2   Name and sketch the lever system that operates during plantar-flexion of the ankle joint.   (3 marks)

3   What do you understand by the terms mechanical advantage and mechanical disadvantage?   (3 marks)

4   Using Newton's second law of motion, explain how an athlete is able to accelerate towards the finish line.   (3 marks)

5   If a sprinter runs at a speed of 8 metres per second for 30 seconds, calculate the distance covered.   (2 marks)

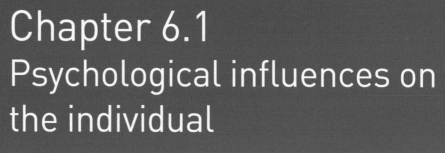

Chapter 6.1
Psychological influences on the individual

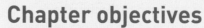

Chapter objectives

After reading this chapter you should be able to:

● Examine the psychological theories and concepts that help to explain the topics of personality, attitudes and arousal levels.

● Discuss how the theories associated with those topics listed above explain the effect on performance of individuals in sport.

● Discuss strategies that can be used to overcome the negative effects of individual psychological effects on performance so that the methods used by coaches to reduce any negative effects on performance can be understood.

In this chapter the study of the psychological influences that affect individual performance will be looked at, and such influences will be discussed with regard to the way they impact on sports performance.

Personality

Personality was defined by the sports psychologist Diane Gill as a 'unique psychological make-up'. This simple definition implies that each person in sport has their own personality profile and that this personality can, and does, have implications for the way coaches and players should approach training and competition. Some players will have similar personality profiles to others, some will be different, and some players will react differently to the same situation. An understanding of these differences can help to make a better performance. Coaches may need to be aware of which players do better under pressure, for example, and players might benefit from a knowledge of how their performance is influenced by personality factors. Some psychologists argue that personality characteristics are innate, others argue that they are learned. This nature versus nurture debate is best discussed using three theories listed below. The nature approach suggests that characteristics are innate and the nurture approach suggests that those characteristics are learned.

Trait theory

The features of **trait theory** are that an individual is born with innate characteristics, called traits, that are stable, enduring and stay the same in different situations. Behaviour is said to be consistent so that the sports performer will behave the same in most situations. Trait theory attempts to predict behaviour because if sports people are always going to behave in the same way, there is a good chance we can expect and predict that same behaviour most of the time.

For example, an **extrovert** basketball player may also behave in an extrovert manner at training, while playing and in team discussions. She might always display the extrovert characteristics of being loud, bright and opinionated!

There are problems with the predictability of trait theory. Can behaviour always be predicted? The problem with trait theory is that it does not take into account personality change. Personality and behaviour can change with the situation. A footballer could be aggressive after being fouled but then calm and apologetic in the post-match interview. Trait theory does not consider that our personalities can be formed by experience. David Beckham played in the 2002 World Cup with concentration, dignity and focus. In 1998 he was petulant and aggressive when sent off in a World Cup game against Argentina. Did his international experience help him to learn a more mature approach to his play? Such development in behaviour could be explained by the social learning approach to personality.

The social learning approach

Social learning theory offers another explanation as to how our personalities develop. Rather than being born with characteristics, we learn them from other people, especially those we hold in high esteem, or significant others, such as role models, friends and parents. Personality traits can be developed by associating with other people and picking up their behaviour, a process called socialisation. We are more likely to learn reinforced behaviour that is seen as successful and powerful and we are more likely to copy behaviour that is consistently shown to us. Behaviour is more likely to be copied if it is witnessed as a live event rather than from a form of media. Therefore players are more likely to copy when taking part in live sport! We learn our behaviour by the following process shown in Figure 1.

Figure 1 The social learning approach

We observe others and copy them, especially if their actions are successful. We can also learn from experience. For example, young football players copy the goal celebrations of professional players if they score a goal playing with their friends. Think of the theory of observational learning in Chapter 2.2 – reinforced behaviour is copied from others when it is successful or loud and bright.

The interactionist perspective

This theoretical concept attempts to explain how aspects of personality are developed and how the behaviour of sportsmen and women can be influenced by both genetic and environmental influences. It combines the two underlying concepts: the trait approach, which suggests that personality is genetically influenced and that we are born with personality traits that will produce consistent behaviour in most situations; and the social approach, which suggests personality is learned from others.

The Lewin approach to personality

The **interactionist perspective** combines social learning and trait theories. It suggests that the traits we are born with are adapted and used according to the situation, so that a player who has the traits of being assertive or

KEY TERM

Extrovert: Extroverts have loud and bright personalities.

KEY TERM

Social learning theory: This theory suggest that behaviour is learned from significant others by socialisation.

STUDY HINTS

Trait theory suggests personality characteristics are innate. Social learning theory says personality characteristics are learned.

KEY TERMS

Trait theory: A theory which suggest that innate characteristics produce consistent behaviour.

Interactionist perspective: A theory which combines trait and social learning to predict behaviour in a specific situation.

Figure 2 Player at rugby scrum is assertive

Figure 3 Rugby player in open play is more assured

well-motivated and dominant would use these traits in a game situation when there is a need to impose a presence on the play. An example would be a rugby player about to form a scrum who would approach the scrum with real intent and begin to pack down with force and determination. That same player, in more open play in the game, may need to think a little more about supporting the player with the ball and approach that situation with a more calm and assured manner.

The interactionist approach therefore accounts for behaviour change and suggests that behaviour is adapted to suit the situation.

Lewin (1935) suggested that the interactionist approach is explained by **Lewin's formula B ƒ(P × E)**, where behaviour is a function of personality and the environment. The interactionist approach attempts to help coaches by predicting how a player will react in a specific situation. The thinking is that since inherent, consistent traits can be adapted to the situation, those traits will produce a typical response.

The Hollander approach to interactionist theory

The idea that interaction can predict behaviour was supported by the work of the psychologist Hollander. He suggested that personality is made up of three features: the core of the performer, the typical responses and the role-related behaviour. The core represents the values and beliefs of the individual; the typical responses are the use of the inherent traits displayed to specific situations; and the role-related behaviour suggests that the performer might adopt or adapt to a very specific role when the situation demands it. According to Hollander, and shown by Figure 4, it is suggested that the more the environment has an influence, the more behaviour is likely to change.

1 The core is stable and solid and not likely to change. Beliefs and values, such as the belief in the benefits of playing a team sport, are underlying.

2 Typical responses are the usual responses the player would make in a given situation.

3 The role-related behaviour implies that further changes to behaviour may be needed as the situation demands.

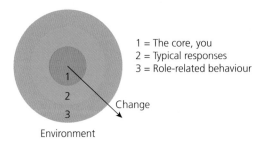

1 = The core, you
2 = Typical responses
3 = Role-related behaviour

Figure 4 The Hollander model

In an example from a team game, it might be that a player has the core values of a strong work ethic and is prepared to work hard for the team in every game. The player is an attacker who typically responds to attacking situations by making the effort to make various runs to find space and then receive the ball from the midfield players. In a close game, however, when the team are under pressure and trying to defend a narrow lead, the player tracks back and employs the role of a defender to help protect the lead, an action needed in that set of circumstances.

Hollander believed that the environment therefore does influence behaviour and he supported the idea of the interactionist theory.

Figure 5 A red card could be avoided if it could have been predicted by the coach

How knowledge of the interactionist perspective can improve performance

A clever coach could use the interactionist idea to help improve team and individual performance by using some of the following ideas, for example.

1 The coach could predict any potential unacceptable or aggressive behaviour and remove the player from the situation by substituting them. This could avoid a potential red card and a sending off!

2 The coach could identify situations that cause inappropriate actions or a dropping off of performance and create similar situations in training so that the player can learn to cope. A nervous player could learn to cope with the effect of being watched by a crowd by getting used to being observed during practice.

3 The coach could use the interactionist approach to change player behaviour by encouraging players to adapt to specific circumstances. If a player is anxious about taking a penalty, the coach could offer advice, support and encouragement during penalty practice so that the player learns to be more in control when taking penalties in future games.

Attitudes

A simple yet effective definition of an **attitude** would be, 'It's what you think about something'. An attitude is an opinion. This is actually not a bad basic definition since an attitude can be described as a value or belief towards something, or more precisely that 'something' is referred to in psychological terms as an 'attitude object'. An attitude has been called a mental and neural state of readiness towards an attitude object and individuals involved in sport will have their own thoughts about sporting issues. Some Premier League football managers have very strong opinions about referees, for example!

Figure 6 Referees are the object of attitudes from football managers

KEY TERMS

Triadic model: The three parts of an attitude: cognitive, affective, behavioural.

Cognitive component: A belief, such as the belief in the ability to win.

Affective component: Relates to feelings and interpretation such as enjoyment.

Behavioural component: The actions of the performer.

Figure 7 Training in the gym could reflect a belief in exercise and a positive attitude

Figure 8 Athlete enjoying a training session shows a positive affective attitude component

Attitude formation

Attitudes are formed by associating with others and picking up their opinions and values, a process called socialisation. We tend to learn attitudes from significant others such as our friends, our parents and our role models. Such attitudes are more likely to be learned if the behaviour we see in those significant others is reinforced or repeated many times. We can almost become familiar with the attitudes of others and accept those attitudes and beliefs as normal. Attitudes can become conditioned by behaviour that is successful and reinforced. Praise from the coach for your performance will develop a positive attitude to your sport and a positive response to your coach! Reinforcement is a way of promoting correct actions according to the principles of operant conditioning. Attitudes can also be negative – when there are negative role models who do not champion the values of sport and when a bad experience such as an injury occurs or when there is no reinforcement offered by the coach to change behaviour.

Attitude components

Regardless of how the attitude was developed, it is made up of three parts, or components. The parts of an attitude, known as the **triadic model**, are as follows.

The cognitive part

This is probably the most deep-rooted part of the attitude and it is simply what you think! The **cognitive** part of the attitude represents your beliefs. Most sports performers believe in their ability to win the game or tournament before they compete.

The affective part

The **affective** part of an attitude concerns the feelings and emotions of the player and how those feelings are interpreted. The affective attitude component is shown when the player enjoys taking part in training and playing. The kind of feeling you might experience when you have had a good work out: 'It was hard work but I enjoyed it!'

The behavioural part

The **behavioural** part of an attitude reflects what you do! It is shown by the actions and habits of the performer. A player in a team sport who goes training a couple of times a week and plays in matches at the weekend displays a good behavioural aspect to their attitude.

Memory tools

Use the acronym **CAB** to remember the attitude components:

- **C** = **c**ognitive
- **A** = **a**ffective
- **B** = **b**ehavioural

Figure 9 Water-polo player trains in the week and plays in games at the weekend to show a positive behavioural attitude

Attitude change

In the examples used to explain the components of an attitude, positive outcomes were described. Unfortunately attitudes can also be negative! Positive attitudes need to be encouraged so participants maintain motivation and effort and continue to take part in exercise.

There are two concepts used to change attitudes – cognitive dissonance and persuasive communication – and they are looked at here.

Cognitive dissonance

Using this method, the coach attempts to put pressure on one or more of the attitude components so that the performer becomes uneasy and is motivated to change their existing attitude. Dissonance means to create a conflict in thinking that causes a lack of harmony and gives an uneasy feeling. The coach can use **cognitive dissonance** in the following ways:

1 The player may be given some new information or presented with a new form of activity so that they begin to question their current attitudes and become motivated to change them. The coach might point out the benefits of a new form of exercise or training method which the player has shown a negative approach to and almost challenge the current thinking of that player. A rugby player may be reluctant to train using a 'dance fit' technique until the coach points out that dancers are able to maintain an intense level of activity for an hour-long session while the rugby player has to rest after a 40-minute half! This challenge might cause the rugby player to think again!

Figure 10 Is a dancer a challenge to a rugby player?

KEY TERM

Cognitive dissonance: New information given to the performer to cause unease and motivate change.

2 Making the activity fun and varying practice may make the session more enjoyable. If the activity is more fun than first thought, it may help to change your opinion.
3 Using rewards as reinforcement may increase the turnout at training and at games if there is a prize for the player of the week.
4 The coach could bring in a specialist or role model player from another club to encourage participation.

Persuasive communication

Sports performers can be talked into changing their attitudes but it is not easy! Attitudes are fairly stable and set as core beliefs and the performer could be quite resistant to change, so attempts at persuasion need to be more than just talk. The communication to the performer needs to be relevant and important and the message given needs to be understood – it has to have real quality! The giver of the message also needs to be of high status, perhaps a role model or expert so the impact of the message is high. The coach may also think of their timing when attempting to persuade the athlete to change their attitude – just after a loss or poor performance, when the player realises that something needs to change, might be the right time to step in!

Positive attitudes give positive outcomes so learning and controlling attitude behaviour is an important way of ensuring sporting success.

Arousal in sport

Arousal is an energised state, a readiness to perform, a drive to achieve! It is a state of activation experienced by sports performers before and during competition. Arousal is always present when playing sport. It can vary on a continuum, from being very low and almost sleep-like to very high excitement. Arousal is important to give competitors some degree of drive and enthusiasm, but too much can cause problems in sport. In this section we look at the theories that explain how arousal affects performance.

Increased arousal in sport can be caused by an increase in the level of competition such as the approach of a major game or championship event, by the effect of an audience, especially if the performer is being watched by an expert, and by frustrating circumstances such as not playing well or losing. The theories of arousal and performance are as follows.

Drive theory

Drive theory is based on the assumption that increased motivation causes increased drive. The more drive we have, the more chance of an increase in performance levels because it is likely more effort will be put into the performance. This theory suggests that as arousal increases, so does performance in a linear fashion; in other words, an increase in drive results in a proportionally increased performance. Performance is said to be a function of drive multiplied by habit, shown by the formula $P = f(D \times H)$, where performance is a function of drive multiplied by habit. Drive theory is summed up by Figure 11.

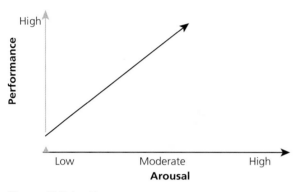

Figure 11 Drive theory

Drive and the dominant response

Increased drive does not always improve performance. It is unrealistic to suggest that performance always keeps improving. At high arousal, less information is processed and the performer tends to concentrate on the '**dominant response**', the response thought to be correct. In experts, the dominant response is indeed usually correct and performance levels remain high. However, with beginners the dominant response may not be developed so the beginner may choose the wrong option and the probability of poor performance increases. Imagine a novice golfer putting against the recent women's golf world number one, Inbee Park. Inbee would perform well under high arousal; the novice would perform as normal – poorly!

If the task is complex, performance may be impaired because there is a lot of information to process and think about, yet at high arousal the ability to process this information reduces and some important cues could be ignored. A simple task does not require much thinking and can be performed well at high levels of arousal. For example, the simple task of a forward roll in gymnastics may still be performed well at high arousal.

The inverted-U theory

The **inverted-U theory** suggests, a bit like drive theory, that as drive and arousal increase, then so does performance, but there the similarities end.

KEY TERM

Drive theory: As arousal increases, so does performance: $P = f(D \times H)$.

KEY TERM

Dominant response: The stand-out response that the performer thinks is correct.

STUDY HINTS

When explaining drive theory, think of it in two parts. The first part is the theory based on the formula $P = f(D \times H)$, and the second part is the link between drive theory and the dominant response. You should aim to explain both.

KEY TERM

Inverted-U theory: Theory linking arousal and performance by stating that increased arousal improves performance to an optimal point at moderate levels of arousal.

According to the inverted-U theory, performance is improved only up to an optimal point which tends to be at a moderate level of arousal. Further increases in arousal can cause performance to deteriorate, therefore, as shown by Figure 12; both under- and over-arousal can be equally bad for performance. Points A and B on the graph show that too little or too much arousal are equally bad for performance.

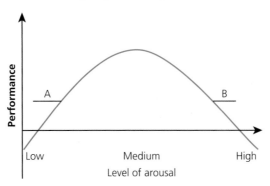

Figure 12 Inverted-U theory showing how increased arousal affects performance

However, just like in drive theory, there is some more explaining to do to fully grasp the details of the inverted-U theory and you must be able to explain both the basic theory and the following additional features of it.

A moderate level of arousal is not always the best for peak performance. The optimum level of arousal can vary depending on the skill level, personality of the performer and the task being undertaken, as explained below.

Experience – novice or expert?

Experienced players are used to dealing with pressure and can deal with tasks effectively, even if they operate with limited information. The 'dominant response' of an expert is likely to be correct so they can produce a high level of performance at high arousal. A beginner might need to operate at a low level of arousal since they would be uncomfortable under pressure.

Personality – extrovert or introvert?

Extrovert personalities may perform happily at high arousal; introverts would prefer to perform at low arousal. This may be because the reticular activating system (RAS), which controls and measures the levels of adrenaline in the body, suggests that extroverts have naturally low levels of activation and can tolerate any increases in arousal; introverts are said to have naturally high levels of adrenaline and therefore would perform best at low arousal.

The task

Gross or fine? Complex or simple?

If the task is gross, such as when doing a stroke in rowing (Figure 14), it can be performed using large muscle group movements at high arousal, without the need for the precise control needed for finer skills such as a table tennis return (Figure 15).

Figure 13 Expert performance by long jumper Greg Rutherford in the 2012 Olympics at high arousal levels

Figure 14 Rowing (a gross skill) can be performed best at high levels of arousal

Figure 15 Table tennis return can be performed at low levels of arousal

A complex skill needs decision making and the ability to process a relatively large amount of information. At high arousal, the ability to process a lot of information is reduced so the performer may require a lower level of arousal to execute a complex skill. A simple skill requires less decision making and can still be executed well at high arousal levels (Figure 17).

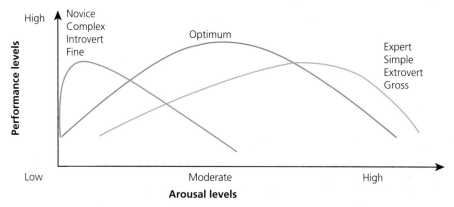

Figure 16 Adaptations to the inverted-U theory showing how the task and the performer can affect the optimal level of arousal for best performance

Catastrophe theory

Catastrophe theory is an adaptation of the inverted-U theory. It suggests that increased arousal causes performance to peak at an optimum level but,

KEY TERM

Catastrophe theory: Theory suggesting that increased arousal improves performance to an optimal point but there is a dramatic reduction in performance when arousal increases beyond the optimal.

Figure 17 In curling, there can be lots of decisions to make in deciding how fast and in what direction to release the stone: a complex skill performed best at low arousal.

KEY TERMS

Somatic anxiety: Physiological anxiety.

Cognitive anxiety: Psychological anxiety.

STUDY HINT

The athlete can recover from the catastrophe if the initial anxiety is low and there is sufficient time!

STUDY HINT

Catastrophe represents a deterioration in performance from which the athlete may not recover.

KEY TERM

Zone: Area of controlled arousal and high level performance.

rather than a gradual deterioration, there is a sudden dramatic reduction in performance. The cause of this slump in performance is a combination of high levels of both **somatic** and **cognitive** anxieties (see below). The player tries to regain control by reducing anxiety and arousal and performance may gradually return to optimal, but only if the initial cause of the anxiety is mild and the performer has the time to recover. More often than not, the performer fails to control their arousal and then starts to panic a little, causing further increases in arousal, which causes a further decline in performance. A diagram of catastrophe theory is shown in Figure 18.

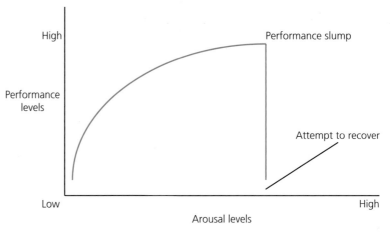

Figure 18 Catastrophe theory

Somatic anxiety is physiological and includes muscular tension and increased heart rate. Cognitive anxiety is psychological and includes loss of concentration and worries about performance. More in Chapter 6.2.

The zone of optimal functioning

The psychologist Hanin studied the inverted-U theory and adapted it. He suggested that increases in arousal can improve performance and that the optimal level of arousal does vary for individual players from low to high levels. But rather than a point of optimal arousal, the best level of arousal for maximum confidence and control in sport is an area, or '**zone**'. A model of the zone of optimal functioning is shown in Figure 20, with an indication that some players find their zone at low arousal, some at moderate arousal and some at high arousal in a mirror of the inverted U, but that this zone is a bandwidth rather than a point. To achieve the zone can be the ultimate experience in sport and individual performers can find their own zone using techniques such as mental practice, relaxation, visualisation and positive self-talk. (These methods are discussed in more detail later in Chapter 6.2 Anxiety in sport.) Once in the zone, performance is said to improve because experience includes the following:

1 Things seem to flow effortlessly.
2 The performer reaches a state of supreme confidence and remains calm under the utmost pressure.
3 The athlete feels that they are in total control of their actions and totally focused on the activity.

The result is a smooth, effortless performance at the highest level. Being in the zone can lead to the peak flow experience, described below.

Figure 20 shows a summary of the zone of optimal functioning, showing how the 'zone' varies for individual performers.

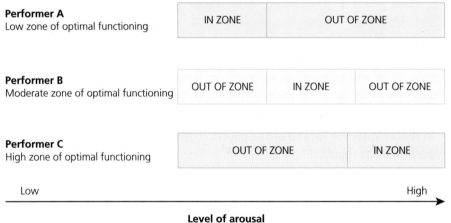

Figure 20 The zone of optimal functioning

Figure 19 Jessica Ennis was 'in the zone' at the London Olympics 2012, winning Gold under the pressure of expectation

The peak flow experience

The **peak flow** is an extension of the feelings and performance levels experienced in the zone. It happens to sports performers when timing, action and movement appear to be perfect. Peak flow is the ultimate intrinsic experience, characterised by a belief in the ability to complete the challenge, clear goals, total focus, effortless movement, and a subconscious feeling of control.

The development of the flow experience is promoted by intrinsic motives which come from a positive mental attitude, high levels of confidence, feelings of relaxation and anxiety control. During peak flow, the performer has total focus on aspects of the task, a high level of confidence in their preparation and fitness levels and a belief that optimum environmental conditions are here at the time of the event. They are good to go! In team sports, the players may have a shared purpose and balanced emotions, even in the games when there is much at stake. The peak flow has no psychological or physiological basis but it does have a positive effect on the player!

Factors affecting the peak flow experience

The peak flow experience can be disrupted by:

1 Poor mental preparation and the failure to reach optimal arousal levels.
2 Environmental influences such as the pressure from the crowd or the frustration caused by a referee decision.
3 The effect of injury or fatigue during the game will also stop the player keeping up with the flow experience.

CHECK YOUR UNDERSTANDING

1 When performing in sport, a player may suffer from an increase in activation known as arousal. Explain the effect of increased arousal on performance according to drive theory.

2 Use catastrophe theory to explain how over-arousal can affect performance.

3 Name three features of the peak flow experience.

4 What would be the optimal level of arousal for an expert rugby player attempting a tackle?

5 What would be the optimal arousal level for a novice golfer attempting a putt?

Figure 21 Germany's World Cup-winning football team had a shared purpose and belief in 2014

SUMMARY

In this chapter we looked at the psychological impact on the individual performer in sport.

The theories and concepts detailed in the chapter described a nature versus nurture approach to sports psychology: the trait or 'nature' approach suggesting that personality characteristics are innate and consistent, that we are born with characteristics that are displayed in most situations, while the 'nurture' approach suggests that characteristics are learned and developed from others.

This nature versus nurture debate does not just occur in the topic of personality. In the topic of attitudes, it is noted that the components of an attitude can be learned from others by conditioning and familiarisation; associating with others who may have a specific trait or consistent belief can cause that belief and associated behaviour to become the norm. Learned attitudes can be hard to change and the concepts of persuasion and cognitive dissonance can help to turn negative attitudes into positive ones.

The theories that explain the relationship between arousal and performance also took a two-sided approach to psychological debate. The drive and inverted-U theories suggested that increased arousal can help performance, yet on the other hand, too much arousal was seen as a negative influence on the performer; the concepts of the zone and the peak flow experience being very much in the former camp, while the catastrophe theory is contained within the latter school of thought. Strategies to reduce the negative influence of all the theories and concepts discussed in this chapter were noted.

The next chapter looks at some more psychological influences on players as they compete.

PRACTICE QUESTIONS

1 According to the inverted-U theory, low levels of arousal produce the best performance when: (1 mark)

   a) the performer is a novice and the skill is gross

   b) the performer is a novice and the skill is fine

   c) the performer is an expert and the skill is gross

   d) the performer is an expert and the skill is fine.

2 The performance and behaviour of sports performers may be affected by their personalities. Discuss this statement using suitable examples, with reference to the interactionist theory of personality. (4 marks)

3 Name and explain one theoretical principle that a coach could use to change a negative attitude into a positive one. (3 marks)

4 When performing in sport, a player may suffer from an increase in activation known as arousal. Explain the effect of increased arousal on performance according to drive theory. (3 marks)

Chapter 6.2
Further psychological effects on the individual

Chapter objectives

After reading this chapter you should be able to:

- Discuss the part that anxiety plays in affecting performance by identifying the types of anxiety that exist when playing sport.
- Evaluate and understand the use of anxiety measures to see how coaches can use data to examine performance.
- Understand the theories that explain the causes of aggression in sport including instinct, frustration–aggression, learned cue and social learning theories.
- Understand the types of motivation that can be used to increase performer effort and task persistence.

Anxiety in sport

In this section we look at the negative aspects on performance of anxiety. **Anxiety** is defined as a state of nervousness and worry, a negative response to a threatening sporting situation. The important point to make about anxiety in sport is that it often arises as a result of the player's perception of the situation. On the eve of an important game such as a cup final, one player is looking forward to competing against strong opponents, believing that any pre-match nerves or anxiety will bring out the best in their performance. Another player from the same team views the situation differently, and might feel anxious due to the fact that tomorrow's opponents are very strong and powerful; the possibility of losing to such a good team causes the player to worry about not playing well and letting the team down. The player displays anxiety. This anxiety can come in different forms and have some damaging effects on the performance.

Figure 1 Trying to win the cup or a big game can cause anxiety. How the player deals with and perceives the threat of competition is important

Competitive trait anxiety

Competitive trait anxiety is when a player feel nerves before most games and could simply be part of the player's genetic make-up. Trait anxiety is displayed before all competitions, regardless of the importance of the event and the possibility of winning. The athlete just feels the nerves every time. This tendency to become anxious in all competitions is known as a trait anxiety.

Competitive state anxiety

Competitive state anxiety is more temporary and is a response to a particular moment in the game or a specific sporting situation. When taking a penalty in a hockey game, for example, the focus of attention and the weight of responsibility is on the penalty-taker and this temporary increase in anxiety can affect the outcome unless the nerves are controlled. The amount of state anxiety experienced can vary throughout the game; it might be high at the start of the game and reduce during the action, and can often depend on the mood of the player at the moment in question.

There is a link between state and trait anxiety. An individual with high trait anxiety is more likely to experience high state anxiety when faced with a stressful situation, especially if it is felt that others are watching or evaluating the performance. If you have the trait, you are more likely to get the state! The psychologist Rainer Martens established the link between state and trait anxiety when establishing the Sports Competitive Anxiety Test or SCAT (see page 179).

Anxiety can be cognitive or somatic

Cognitive anxiety is psychological and refers to the irrational thinking and worries that may occur during and before performance. The performer may believe that they do not have the ability to complete the task, and may experience nervousness and even a loss of concentration. Playing in a game when called upon to mark a bigger and more physical opponent may lead the player to think they will not be able to cope. Such thinking is irrational since the player may well have the ability to deal with the situation, but anxiety means the personal perception is different.

Somatic anxiety is physiological. It is the response of the body to the individual's belief in their lack of ability to complete the task. Symptoms might include increased heart rate, sweating, muscular tension and, in extreme cases, may even cause sickness! These experiences may be felt at their worst at the start of a game but fortunately they often reduce as the game gets underway. The effects of somatic and cognitive anxiety on aspects of performance are shown by the graphs in Figures 4 and 5.

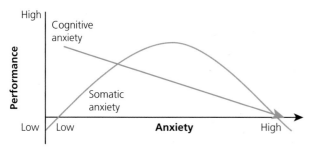

Figure 4 The relationship between cognitive anxiety, somatic anxiety and performance

KEY TERMS

Anxiety: A level of nerves and irrational thinking.

Competitive trait anxiety: A disposition to suffer from nervousness in most sporting situations.

Competitive state anxiety: A nervous response to specific sporting situations.

Somatic anxiety: A physiological response to a threat such as increased heart rate.

Cognitive anxiety: A psychological response such as worrying about losing.

Figure 2 Taking a penalty in hockey can cause state anxiety

Figure 3 Trying to mark Ronaldo may lead to a lack of belief in your ability and give cognitive anxiety!

The graph in Figure 4 shows that somatic anxiety has an identical effect on performance as increased arousal does in the inverted-U theory. Increases in somatic anxiety can improve performance up to a point, after which further increases in somatic anxiety will impair performance. However, cognitive anxiety has a negative linear effect. In other words, the greater the cognitive anxiety, the worse the performance.

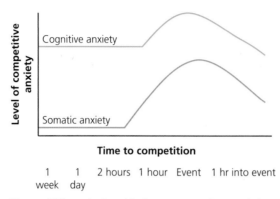

Figure 5 The relationship between anxiety and time to competition

The graph shown in Figure 5, anxiety in the approach to competition, shows that somatic anxiety tends to increase just before a competition or major game is due to begin and reduces as performance is underway. Cognitive anxieties are present much earlier and just because the performer is not showing any physical signs of anxiety does not mean that worries about the forthcoming event are not present. The coach and player should therefore begin to control cognitive anxiety well before the game and introduce techniques to control somatic anxiety as the game approaches.

Anxiety measures

There are three methods of measuring anxiety in sport: self-report **questionnaires**, observation and physiological testing. Such measures are extremely useful to the coach since knowledge of how players deal with and experience anxiety will help the coach to make informed decisions: which players can remain calm enough to take the penalty, for example?

Questionnaire

A questionnaire asks the performer to answer a series of questions about their emotions in different situations. The advantages of this method are that it is quick, cheap and efficient so that large numbers of players can be assessed quickly. Once assessed, the coach can have a set of results that can be compared easily.

However, the results of such self-report questionnaires can be sometimes invalid due to some drawbacks with the method. These disadvantages are:

1 Players may not understand the question being asked and their answer may be one that they think they ought to give rather than the actual truth – the socially desirable answer is given rather than the actual one!

2 Answers may also depend on mood state. The answers given after a win may not be the same as those given after a loss, for example.

3 The questions are inappropriate so that biased results are given, e.g. if the question leads to an answer rather than asking for one.

4 The responses can be influenced by the time it takes to do all the questions; rushing to complete the answers may lead to an incorrect response.

An example of a questionnaire used by sports psychologists to measure anxiety is the **Sports Competition Anxiety Test** or **SCAT**. The questionnaire, developed by Martens in 1977, consists of a series of 15 statements designed to measure how the player responds to competitive sporting situations.

KEY TERM

Sports Competition Anxiety Test (SCAT): A questionnaire used by sports psychologists to measure anxiety.

ACTIVITY

A copy of part of the SCAT test is given below. Complete the test and then use your score to assess your own level of pre-competitive anxiety.

SCAT test

Below are some statements about how people feel when they compete in sports and games. Read each statement and decide if you 'hardly ever', 'sometimes' or 'often' feel this way when you compete in sports and games. Tick the corresponding boxes. There are no right or wrong answers; try not to spend too much time answering the questions. Remember to choose the word that describes how you *usually* feel when you compete at sport.

STATEMENT	RESPONSE		
	Hardly ever	Sometimes	Often
1 Competing against others is socially enjoyable.			
2 Before I compete I feel uneasy.			
3 Before I compete I worry about not playing well.			
4 I am a good sportsperson when I compete.			
5 When I compete I worry about making mistakes.			
6 Before I compete I am calm.			
7 Setting a goal is important when competing.			
8 Before I compete I get a queasy feeling in my stomach.			
9 Just before competing I notice my heart beats faster than usual.			

How to score the SCAT test

For each statement, three responses are possible: a) hardly ever, b) sometimes and c) often. The test items are Questions 2, 3, 5, 6, 8 and 9. The spurious items in Questions 1, 4 and 7 are not scored. Questions 2, 3, 5, 8 and 9 are scored according to the following key:

Hardly ever = 1, Sometimes = 2, Often = 3

Item 6 is scored as follows:

Often = 1, Sometimes = 2, Hardly ever = 3

The higher the score, maximum 18, the higher is your competitive anxiety.

The SCAT test was extended by Martens in 1990 to become the **Competitive Sport Anxiety Inventory**, or **CSAI 2**. Examples of questions used in the CSAI are:

KEY TERM

Competitive Sport Anxiety Inventory (CSAI): A questionnaire used by sports psychologists to measure anxiety.

1 I have self-doubts

   Not at all   Somewhat   Moderately   Very much so

2 My body feels tense

   Not at all   Somewhat   Moderately   Very much so

3 I feel at ease

   Not at all   Somewhat   Moderately   Very much so

4 My heart is racing

   Not at all   Somewhat   Moderately   Very much so

Note these are only sample questions from the test, the full version can be seen at www.brainmac.co.uk

From the questions, it is obvious that this test can distinguish between somatic and cognitive anxieties and should be completed an hour prior to the event to gain an accurate result. The test also includes a measure of the confidence levels of the performer, so it is split into three parts with nine questions in each part, giving a maximum score of 36 for cognitive anxiety, somatic anxiety and confidence. The idea is that the coach can see how players might behave in competitive situations and be able to plan accordingly. A weakness in dealing with stress and anxiety can be identified, especially if the anxiety identified is cognitive and happens prior to the event. While some somatic anxiety can help performance, the coach should use techniques to reduce both cognitive and somatic anxiety to improve results.

ACTIVITY

Some results of the SCAT test are given below. Study the results of the three different performers and then suggest how you would use the results in the situations described below if you were the team coach. The maximum score is 30 and the minimum is 10. The higher the score, the greater the level of competitive anxiety.

Player A: SCAT score 22
Player B: SCAT score 26
Player C: SCAT score 15

Which player(s) would you?

a) Nominate to take penalties.

b) Pick as your captain.

c) Pick as a team mentor.

d) Introduce to anxiety control techniques.

e) Substitute in a close and aggressive match.

Observation

Anxiety can be measured by simply watching sports people, either in their familiar training environment or during the game. This realistic approach gives **observation** studies an advantage in that they are true to life. But there are disadvantages with this form of research in that results are based on the opinion of the observers and, where numerous observations are made, these opinions can vary, making the results highly subjective. The observers also need to know what the people they are watching behave like normally so that changes from the norm can be

KEY TERM

Observation: Gaining a measure of (in this case) anxiety simply by watching the performer.

noted. So the process then becomes very time consuming and may need more than one observer to complete. If the people being observed in sport realise they are being watched, then their behaviour might change or they might feel more uneasy and suffer some anxiety, thus making the results invalid. Sometime sports people can be observed in more controlled situations to reduce the anxiety, but once the performer is taken away from their normal environment, they might begin to realise they are being watched!

Physiological measures

Anxiety can be measured by using a physical response from the body. Such responses to anxiety include increased heart rate, increased levels of sweating, increases in the rate of respiration and even levels of hormone secretion.

The advantage of such measures are:

1 They are factual so that comparisons can be easily made.
2 Responses to anxiety could be measured in training or even real game situations. With recent advances in technology, heart rate can be measured by an electronic device contained within the clothing of the performer and relayed immediately to the coach, who could judge anxiety while the game is in motion.

The difficulty with such measures are:

1 Training is often required so that coaches can learn how to use the devices; the cost of them may deter amateur performers from using them.
2 In some cases actually wearing the measuring device, such as a heart rate monitor, may restrict movement in sport.
3 The fact that the performer is aware that they are being measured may cause additional stress and give a false reading.

Figure 6 Being watched by an observer can increase anxiety and make results invalid. The boxer Christopher Eubank Jnr has been studied by his famous father, Chris.

Figure 7 Wearing a heart rate monitor may increase the stress on a sports performer

> **CHECK YOUR UNDERSTANDING**
> 1 Name two features of cognitive anxiety.
> 2 Name two features of somatic anxiety
> 3 Name three ways of measuring anxiety in sport.
> 4 Using a table, give one advantage and one disadvantage of each method named in the answer to the question above.

> **STUDY HINT**
> The disadvantages of the anxiety test measures could make results invalid and unreliable.

Aggression in sport

The concept of **aggression** in sport is often misunderstood and interpreted incorrectly by observers who mistake aggressive behaviour for assertive behaviour. **Assertion** might be welcome since it is a display of well-motivated behaviour; aggression should be unwelcome since it may result in injury and a performance that is affected by over-arousal.

To clear up the definitions, aggression is:

KEY TERMS

Aggression: Intent to harm outside the rules; hostile behaviour.

Assertion: Well-motivated behaviour within the rules.

- the intent to harm
- outside the rules
- reactive
- out of control
- deliberate and hostile.

Punching someone after a foul in rugby or the deliberate attempt to hurt an opponent as a challenge is about to happen are both examples of aggression. The intent to harm is in the aggressor's head before it happens.

Figure 8 A deliberate foul is pre-meditated and intends to harm

Assertion is:

- controlled
- well motivated
- generally within the rules
- goal-directed
- not intended to harm.

Examples are a hard and fair tackle in rugby or the 50/50 challenge in a team game when both players are going for the ball with determination. There is no original intent to harm each other, although injury may occur as a result of the players' actions.

The problem with these definitions is that there is sometimes difficulty in placing sporting actions in the aggression or the assertion category. In boxing, for example, it is within the rules to punch your opponent and there is also an intent to harm when you punch someone! Aspects of both definitions of aggression and assertion occur here, so how would you classify boxing?

In the boxing example, there is a grey area between the definitions of aggression and assertion. A punch is within the rules in boxing, yet it has an intent to harm!

This grey area is indicated by Figure 10. This middle ground or grey area can occur when there is an aim or intent, but the action is within the rules. When making a tackle in rugby, for example, the defender may make contact with the ribs of the attacker. This is within the rules but there is also some intent to cause some pain so the attacker drops the ball.

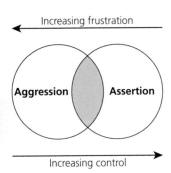

Figure 9 Is a punch in boxing aggression or assertion?

Increasing frustration

Aggression   Assertion

Increasing control

Figure 10 The overlap between aggression and assertion

Causes of aggression in sport

The theories of aggression

There are four theories, detailed below, that attempt to explain how aggression is caused.

Instinct theory

Instinct theory is an evolutionary theory which claims that all performers are born with an aggressive instinct that will surface with enough provocation.

It is claimed that humans retain some of ritualistic aggressive animal instincts that will surface under threat. An example of the evolutionary aspects of instinct theory was when territory was invaded, with the need to defend your territory evoked. Relate this to current sporting situations and when playing at home, sports performers will defend vigorously their home record and try everything to win, even aggression.

Aggressive instincts can surface as a reaction to a bad foul; when the threat of injury is presented, you might react by defending yourself, perhaps by committing an aggressive act! It is suggested that once the aggressive act has been undertaken, the aggressor may then begin to calm down and experience an emotion called **catharsis**, when a more controlled approach is restored. Observers therefore see sport as an outlet for aggression that could otherwise surface in a different situation and see catharsis as a benefit of playing competitive games.

The problem with instinct theory is that not all aggression is reactive and spontaneous – some aggression is learned and pre-intended. Rather than experience catharsis, some players increase their aggression during the game and can display that aggression when not playing, as well as during the game. In terms of evolution, not all our ancestors were aggressive – some of them gathered their food!

The frustration–aggression hypothesis

This theory suggests that inevitable aggression occurs when goals are blocked and the performer becomes frustrated.

The theory argues that once a performer has been prevented from achieving their aim, there will be a building frustration that leads to aggressive tendencies. The built-up frustration can be reduced if an aggressive act is initiated by the performer – the aggressive drive will be reduced. The process of reducing the aggressive drive is called catharsis. However, if the performer is unable to release the aggressive drive, then a form of self-punishment will occur and even more frustration will lead to an increased aggressive drive.

A player who is fouled in a game of football when about to run through towards the goal might immediately retaliate with a push or blow to the player who fouled him. Once this initial skirmish is over, the released aggression will calm the situation down and catharsis might occur. However, if the fouled player is unable to retaliate, perhaps due to the interference of other players, then he might harbour their aggressive instinct and remain frustrated until he is able to hunt out the player who fouled him and seek revenge with a foul of his own.

STUDY HINTS

Remember to name the theories correctly to explain the causes of aggression and be prepared to evaluate each theory. For example, the instinct theory suggests that aggression is innate and reactive, but is all aggression spontaneous (see below)?

KEY TERMS

Instinct theory: When aggression is spontaneous and innate.

Catharsis: Cleansing the emotions; using sport as an outlet for aggression.

STUDY HINT

Instinct theory says aggression is innate.

STUDY HINT

The frustration–aggression hypothesis suggests, similar to instinct theory, that a performer has innate aggressive tendencies.

Figure 11 A poor shot over the bar may lead to frustration

Catharsis

Catharsis is a term for 'letting off steam' or a cleansing of the emotions. Sport can be seen as a release for channelling aggression. It is argued that if the aggressive intent is given an outlet, then the aggressive drive will be reduced. In terms of the frustration–aggression hypothesis, catharsis may be experienced once the frustrated player has had a chance to get rid of the aggressive inclination. Unfortunately, more aggression may occur if the chance to experience catharsis does not occur.

Reasons why you might react with aggression due to frustration in sport could include: losing, poor play by you, poor play by a team mate, disagreement with referee, a hostile crowd, pressure of success, a high-pressure game, being fouled.

However, not all frustration leads to aggression; some players can manage to control themselves, even when a little wound up.

Aggressive cue hypothesis (Berkowitz)

Aggressive cue hypothesis also suggests that increased frustration will lead to increased arousal levels and a drive towards aggressive responses. However, such aggressive responses will only occur if certain learned 'cues' are present to act as a stimulus for the performer to act aggressively. Such 'cues' could have come, for example, from a coach who has allowed a basketball player to push away an opponent who is marking him too closely. An opponent who marks too closely in future may also get a push! This theory begins to generate the idea that aggression can be learned from significant others such as coaches and fellow players. In social learning theory in the personality section, it was noted how behaviour can be learned from others; this theory and the next explain a nurtured production of aggression. In football, it has become common to see players push and grab each other as they jostle for position when a corner kick is taken. The coach may have encouraged such foul play by telling the players not to be pushed out of position at a corner kick so they learn to push their opponents out of the way: the taking of the corner kick is the cue for the aggressive act.

Figure 12 A corner kick in football could be a cue for aggression

Other cues for aggressive acts may include a sporting venue such as the away pitch of your local rivals in a local derby, sporting equipment such as bats and boxing gloves, even other people in sport, such as your main rival for the title.

Social learning theory

Here aggression is also seen as a learned response. Aggression can be copied from others, particularly if such behaviour is reinforced. Bandura suggested that aggression is learned through the following process:

observe → identify → reinforce → copy

For example, you see an experienced player foul an opponent off the ball as she is about to receive a pass, unobserved by the referee. The foul distracts and unsettles the opponent and is successful in preventing a score. You copy the act next time.

Aggression is learned from significant others or those we hold in high esteem, such as role models, our team mates or our coach. **Social learning theory** is particularly important in sport since live behaviour is more likely to be copied than recorded behaviour. Aggressive behaviour is more likely to be copied if it is consistent, powerful and bright.

Figure 13 A skirmish in a team game or a dispute in a game between two players often leads to others joining in if they have learned this is the thing to do!

The difficulty with social learning theory is that, as we have discussed, aggression can be instinctive and reactive rather than being learned. Some players react aggressively without being in a situation where they could observe and copy others.

Memory tools

The four theories of aggression could be recalled by using the acronym **AS IF**:

- **A** = **A**ggressive cue hypothesis
- **S** = **S**ocial learning theory
- **I** = **I**nstinct theory
- **F** = **F**rustration aggression hypothesis

Preventing aggression

Aggression is not desirable in sport since it can cause injury, a loss of concentration and an increase in arousal and anxiety in the player. Coaches, players and importantly the referee can play a part in reducing aggression in sport. They may do some or all of the following;

- Do not reinforce aggressive acts in training.
- Punish aggression with fines.

STUDY HINT

The aggressive cue hypothesis and the social learning theory suggest that aggression can be learned, that it is nurtured. Is it?

- Punish players by sending them off.
- Substitute an aggressive player or remove them from the situation.
- Reinforce non-aggression, for example, give a fair play award.
- Talk to players to calm them down,
- Promote peer-group pressure within the team.
- Walk away from the situation,
- Apply the rules consistently and fairly.
- Use mental rehearsal or relaxation to lower arousal.
- Point out responsibilities to the team.
- Point out non-aggressive role models.
- Set non-aggressive goals.
- Channel aggression into assertion.
- Apply sanctions immediately.

ACTIVITY

Look at all the methods used to reduce and prevent aggression in sport listed above. Put them in a copy of Table 1, under the headings: Players, Coaches, Officials. (You can list each method more than once in each column.)

Table 1 Strategies used to prevent aggression

PLAYERS	COACHES	OFFICIALS

KEY TERMS

Motivation: A drive to succeed.

Intrinsic motivation: Motivation from within.

Extrinsic motivation: Motivation from an outside source.

Tangible rewards: Rewards that can be touched or held, physical.

Intangible rewards: Non-physical rewards.

STUDY HINT

Motivation is the drive to succeed.

Motivation

Keeping individual sports performers and members of teams motivated is a high priority for sports coaches. **Motivation** keeps the players on track and means that they are persistent and consistent in giving their best in every game.

Motivation is described as being the drive needed to succeed. It is the external stimuli and internal mechanisms that drive and direct behaviour. Motivation can therefore be intrinsic, which means it comes from within the performer and is an inner drive. **Intrinsic motivation** would show itself with a feeling of pride and satisfaction at having completed a task, such as when a climber completes a difficult route or when a runner completes a marathon. The objective having been met gives a sense of self-satisfaction.

Extrinsic motivation comes from an outside source such as the coach or other players; it could even come from spectators cheering you on such as the crowds that support and encourage the runners in the London Marathon or in a 10k running event. Extrinsic motivation can be presented in two forms: tangible and intangible. **Tangible rewards** are those that are physical and can be touched or held, e.g. the certificates achieved by youngsters as they make progress in early swimming classes or the cups and trophies won by professional players as they win the league or cup competition. There is a wide range of rewards on offer! **Intangible rewards** are non-physical and concern the praise and encouragement that could be gained from the coach, the applause from the crowd, the positive comments given by the press, and even the breaking of a personal best time when you may not get a certificate but you know you have done it!

Figure 15 The crowd cheering you on during a running event gives extrinsic motivation

Figure 14 A climber completing a route gains a sense of satisfaction and pride

Coaches and players must be careful not to place too much emphasis on extrinsic rewards, since over-use may lead to a loss in value and incentive. If there is always a trophy or badge on offer, then this might become the norm rather than the exception and players may even compete to get the reward and not for the true value of the game. Extrinsic rewards may also place pressure on players to get the reward and could even lead to cheating as players bend the rules to gain the trophy. Extrinsic motives can undermine the intrinsic reasons for competing; players may start to compete just to get a reward and not for the benefits in exercise, health and skill improvements that competing could bring.

Intrinsic motivation is better because it is stronger and longer lasting. The coach should maintain intrinsic and extrinsic motives by using some of the following tactics and strategies.

- Offering rewards and incentives early on, such as a 'player of the week' award.
- Making the activity fun and enjoyable, perhaps by including mini-games and easier tasks to allow success.
- Pointing out the health benefits of doing the task.
- Breaking the skill down into parts, to allow success on each part.
- Pointing out role models to whom the performer can aspire.
- Making the performer feel responsible for any success achieved by giving praise.
- Attributing success internally, in other words telling the performer that a good result was down to them, they played well!
- Setting goals or targets that are achievable by the performer.
- Using feedback to inspire and correct errors.

Methods of feedback are discussed in Chapter 2.2.

ACTIVITY

Study the list of ways that a coach could use to motivate players in their charge. Suggest which of the methods listed could be used for a novice and which could be used for a more advanced performer.

CHECK YOUR UNDERSTANDING

1 What is motivation?
2 What is the difference between intrinsic motivation and extrinsic motivation?
3 What is the difference between tangible and intangible rewards?
4 Which type of motivation is more permanent?
5 How could a coach ensure that the motivation levels of experienced players in their team are maintained?

SUMMARY

In this chapter we looked at the psychological impact on the individual performer in sport with regard to the theories of aggression, anxiety and motivation.

The theories of aggression continued the theme of nature versus nurture looked at in Chapter 6.1, with the instinct theory and the frustration–aggression hypothesis being in the nature camp and the learned cue and social learning theories taking the nurture stance.

The concepts of anxiety and anxiety types were identified and it was suggested that anxiety can produce negative cognitive (psychological) and somatic (physiological) effects. We then looked at how these effects can be measured and reduced – vital for top-class sports performance!

The various types and methods of motivation were discussed as a means of improving and maintaining drive and effort in players.

While this chapter studied individual performance, in the next chapter the effect of more psychological aspects on performance will be looked at in terms of a collection of individuals: the team!

PRACTICE QUESTIONS

1 Two players from opposing teams both challenge for the same ball during a game. One player gets injured during the clash. This is an example of: (1 mark)

   a) aggression

   b) instrumental aggression

   c) foul play

   d) assertion

2 Sport performers can experience anxiety during performance. Explain the different types of anxiety that can be experienced in sport and use examples to show how these types of anxiety can have a negative effect on performance. (4 marks)

3 Aggression is an unwelcome aspect of team performance. Explain why aggression might occur during team games. (5 marks)

4 To achieve good results, sports performers need to be motivated. Explain the different forms of motivation that may be available to help the sports performer succeed. (4 marks)

Chapter 6.3
Psychological influences on the team

Chapter objectives

After reading this chapter you should be able to:

- Examine the differing psychological effects when others are present during sports performance, based on the model by Zajonc, 1965.
- Understand the changing dynamics of sports groups and how these dynamics can affect results by looking at the psychological concepts of cohesion, the work of the psychologist Steiner and the problems that occur during team performance, such as poor co-ordination and social loafing.
- Discover strategies that coaches and players can use to prevent the negative psychological influences that could hinder team performance, including the principles of effective goal setting.

In this chapter, the individual psychological influences discussed in Chapters 6.1 and 6.2 are taken a little further to look at what happens when individuals have an effect on the team. For example, we have seen how motivation can help individuals; we can now look at how a loss of motivation can cause an effect called social loafing. We have looked at the effects of arousal and anxiety on performance and we can now examine how being watched causes increases in both arousal and anxiety that can influence sports performance and results.

Social facilitation and inhibition

This section looks at the effects of others who might be present and watching when sport is played and those effects are very different.

The theory behind the influence of others on performance was proposed by the psychologist Zajonc (in 1965) and to define the effects of others on performance the following acronym, BEDTOP, is useful: the behavioural effects due to others present.

Memory tools

A definition of social facilitation can be recalled using the phrase 'BEDTOP'.

The behavioural effects due to others present (BEDTOP)

At the Tour de France cycle race that started in Yorkshire in 2014, large crowds were present along almost the whole route. The support and encouragement of the crowd led to an enjoyable experience for the riders, who were top-class professionals. The crowd support helped to bring out the best in the cyclists. Imagine, however, if those cyclists had been beginners – the effect of the large crowd could have made them very nervous and had a damaging effect on their performance.

Figure 1 The crowd at the Yorkshire section of the Tour de France in 2014 had an effect on the cyclists

KEY TERMS

Audience: Those who just watch the event.

Co-actors: Those who are doing the same task but are not involved in direct competition.

Zajonc suggested that in sport there are four types of others who can be present when playing sport. They are:

1 **The audience:** Those people who are watching, either as spectators at the event or as the large TV audience watching national events. Their very presence causes pressure.

Figure 2 The audience watching a snooker match are passive but have an effect on the players

2 **The co-actors:** Those who are doing the same thing at the same time but who might not be in competition, such as the jogger on the opposite side of the road or another cyclist who passes by while out on a training ride.

Figure 3 Coming across a fellow jogger means that you have a met a co-actor

3 **The competitors:** Sometimes called the **competitive co-actors** since they are now in direct competition, e.g. the cyclists in that Tour de France or the runners in a 100-metre competitive race.

Figure 4 The athletes in a 100-m race are fellow competitors

4 **The social reinforcers:** These are the people who have a direct influence on the performance and their presence is a part of the event, such as the coach.

A diagram to show the Zajonc model is given in Figure 6.

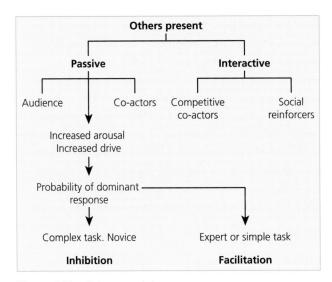

Figure 6 The Zajonc model

The first two types of others present in sport, the audience and the co-actors, are said to be passive in that they do not exert a direct influence on the event but their mere presence causes an increase in arousal – the players are aware of being watched! The competitors and the social reinforcers are more actively involved in the event and can give encouragement, advice or cause distractions.

The response of the sports performer to being watched depends very much on their level of experience and on the degree of difficulty of the skill being undertaken. Put simply, a beginner will experience anxiety and over-arousal when being watched and will perhaps not be able to cope with the pressure from the crowd, causing a poor execution of skills, or **social inhibition**. An expert will be able to cope with the demands of the crowd and will be motivated and encouraged by the support: skills performance can be enhanced, known as **social facilitation**.

Figure 5 The coach watching the game has a direct influence on the outcome: a social reinforcer

In addition, if the skill being performed is simple, then the presence of co-actors can help. Trying to be the last person to stop when doing sit-ups with a group could be an example – you don't want to be the first one to give in!

When complex skills are being performed, the presence of others can have a negative effect. It is suggested that since the complex skill requires the interpretation of numerous items of information, then the ability to process this information is reduced when under stress. Increased levels of arousal can mean that the performer is unable to deal with a lot of information – as arousal levels increase, then the ability to process information decreases.

Performance and the dominant response

There is a strong link between drive theory and the effects of an audience because the presence of others has the immediate effect of increasing the level of arousal. As discussed in Chapter 6.1 on arousal, the drive theory explains how increased arousal affects performance.

Zajonc suggested that if the performer is an expert, it is likely that the responses they use are well learned and familiar to them. When performing in the presence of others, such well-learned responses are performed automatically, with ease, and there is no pressure on the performer. The response is made simple because it can be done without much thought or attention. The response will be correct, even when performed under pressure. Indeed the effect of the crowd may be to lift the performer and promote facilitation. When Andy Murray won at Wimbledon in 2013, he engaged in long rallies with his opponent, Novak Djokovic, during which the shots made were consistently accurate, and the home crowd facilitated his efforts.

On the other hand, a novice is unlikely to have learned responses that are performed automatically and may not even be able to identify the correct response and may produce an incorrect action. Therefore, responses are made complex as the novice uses a lot of attention to find the right answer and the effect of the crowd is to add to this pressure and cause inhibition.

A novice cricketer might be unable to make the right choice of shot to play when attempting to hit the ball thrown by a more experienced bowler in front of a crowd. Increased pressure and arousal may result in a very short innings!

Evaluation apprehension

Sometimes the people who are watching may be considered by the performer to be important or experts in the sport. Imagine being watched by a professional scout or by a top-class coach while playing in a game. The effects of the audience would be intense: it could really motivate the performer to play well but it could also increase anxiety and arousal to very high levels, meaning that there is a significant reduction in performance, or inhibition. The perception of the players when someone significant is watching is that, not only are they being observed, but in addition there is a judgement being made on the performance. This is called **evaluation apprehension**, defined as the perceived fear of being judged.

Evaluation apprehension can occur if the people watching are known to the player. If your family have watched you when you took part in sport, it may be that you expected some comments from them on your performance after the event! Evaluation apprehension can also be more acute if the performer is feeling less confident about the outcome, since they may already be feeling

KEY TERM

Evaluation apprehension: The perceived fear of being judged.

a little unsure, in addition to the pressure from an expert audience. Indeed, if the audience is seen to be expert or knowledgeable, such as a scout from a professional club, or the audience is critical, then the effects of evaluation apprehension could be worse. An audience that just watches the event and makes no comment may cause a real sense of unease in the performer, while an openly critical audience can add to the pressure.

In the example of Andy Murray, he is often watched by his mother Judy: it could be assumed that mum evaluates his performance.

Figure 7 When parents watch their children play sport, it may cause evaluation apprehension

Preventing social inhibition

To limit the effects of social inhibition and evaluation apprehension, there are some strategies that the coach and player can employ. These are:

1 **Getting the players familiar with playing in front of a crowd.**
   The coach should allow the team to train with the distraction of an audience so that they get used to being watched – a concept called familiarisation. In some team sports, young players can often be taken to the game by parents who will then stay and watch, but perhaps the coach could add a few more audience members to the list and get some unfamiliar faces to add their support. In this way, the audience is built up gradually so that the players get used to being watched and learn to cope with it.

2 **Gradually introducing evaluation.**
   Not only should the audience be built up gradually, but so should the level of assessment and evaluation of the performance. Informal team chats about the game and asking the players what they thought of their performance could be a starting point. This may lead to formal assessment sheets, statistics and one-on-one interviews, as the players become more experienced, so that their performance comes under review and they can deal with such scrutiny. Support from team mates and other peer groups helps to encourage players through games when a large crowd is present. The coach could even try to reduce the importance of the event, if possible, perhaps by stating, for example, that the league title does not depend solely on this game and a loss or draw would not be disastrous!

3 **Improving focus and concentration.**
   The players could try to really focus on the game and not the audience so they focus attention on the things that matter and not the things that are irrelevant. They may use the process of selective attention to good effect.

ACTIVITY

Think back to your early years of playing sport. How did you feel when someone you knew came to watch? Did that audience help or hinder your performance?

ACTIVITY

Make a list of the ways a coach or player could reduce the effects of social inhibition. Check your list against the points above.

CHECK YOUR UNDERSTANDING

1 Using examples, identify the four types of others, according to Zajonc, who could be present at a sporting event.
2 What is evaluation apprehension?
3 What strategies could a coach use to limit the effects of evaluation apprehension?
4 How does drive theory help explain the effects of an audience on performance?

Group dynamics

A team is more than just a group of individuals. Those individuals have to work together to achieve a goal and they may have to perform different functions such as attacker or defender to make the team unit complete. A team has the following characteristics:

- **A collective identity:** This means that the team can be recognised easily since they are usually wearing the same colour kit. Often team members will feel a strong affiliation to the team and gain a sense of pride when they wear the team clothing on the way to games. This affiliation is important to give motivation and a sense of belonging to the team.

Figure 8 A team is identified by their kit. It seems they belong together!

- **Interaction:** The team members should operate in their own role successfully and also be able to link this role with other members of the team. Interaction can be seen as the way that team players work together to complete a task. In netball, for example, the defence and central players may each mark a specific opponent and also communicate with each other to cover any opposition attacks.

- **Communication:** To help with interaction, the individual players in the team should talk to each other and communicate non-verbally in the way that rugby players would use a coded call or a hand signal to indicate where the ball is being thrown at the 'line out'.

Figure 9 At a line out in Rugby Union, players must communicate their calls

- **A shared goal or purpose:** The prospect of achieving success is what often keeps players in the team and working for each other. All the players should want to aim for the same goal to have maximum motivation.

When the team forms and as the characteristics mentioned above begin to develop, the psychologist Tuckman (1965) suggests there are four stages of group formation through which the group must pass in order to start working as a unit. Tuckman's theory is based on the study of groups and in sport, a group could be classed as a sports team. The stages of group formation are:

1 **Forming:** In this short first stage, the group comes together and gets to know each other, with individuals often finding out how they feel about the team and if they think they will fit in. An assessment is made on the strengths of the individual compared to the strengths of others in the group.

2 **Storming:** This is a stage of potential conflict when individuals may compete with others to establish position, status or role in the team. It may be that two players are competing for the same position and the coach or captain should resolve such issues as quickly as possible to ensure players may accept an alternative. During 2015, Wayne Rooney, a striker for Manchester United, often accepted the role of midfield player in order to help the team play other new strikers in their preferred roles.

3 **Norming:** Once conflicts have been resolved, the team begins to settle down and co-operate, with the intention of achieving their goals. Group standards are accepted and the cohesion of the team develops.

4 **Performing:** In this stage, all the players are now interactive and working together to achieve their goals. The team members support each other and understand their role in the team.

The length of time it takes to complete this process can vary, depending on the size of the group, the difficulty of the task and the experience of the players. Some club teams are established and can welcome new players quickly, going through the stages in a short time span. Representative teams (one in which a player represents the county or area) and international teams may take longer since the players have to learn unfamiliar tactics and new roles within a limited time span during infrequent meetings.

Sometimes in sport there are teams that have the best players and the best facilities and yet they under-perform and do not achieve the results of which they are capable. Think of the England International football team in the World Cup of 2014 – they did not even qualify for the final stages of the tournament. On the other hand, there are occasions in sport when a team achieves unexpected success with players of less than international standard. Perhaps the FA cup success of Wigan who beat Arsenal in the 2013 final is an example. The reasons behind such sporting surprises are to do with how the players work together, how they are motivated and how they integrate as a team. How do the parts become whole?

In this section, the factors and influences on the team and its players that can influence performance in a positive and negative way are looked at. This integration of team members and how they work together is called the **cohesion key**. In Chapter 6.1, the influence of positive attitudes on cohesion was examined; other influences on cohesion are studied here.

ACTIVITY

Provide a phrase that summarises each of the four stages of group formation.

Figure 10 Wayne Rooney accepted a midfield role to help the team

STUDY HINTS

Don't just name the four stages of group formation. Use a key phrase to explain each stage. For example, forming means getting to know others in the group.

Figure 11 Wigan lifting the FA Cup in 2013 was a result of working together as a team

Figure 12 The British 4x400-m relay team dropped the baton in the 2011 European Championships – an example of poor co-ordination and cohesion

Cohesion in sport

Cohesion is the tendency of members of the team to work together to achieve what they want to achieve. Some psychologists argue that the team has to be cohesive in order to achieve any success; others argue that cohesion will develop as the team becomes successful. Regardless of whether cohesion or success comes first, there is little doubt that cohesion is needed for the team to achieve their aims. Cohesion looks at the forces acting on the team members that help to keep the team integrated and on task. In some sports, the cohesion involves every team member working hard at the same thing, as in rowing when all the crew must literally pull together! This is **co-action**. In other sports, each player may have a different role and this role must be integrated with the roles of the other team members. This is **interaction**.

Figure 13 Rowing is an example of co-active cohesion

There are influences on the team members that will help them to work together. These influences were summarised by the psychologist, Carron, who stipulated that there were four main influences on the team; these are known as **Carron's antecedents**, or the things that must be in place for cohesion to be effective. Carron's antecedents are not, at the time of writing, directly on the specification, but they are a useful way of looking at the influences on cohesion, hence the inclusion here. Carron's antecedents are:

1   **Environmental factors:** These include the size of group and the time available. The longer the group are together, the more time they will have to learn each other's roles. The size and structure of the group can effect cohesion because the larger the group, the better the chance of more productivity. But with a large group, there is more chance of **social loafing** and the **Ringlemann effect** developing (see pages 201–2)! Motivation may be reduced in a larger group. A mix of age and gender may reduce cohesion and the desire to reach common goals. When the group gets too large, a sub-division or 'clique' can form.

2   **Personal factors:** This refers to the similarity of group members in terms of their aspirations, their opinions and values, whether they are happy with the role they play in the team and even how fit they are.

3   **Leadership factors:** The leadership style chosen by the coach or captain is important here, as is how the captain or coach gets on with the others in the team. Tracey Neville was appointed coach to the England netball team in 2015 since she has excellent leadership qualities.

4   **Team factors:** Team success is important here and the more success is achieved and the more each team member wants to be successful, the higher cohesion will be. The team will have experience of both wins and losses and the experience gained from these results is useful in learning for future games. The longer the team has been together, the more chance of cohesion. Sometimes if the team is threatened from another group, perhaps with a statement suggesting that they are 'going to thrash us, such threats tend to bind the team in response and eliminate any cliques within the team. The Barcelona football team has a long history of success in Spain and Europe, despite many attempts to beat them!

Figure 14 Netball is an example of interactive cohesion

KEY TERM

Carron's antecedents: The factors that might influence cohesion.

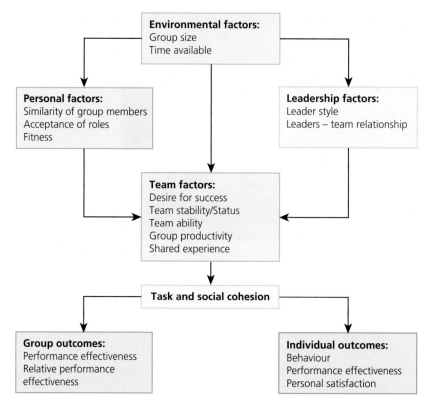

Figure 15 A model of Carron's antecedents and how they affect cohesion

Task and social cohesion

There are two types of cohesion.

1 **Task cohesion** looks at the end result and involves every player working together to achieve the goal, either by doing their own role well, so that the other team members can also make their contribution, or by working hard, along with everyone else on the task.

2 **Social cohesion** looks at the interaction of the individuals in the team and how they work with each other. It may be that there is a degree of trust in each other's ability and that there is support for each team member. They may even socialise with each other away from the game. As an example, the American gymnast Nicole Anderson was quoted as saying, 'I had a couple of friends from cliques at school but my true friends were my gymnastic team mates. I grew up competing with them for ten tears.'

In terms of results, it is better if the team has both task and social cohesion. Social cohesion will help the team to be interactive and will help communication and team spirit, but social cohesion can be a negative influence on the group. It might produce sub-groups or 'cliques' that mean some members of the team will not co-operate, or at training they may not contribute to team questions or suggestions on tactics. It may be that outside of team training and playing, some members of the team may not see each other. When social cohesion is strong, members of the team may socialise outside of the team environment.

Task cohesion, however, is really important and can over-ride the problems of social cohesion. The performance and results of the team may still be good, even if players do not socialise, but without task cohesion those results would be poor. There may be members of a team who do not get on socially but once out on the field of play, they will work hard for the cause. The players may not be top-class elite performers but the desire for success drives the team towards achieving their goals. Task cohesion provides motivation in the sense that all members of the team will work hard to win the cup or league title – the prize on offer becomes more important than any social differences.

STUDY HINT

In any definition of cohesion, remember to include both task and social cohesion in your answer.

Figure 16 Winning a title might indicate strong task cohesion, as shown by the British cycling track pursuit team at the 2012 Olympics

Steiner model of team performance

Steiner (1972) proposed that the results of group efforts could be based on an equation that sums up the influences on cohesion. The thinking behind the equation is that it is not always the case that having the best players produces the best results – those players have to be moulded by the coach into a cohesive unit and maintain levels of motivation.

The Steiner model is given in Figure 17.

Actual productivity = Potential productivity − Losses due to faulty processes

Figure 17 The Steiner model

The **actual productivity** looks at the performance of the **team** at a given time, at the end of the game. It is the result, the end outcome: a win, a loss or a draw.

The **potential productivity** concerns the team's best possible outcome that could happen if everything went perfectly during the game. Group potential is affected by the skill level and ability of the players compared to the opponents and how difficult the task ahead may be. Sometimes having the very best players and best facilities for practice does not mean that the team will be victorious. The players need to integrate and interact as a team – they need cohesion! In the example of the 2014 Football World Cup, the England team hopefully selected the best players and the team were faced with difficult group opponents in Italy, but were still expected to qualify for the final stages of the competition. However, the team under-performed and did not live up to expectations or potential by failing to win a game!

KEY TERMS

Actual productivity: The outcome of group performance.

Team: A group that has interaction, shared goals, an identity and communication.

Potential productivity: The best performance based on player ability and group resources.

Figure 18 England World Cup team in 2014 showed poor cohesion

The faulty processes

The **faulty processes** are simply the things that go wrong! They are the factors which prevent the team from reaching its true potential and fall into two types: co-ordination problems and motivational problems.

Co-ordination problems occur when players in the team fail to listen to the coach's instructions or employ the incorrect tactics. For example, the players may have been told to be patient in their approach to attacking situations during a hockey game and pass the ball around before looking for an opportunity. Instead, the players go for more risky long passes which get frequently intercepted! The players in the team might also fail to communicate with each other. For example, two defenders in a rugby game go to tackle the same player, leaving another attacker free to receive a pass because they did not tell each other which player to defend against. The players may also misunderstand their role in the team: perhaps a player assigned to a 'sweeper' role behind the defence in the hockey team keeps venturing too far up field, leaving gaps in the defence.

The motivational problems in the team can affect performance when players suffer from too much or too little arousal or they lose the drive to win, with a resultant reduction in effort and concentration.

Social loafing

Motivation problems can also happen when players begin to feel under-valued and think that their efforts are not being recognised. **Social loafing** is the loss of motivation in individuals within the team due to lack of performance identification – their efforts have gone unnoticed. Players who are social loafers will often coast through the game and even hide behind other team members who they think might cover for them. They tend to take easy options in the game and make a limited contribution to the team cause.

Causes of social loafing

Social loafing may be caused by a lack of confidence when the player does not believe in their ability to compete with the opposition. Players may develop a negative attitude (see Chapter 6.1), perhaps not liking the position they have been selected to play in. The coach or captain may have displayed poor leadership by not offering incentives and reinforcement, such as a player of the match award. Players may therefore think any effort will not be recognised or valued. The players may not understand the role they need to play in the team or they may not accept that role with enthusiasm. Players may even lack fitness and not be able to maintain their role in the team for the whole game. The goals set by the coaches, especially those related to the task, may be too general and lack meaning. The goal of just winning the game is not specific enough – players may need to know more about how their own contribution can help. 'Stop the attacking options to the right' may be more meaningful. The sub-groups or cliques that may form in the team may also affect social loafing.

Liverpool player Mario Balotelli has been described as a social loafer when he seemed to lack motivation during games.

The Ringelmann effect

In a similar concept to social loafing, the study by Ringelmann, completed over a century ago, may still have some significance. A study of tug of war found that the individual effort within the group reduced with increasing group size. Individuals tried hard on the rope pull when their efforts were highlighted but tended to reduce their effort in a team of eight.

Figure 19 Ringelmann based his conclusion on tug of war and found that group performance decreases with group size

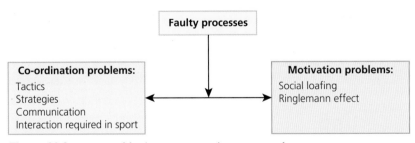

Figure 20 Summary of faulty processes in group performance

Avoiding social loafing

To avoid the negative aspects of social loafing, the coach should make sure that the efforts of the players are recognised and rewarded. This can be done by giving the players specific roles to play in the team, such as specific responsibility for marking a particular player on the opposition. The coach could use statistics such as tackle counts, number of assists or pass completion rates to highlight individual performance. The coach should use a goal-setting strategy, setting goals that are realistic and specific and not just based on the result. Even in defeat, a player can improve on performance!

The coach might use video analysis, a form of sports analytics discussed in Chapter 7.1, to highlight the performance of the individual and use feedback to evaluate and assess that performance. In training, the coach should avoid situations when social loafing could occur by using small-sided games and varying the practice to maintain motivation. The coach should also make sure that conditioning is up to standard so that the players stay fit!

> ### ACTIVITY
>
> #### Promoting cohesion, reducing the effects of social loafing and solving co-ordination problems
>
> Strategies used to achieve the above results include those listed below, some of which are discussed in the previous paragraph and some of which are added here.
>
> - setting individual goals
> - setting more challenging goals
> - involving all players in goal setting
> - giving specific roles within the team and making sure this role is clear and accepted
> - making tactics clear
> - promoting motivation with rewards
> - establishing a group identity
> - using statistics to highlight individual performance
> - using team meetings to resolve conflict
> - maintaining communication with open discussion
> - rewarding exceptional contribution to the team.
>
> Copy and complete Table 1 to suggest which of the above strategies could be used to specifically reduce social loafing and co-ordination problems and promote cohesion. You can use the same strategies more than once.
>
> **Table 1**
>
> | REDUCE SOCIAL LOAFING | REDUCE CO-ORDINATION PROBLEMS | PROMOTE COHESION |
> |---|---|---|
> | | | |
> | | | |
> | | | |

CHECK YOUR UNDERSTANDING

1 What are the features of a team or group?
2 Name and explain the four stages of group formation.
3 What do you understand by the term social loafing?
4 What are the co-ordination problems that can affect team cohesion?
5 What might affect the potential productivity of a sports team?

KEY TERM

Goal setting: Setting targets.

Goal setting

One of the strategies used to help reduce the effects of social loafing and to improve cohesion is for the coach and player to set goals or targets for future reference. **Goal setting** is a strategy used widely in sport since it has a number of benefits for the performer.

Benefits of goal setting

Setting goals improves performance. The benefits of goal setting are:

1 Increasing motivation and making sure that the participants in the sporting activity keep on trying. Players can become what is called task persistent, since there is a target to aim for that requires some effort to

reach, but once the player has succeeded in reaching that target, a sense of pride and satisfaction is experienced. This sense of pride increases intrinsic motivation.

2 Improving confidence since the performer can experience an improvement in technique or in results as the target is being reached.

3 Regulating and sustaining effort. As the player continues to strive to reach a target, they might begin to try a little harder as the goal nears completion. The coach needs to adjust the target to account for a specific competition or event so that a short period of effort is applied in the build-up to competition.

There are different types of goals that a sports performer could use. These are discussed below.

Outcome goals or product goals

These goals concern the results and are success-based. An example might be winning a trophy or making the play-offs at the end of a season. **Outcome goals** need not necessarily be based on winning. An athlete could be set the goal of a top-three finish and if this goal is realistic, then motivation is maintained. The athlete may not be concerned with the manner or technique used in the performance, as long as the goal is reached. Such performances are said to be outcome orientated. However, there is a danger here that the goal may not be achieved and then motivation can be lost; if the athlete is less experienced or less talented, a performance type goal may be best. Outcome goals involve a comparison with others and if the athlete begins to think they are not as good as other competitors, motivation may be lost. To avoid such social comparisons, it may again be important to use a performance goal – see below.

KEY TERM

Outcome goal: A goal set against the performance of others and based on a result.

Figure 21 Goals do not have to be about winning: a personal best or improvement in technique can be more effective. Such goals are more task related

Task-orientated goals

Goals based on the task are not just about winning. **Task-orientated goals** are concerned with improvements in technique or performance. This means that an athlete could still achieve their goal, even if they do not win the race, because their performance or technique has improved to the target set. Motivation is still maintained when performance or process goals are used: a personal best time can still be achieved when finishing third! The athlete does not compare against others but makes an evaluation based on their own past performances.

KEY TERM

Task-orientated goal: Getting a better performance.

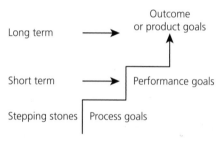

Figure 23 Goal-setting summary

Performance goals

Performance goals are judged against other previous performances in an attempt to improve personal achievements, rather than being based on a comparison with others; for example, achieving a personal best time in swimming. To achieve this time, it might be appropriate to break down the performance into techniques used at various parts of the race. A better turn, a faster reaction to the starter and a better arm action may be part of the process and involve the use of specific process goals.

Process goals

Process goals are concerned with improvements in technique. For example, to achieve that personal best time, a swimmer might improve their techniques on the arm action and at the start of the race. The swimmer could work on aspects of each technique, using training drills and practice methods. The process goals can be used as a base so that a better performance can be achieved. Improved technique should result in better performance.

Figure 22 A swimmer may improve their technique at the start of a race as a process goal

Goals set by a player should include both process and performance goals and not just be focused on the outcome. If goals are only concerned with the end result, then motivation might be lost because the performer perceives the win as too difficult to achieve. Goals should focus on personal improvement and technique and be more performance-based. In a Marathon, there is only one winner but a chance for everyone to achieve a personal best.

Performance goals reduce anxiety in competition and provide more consistent motivation. Outcome goals focus on gaining a prize and provide a basis for comparison – they are more likely to cause stress, particularly if the prize is not gained. Short-term goals provide a means for reassurance.

Factors to consider when setting goals

In order to make goal setting effective, coaches and players should take into account the following principles.

The SMARTER principle

According to the National Coaching Foundation, coaches and performers should ensure that goals are:

- **Specific:** Goals should be clear and precise, perhaps using data. These goals should be specific to the performer and the sport. These goals should be clear and relevant to improve specific aspects of the performance. An example from rugby: improving your defence is too general, whereas improving your left shoulder tackles by making firmer contact is a specific goal.

Figure 24 A rugby tackle could be a specific target to improve a player's defence

- **Measured:** Some form of assessment should occur to aid motivation. The performer should have access to statistics. Distances, times or numbers of passes are examples. Measurement allows the performer to see how much progress is being made towards completing the goal. In sports such as gymnastics, when there is a judgement to be made on the performance by the coach, then any feedback given should be precise to allow progress to be measured.

- **Achievable:** The performer should be able to reach their goal. By reaching the target with a controlled amount of effort, motivation and self-satisfaction are improved and the willingness to extend the target can be achieved.

- **Realistic:** The goals should be within reach to promote motivation and sustain effort, yet not too difficult so that they are impossible to reach. Goals should be achievable with effort so that the player gains satisfaction and confidence from reaching them. If the goal set is too difficult, it may cause anxiety.

- **Time-bound:** Short-term and long-term steps should be clearly defined so that there is a clear deadline for coach and player to assess if the goal has been reached. Player and coach can then gauge progress and keep motivation levels high.

- **Evaluate:** The performer and coach should evaluate how and when the goal was achieved so that future attempts at reaching targets can be assessed. The coach and player should consider the methods that worked well and the methods that were not so successful, so that only the best ways to succeed are used in the future.

- **Re-do:** If the goal has not been reached, if progress is slow or after evaluation the performer thinks that something could have been done better, do it again! The target can be adjusted to help ensure success.

Figure 25 Feedback given to a gymnast should be precise to allow performance to be measured

Table 2 Examples of goal setting

Goal-setting principle	Description	Example
Specific	Positional and sports specific	A netball centre aiming to improve agility
Measured	Assessed with statistics or scores	A swimmer aiming to reduce their 50-metre freestyle time by 0.2 seconds
Achievable	Within reach with effort	A team player aiming to increase the number of tackles made each game
Realistic	Within performer ability	A high jumper who can already jump 1.20m could aim for 1.25m
Time-bound	How long? Deadlines	A team aiming to be in the top four of the league halfway through the season
Evaluate	Look at successes and failures	The team did not quite make the top four, despite excellent attacking play, because of poor defending
Re-do	Re-visit the failures	Aim to be in the top four at the three-quarter point in the season, with improved defensive techniques

ACTIVITY

Imagine you are a swimmer with the long-term goal of trying to achieve a qualifying time for the Regional Finals. What short-term goals could you set to help achieve your aims?

CHECK YOUR UNDERSTANDING

1 What are the benefits of goal setting?
2 Name three types of goals.
3 Why could goals that are set just on winning have a negative impact on performance?

SUMMARY

In this chapter the psychological influences that make team performance successful and unsuccessful have been studied. It seems that sports psychology is a really important consideration for sports coaches since we have seen how it can both help and hinder performance.

The effects of others being present when sport is taking place can either facilitate or inhibit performance, according to the theory of Zajonc.

In terms of team dynamics, cohesion can really help a team become successful, while lack of cohesion, according to Steiner, can have a negative effect on performance, with the influence of social loafing and co-ordination problems affecting the team work ethic.

Goal setting is a method used by coaches and players to improve performance outcomes, taking into account the SMARTER principles.

The strategies discussed here will help to improve rather than hinder performance and these form a major role in using sports psychology to the advantage of players and coaches.

PRACTICE QUESTIONS

1 According to Zajonc, the crowd cheering on their team during a match is best described in terms of the type of others present as: (1 mark)

   a) co-actors

   b) social reinforcers

   c) audience

   d) competitors

2 What do you understand by the term 'evaluation apprehension'? Explain how the concept of evaluation apprehension can affect performance. (3 marks)

3 Steiner suggested that the relationship between the individual members of a team and their overall performance may be expressed as:

   Actual productivity = Potential productivity – Losses due to faulty process

   Explain the terms 'actual productivity' and 'potential productivity' and the factors that might affect them. (3 marks)

4 Suggest potential causes of the losses due to faulty group processes. (4 marks)

5 Team leaders set goals to motivate their teams. What are the characteristics of effective goal setting? (4 marks)

Chapter 7
The role of technology in physical activity and sport

Chapter objectives

After reading this chapter you should be able to:

- Gain an overview of the use of technology in data collection, including an understanding of key terms including sports analytics; quantitative and qualitative; objective and subjective; and ensuring validity and reliability in data collection.
- Understand the use of video and analysis programmes in physical activity and sport.
- Understand testing and recording equipment in physical activity and sport, e.g. the metabolic cart for indirect calorimetry.
- Understand how GPS and motion-tracking software and hardware are being used in physical activity and sport.
- Understand how to maintain data integrity when using technology.

Use of technology in data collection

Some key terms defined and applied

High quality **research** is vital to understanding all aspects of sport, exercise and health. When undertaking research and collecting information using technology, it is important that you are able to understand some important terms you might come across during your studies of data collection and analysis, as outlined and explained below.

KEY TERMS

Research: A systematic process of investigation and study carried out with the aim of advancing knowledge.

Sports analytics: The analysis of sports data using analytical tools and methods for data to be subjected to analytical procedures in order to try to improve results.

At the outset of this chapter it is important that you are able to understand the term **sports analytics**, as defined above. It is also useful to be able to relate such analytics to current examples of its usage in the world of sport, a number of which will be outlined later in this chapter. In cricket, it can be used to study and give detailed averages and 'tendencies or potential weaknesses' of opponents which bowlers can look to exploit. Opta is a company that has statisticians gathering and analysing sporting data collected in order to create the best predictions possible. Professional sports such as cricket and football have embraced companies such as Opta in their quest to fine-tune and optimise performance, give detailed analysis on opponents, as well as help in the effective recruitment of new talent.

There are a number of other terms in addition to sports analytics identified in the specification for this area of the syllabus (e.g. the role of technology in performance evaluation and sport).

Technology is being used in sport and physical activity to collect a variety of different types of data suitable for different requirements, aiming to ensure it is as reliable, valid and objective as possible, as explained below.

Quantitative and qualitative research (see also Chapter 4.2)

Quantitative research is a formal, objective and systematic process used to gather **quantitative data** (i.e. factual information and numerical data). Most fitness tests use quantitative data. (e.g. the VO_2 max test on a treadmill).

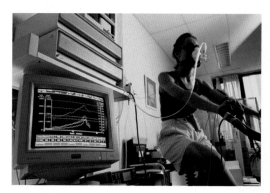

Figure 1 The VO_2 max test in action

Qualitative research is generally focused on words as opposed to numbers. The **qualitative data** collected is subjective as it looks at feelings, opinions and emotions (e.g. a group of coaches expressing an opinion when judging a gymnast performing a competitive routine).

Examples of gathering **quantitative data** in sport in order to try to prove a hypothesis being tested include the following.

● In sport psychology, the potential positive link between motivational self-talk and its relationship to improving self-paced skills (e.g. a golf putt).

● In exercise psychology, research of a quantitative nature (e.g. on a numerical scale) could compare the relative effect of different environments on exercisers' moods (e.g. cycle trails in wooded areas versus cycling lanes in urban areas).

Qualitative research data is used to try to gain a better understanding of a participant's experiences. In sport psychology, qualitative methodology such as open-ended questions with focus groups can be used to explore the feelings of anxiety among athletes prior to performance at major sporting competitions. In exercise psychology, in-depth interviews could be used to help establish whether more frequent exercisers have a more accurate understanding of their injuries than less frequent exercisers.

Objective and subjective (see also Chapter 4.2)

Objective data is information received based on facts. It is measurable and observable and therefore highly suitable or meaningful for decision making when feeding back to sports performers (e.g. performance analysis of a swimmer at the English Institute of Sport).

Subjective data is information based on personal opinions, assumptions, interpretations, emotions and beliefs. With an emphasis on personal opinions, it is seen as less suitable or meaningful when feeding back to performers (e.g. a parent talking to their child at half time during a hockey match, giving their opinion of their performance in the first half!).

Validity and reliability

Data collection when using technology should be both valid as well as reliable.

Validity

To assess the **validity** of data collection an important question to ask is:

Does the data collected measure exactly what it sets out to do?

Reliability

Reliability is when the data collected is consistent and similar results are achieved when the data collection process is repeated at a later date. In quantitative research, reliability can be when one researcher conducting the same test (e.g. skinfold measurements) on the same individual on a number of occasions and getting the same or very similar results. Alternatively, it can be different researchers conducting the same test on the same individual and getting the same or very similar results.

In qualitative research, reliability relates to the same researcher placing results into the same categories on different occasions, or different researchers placing results into the same or similar categories. Reliability can be affected by errors that occur when researchers do not know how to use equipment correctly, e.g. use of skin-fold calipers when assessing body composition. Accuracy can also be affected by poorly maintained equipment, e.g. weighing devices giving initial incorrect readings which affect calculations e.g. body mass index (BMI).

The validity of data is pre-requisite to data reliability. If data is not valid, then reliability is questionable. In other words, if data collected is *not* valid, there is little or no point in discussing reliability because data validity is required before reliability can be considered in any reasonable way.

Video and analysis programmes

Coaches and athletes are using video, DVD, or digital technology as a medium more frequently to analyse individual technique, as well as team performances. At an individual level, video analysis can also be used to analyse gait and biomechanical aspects of performance, with any information gained also potentially able to help in injury rehabilitation. (See Chapter 5.1 for a more detailed coverage of biomechanics in sport.)

KEY TERMS

Objective data: Fact-based information which is measurable and usable (e.g. the level achieved on the multi-stage fitness test which links to a VO_2 max score).

Subjective data: Data based on personal opinion which is less measurable and often less useable!

STUDY HINT

Validity can also relate to the extent to which inferences, conclusions and decisions made on the basis of data are appropriate and meaningful.

KEY TERMS

Validity: Refers to the degree to which the data collected actually measures what it claims to measure.

Reliability: Refers to the degree to which data collection is consistent and stable over time.

Figure 2 Motion analysis picture of a golfer

KEY TERM

Video motion analysis: A technique used to get information about moving objects from video.

KEY TERM

Performance analysis (PA): The provision of objective feedback to a performer who is trying to get a positive change in performance. (Feedback can be gained on a variety of performance indicators including: the number of passes made; pass completion success rates; distance run in kilometres; number of shots attempted; number of shots on target, etc.)

Video motion analysis usually involves a high-speed camera and a computer with software allowing frame-by-frame playback of the footage on video. It is useful in the individual analysis of technical performance (e.g. to identify and correct problems with an athlete's technique such as the angle of release when throwing a shot; or ball release velocity and arc of travel when fielding and throwing in cricket; or the head and body position when taking a shot at goal in football). Such analysis can take place either immediately after performance (e.g. at the side of a track) or it can be undertaken in a more controlled laboratory environment.

The process of motion analysis has developed into two distinct sport science disciplines:

● **Notational match analysis**: used to record aspects of individual or team performance.
● **Biomechanics**: used to analyse the sporting impact of body movements. (This is sometimes called kinematics.)

The two disciplines use similar methods to collect data and both rely on IT for data analysis. The main thing they have in common is the use of **measured observation (i.e. quantitative analysis)** during or after an event to **quantify performance** in an accurate, reliable and valid way.

An English Institute of Sport (EIS) report has shown that, on average, athletes and coaches can only recall about 30 per cent of performance correctly, so performance analysis can help us with the other 70 per cent. So you can tell the athlete what actually happened, as opposed to what they thought had happened!

Performance analysis (PA) is now acknowledged as an important aid to performance enhancement at all levels and failure to use it might result in poor immediate decisions being made (e.g. in competition), as well as in the longer term in relation to an athlete's training programme.

There are a variety of PA techniques used by coaches and sport scientists to provide them with task, performance and physiological data. Within a training environment, immediate visual feedback software is useful to provide images pre- and post-training feedback for the athlete and coach to compare. (See Chapter 2.2 for further information on types of feedback.)

In a competitive environment, the coach and performer might look at the stats of their opponent(s) before discussing the data, alongside other past experiences against this opposition, to come up with a game-plan to win (using particular strategies/tactics to outwit their opponents).

CHECK YOUR UNDERSTANDING
Identify three potential problems a sports coach might have if they choose not to use video analysis programmes, but rely instead on their own observation and analysis skills.

ACTIVITY

Visit one of the following links to find out more about PA and motion analysis software used in sport.
Dartfish: www.dartfish.com
Dartfish is video software which enables individuals to view, edit and analyse videos of technique, e.g. running style or high jump performance in athletics.
Upmygame: www.upmygame.com
Upmygame is a video analysis app you can use to connect with top coaches which gives you access to drills, practices, etc. which can be used to improve your own technique or someone you are coaching.
Prozone: www.prozonesports.com
Prozone can be used to analyse and improve player performance via use of high definition cameras which provide detailed performer/team analysis in football. It provides a service to 'tag' or 'code' the video with a player's actions, and delivers results to the coach/performer after the match via PA software (e.g. number of successful tackles made).

STUDY HINT

The main purpose of motion analysis is to improve individual and/or team performance, as well as analyse opposition patterns of play to gain a tactical advantage.

With rapid advances in IT and digital photography, PA is increasingly being used by the world's top sports performers and coaches to maximise performance. PA has to prove its use as an accurate, valid and reliable record of performance by gaining systematic observations that can be analysed with a view to bringing about positive change in performance. Examples of its use include notational match analysis to record individual and team performance (e.g. in basketball, the ratio of shots taken to baskets scored; in netball, the identification of strengths and weaknesses of an individual player to provide a technical focus for future training sessions).

STUDY HINTS

If you have access to motion analysis software at your school, college or sports club, it might be useful to help with your coursework by analysing in detail your technique or performance (in the role of performer) or the technique or performance of someone else (in the role of a coach).

ACTIVITY

Choose an invasion game where opponents are in direct competition with one another (e.g. hockey, netball, rugby, football, basketball, etc.) and attempt to design and complete your own simple player analysis. Focus on one player involved in the match and gather data on one aspect of skill or technique (e.g. passing) used in the activity selected.

You can look at the number of passes made in a set time period. This can then be expressed as a ratio or percentage of successful passes during the time observed.

CHECK YOUR UNDERSTANDING

Imagine you are a basketball coach and you have the shooting data in Table 1 available on your main two offensive players. This information can be used to help feed back to the players concerned, as well as inform future shooting strategies.

1 Use the data in Table 1 to explain which player (i.e. Player 1 or Player 2) has been the most successful at shooting.
2 What other additional information would you need to consider when making your judgement on the relative shooting capabilities of Player 1 and Player 2?
3 How could you use the data to inform your offensive players shooting strategies in their next match?

Table 1 Basketball shooting data

	NO. OF LAY UPS ATTEMPTED	NO. OF LAY UPS SCORED	NO. OF SET SHOTS IN KEY ATTEMPTED	NO. OF SET SHOTS IN KEY SCORED	NO. OF 3-POINT SHOOTING ATTEMPTS	NO. OF SUCCESSFUL 3-POINT SHOTS
Player 1	5	5	4	3	4	1
Player 2	5	4	5	3	4	1

Testing and recording equipment

An overview of indirect calorimetry and metabolic cart

Indirect calorimetry is a technique where headgear is attached to a subject while they breathe for a specific amount of time. Their inspired and expired gas flows, volumes and concentrations of O_2 and CO_2 are all measured. It therefore involves the continuous measurement of oxygen consumption and carbon dioxide production. It is a non-invasive technique and is regarded as being relatively accurate.

The equipment used when measuring indirect calorimetry is also known as a **metabolic cart**.

A metabolic cart is an electronic medical tool used to measure the body's metabolism through the amount of heat produced when the body is at rest. The metabolic cart uses a process called **calorimetry** to get this measurement. The result can help tell doctors more about a person's overall health condition.

The various parts of the device, which include a computer system, monitor, and breathing tubes, are typically mounted together on a mobile push cart, hence the name, which can easily be moved from one room to another. It uses two factors to calculate the heat production. One is the intake of oxygen for the body. The other is the output of carbon dioxide. These two figures will provide the result for the metabolic cart, which is generally measured as resting energy expenditure (REE). The REE for a patient can vary quite a bit. The results can change according to a range of conditions. Between individuals, the REE changes with regard to a person's overall weight or height to weight ratio. Age and gender can also influence the result of this test. In addition, the chemistry of the body in response to various drugs will change the outcome.

KEY TERMS

Indirect calorimetry: The measurement of the amount of heat/energy generated in an oxidation reaction by determining the intake or consumption of oxygen or by measuring the amount of carbon dioxide released and translating these quantities into a heat equivalent.

Metabolic cart: A device which works by attaching headgear to a subject while they breathe a specific amount of oxygen over a period of time.

Calorimetry: Measurement of the heat/energy eliminated or stored in any system.

Therefore due to average differences in size, it is lower in women when compared to men. Smoking and drugs such as amphetamines can both increase someone's REE.

Memory tools

Resting energy expenditure (REE): The amount of energy, usually expressed in Kcal, required for a 24-hour period by the body during rest.

Indirect calorimetry and use of a metabolic cart can therefore help individuals:

- To determine their energy requirements and response to nutrition over time.
- To calculate energy expenditure which allows determination of nutritional requirements/caloric needs.
- Who are classified/potentially classified as obese.
- In the calculation of their REE, which helps medical staff determine the amount of food and nutrition needed.

Possible difficulties or sources of error affecting the validity and reliability of using indirect calorimetry via a metabolic cart include:

- Inaccuracies from air leaks.
- Possible inaccuracies from measurement/recording errors.
- Difficult to use on children.
- Overfeeding/underfeeding may occur based on results received.
- Single snap shots are worse than 'average results/studies' over a longer period of time.
- The process actually measures consumption, not needs.

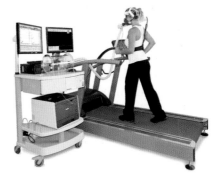

Figure 3 A metabolic cart in use

> **CHECK YOUR UNDERSTANDING**
> Identify different reasons for individual variations in an individual's REE over a period of time.

Use of GPS and motion-tracking software and hardware

GPS software tracking systems are very useful when helping coaches monitor players during matches, as well as in training. Such systems give coaches a vast amount of information immediately, at the touch of a button on a computer! They track the speed, distance and direction of individuals being monitored.

GPS can also provide data which helps improve performance via monitoring success rates in technical performance. In high contact sports (e.g. rugby) it can measure the impact in 'G' forces. It can also help coaches to make objective decisions about possible replacements and substitutions. This can help decrease the risk of injury as GPS can help gauge a performer's fatigue level. If a performer is recovering from injury, GPS can be used to manage the workload during their rehabilitation.

GPS technology has recently entered into the world of football and many believe it will become increasingly popular in the coming years. For footballers to stay competitive and reach their goals, they have to work harder than their competition. This can be made easier for them by using GPS tracking. In essence, the GPS tracking of players today is used to gather meaningful data on different aspects of a player's performance. GPS tracking of players allows the measurement and monitoring of a player's speed and distance covered during a game or a training session. GPS tracking is also used to measure a player's heart rate, pace, recovery time and the amount of

KEY TERMS

Software and hardware: Computer **software** is any set of machine-readable instructions which direct a computer's processor to perform specific operations. Computer **hardware** is the physical component of computers.

GPS (Global Positioning System): A space-based navigation system that provides location and time information.

ACTIVITY

Think about and write down three pieces of information a rugby coach might receive from a GPS tracking system during training and matches.

dynamic acceleration. A number of reasons can therefore be given for using GPS technology for player performance and work tracking. These include:

- Makes better use of training time/ensures training meets game demands.
- Improves the tactical analysis undertaken at a club.
- Helps a coach compare player performance and potentially 'pick the best players' for the team based on GPS data.
- Helps to get injured players successfully through rehab at a faster rate.

In addition to the use of GPS to aid elite performer development, it has recently been developed to enable athletes at all levels to benefit from the information which can be gained from the technology. Strava software is just one example of how elite and non-elite athletes alike can improve their performance via the new GPS technologies becoming available.

Such GPS tracking systems involve lots of athletes from all over the world who, alone or together, are working hard and are determined to achieve their best. It helps people to connect, compare and compete with one another via mobile and online apps! GPS technology also lets individuals track their swims, rides and runs on their smartphones or through the use of dedicated GPS devices. It helps them to analyse and quantify their performance and use the data to provide motivation to improve their performance.

Figure 4 Tracking performance via GPS technology

Monitoring data integrity

The overall intent of **data integrity** is to ensure data is entered into the system and recorded exactly as intended and, when retrieved later, to ensure the data is the same as when it was originally recorded.

Data integrity can be compromised in a number of ways, including through:

- human error when data is entered
- errors occurring when data is transmitted from one computer to another
- software bugs or viruses
- hardware malfunction such as disk crashes.

Ways to minimise threats to data integrity include:

- regularly backing-up data
- controlling access to data and protecting against malicious intent via security mechanisms

KEY TERMS

Data integrity: Maintaining and ensuring the accuracy and consistency of stored data over its entire lifetime.

Data integrity using sport analytics: Refers to the validity of data (i.e. its relevance/meaningfulness).

- designing interfaces which prevent the input of invalid data; taking care when entering data
- using error detection and correction software when transmitting data
- not leaving a computer unattended for anyone to access.

SUMMARY

As a result of studying this section, you should be able to explain, using practical examples in sport or physical activity, how technology and video and analysis programmes, as well as GPS and motion-tracking software, can all be used to help collect data to inform and improve performance. You should also understand how such data can be collected to ensure objectivity, validity and reliability.

In addition, you should be able to understand how a metabolic cart can be used to measure a person's calorimetry at rest and how such a measurement can be used to help gain an understanding of an individual's overall level of health and fitness.

PRACTICE QUESTIONS

1 Which of the following statements best describes 'objective data' in relation to a netball performer? (1 mark)

   a) Her shooting technique looked poor at times.

   b) Her passing technique looked good in the match.

   c) Her shooting technique in the match was 80 per cent overall.

   d) Moving free was the weakest aspect of her performance.

2 Define and give examples of quantitative data research in relation to assessing an individual's physical fitness levels. (2 marks)

3 Technology can be used to optimise performance over a long-term timeframe (e.g. months). Identify possible benefits of using video technology to help refine technique towards 'the perfect model'. (2 marks)

4 Define the term 'indirect calorimetry'. (2 marks)

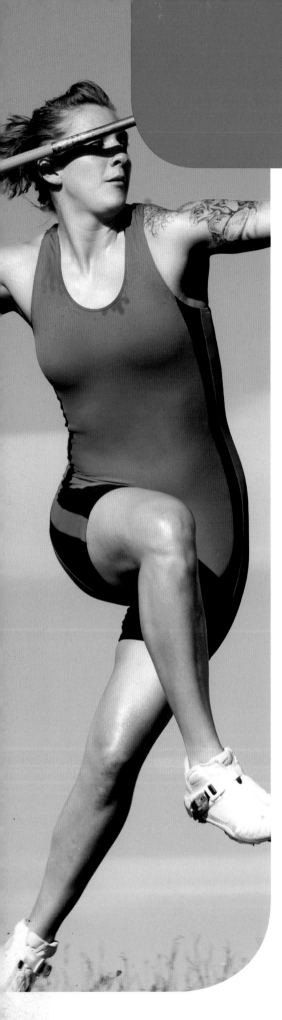

Chapter 8.1
Tackling the AS examination

As a student of AQA AS Physical Education, you will know that preparing for your examination in the correct manner is crucial to your success. Before starting to revise, you should familiarise yourself with the structure of the AS paper and what skills you are likely to need on the day of sitting the paper.

Structure of the paper

There is only one paper for AQA AS Physical Education, which involves a mixture of different question types:

● Multiple-choice questions

● Short answer questions

● Extended answer questions.

As the paper is two hours long and includes 84 marks, you have just under one and a half minutes per mark. Be prepared to give yourself at least one minute per mark, or slightly longer on questions that require more thinking time. Remember that your examination is worth 70 per cent of your final mark, so you do not want to rush and you should follow strict time parameters to ensure that you can answer all of the questions on the paper.

The 84 marks will be structured into three sections that all contain multiple-choice, short answer and extended questions.

The three sections are:

● Section A: Applied physiology

● Section B: Skill acquisition and sports psychology

● Section C: Sport and society and technology in sport

> **CHECK YOUR UNDERSTANDING**
> Remember the examination at AS:
> ● is two hours' long
> ● is worth 84 marks
> ● includes multiple-choice, short answer and extended questions
> ● can be completed in just under a minute and a half per mark.

It is important that you remember to bring black pens and a calculator into the examination. As the examination may include data or some simple mathematical calculations, the calculator is a requirement.

Multiple-choice questions

Multiple-choice questions will involve a series of options, which have a 'circular area' to colour in at the end of each option.

For example, if you were asked about Tuckman's stages of group formation, you would select the answer by colouring in the circle at the end of the correct answer:

A: Forming, storming, norming, performing ⦿

B: Storming, forming, norming, performing ◯

C: Performing, storming, norming, forming ◯

D: Norming, storming, performing, norming ◯

Figure 1 An example of a completed multiple-choice question

Remember, it is easy to fall into the trap of rushing with such questions, so be careful to stick to your time plan and take at least a minute to think through which answer is correct. You do not want to be left with 'dead time' – i.e. time left at the end of the examination, staring into space!

Short answer questions

Short answer questions do not necessarily allow you to bullet point the answer. If a question asks you, for example, to discuss, you will need to explain in detail both sides of an argument. Remember, it is only the command words of 'state', 'name', 'identify' and 'list' that allow you to simply list your answers. See the guide to command words below.

Extended question

Each of the three sections within the paper will include an **extended question** which requires you to write your answer in continuous prose, i.e. sentences and paragraphs. The following points are strongly advisable and should be noted:

1 Start by reading the question … and then read it again.

2 It is important to make sure that you have understood the question before starting your answer.

3 Follow the tips below (in Further tips and advice, page 220) regarding the use of Time, Topic, Command and Context (TTCC).

4 Think about making a short plan before starting to write to ensure that your answer will have a suitable structure and flow.

5 Remember that the extended questions require extended answers. There is a large space available as you are expected to develop your answers. Keep asking yourself: 'Have I explained that point in enough detail?'

When writing your extended answer, it is important to focus on several points:

- The level of your knowledge.
- The accuracy of what you are writing.
- The detail included in your answer.
- How the knowledge you have demonstrated has been applied to the question.
- The degree to which the language you have used has made use of correct terminology.
- The degree to which you have addressed the command word – see the guide to command words below.

Command words

When answering questions, it is vital to take your time to understand what the question is actually asking you.

The following list gives an accurate explanation of what each potential command word actually means:

- **Analyse:** Break down into component parts. Separate information into components and identify their characteristics.
- **Apply:** Using the information given, put it into effect in a recognised way.
- **Assess:** Make an informed and/or accurate judgement.
- **Calculate:** Complete a calculation to work out the eventual value of something.
- **Comment:** Look at the information provided to present an informed opinion.
- **Compare:** Identify similarities and or differences.
- **Complete:** To finish or complete a task by adding to the information already given.
- **Consider:** Often used to test analysis and evaluation. Involves reviewing and responding to information that is given.
- **Contrast:** To identify differences between things.
- **Define:** Provide or specify a meaning/definition.
- **Describe:** To set out the characteristics of something.
- **Discuss:** To give both sides of an argument. To present key points about different ideas or strengths and weaknesses of an idea.

  NB This can be a problematic command word, in that students do not always provide both sides of the argument. It is good practice to open a sentence with an introductory statement about what side of the argument is being proposed. For example:
  - 'The first advantage is that…'
  - 'The second advantage is that…' followed by…
  - 'The first disadvantage is that…' etc.
- **Evaluate:** To judge the 'worth' of something from available evidence.
- **Explain:** To set out purposes or reasons in detail.

  NB This is a particularly problematic command word for students, whose answers often lack the detail to provide the purposes or reasons. When linked with 'Name' to form 'Name and explain', students often name what is required without providing the explanation.
- **Give:** Simply providing an answer from knowledge or recall.
- **Identify:** To simply name.
- **Interpret:** To use the information given and translate into a recognisable form.
- **Justify:** To support a case or idea with evidence.

  NB This is often problematic for students who do not provide enough detail in their answer to support the case being proposed. For example, if a question was to ask you to, 'Justify why a cognitive performer is more likely to need to make use of visual guidance', the answer should support the given case with detail:
  'The cognitive performer will need to make use of visual guidance as they have not developed a mental picture of how the skill should look. They are also less likely to be able to replicate the skill using verbal guidance only.'
- **Label:** Provide appropriate names on a diagram.
- **List:** Provide a list of the recognised terms or names.
- **Name:** Identify using a recognised technical term or give a name.

- **Outline:** Setting out the main characteristics.
- **Plot:** Mark or plot on a graph.
- **State:** To express clearly and briefly.
- **Sketch:** Draw roughly/approximately.
- **Suggest:** Presenting a possible or plausible case/solution.

Revision ideas

There is no one tried and tested way to revise that works for everyone. You must find your own method but remember to replicate examination conditions in that:

- You cannot bring notes in.
- You are under time pressure.

Mind maps

Mind maps or spider diagrams can be a great way to build up your ability to recall information without having the benefit of your notes. Simply choose a specific topic area and without your notes, write down what you can remember. When you feel you cannot remember any further information, consult your notes then start again.

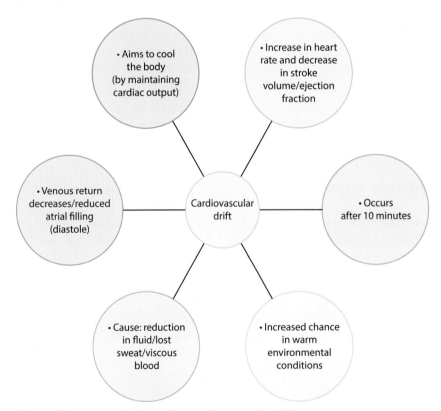

Figure 2 A sample mind map for cardio-vascular drift

Previous examination questions

It may be helpful to study previous examination questions. The examination board produces sample assessment materials and mark schemes, which can be of great benefit for you to test yourself on the types of questions that could appear in the paper. Remember that the specification before 2016 also contained a wealth of questions and mark schemes that are still relevant today. Try to test your knowledge under the actual timed conditions you will face in the paper. Remember, there are also practice questions included at the end of each chapter.

Revision cards

Revision cards are a great way to re-write your notes in a small, concise but manageable format. Create topic cards with the main points to remember or create questions on one side with the answers on the other.

Study buddies

Study buddies can be great in that you can ask each other questions and learn from each other. It is often a good idea to use past examination questions to both try and then compare each other's answers. You can download old AQA questions via the website: www.aqa.org.uk.

This textbook

This Hodder textbook provides detailed, informative content on the course, as well as many opportunities to check your understanding. The memory tools are a great way to test your recall, and the practice questions are designed to assess you while providing an indication of the depth of response required. Don't forget the study hints and where possible, as you read through each chapter, actually do 'check your understanding'.

As the examination approaches, why not attempt to use one of the ideas above along with the textbook? For example, try to write a mind map on a topic area and use the book for reference to fill in any gaps. You could then test yourself and perhaps a study buddy using the practice questions.

Another easy and productive way to use the textbook for revision is to start by looking at the chapter objectives, as a guide on what to revise within each chapter. Can you identify and explain what each point suggests without reading any further?

Further tips and advice

As a definitive plan for exams, it may be an idea to adopt the principle of Time, Topic, Command, Context (TTCC). In simple terms this involves going through four stages when answering questions:

1 **Time:** Look at the number of marks and multiply this by at least 1; e.g. for a four-mark question, you should take at least four minutes (possibly slightly longer).

2 **Topic:** Once you know how long you have got, read the question to work out what the topic area being examined is. This may involve reading the question several times.

3 **Command:** Check that you have seen and highlighted or underlined the main command word/s within the question so that you know what is being asked. For example, if you see 'Explain', it means you need to give detail and set out reasons.

4 **Context:** Read the question again (and again, if necessary) to work out the context, i.e. what is it actually asking me to do?

If you were looking at the following question, the four stages of TTCC can be applied.

Question: Explain what happens to tidal volume and residual volume as a result of the onset of exercise. (2 marks)

● **T**: 2 marks = take at least 2 minutes
● **T**: The topic is tidal volume and residual volume (lung volumes)
● **C**: The command word is explain – give detail/set out reasons
● **C**: The context is to explain in detail and give reasons as to what happens to tidal volume and residual volume if you start exercise, providing at least two points (one for each). As 'Explain' is the command word, it would not be enough to state that tidal volume increases – it needs to be explained.

It is also important never to miss out answers to questions altogether. You may pick up marks even with an educated guess!

Chapter 8.2
Tackling the non-examined assessment

Introduction and assessment weightings

As a student studying AQA AS Physical Education, you will be required to carry out a non-examined assessment. You may well call this the 'practical' part of the course but it is officially called the non-examined assessment (NEA).

This part of the course is worth 30 per cent of your overall mark and will be assessed by the teaching staff in your school or college, although moderation of marks will be carried out by external AQA staff.

- The maximum number of marks you can score for the NEA is 90.
- This is split into 45 marks for the practical task (performing or coaching) and 45 marks for an analysis and evaluation task.
- The performing or coaching task is split into three multiplied by 15 marks for three areas of assessment.
- The analysis and evaluation task is split into 20 marks for the analysis and 25 for the evaluation.

Table 1 Non-examined assessment

Performance or coaching task (45 marks)		Analysis and evaluation task (45 marks)	
Area of assessment 1	15 marks	Analysis	20 marks
Area of assessment 2	15 marks	Evaluation	25 marks
Area of assessment 3	15 marks		

Practical task: One role and one activity

As a student, you will assume one role (after discussion and agreement with your teachers). The potential options are **performer** or **coach**. Whether you choose to perform or coach your chosen activity, it must come from the agreed activity list, as stated in the table at the end of this chapter. You will notice that each activity has three areas of assessment, i.e. three things you will be assessed in.

The performance role

If you choose to adopt the performance role, there are several factors to consider:

- The performance *must* be done in a fully recognised version of the activity – e.g. an 11-a-side football match.
- There are two exceptions to this:

  Climbing – the climbs chosen must have natural features that appropriately challenge the climber.

Dance – the dances chosen must simply be performed in a formal environment in front of an audience, e.g. a dance show.

- Your actual performance will be assessed in a practical setting and is worth 45 of the 90 marks available.
- The other 45 marks will come from completing an analysis and evaluation task (analysing and evaluating your performance **or** analysing and evaluating the performance of the person you have coached). Alternatively, you can choose to analyse another person if you so wish, e.g. one of your peers. There is detail about how to complete this section later in the chapter.

The areas of assessment for a performer

As previously mentioned, your practical performance is scored out of 45. Each area of assessment is scored out of 15. For example, a footballer can score:

- Area of assessment 1: 15 marks (attacking core skills)
- Area of assessment 2: 15 marks (defensive core skills)
- Area of assessment 3: 15 marks (tactics and strategies)

Areas of assessment 1 and 2

The assessment of areas 1 and 2 can be summarised by:

- How well you perform suitable core skills in a full competitive context.
- How accurate and/or successful you are in applying these core skills.
- The level of competition you are performing at.
- The level of appropriate fitness you have for your activity.
- The level of psychological control you have for your activity.

As with all activities, the example above for football would involve being assessed in a set list of 'core skills'. Attacking core skills to be assessed within a fully competitive game (for outfield players) include:

- Receiving the ball – control using both feet and thigh
- Passing – (dominant foot) short/long – along the floor, lofted, chip and driven
- Dribbling – close control, use of inside and outside of dominant foot
- Shooting – short and long range with dominant foot
- Half volley, header

Similarly, defensive skills are the stated skills in the specification that are used while defending. Different activities have different versions of areas of assessment one and two. Remember that your ability to execute the core skills/techniques outlined in the specific activity criteria (in a fully competitive situation/equivalent scenario) is key to your final mark awarded.

Don't forget to review Chapter 2.1, Skill acquisition, and Chapter 2.2, Principles and theories of learning and performance to remind yourself how students have acquired skills. You are not assessed on your knowledge of this in the NEA but it is good to revise your knowledge of this!

Area of assessment 3

The assessment of area 3 can be summarised by:

- The level of motivation/commitment you have within your activity.
- Your understanding and application of rules within your activity.
- Your ability to use core strategies/tactics or the ability to compose/choreograph routines for your activity. (NB The levels of competition are considered.)

Figure 1 Perform or coach?

PRACTICAL TIP

If you are asked by your teacher to obtain footage of yourself, it is advised that the footage you collect should show you performing at the highest standard possible. For example, if you are a county netballer, get evidence of you playing in a county match.

This is perhaps a particular consideration if you play more than one sport at a high level. For example, is there one sport you perform in that is easier for you to gain quality evidence of you performing at the highest standard possible?

Figure 2 Attacking

Figure 3 Defending

Figure 4 Applying tactics and strategies

- The number of errors you make when applying, core strategies and tactics.
- If you use choreography, the use of motifs, heights and use of space (so as to engage with the audience).
- The use of different skills and techniques as a result of the choices made regarding core tactics/strategies or choreography.

All activities have stated tactics and strategies for area of assessment 3. For the football example provided above, the core tactics and strategies you are assessed in while performing are:

- Role at corners
- Set play
- Role in formation. Tracking back
- Man-to-Man marking
- Range of passing
- Decision making – when to pass/dribble/shoot or when to tackle/jockey.

The success of how you use core tactics or strategies should be to outwit opponents (if necessary). Assessment will also include how successful or otherwise the core tactics/strategies have been within your performance.

Recording evidence

It can be difficult capturing evidence of yourself performing at your best. Your teacher may decide that the best way to evidence the mark they have awarded you is to use video or DVD evidence. A sample of student marks will have to be moderated by the examination board, so it is vital that evidence exists of you performing to the standard at which your teacher has assessed you. If you are asked by your teacher to provide them with video evidence of you performing outside of school, please remember a few simple rules:

- You should be seen performing at the highest level possible.
- Don't forget, it must be the full recognised version of the activity – 5-a-side football will not do!
- It must be clear and the person watching it must be able to actually see you!
- You may need to gain several examples from several different competitive contexts.
- Team sports require a 'player cam' approach, i.e. the camera should follow you but also be on a wide enough setting to see what is going on in the game.
- The mark awarded will not be based purely on the level you are performing at. Even if you are an international performer, there must be an appropriate amount of evidence of you actually performing.
- It is sometimes advisable to include 'voice over' on top of the footage. For example, in a game of rugby there may be 30 bodies covered in mud! In this case, it will help your cause to gain marks if you commentate as to where you are and what you are doing.
- For the person assessing you, some activities are easier than others to work out the tactics and strategies you are using. It may be obvious to see that a badminton player is deliberately using drop shots to drive their opponent forwards; however in an activity like golf, it may be better to explain your tactic/strategy to the camera prior to playing the shot.
- Don't forget that Chapter 7.1 on the role of technology in sport may provide you with some ideas on video analysis.

Table 2 shows how you can submit your recorded evidence.

Table 2 How to submit your footage

Unedited footage with written notes
Unedited footage may be very long, with lots of irrelevant sections where you are not involved. You do not need to edit this as you could simply produce a written account of the sections that you feel your teacher should watch. *For example:* netball footage: 1:10 – I pass the ball to the WA 1:55 – I make an interception 1:58 – I pass to Centre 2:35 – I double dodge to lose opponent, catch pass from GK and set up attack with the C, etc.

The coaching role

If you decide to choose the coaching role, there are several factors to consider:

● The coaching *must* be done in a fully recognised version of the activity – e.g. an 11-a-side football match.

● There are two exceptions to this:

   Climbing – the climbs chosen for which the coaching takes place must have natural features that appropriately challenge the climber.

   Dance – the dances chosen to be coached must simply be performed in a formal environment in front of an audience, e.g. a dance show.

● Your actual coaching will be assessed in a practical setting and is worth 45 of the 90 marks available.

● The other 45 marks will come from completing an analysis and evaluation task (analysing and evaluating the performance of the person you have coached).

The key to being a successful coach at AS Level is your ability to improve (refine) the skill level and performance of the person/people you are coaching. This process will follow three distinctive stages:

Figure 5 Watch the performer/s performing in a fully competitive context. **Analyse** their strengths and weaknesses (see key points below)

Figure 6 Remove the performer/s from the competitive context to **modify** the weaknesses using appropriate drills/intervention/communication (see key points below)

Figure 7 Refinement occurs when the performer/s is put into the full competitive context again

As you can see in Figures 5, 6 and 7, the process of coaching involves analysis, modification and refinement. However, other variables are also taken into account by your teacher when awarding marks:

● Your ability to communicate to the performer/s.
● Your ability to use appropriate terminology/language/terms.
● How well the person/people understand(s) you when you coach.
● Your choice of appropriate drills/technical intervention to cause refinement.
● The timing of your intervention, e.g. when to provide analysis.

Key points for a coach

As a coach, you will be expected to analyse the performance of an individual within a fully competitive/performance context to **identify one core skill** to be developed to enhance performance.

You should deliver a planned progressive session to modify the chosen core skill so that performance of this skill is refined.

This process should be **repeated for each of the areas of assessment** (one core skill from area of assessment 1, one core skill from area of assessment 2 and one core skill from area of assessment 3).

The areas of assessment for a coach

Your coaching is scored out of 45. Each area of assessment is scored out of 15. For example, for a netball coach:

● Area of assessment 1: 15 marks (coaching of attacking core skills)
● Area of assessment 2: 15 marks (coaching of defensive core skills)
● Area of assessment 3: 15 marks (coaching appropriate tactics and strategies)

Areas of assessment 1 and 2

The assessment of areas of assessment 1 and 2 for a coach can be summarised by

- How well you demonstrate your coaching when analysing core skills/techniques in a fully competitive/performance context.
- How consistent and accurate you are when analysing, modifying and refining the chosen core skills/techniques to progress and modify performance.
- How good your communication skills are, including your use of relevant technical terminology.
- How well you can adapt your language/terminology to ensure the performer understands your comments.
- How well you choose appropriate exercises/activities designed to modify and refine performance suitable to the level they perform at.

Remember, as with the performance role, there is a set list of what constitutes an 'attacking skill'. The chosen skill to coach must come from this list for each area of assessment. Within the example above, when coaching a netball player for area of assessment 2, the coach could choose to coach any of the stated defensive core skills:

- Footwork
- Marking a stationary player – blocking the pass/shot
- Intercepting from standing, or
- Rebounding (if appropriate).

Area of assessment 3

The assessment for area of assessment 3 can be summarised by:

- How well you demonstrate levels of motivation/commitment.
- How consistent, accurate and successful you are at analysing, modifying and refining tactics/strategy/choreography.
- How competent you are even when refining and modifying advanced tactics/strategy/choreography.
- How well you communicate, including your use of relevant technical terminology.
- How well you adapt your language/terminology to ensure the performer understands your comments.
- How well you choose exercises/activities designed to modify and refine performance suitable to the level the performer is at.
- How much refinement takes place due to your intervention so that performers make excellent progress.

For area of assessment 3, coaching tactics and strategies refers to coaching the tactics or strategies the performer uses. For example, they may be too attacking and require coaching to develop the defensive side of their game. A swimmer may need coaching to develop an appropriate breathing rate to maximise their potential to win the race, etc. In the example above, a netball coach may coach appropriate tactics or strategies to allow the performer/s to outwit their opponents/markers. Thus the coach maximises the performer's opportunities for success.

Analysis and evaluation task

As mentioned in the introduction to this chapter, half of your NEA mark comes from submitting an analysis and evaluation task. The task is worth 45 marks.

> **PRACTICAL TIP**
>
> As a coach, it is important that you provide analysis at the right time. Don't talk for the sake of talking – provide informative feedback once you have worked out what is relevant to say. Also, although pre-planned drills can be helpful, you should not always stick to a plan as you must adapt to what is in front of you. For example, if your performer suddenly starts performing a skill poorly, then that is the one you should coach.

As a student, you will be required to analyse and evaluate, using appropriate theoretical content from the specification. This analysis and evaluation will be about one performer (you or another person) performing one activity from the specification.

Just to make it clear:

- You can analyse and evaluate your own performance (or the person you have coached); **or**
- You can analyse and evaluate the performance of another person.

In producing the task, you can complete it in one of two ways. It is possible to submit:

- A written piece of work; **or**
- A mixture of written work (e.g. essay style/ PowerPoint slides, etc.) **and** additional verbal explanation (e.g. providing more detail on the PowerPoint to explain it further).

Analysis (20 marks)

Performers

You have to analyse how well you or another person has performed in a fully competitive context, e.g. an 11-a-side game of football. The activity being performed must be an activity included in the activity list.

Coaches

You have to analyse how well the person you have coached or another person has performed in a fully competitive context, e.g. an 11-a-side game of football. The activity being performed must be an activity included in the activity list.

Both performers and coaches

Step one

You have to identify one weakness from area of assessment 1 only. As an example, a netball player will have to choose a weakness in their attacking play (e.g. shooting). However, if you would prefer to outline more than one weakness for area of assessment 1, this is also acceptable, e.g. poor start and leg technique in swimming. However, if you choose to do this, you will only discuss how to improve <u>one</u> of these weaknesses in your evaluation (see Evaluation).

Step two

Now you have identified your weakness, you must analyse it. Analyse involves breaking something down, so in this case, you must break down the technique that was used when the weakness occurred. Analysis involves looking in detail at the weakness you have identified in step one, observing (in technical terms) what has caused it, and assessing the impact this weakness has had on the performance.

Here are some activity-specific examples of what the weaknesses may be. However, you can choose whatever you like as long as the area of assessment 1 weakness is a skill.

Table 3 Sport-specific examples of weaknesses

Activity	Area of assessment 1: Weakness example
Rugby	Attacking weakness: Poor kicking
Hockey	Attacking weakness: Poor aerial pass
Badminton	Attacking weakness: Poor smash
Horse riding	Ride 1 without jumps: Poor transitions
Swimming	Race 1: Poor tumble turn
Dance	Dance 1: Poor travel/elevation
Sculling	Race 1: Poor body position during stroke

In choosing a weakness for area of assessment 1, remember that the weakness must be a skill. This is important as your understanding of the technique used and the impact that this poor technique has had on performance will form part of your assessment.

Remember you can learn about skills in the Chapter 2.1 on skill acquisition!

Although no word count is put on your weakness, you should aim to identify what the detail behind the weakness was concisely – i.e. don't waffle!

A potential structure for your analysis is shown in Table 4:

Table 4 Analysis section: Weakness 1

Person being analysed	Activity performed
Area of assessment 1:	**Weakness identified:**
Background information (e.g. where appropriate – Who was performing? Against who? When? What was happening at the time? What was the score? How had they been performing?)	
Explanation of the weakness (analysing the technique used) and the impact this weakness had on the performance:	

Figure 8 Skills analysis in basketball

Major points to consider about your analysis

- Make sure your area of assessment 1 weakness is a skill, e.g. passing. Something like cardiovascular endurance is not a skill – it is an aspect of fitness. This will allow you to fully explain the technique that was used and what was incorrect about it.

- Aim to use technical terms relevant to the activity being analysed.

- Mention as many aspects of the technique as you can, e.g. you will need to mention many body parts! Where were your or their eyes looking? What angle was the top half of your or their body at? What were your/their arms or hands doing? How flexed was your/their hip? Was the angle at your/their knee correct? What were your/their feet doing, e.g. plantar-flexed?

- It is not enough to just provide a detailed account of technique used. You must also explain the *impact* that the poor technique has had on the performance. An example of this is briefly shown below for driving in golf.

The player's stance was wider than shoulder-width apart with the club head further away from his feet than it needed to be. Although the base was strong, the hands had dropped low and there was obvious potential to open the club face on the backswing. As the player was level par standing on the tee, the slicing action of the club caused the ball to move from left to right and caused the ball to fly over the fairway and into deep rough on the right. The player's grip was slightly 'open', with the right hand too far away from the interlocking left, causing a lack of control in the backswing. As the player swung the club outside of the natural line, the club face opened in the backswing and was extremely open at the top of the backswing. The backswing went past the linear line to the target and as a result, the follow-through was long and rushed, causing the club face to remain open and slice across the ball. Player X lost distance due to the trajectory of the ball and his drive finished 190 yards from the green in deep rough. Although he had lost distance, he also lost a good line into the green which could have been possible from the middle of the fairway. The line into the pin was now over two bunkers and a small hill in front of the green, meaning that the second shot would be 'hit blind'. Player X's body language showed how frustrated he was and he subsequently double-bogeyed the hole. Not only did his overall confidence take a dip, but he was also less confident about using his driver off of the tee for the remainder of his round.

- In analysing your weakness, it is advisable to make reference to an elite named performer who you feel uses the perfect technique. Some comparison to this person may help you to fully explain the weakness/es that you have. This should not be a cursory mention that, for example, Kobe Bryant uses the perfect technique, but should draw upon and explain that technique that he uses.

Evaluation: 25 marks

The evaluation section of your work links the weaknesses you have identified in your analysis to the theoretical areas of the course that can explain why the weakness occurred and how performance can be improved. For the weakness/es you have identified, you must suggest an appropriate cause and corrective measure, which have to come from the theoretical content within the specification. Evaluation basically means to look at something's 'worth' or 'appropriateness'. In this case, that 'something' is the theoretical principles included in the PE specification.

For example, if your weakness was kicking in Rugby, you need to choose an appropriate aspect of the course which explains why that weakness exists and an appropriate theoretical area to correct the weakness.

- **For example:** Poor kicking in Rugby
- **Possible cause:** Over-arousal
- **Possible corrective measure:** Cognitive stress management techniques

Remember, any relevant aspects of the theoretical content can be used. Use the theoretical content included within this textbook to help you choose appropriate areas of the course.

You have some options when completing the evaluation:

- You may choose just one theoretical area for the cause/corrective measure (to show how well you understand that aspect of the theory); **or**
- You may make reference to more than one relevant theoretical area for your cause/corrective measure (to show your knowledge across several areas and how they link together).

The diagram in Figure 10 outlines the key criteria you must meet in order to complete your evaluation effectively.

Figure 9 The rugby kick: How it should be done!

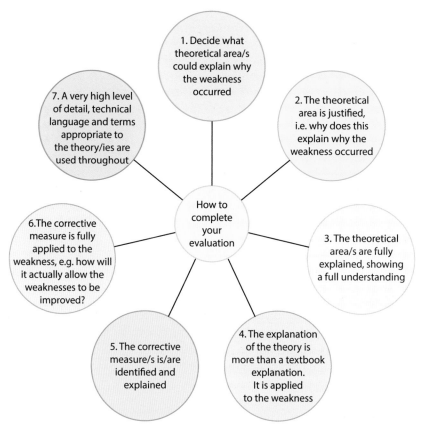

Figure 10 The key criteria you must meet in order to complete your evaluation effectively

1. Decide what theoretical area/s could explain why the weakness occurred

2. The theoretical area is justified, i.e. why does this explain why the weakness occurred

3. The theoretical area/s are fully explained, showing a full understanding

4. The explanation of the theory is more than a textbook explanation. It is applied to the weakness

5. The corrective measure/s is/are identified and explained

6. The corrective measure is fully applied to the weakness, e.g. how will it actually allow the weaknesses to be improved?

7. A very high level of detail, technical language and terms appropriate to the theory/ies are used throughout

How to complete your evaluation

A potential structure for your evaluation is shown below in Table 5.

Table 5 Evaluation section: Weakness 1

Name of performer	Activity performed
Area of assessment 1:	**Weakness identified:**
Theoretical cause for the weakness identified:	
Corrective measure identified:	
Explanation:	

Final checklist

1　Choose which activity you are going to do from the list in Table 6.

2　Choose which role you will undertake – performer or coach.

3　Liaise with your teacher about how you will be assessed/how evidence will be gathered.

4　Carry out your performance or coaching.

5 You will need one weakness (or more) from your area of assessment 1.

6 Make sure weakness/es allow you to demonstrate your knowledge of technique for area of assessment 1.

7 Complete your analysis and evaluation task on yourself, or the person you coached or another person.

8 Choose an appropriate part/s of the theoretical course which explain why the weakness existed (**the causes**).

9 Choose an appropriate part/s of the theoretical course to explain how to correct the weakness (**the corrective measures**).

In conclusion, your analysis and evaluation task is your chance to show that you understand the technique used when performing and the impact poor technique has on performance. It also allows you to demonstrate your knowledge of tactics and strategies, while linking the knowledge you have gained from the theoretical side of the course to the identified weaknesses.

Good luck!

Table 6 Official activity list

Activity	Relevant comments	Assessment 1	Assessment 2	Assessment 3
Amateur boxing		Attacking skills	Defensive skills	Tactics and strategies
Association Football	Cannot be five-a-side or futsal	Attacking skills	Defensive skills	Tactics and strategies
Athletics		Event 1	Event 2	Tactics and strategies
Badminton		Attacking skills	Defensive skills	Tactics and strategies
Basketball		Attacking skills	Defensive skills	Tactics and strategies
Camogie		Attacking skills	Defensive skills	Tactics and strategies
Canoeing (Flat water) (White water)		Event/race 1 Downstream skills	Event/race 2 Upstream skills	Tactics and strategies
Cricket		Attacking skills	Defensive skills	Tactics and strategies
Cycling	Track or road cycling only	Attacking skills	Defensive skills	Tactics and strategies
Dance		Dance 1	Dance 2	Choreography
Diving	Platform diving	Attacking skills	Defensive skills	Tactics and strategies
Gaelic football		Attacking skills	Defensive skills	Tactics and strategies
Golf		Short irons (7-wedges), putting	Long irons (Driver-6 iron)	Tactics and strategies
Gymnastics	Floor routines and apparatus only	Piece of equipment 1	Piece of equipment 2	Tactics and strategies
Handball		Attacking skills	Defensive skills	Tactics and strategies
Hockey	Must be field hockey, not ice hockey or roller hockey	Attacking skills	Defensive skills	Tactics and strategies
Equestrian		Flatwork	Jumping	Tactics and strategies
Hurling		Attacking skills	Defensive skills	Tactics and strategies
Kayaking (Flat water) (White water)		Event/race 1 Downstream skills	Event/race 2 Upstream skills	Tactics and strategies
Lacrosse		Attacking skills	Defensive skills	Tactics and strategies
Netball		Attacking skills	Defensive skills	Tactics and strategies

Activity	Relevant comments	Assessment 1	Assessment 2	Assessment 3
Rock climbing	Can be indoor or outdoor	Climb 1	Climb 2	Tactics and strategies
Rowing		Bow side	Stroke side	Tactics and strategies
Rugby League	Cannot be tag rugby	Attacking skills	Defensive skills	Tactics and strategies
Rugby Union	Can be assessed as sevens or fifteen-a-side. Cannot be tag rugby	Attacking skills	Defensive skills	Tactics and strategies
Sculling		Race 1	Race 2	Tactics and strategies
Skiing	Outdoor/indoor on snow. Must not be on dry slopes	Race 1	Race 2	Tactics and strategies
Snowboarding	Outdoor/indoor on snow. Must not be on dry slopes	Race 1	Race 2	Tactics and strategies
Squash		Attacking skills	Defensive skills	Tactics and strategies
Swimming	Not synchronised swimming	Race 1	Race 2	Tactics and strategies
Table tennis		Attacking skills	Defensive skills	Tactics and strategies
Tennis		Attacking skills	Defensive skills	Tactics and strategies
Trampolining		Compulsory routine	Voluntary routine	Tactics and strategies
Volleyball		Attacking skills	Defensive skills	Tactics and strategies
Specialist activity	**(Certified learning need)**			
Boccia		Throws at the jack	Blocking throws	Tactics and strategies
Goal ball		Attacking skills	Defensive skills	Tactics and strategies
Powerchair football		Attacking skills	Defensive skills	Tactics and strategies
Polybat		Attacking skills	Defensive skills	Tactics and strategies
Table cricket		Batting skills	Fielding skills	Tactics and strategies
Wheelchair basketball		Attacking skills	Defensive skills	Tactics and strategies
Wheelchair football		Attacking skills	Defensive skills	Tactics and strategies
Wheelchair Rugby		Attacking skills	Defensive skills	Tactics and strategies

Answers

Chapter 1.1 The cardiovascular system

Answers to Check your understanding questions

(p.5)

As an individual runs on a treadmill, his or her chemoreceptors will detect an increase in carbon dioxide levels and blood acidity. Name the other receptors, explain what they detect and describe the effect this has on heart rate.

- Baroreceptors
- Increase in blood pressure results in a decrease in heart rate
- Proprioceptors
- Increase in muscle movement results in an increase in heart rate

(p.8)

1 Define the terms cardiac output and stroke volume and explain the relationship between them.
- Cardiac output = the volume of blood pumped out by the heart ventricles per minute.
- Stroke volume = the volume of blood pumped out by the heart ventricles per contraction.
- Cardiac output = stroke volume × heart rate.

2 What are the effects of a period of training on resting stroke volume and cardiac output?
- Stroke volume increases.
- Cardiac output stays the same.

(p.12)

Describe the mechanisms that are used to return blood to the heart.
- Skeletal muscle pump where muscles contract and compress veins
- Respiratory pump where pressure changes caused by the muscles compress veins
- Pocket valves prevent back flow.

(p.14)

During a 400-metre hurdle race, the oxyhaemoglobin curve shifts to the right. Explain the causes of this change to the curve and the effect that this change has on oxygen delivery to the muscles.
- Increase in blood temperature
- Increase in blood carbon dioxide levels
- Decrease in blood pH
- Bohr shift
- Oxygen delivery is quicker.

(p.16)

During a game of football, a player's arterio-venous oxygen difference (A-VO₂ diff) will increase. What is the significance of this increase in A-VO₂ diff to the player?

- This is the difference between the oxygen content of the arterial blood arriving at the muscles and the venous blood leaving the muscles.
- Because more oxygen is needed by the muscles for energy production.
- As a result, arterio-venous oxygen difference increases, resulting in an increase in the delivery of this extra oxygen in the blood.
- This leads to improved performance.

Answers to Activity questions

(p.3)

1 **Name the four chambers of the heart.**
- Right atrium, left atrium, right ventricle, left ventricle

2 **Which chambers are larger? Explain why.**
- Ventricles as they have to pump the blood further.

3 **Which side of the heart is larger? Explain why.**
- Left as this has to push blood around the body as opposed to the right side to the lungs.

4 **Name the main blood vessels that enter and leave the heart.**
- Vena cava from the body into right atrium
- Pulmonary artery from right ventricle to lungs
- Pulmonary vein from lungs to left atrium
- Aorta from left ventricle to body

5 **What are the names of the valves in the heart and where are they located?**
- Tricuspid valve between right atrium and right ventricle
- Bicuspid valve between left atrium and left ventricle
- Semi lunar valves in the pulmonary artery and aorta

6 **What is the main function of valves?**
- To prevent back flow.

7 **Starting at the venae cavae, place the following structures in the correct order that a red blood cell would pass on its journey through the heart.**
Aorta   Left ventricle   Lungs   Pulmonary artery   Bicuspid valve   Right ventricle
Left atrium   Tricuspid valve   Pulmonary vein   Right atrium

1 Right atrium	6 Pulmonary vein
2 Tricuspid valve	7 Left atrium
3 Right ventricle	8 Bicuspid valve
4 Pulmonary artery	9 Left ventricle
5 Lungs	10 Aorta

(p.3)

Rearrange these words so they show the correct order that the impulse travels in:

AVN   purkinje fibres   ventricular systole   atrial systole   bundle branches   SAN   bundle of His

SAN   atrial systole   AVN   bundle of His   bundle branches   purkinje fibres   ventricular systole

(p.7)

Now sketch a graph to show heart rate during a game of football.

Any answer that shows the graph fluctuating up and down throughout, such as the one below:

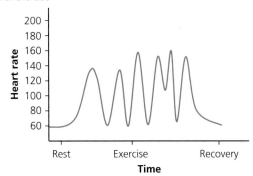

(p.8)

Look at Table 1 and comment on the difference between cardiac output at rest and during exercise for both the trained and untrained performer.

● Stays the same for both performers at rest.
● Much higher for the trained performer during exercise.

(p.10)

Knowing the structure of the blood vessels will help in your understanding of this topic. Identify the characteristics of each blood vessel and explain the reason for these specific characteristics.

● Veins have thinner muscle/elastic tissue layers because blood is at low pressure and they have a wider lumen so they have mechanisms such as valves to prevent back flow.
● Arteries are very elastic as they have to cope with high blood pressure; a smaller lumen to help increase resistance and a smooth inner layer so blood can flow freely.
● Capillaries are only wide enough to allow one red blood cell to pass through at a given time. This slows down blood flow and allows the exchange of nutrients with the tissues to take place by diffusion. They are also one cell thick which means they have a short diffusion pathway.

(p.11)

Copy and complete Table 2, then identify the pressure of blood in each of the blood vessels.

Blood pressure			
Artery	**Arteriole**	**Capillary**	**Vein**
High and in pulses	Not quite as high	Pressure drops throughout the capillary network	Low

(p.11)

Look at the graph (Figure 8) and give three key points about blood pressure.

Choose any three from:

- Pressure highest in arteries
- Pressure lowest in veins
- Pressure drops significantly in capillaries
- Systolic pressure is higher than diastolic pressure

(p.15)

Look at Figure 12 and give reasons for the percentage change in cardiac output during exercise.

- Stays the same for both performers at rest
- Much higher for the trained performer during exercise

(p.16)

Copy out Table 3 and construct sentences to connect the key words in the spaces below.

1	brain		blood flow
The brain requires oxygen for energy to maintain its function so needs a constant blood flow.			
2	eat	competition	gut
It is important to not eat an hour before competition as more blood will go to the gut for digestion and less to the muscles.			
3	vasomotor centre	chemoreceptors	medulla oblongata
Chemoreceptors detect an increase in carbon dioxide and send impulses to the vasomotor centre in the medulla oblongata.			
4	vasoconstriction	vasodilation	arterioles	blood flow
Vasodilation of arterioles increases blood flow and vasoconstriction decreases blood flow.				

Answers to Practice questions

(p.17)

1 **Why does blood flow to the brain remain the same at rest and during exercise?**
- The brain requires oxygen
- For energy
- To maintain function

2 **Why should an athlete not eat at least one hour before competition?**
- During exercise, more blood goes to the gut for oxygen to provide the energy to digest food.
- This means less blood available to the muscles.
- And can result in a decrease in performance.

3 **How is oxygen transported in the blood?**
- It dissolves into plasma and combines with haemoglobin to form oxy-haemoglobin.

4 **Explain how blood is redistributed to the working muscles.**
- An increase in CO_2 is detected by chemoreceptors.
- An increase in movement is detected by proprioceptors.
- They send impulses to the vasomotor centre in the medulla of the brain.

- Through the sympathetic nervous system, the brain sends impulses, causing vasodilation to areas needing blood such as the muscles, and vasoconstriction to areas not needing as much blood such as the kidneys/liver/gut.
- Pre-capillary sphincters relax so blood flow is increased.

5 **During exercise, heart rate will increase to meet the extra oxygen demand required by the muscles. Explain how the increasing level of carbon dioxide in the blood raises heart rate.**
- This is detected by chemoreceptors.
- Nerve impulses are sent to the medulla.
- Sympathetic nervous impulses are sent to the sinoatrial node/SAN/SA node.
- Decrease in parasympathetic nerve impulses.

6 **Just before the start of an 800m race, the athlete will experience a change in heart rate. What change occurs in the athlete's heart rate and why does this happen?**
- Increase in heart rate prior to exercise
- Caused by the release of adrenaline.

7 **Explain what is meant by the term cardiovascular drift.**
- Heart rate increases/beats more and decrease in stroke volume.
- Fluid lost as sweat.
- Reduced plasma/blood volume.
- Reduced venous return.
- Starling's Law.
- Cardiac output also increases due to more energy needed to cool body/sweat.

8 **Gymnastic performance will demand an increase in blood supply to the active muscles. The table below shows how various measurements concerned with the heart vary during rest and activity. Using the information in Table 4, calculate the cardiac output at rest.**
- Cardiac output = stroke volume × heart rate
- = 70 × 70
- = 4900ml or 4.9 litres

9 **What is understood by the term 'Starling's law' of the heart'?**
- Increased venous return
- Greater diastolic filling of the heart
- Cardiac muscle stretched
- More force of contraction
- Increased ejection fraction

Chapter 1.2 The respiratory system

Answers to Check your understanding questions

(p.23)

Figure 6 shows the spirometer trace of a badminton player. What lung volumes are represented by A, B, C and D?
- A = inspiratory reserve volume
- B = expiratory reserve volume
- C = tidal volume
- D = residual volume

Answers to Activity questions

(p.19)

Rearrange the following words to show the correct passage of air:

larynx nose trachea pharynx alveoli bronchioles bronchi

nose, pharynx, larynx, trachea, bronchi, bronchiole, alveoli.

(p.24)

Draw a simple diagram to show the movement of oxygen from the alveoli to the muscles and the movement of carbon dioxide from the muscles to the alveoli. On this diagram label the partial pressures of oxygen and carbon dioxide and show the diffusion directions.

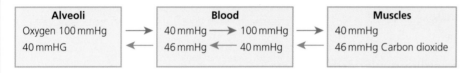

(p.25)

Use the information from Figure 8 to explain how oxygen and carbon dioxide move between the two locations.

- By a process of diffusion where a gas moves from an area of high concentration to an area of low concentration.
- The partial pressure of oxygen is higher in the alveoli and lower in the capillary; carbon dioxide has a lower partial pressure in the alveoli and higher partial pressure in the capillary.
- The oxygen therefore diffuses from the alveoli to the capillary and the carbon dioxide from the capillary to the alveoli.

Answers to Practice questions

(p.28)

1 Which of the following statements is correct?
   a) Tidal volume is the amount of air breathed in after a normal breath.
   b) Expiratory reserve volume is the amount of air that can be breathed out.
   c) Minute ventilation is inspiratory reserve volume *plus* expiratory reserve volume.
   d) Inspiratory reserve volume is the amount of air that can be forcibly inspired after a normal breath.

a) Tidal volume is the amount of air breathed in after a normal breath.

2 During exercise, the demand for oxygen by the muscles increases. How does an increase in blood carbon dioxide change breathing rate?
   - The increase in carbon dioxide is detected by chemoreceptors (in carotid arteries/aortic arch/medulla).
   - Chemoreceptors send nerve impulses to the respiratory control centre in the medulla of the brain.
   - The medulla then sends nerve impulses to the breathing muscles via the phrenic nerve/sympathetic system.
   - This increases the rate of contraction of the diaphragm and external intercostal muscles, so breathing increases.

3 Gas exchange and oxygen delivery influence performance in sporting activities. Explain how oxygen diffuses from the lungs into the blood and how it is transported to the tissues.
   - One mark for a definition of diffusion – high concentration/partial pressure to low/down a diffusion gradient.
   - At the alveoli this is a short diffusion pathway.

- There is a high pO2 in alveoli and a low pO2 in the blood so oxygen moves from the alveoli into the blood.
- Oxygen is transported by combining with haemoglobin to form oxyhaemoglobin.
- Some oxygen is transported by dissolving in plasma.

4 **Define tidal volume and identify what happens to this respiratory volume during exercise.**
- The volume of air breathed in or out per breath.
- This volume increases during exercise.

Chapter 1.3 The neuromuscular system

Answers to Check your understanding questions

(p.31)

A basketball player will use type IIb fibres to jump as high as possible to win a rebound. Can you give two characteristics of this fibre type?

Two from:
- Fast contraction speed
- Large motor neurone
- High force produced
- Fatigues quickly

(p.34)

A weightlifter needs to produce as much force as possible. Describe how the weightlifter can use motor units to achieve a maximal contraction.
- Lots of motor units recruited
- Large number of motor units for a stronger contraction
- All or None Law/explanation
- Spatial summation – simultaneous impulses received at different places on the neurone need to add up to fire the neurone
- Use of fast twitch motor units produces more force
- Wave summation – repeated nerve impulse with no time to relax
- Consequently calcium summates in the muscle cell
- Tetanus/tetanic (smooth sustained muscle contractions)
- Leads to a more powerful contraction
- Fast twitch motor units used

Answers to Activity questions

(p.30)

Copy and complete Table 1. Can you think of three sporting examples for each category?
- **Slow twitch:** marathon, cross-country skiing, Tour de France
- **IIa:** 1500m, 200m swim, floor routine in gymnastics
- **IIb:** power lifting, 100m sprint, smash in tennis

(p.31)

Each of the characteristics you have just learned can be divided into two groups. They can either be a functional characteristic or a structural characteristic. A functional characteristic is what the fibre does and a structural characteristic is the make-up of the fibre. Copy and complete Table 3 and place each of the characteristics from Table 2 into the relevant category.

Contraction speed ms	functional
Motor neurone size	structural
Motor neurone conduction capacity	functional
Force produced	functional
Fatigability	functional
Mitochondrial density	structural
Myoglobin content	structural
Capillary density	structural
Aerobic capacity	functional
Anaerobic capacity	functional
Myosin ATPase/glycolytic enzyme activity	functional

Answers to Practice questions

(p.36)

1 The training that elite performers undertake may include proprioceptive neuromuscular facilitation (PNF) stretching. Explain the role of the muscle spindles and Golgi tendon organs in PNF stretching.

- Golgi tendon organs activated/detect stretch
- Muscles relax
- Inhibits stretch reflex/overrides/stops muscle spindles
- Designed to prevent overstretching/protective
- Allowing greater range of movement to be used
- CRAC (contract/relax/antagonist/contract)

2 Contraction of different types of muscle fibres involves the use of motor units. What do you understand by the term motor unit?

- Motor neurone and muscle fibres
- All fast twitch or slow twitch
- All or none law

3 How are motor units involved in the process of spatial summation?

- Causes an increase in strength of contraction/more force in muscles
- Use bigger/larger motor units
- More motor units
- Fast-twitch units produce more force than slow-twitch units

4 Describe the characteristics of the main muscle fibre type used by marathon runners.

- Slow oxidative fibre/type 1
- Slow motor neurone conduction capacity
- High numbers of mitochondria
- High myoglobin content
- High capillary density
- Low force production/less powerful

Chapter 1.4 The musculoskeletal system and analysis of movement in physical activities

Answers to Check your understanding questions

(p.42)

1 Label the joint actions in the elbow and shoulder for Figures 14 and 15.

2 Label the joint actions in the ankle, knee and hip in both legs.

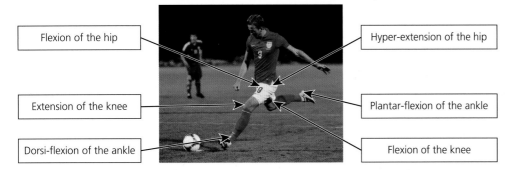

(p.44)

Figure 19 shows a javelin thrower just prior to delivering his throw. As the thrower prepares to throw the javelin, identify the joint action and main agonist occurring at the elbow and shoulder joints during this movement.

	Elbow	Shoulder
Joint action	Flexion	Horizontal abduction
Main agonist	Biceps	Latissimus dorsi

Answers to Activity questions

(p.39)

As the syllabus only requires knowledge of the hip, shoulder, elbow, knee and ankle, copy and complete the table (Table 1: Articulating bones at the five examined joints) and identify the articulating bones.

Joint	Joint type	Articulating bones
Ankle	**Hinge**	Talus, tibia, fibula
Knee	**Hinge**	Tibia, femur
Hip	**Ball and socket**	Femur, pelvis
Shoulder	**Ball and socket**	Humerus, scapula
Elbow	**Hinge**	Humerus, radius and ulna

(p.42)

Copy and complete Table 2.

Joint	Joint actions
Shoulder	Flexion, extension, hyperextension, abduction, adduction, horizontal abduction, horizontal adduction
Elbow	Flexion, extension
Hip	Flexion, extension, hyper-extension, abduction, adduction, horizontal abduction, horizontal adduction
Knee	Flexion, extension
Ankle	Plantar-flexion, dorsi-flexion

(p.46)

Answer the following questions for the movements involved in a press-up.

1 Perform the downward phase of a press-up.
 ● What is happening at the elbow joint?
 ● Which muscle is contracting?
 ● What type of contraction is it performing?

   Answers:
   ● Flexion
   ● Triceps
   ● Eccentric

2 Now perform the upward phase of a press-up.
 ● What is happening at the elbow joint?
 ● Which muscle is contracting?
 ● What type of contraction is it performing?

   Answers:
   ● Extension
   ● Triceps
   ● Concentric

3 Try to hold the press-up in the downward phase.
 ● Which muscle feels as if it is contracting?
 ● What type of contraction is it performing?

   Answers:
   ● Triceps
   ● Isometric

(p.46)

Answer the following questions for the movements involved in a squat.

1 Perform the downward phase of a squat.
 ● What is happening at the knee joint?
 ● Which muscle is contracting?
 ● What type of contraction is it performing?

Answers:

- Flexion
- Quadriceps
- Eccentric

2 Now perform the upward phase of a squat.
  - **What is happening at the knee joint?**
  - **Which muscle is contracting?**
  - **What type of contraction is it performing?**

    Answers:

    - Extension
    - Quadriceps
    - Concentric

3 Try to hold the squat in the downward phase.
  - **Which muscle feels as if it is contracting?**
  - **What type of contraction is it performing?**

    Answers:

    - Quadriceps
    - Isometric

Answers to practice questions

(p.47)

1 Which of the following statements is correct?
  a) **Flexion, extension and hyper-extension occur in a sagittal plane about a transverse axis.**
  b) **Flexion, extension and hyper-extension occur in a transverse plane about a longitudinal axis.**
  c) **Flexion, extension and hyper-extension occur in a frontal plane about a sagittal axis.**
  d) **Flexion, extension and hyper-extension occur in a transverse plane about a sagittal axis.**

a) Flexion, extension and hyper-extension occur in a sagittal plane about a transverse axis.

2 **Figure 22 shows a weightlifter performing a squat. Using the picture, identify the joint action, main agonist and the type of muscle contraction occurring at the hip and ankle joints as the weightlifter performs the downward phase.**

	Hip	Ankle
Joint action	Flexion	Dorsi-flexion
Main agonist	Gluteals	Gastrocnemius
Type of muscle contraction	Eccentric	Eccentric

3 **Figures 23 and 24 show a gymnast performing a press-up during a fitness session:**
  a) **Using Figures 23 and 24, name the main agonist and antagonist acting on the elbow as the gymnast moves from the position A to position B.**

    Agonist = triceps

    Antagonist = biceps

  b) **Name the type of muscle contraction that occurs in the main agonist:**

    At position A while the gymnast is stationary: Position A = isometric

    As the gymnast moves from position A down to position B: Position B = eccentric

Chapter 2.1 Skill characteristics and their impact on transfer and practice

Answers to Check your understanding questions

(p.49)

Skills are learned and efficient. State another three characteristics of skill.

Three from:

- Accurate
- Aesthetically pleasing
- Consistent, controlled
- Goal directed, fluent

(p.53)

Classify a sprint start in athletics under the following continua:

- **Open – closed**
- **Self-paced – externally paced**
- **Discrete serial – continuous.**
- *Closed:* environment predictable.
- *Externally paced:* starter gun controls,
- *Discrete:* clear beginning and end.

(p.54)

1 **In team sports, skills can be classed as open or closed. Using an example from a team game, explain what is meant by both an open and a closed skill.**
   - During an open skill the environment is unpredictable, e.g. pass in hockey.
   - During a closed skill the environment is predictable, e.g. penalty in football.

2 **What are the characteristics of skilled performance?**
   Skill is learned, consistent, controlled, aesthetically pleasing, accurate, (economical, efficient or fluent), accurate, goal directed.

(p.56)

1 **Explain what you understand by the term positive transfer and give an example of two skills that might promote positive transfer when performed in practice.**
   - When one skill helps the learning and performance of another.
   - For example, a basketball pass and a netball pass because the actions are similar (equivalent).

2 **Consider the skills of a throw in the game of rounders and a javelin throw. What type of transfer do you think could take place between these two skills? Can you explain your choice?**
   - Negative. The actions are not the same even though there might be similarities in the environment.

(p.57)

Name three advantages of using whole practice.

Any three of:

- Whole practice gives a feel of the task with movements complete
- Gives fluency

- Is efficient
- Forms a mental image
- Is realistic and applies consistency

(p.58)

What are the advantages of using the whole-part-whole method of practice?

- Gives motivation
- Maintains fluency/links between subroutines
- Highlights a weakness
- Corrects errors
- Gives immediate feedback

(p.59)

When would you use progressive part practice?

- When there is danger
- When you have time
- For a performer who is a beginner, unfit or less motivated
- When the skill is serial, complex or low organised

(p.60)

What is the difference between massed practice and distributed practice?

- Massed practice is non-stop with no rest intervals
- Distributed practice allows a rest interval

(p.61)

For what type of skills would you use varied practice?

Open skills, complex skills, continuous skills, externally paced skills

(p.62)

What are the advantages of using mental practice?

It improves motivation and confidence, it builds motor programmes, it improves reaction time, it lowers anxiety, it develops thinking, it can be done when injured.

Answers to Activity questions

(p.53)

In this section various examples have been used to explain the different skill classifications. Review each of the classifications that have been discussed and see if you can think of an example of your own to illustrate the criteria of each classification.

Answers as appropriate.

(p.62)

Having discussed the different types of practice, pick a skill from a sport of your choice and attempt to classify that skill according to the criteria highlighted earlier in this chapter. Having classified your skill, now suggest the types of practice you might use to learn your chosen skill. Give reasons for your choices.

Answer: Any appropriate example.

Answers to Practice questions

(p.64)

1 The skill of a free throw in basketball is an example of a skill that can be classified as:

    a) open, externally-paced and discrete

    b) closed, self-paced and discrete

    c) open, self-paced and discrete

    d) closed, externally-paced and continuous.

b) closed, self-paced and discrete

2 What do you understand by the term 'transfer of learning'? Explain the forms that transfer can take.

- Skills learned in one activity affect another.
- Positive – enhances the learning of a new skill.
- Negative – one skill hinders the learning of another.
- Bilateral – transfer of skill from one limb to another.
- Zero – no influence on skill.

3 The sport of athletics is a major feature of the Olympic Games. State a skill in athletics that you think is closed, a skill that you think is serial and a skill that you think is gross. Give reasons for your choices.

- Closed – shot putt, predictable environment.
- Serial – triple jump. Several discrete skills linked in order to produce a more continuous movement.
- Gross – 100m sprint – large muscle groups used.

Other examples may be used.

4 Swimming may be taught using either the whole method or part method. What are the advantages of using the whole method and the part method?

Answer: five from:

Whole method: sub max of 3 marks

- Develops (kinaesthesis) feel of movement
- Builds up a cognitive picture/ mental picture/ know what to do
- Link together the spatial and temporal elements of the skill/ correct order of sequence
- Gives consistency
- More realistic

Part method: sub max of 3 marks

- Reduced demands for complex skills/ less information to process
- Allows confidence and understanding to grow quickly
- Helps with motivation
- Useful in dangerous situations – swimming
- Can reduce fatigue in physically demanding skills
- Allows the opportunity to focus on particular elements/ work on one part at a time
- Provides stages of success
- Low organisation skills can be broken down easily

Chapter 2.2 Principles and theories of learning and performance

Answers to Check your understanding questions

(p.67)

Name two features of the cognitive stage of learning.

- It is used by a beginner, performance is uncoordinated, motor programmes are not formed.
- Trial and error is used, understanding is developing.

Name some aspects of performance linked with the autonomous stage of learning.

- Efficiency
- Smooth movement
- Able to concentrate on detail
- Can use motor programmes
- Used by experts

(p.68)

1 What type of feedback would you use for a performer in the associative stage of learning?

Extrinsic, then intrinsic, knowledge of performance.

2 How could a coach make sure that the feedback given to players has the best results?

Make it appropriate to the learner, e.g. positive for a novice. Make it relevant and understood, make it brief or break it up into parts, set goals with the feedback.

(p.71)

After practising the same closed skill for a period of time, a performer may reach a period when the performance does not improve, which is called a plateau. What could the performer do to overcome the plateau?

- Change the coach
- Take a rest
- Set new targets
- Vary practice to make it more fun
- Use reinforcement
- Ensure the plateau concept is understood

(p.73)

Explain what you understand by visual guidance. What are the advantages and disadvantages of using this method?

Visual guidance: Can be seen, demonstrated

Advantages: Visual, creates mental image, build sub-routines, good for beginner, highlights weakness

Disadvantages: Copied incorrectly if not accurate, may be out of performer capabilities. Too much information may confuse performer

(p.74)

What is mechanical guidance? What are the advantages and disadvantages of using this method?

Mechanical guidance: using an artificial aid

Advantages: Safe, builds confidence, gives early feel of skill

Disadvantages: Performer may over rely on it, could lose motivation, may interfere with feel of task if used too much

(p.77)

1 **Name three important features of operant conditioning.**
   - It is based on trial and error learning
   - It attempts to shape behaviour using reinforcement
   - It can be helped by manipulating the environment

2 **State whether the following are examples of positive reinforcement, negative reinforcement, or punishment:**
   a) **A coach stops shouting at a player when they make a good tackle.**
   b) **A coach brings in the team for extra training after a heavy defeat.**
   c) **A coach gives the goalkeeper the player of the match award.**
      - Positive reinforcement (c)
      - Negative reinforcement (a)
      - Punishment (b)

(p.78)

During learning, the coach may use a demonstration to show key points of a skill. From your understanding of the process of observational learning, what can the coach do to make sure such demonstrations are more likely to be copied and understood?

Model answer:

To make sure that demonstrations are copied, coaches should repeat the demonstration and make sure that every time the demonstration is shown it is accurate and clear. The coach could use role models of similar ability to the performer to encourage the performer that they have the ability to succeed in the task. The coach should offer reinforcement and praise and the coach could highlight specific cues within the demonstration. Mental practice may be used to emphasise the key points of the demonstration. Complex tasks should be shown from different angles. The demonstration should be repeated.

(p.79)

1 **What is the zone of proximal development?**

The next stage of learning needed to improve the skill.

2 **What are the three stages of Vygotsky's constructive learning theory?**
   - What can I do alone?
   - What can I do with help?
   - What can I not do?

(p.80)

What are the advantages of using insight theory to learn new skills in sport?
- It gives a specific role
- Develops thinking

- Promotes understanding
- Gives self-satisfaction and motivation

Answers to Activities

(p.68)

Complete the table to show the types of feedback that are appropriate for each stage of learning.

Stage of learning	Type of feedback
Cognitive	Positive to motivate. Extrinsic since player lacks internal knowledge. Knowledge or results to give an initial feel.
Associative	Extrinsic as the player enters this stage. Intrinsic as the player develops in this stage Knowledge of performance.
Autonomous	Negative to correct technical errors. Intrinsic to amend feel of movement with experience. Knowledge of performance to fine tune skills Extrinsic could be used as long as the coach gives detailed technical advice.

(p.71)

Copy and complete Table 2 about the causes of and cures for learning plateaus.

Cause	Cure
Lack of motivation	Rewards reinforcement
Fatigue	**Rest**
Poor coaching	Change coach
Boredom	**Different practices**
Targets too low	Set new challenge/goals
Limit of ability	**Explain the plateau concept**

Answers to Practice questions

(p.81)

1 A coach giving a player a fine for being late for training is an example of:

a) negative reinforcement

b) positive reinforcement

c) punishment

d) manipulating the environment.

c) punishment

2 Describe the theory of operant conditioning and show how a coach might use it to improve performance.

- Operant conditioning is the use or reinforcement to ensure the repetition of a correct action.
- Based on trial and error.
- Manipulates environment, use of targets.
- Shapes behaviour.
- Positive reinforcement, for example, a coach giving praise.
- Negative reinforcement, for example, a coach stopping shouting at a player after a correct action.
- Punishment, for example, a red card for being sent off!

3 **Name the three stages of learning that a sports performer experiences while developing their skills and describe the characteristics of the level of performance associated with each stage.**

- Three stages: Cognitive, Associative, Autonomous
- Cognitive characteristics: Beginner, unco-ordinated, trial and error, understanding early actions.
- Associative characteristics: Smoother performance, motor programme forming, practice, modelling.
- Autonomous characteristics: Expert, detailed efficient, motor programme developed.

4 **Bandura's model of observational learning uses four principles to help sports performers learn skills by copying demonstrations. Explain how the terms attention, retention, motor production and motivation help the process of learning.**

Attention:

- How attractive/successful/powerful or if the behaviour is functional
- Demonstration can be seen/is accurate

Retention:

- Can observer retain the skill in memory/involves cognitive skills
- Demo is meaningful/relevant/realistic/succinct and clear

Motor production:

- The abilities/skills to complete the task
- Opportunity to practise/complex skills show progression

Motivation:

- Drive needed to complete the task
- Reinforcement/praise/feedback/sense of pride/sense of satisfaction

5 **When a sports performer continually practises a closed skill for a period of 20 minutes, they may reach a stage when there is no improvement in their performance, called a plateau. Suggest reasons why this plateau effect may have occurred. How could the plateau effect be overcome?**

Plateau causes:
- Boredom
- Fatigue
- Lack of motivation
- Limit of task or limit of ability
- Poor coaching
- Targets set too low

Plateau solutions:
- Vary practice
- Give a rest
- Offer rewards or praise
- Extend the task/Set a new challenge
- Change coach
- Set more challenging goals
- Point out the plateau concept

6 Explain the term insight learning and show how this approach can have a positive effect on performance.

Choose three from:

- Using experience to solve problems.
- Gives a role
- Promotes understanding
- Develops ability to think
- Gives motivation and self-satisfaction
- Concentrates on whole skill

Chapter 3.1 Emergence of the globalisation of sport in the twenty-first century

Answers to Check your understanding questions

(p.84)

Explain three characteristics of pre-industrial football.

Any three from:

Characteristic	Explanation
Played occasionally	Because of limited free time; linked to seasons/religious festivals
Local	Because of limited transport/communications
Limited organisation/few rules	Because the lower class in society were illiterate
Violent	Because society was harsh/violent in nature
Lower class participation	Mob games were viewed as suitable activities for the lower classes
Rural	Society was agrarian in nature with the population spread out in the countryside
Natural/simple	Because people used what was readily available to them, e.g. open fields

(p.85)

In what ways was real tennis different from most other popular recreation activities, e.g. mob football?

Four points on real tennis from:

- It was courtly/exclusive/played by the upper class.
- It had complex written rules.
- It was non-violent; had etiquette; respect for opponents.
- It was played regularly.
- It was played in purpose-built facilities; used specialist equipment.
- It was non-local; upper class could travel to play.
- It required the use of complex skills (not violence!).

(p.88)

Identify four ways in which the leisure opportunities for the working classes improved as a result of industrialisation.

Choose from:

- Improved health and fitness led to more energy/improved general well-being.
- Increased income/more time to play sport due to increased wages and decreased working hours.

- Positive influence of the new middle class which led to more provision/increased acceptability of working class participation.
- Employer provision/industrial patronage led to factory teams being formed/broken time payments being made.
- Improved transport/communications led to increased travel distances/regular nationwide fixtures.
- Improved public provision, e.g. public parks.

(p.89)

Identify the impact of developments in transport on sporting opportunities for the working classes.

Choose from:

- Development of the railways allowed transport of teams and spectators; spectator sport developed.
- Fixtures could be played more regularly.
- Competitions developed nationally (e.g. FA Cup; Football League).
- Professional sport developed.
- Improved access to the countryside was possible (e.g. for rambling/climbing).
- Road developments led to developments in cycling clubs.

(p.89)

Identify how the Church encouraged the post-industrial game of football.
- Via giving its 'approval'.
- By providing facilities – a place to play e.g. on church land or in church halls.
- Via establishing it as a social activity to increase the opportunity to play the game, e.g. in Sunday School teams.
- Via establishing clubs/youth sections in the church which encouraged football, e.g. the Boys Brigade.

(p.91)

Why did local authorities in the nineteenth century start to provide recreational and sporting activities for their local communities?
- To increase the health and fitness/personal hygiene of the working class.
- Via civic responsibility in times of social responsibility/philanthropy.
- To gain prestige for the local area.
- To increase social control/civilise society; temperance movement wanted to keep the working class out of the pubs and away from alcohol.
- To improve productivity of the workforce.

(p.92)

Why did some NGBs try to prevent professionals from competing in their sport?
- Due to the desire of the upper class/middle class to maintain control of sport.
- To preserve amateur ideals in sport.
- To maintain 'exclusivity' – the upper class and middle class did not want to mix with the working class.
- Because they did not like losing to (working class) professionals!

(p.99)

Suggest three reasons why women's participation in football has increased during the twentieth century through to the current day.

Any three from:
- Equal opportunities; decreased discrimination; increased social acceptance led to more women believing that…
- It is acceptable to play football.

- Growth in the professional game for women.
- Increased media coverage; more female role models to aspire to.
- Increased demand from women to play football.
- Improved/increased PE provision.
- Increased FA approval; integration into FA programmes through to international level.
- Improved funding at grassroots level, e.g. via Sport England/FA.
- Increased leisure time for women; general decrease in traditional domestic responsibility role for women.

(p.101)

Identify the factors which led to tennis increasing women's participation in physical activity in the late nineteenth century.

- Women could play in seclusion/privacy of their own garden, away from view.
- Tennis became a social game which could be played as a mixed-sex activity.
- It was an opportunity to be athletic/energetic, but it did not need to be vigorous – women could retain their decorum and stay 'ladylike'!
- No special kit was initially required; women could dress modestly to play tennis.
- Acceptance of exercise in fresh air as therapeutic.
- Positive female role models, e.g. Lottie Dodd as an early Wimbledon champion.
- The middle classes set up tennis clubs to join.

(p.102)

State three characteristics of lawn tennis as a 'rational recreation' activity.

Any three from:
- Played regularly because players had more free time to play.
- Middle class development/invention which spread nationwide – they created clubs/set up an NGB for tennis.
- High levels of structure/skill – due to rationalisation of tennis.
- Rules were produced to help standardise the game.
- It was a social game for both sexes; it was considered as a 'suitable activity' for women to play as it was civilised and could be played in 'appropriate' clothing, preserving a woman's modesty.
- It required equipment/facilities which the middle classes could provide/afford, e.g. a game played in the suburban gardens of their homes.

(p.105)

Identify the characteristics of a sport which make it attractive for TV coverage.

- National relevance/traditional part of culture/large audiences.
- High levels of skill in evidence/professional sport/high profile/competitive.
- Competitive/opponents potentially well matched.
- Demonstrate aggression/physical challenge/entertainment.
- Understandable rules/scoring systems.
- Relatively short time scale.
- Well-known performers/role models.
- Linkage to sponsorship/business/players are contracted.

(p.83)

Identify three ways in which the game of Haxey Hood reflects the characteristics of pre-industrial Britain.

- Male dominated/played by 'young men'
- Annual/occasional/irregular
- Localised/played in a village/rural location
- Violent
- Large numbers took part/few rules

(p.83)

The linkage between socio-cultural factors in pre-industrial Britain and popular recreation activities of the time:

Socio-cultural factor in pre-industrial Britain	Popular recreation characteristic to reflect this
Limited transport/communications	Sport was localised
Illiteracy/uneducated	Limited organisation/simple rules/uncodified
Harsh society	Violent/highly aggressive
Seasonal time/long working hours	Occasional/part of a festival occasion
Pre-industrial/pre-urban revolutions	Rural/natural/simple
Two-tier society/feudal system	Gentry/upper class activities were clearly separated from lower-/peasant-class activities

(p.85)

Summarise five characteristics of real tennis.

Choose from:

- Exclusive/courtly in nature
- Played by upper class males
- Written rules
- High moral code
- Played regularly
- Purpose built facilities/specialist equipment
- Non-local
- Highly skilled/highly technical

(p.86)

Wenlock research activity

Solutions as appropriate based on task set, e.g. simple rules due to lack of literacy; locally based due to lack of transport; annual due to lack of time, etc.

(p.89)

Identify three ways in which improved literacy positively influenced the development of rational recreation.

Any three from:

- Generally increasing knowledge and awareness of sport via specialist newspapers which could be sold to the masses
- E.g. when fixtures were taking place

- E.g. what the results were
- Increasing knowledge of sporting heroes/role models in the newspapers they could read
- Rules could be developed as more sections of society could understand them

(p.90)

Copy and complete Table 2 comparing pre-industrial socio-cultural factors relating to popular recreation with post-industrial factors relating to rational recreation.

Pre-industrial factors	Post-industrial factors
Seasonal time/agricultural time	Machine time/industrial time
Limited transport/communications	Improved transport/communications
Widespread illiteracy	**Increased literacy**
Uncivilised lifestyle; limited law and order	**Civilised lifestyle; increased law and order**
Feudal society; two-tier society	Emergence of new middle class; three-tier society
Limited technology	**More advanced technology**

(p.92)

FA website activity

Use own solutions, as appropriate.

(p.94)

Corinthian Casuals research activity

Use own solutions, as appropriate.

(p.94)

Amateurism and professionalism in eighteenth- and nineteenth-century Britain and three key differences between the gentleman amateur and the professional.

Any three from:

Amateurs	Professionals
Upper class	Working class
Wealthy	Poor
Lots of time for participation	Limited time for participation
Played sport for the love of it – sportsmanship ethic	Played sport to win – gamesmanship/cheating/corruptible

(p.97)

Consider how improved transport aided the development of Association Football as a 'national game' from the mid-nineteenth century onwards.

- **Travel:** teams and fans could travel further in a faster time.
- **Affordable:** travel was at an affordable cost for the working class.
- **Rules:** regular fixtures created a need for rule standardisation/codification.
- **Competitions:** national competitions developed, e.g. Football League and FA Cup.

(p.99)

Information from UEFA Women's infographics

- Number of female players has grown five times since 1985.
- There are 7461 qualified female referees.
- There are 21,164 qualified female coaches.
- 53 associations in UEFA have a national women's team.
- Seven European countries have more than 60,000 female players.

(p.104)

Three different ways the 'golden triangle' can lead to disadvantages for sport:

Choose three from:

- Increased deviancy
- Due to increased pressure to win/win at all costs
- Due to massive financial rewards
- Certain sports dominate TV schedules and others get limited media attention
- Sponsorship opportunities link to level of media attention (therefore unequal)
- Sponsors may become over-dominant (e.g. via requests for personal appearances at corporate events).

(p.105)

Identify three different types of media you might use to 'follow sport'.

Choose three different types of media from:

- TV
- Newspapers
- Radio
- Social media
- The internet

(p.107)

Think about and list four positive effects the media can have on a sport.

Choose from:

- Increased participation in a sport, e.g. via positive role models to identify with and inspire participation.
- Increased funding/sponsorship opportunities/advertising income to the sport; increased income via TV rights.
- Myths and stereotypes can be broken, e.g. ability of women to play sports such as football to a high level.
- Minority sports are highlighted and promoted.
- Sport is made more entertaining/attractive to the viewer via changes made to a sport to speed up the action/scoring, e.g. T20 Blast cricket.
- Positive impact of introduction of technology via media innovations, e.g. referees being miked up so the audience can hear them; referees being given technological assistance when taking difficult decisions, e.g. via Hawkeye.

Answers to Practice questions

(p.109)

1 Which of the following is a characteristic of popular recreation?
   a) Regularly played
   b) Officials present

c) **Highly violent**

d) **Highly structured**

Answer:

c) Highly violent

2 State the characteristics of popular recreation.

- Occasional/irregular
- Few simple rules
- Violent/damage to property/force not skill based
- Male-dominated/wagering
- Low structure/unlimited numbers/no set space/limited facilities/limited equipment
- Local
- Lower class development

3 Identify key characteristics of rational recreation.

- Refined skills/skill based/tactical
- Played in 'purpose-built' facilities; use of sophisticated equipment
- Regionally/nationally played
- Respectable
- Regular participation
- Rule based/codified; complex written rules
- Referees/officials

4 List and explain the different socio-cultural factors which influenced the development of rationalised sport in late nineteenth-century Britain.

- Development of transport/railways
- Increased accessibility for sporting events/played regionally/nationally; increased fixtures/competitions/leagues
- Emergence of urban middle-classes/factory owners/philanthropists/patronage
- Set up factory teams/provided facilities to play sport/ provided time off work to play and watch sport; early development of professional sport, e.g. via broken time payments
- Public schools/Old Boys
- Set up teams/set up NGBs/provided rule structure/codification
- Urbanisation
- Purpose-built facilities in limited space/large numbers in relatively small area needed entertaining/occupying/ public provision for sport gradually increased
- Church
- Set up church teams/provided facilities to play sport/set up organisations such as YMCA/Boys Brigade, etc.; creation of a sense of community
- Legal acts/Factory Acts/Industrialisation
- Increased free time to participate and watch sport/increased disposable income/improved health as a result of improved working conditions
- Increased communication via newspapers as society became more literate
- Increased knowledge/awareness of sport

5 Discuss the effects of industrialisation on sporting opportunities for the working classes.

Initial/First half of nineteenth century:

- Loss of space/ overcrowding

- Lack of time/long working hours
- Lack of disposable income/poverty/low wages
- Poor health/hygiene/little energy left after work
- Loss of rights to play mob games due to changes in criminal laws

Later/Second half of nineteenth century:
- Health/hygiene improved (e.g. public baths provision)
- More time for sport/Factory Acts/Saturday half day
- More disposable income for sport as wages gradually rose
- Middle-class philanthropists/patronage, e.g. factory teams/facilities
- Church/Public School Old Boys set up teams/provided facilities
- Improvements in transport/communications

6 'Victorian vicars made super sports.' During the late nineteenth century, the Church set up organisations, formed sports teams and provided facilities for sports participation among the working classes. Why did it do this?
- Improve attendance at church
- Social control/improve behaviour of working class/keep them out of trouble
- Sport had rules/had developed rationally, therefore more acceptable to them

7 Outline reasons why opportunities to reach elite level sport were restricted for the working class in the late nineteenth century.
- Elite sport was for upper class in the main
- Expense to participate meant limited opportunities for working classes
- Lots of time was needed to participate – limited for working classes
- Limited public provision
- Upper/middle classes controlled NGBs
- Upper/middle classes selected teams/restricted access to clubs
- Less equality of opportunity in society in general, e.g. gender

8 What factors led to an increase in the status of professional sports performers in twentieth-century Britain?
- More respected for their talents
- Higher profile/increased media coverage/role models
- Professionals used to be working class/lower status
- Social class no longer a barrier to participation
- Society now values 'materialism' more
- Sport seen as a 'way out'

Chapter 3.2 The impact of sport on society and of society on sport

Answers to Check your understanding questions

(p.111)

Define the terms primary socialisation and secondary socialisation.
- *Primary socialisation* = socialisation during the early years of childhood
- *Secondary socialisation* = socialisation which occurs during the 'later years', i.e. as teenagers/as adults

(p.112)

Identify different reasons why aerobics is a popular pastime among women compared to a sport such as rugby.

Aerobics is more popular because:

- Good for weight loss/body toning/health and fitness
- Non-contact activity
- Socially acceptable/fits female stereotype/positive female role models
- Gradual increase in leisure time/disposable income
- More equality of opportunity in society generally
- More opportunities to do it
- Can be performed recreationally/socially/at own level
- Women-only classes/sessions

(p.116)

How can participation in sport and other physical activity be increased among individuals in the working class?

Participation can be increased via:

- Increased publicity/advertisement of opportunities available
- Making sure they are affordable/decrease costs/subsidise
- Provide taster sessions
- Provide appealing activities
- Invest in areas of social deprivation

(p.117)

The participation of ethnic minorities in sport can be negatively affected by discrimination. Explain what is meant by the term 'discrimination'.

Discrimination is:

- Treating people differently
- Acting on a prejudice/excluding from participation
- Based on stereotyping on the basis of race/ethnicity

(p.117)

Explain the benefits to society of increasing participation rates in sport and physical activity.

Benefits to society of increased participation rates:

- Increased health and fitness results in less strain on the NHS/decreased obesity
- People spend money on hiring facilities/buying equipment which results in economic benefits/employment opportunities
- People participate together, leading to social integration/community integration
- Increased skill levels results in improved morale/confidence in the population
- Keeping people out of trouble, positively occupied in physical activity decreases crime

(p.123)

Identify barriers to sports participation which still exist for ethnic minority groups in twenty-first century Britain.

Barriers to participation for ethnic minority groups:

- Racism/discrimination still exists
- Actively discouraged by parents/peers

- Low status given to sport/preference for academic work
- Conflict with religious observances/dress codes
- Fewer ethnic minority role models/less media coverage
- Stereotyping/channelling still exists
- Fear of rejection/lower self-esteem

Answers to Activities questions

(p.111)

Consider the various purposes of play for young children during the primary socialisation process.
- Improving physical skills/co-ordination
- Improving social skills/communication/ability to make friends
- Improved morality/learn how to share
- Improved safety awareness/awareness of the environment
- Increased creativity/cognitive skills/decision-making

(p.112)

Consider the various purposes of physical education during the secondary socialisation process (i.e. what skills/values do children develop as a result of their PE experiences in secondary school?).
- Improved health and fitness
- Improved physical skills/competencies
- Improve social skills/leadership skills/social skills
- Improve moral skills
- Improve decision making skills
- Preparation for active leisure

(p.113)

Note down three key points about Cricket for Change as a scheme designed to help bring about social change.
- Scheme aimed at disadvantaged children
- Scheme aims to promote mutual respect and improve relationships within local communities
- Scheme provides free to access structured participation in cricket

(p.113)

Identify any myths about women which may negatively affect their participation in sport or physical activity.
- Myths about their physical capabilities (e.g. lack strength/power, etc.)
- Myths about their psychological attributes (e.g. lack aggression/determination)
- Myths about their skill levels (e.g. less entertaining to watch)
- Myths about traditional domestic/childcare role

(p.114)

Identify a sporting activity linked to those from a middle- or upper middle-class group and give reasons why there is limited access to this activity for those in 'lower' social classes.

For example, polo:
- Access restricted to upper class
- Due to lack of access to clubs/facilities

- Due to very high costs involved
- Due to strong traditional association with 'nobility'/high social class

(p.115)

Compare the possible differences between sports facilities at a state school with those of a private school in the area you live in.

Solutions dependant on local area lived in.

(p.115)

Look at the data in Figure 1 from 2011–12 which illustrates the Sport England Active People results on sports participation linked to socio-economic groups (i.e. social class). What does the data illustrate to you about social class and its impact on participation in sport?

- The data illustrate the differential which still exists in sports participation once a week based on the socio-economic group belonged to.
- A significantly higher proportion of adults from the highest socio-economic groups take part in regular sport (42.7%) compared to those from the lowest socio-economic groups (27.1%).

(p.121)

Research sports such as Boccia and Goalball to try to find out how they have been designed to help individuals with visual impairments get involved in sporting activity.

Solutions as appropriate to activity researched. For example:
- Improve confidence
- Increased access to clubs/equipment necessary to participate
- Access to activities specifically designed to meet their 'needs' in a safe environment

(p.124)

Suggest what sports or sports events women appear most frequently in on TV and/or in newspapers and what impact you think this might have on women's participation in sport.

- Common sporting events include: tennis, athletics, football.
- Global events include Olympic coverage and more recently World Cup women's football.
- Increased coverage in such sports/sports events can lead to more role models to aspire to/copy which can increase their participation in sport.

(p.124)

Summarise the times to women's participation in sport and physical activity in the acronym TRIPS, where T = Time, R = Role models, I = Income costs, P = PE programmes and S= Sponsorship

Students' own answers.

(p.126)

Identify two key facts from the data in Figure 9 illustrating participation patterns among women in team sports.

Facts from team sports data:
- Football is the most popular team sport for women.
- Team sports are participated in far more by men compared to women, e.g. men's football is nearly three million compared to just over a quarter of a million women.

(p.126)

What important sports participation 'trends' are illustrated by the demographics figures in Figure 10 comparing participation in sport by various groups in society from 2005–6 to 2011–12?

- **General population**: in the general population, participation in sport has increased (by 3.5%).
- **Age**: in terms of age, younger age ranges (i.e. 16–24) are far more likely to participate than the older age range (NB: participation in the 16–24 age range has slightly decreased by 4 per cent).
- **Gender**: participation in sport for men and women both increased (3.9 per cent for men and 3.3 per cent for women); participation by men is 10 per cent more likely than for women.
- **Ethnicity**: participation in sport has increased among both the 'white' population as well as the BME population: 3.3 per cent in white population, compared to 5.3 per cent in BME population. This is a larger percentage increase for BME group compared to the white group and brings the two very close.
- **Disability**: participation in sport has decreased for those with a disability (2.9 per cent); non-disabled individuals are almost twice as likely to participate as those with a disability.
- **Disabled individuals** are the lowest participators of sport when compared to other 'disadvantaged groups' such as ethnic minorities and women. Only individuals who are 75+ have a lower percentage participation than disabled population in general.

(p.129)

Do some research to identify how the CSP in your area is working to increase participation (e.g. how it is delivering the Sportivate programme aimed at increasing participation in young people). What do you think the advantages and disadvantages are of a 'regional approach'?

Information on CSP as appropriate to the local area researched.

Answers to Practice questions

(p.132)

1 Which of the following statements best define the term 'socialisation'?

d) A lifelong process whereby members of society learn the values, ideas, practices and roles of that society.

2 Define the following terms: stereotyping and prejudice.

- **Stereotyping** = standardised/over simplified/shared image of a group
- **Prejudice** = formation of an unfavourable opinion of an individual, often based on inadequate facts

3 Identify the benefits to the individual of participating in club sport.

- Increased health and fitness; decreased obesity
- Positive use of free time; keep people out of trouble
- Increased job opportunities
- Increased self-esteem/self-confidence via personal 'success'/improvement
- Improvement in social skills/community integration
- Improved morale

4 Give reasons why disabled sports participants have improved opportunities to take part in sport in the early twenty-first century compared to the late twentieth century.

- Increase in equality of opportunity/inclusion/social acceptance
- Adapted equipment/improved access to facilities/increase in number of specialist facilities
- More sporting activities available (adapted/specifically designed for the disabled)
- More competitions/clubs to enter/join
- Increase number of specialist coaches/trained staff

- Technological advancements/improved technology
- Increased media coverage of disability sport/more role models from disability sport/Paralympic effect
- Increased awareness of 'needs' in PE programmes
- Via work of organisations such as EFDS/Sport England
- Additional funding for target groups such as disability

5 **Identify the economic barriers which may account for the lower rate of participation of women in sport and physical activity.**
- Costs involved/fewer resources/social acceptance
- Fewer sponsorship opportunities available
- Fewer full-time sporting opportunities
- Long working hours/less leisure time available

6 **Identify schemes and initiatives Sport England has put in place to improve opportunities for women and young girls to participate in sport.**
- I Will If You Will
- Women in Sport (via WSFF)
- Active Women
- This Girl Can
- Breeze
- Back to Netball
- US Girls

Chapter 4.1 Diet and nutrition and their effect on physical activity and performance

Answers to Check your understanding questions

(p.135)

Why should a games player have a diet rich in fat?
- Energy source
- Important to last the match
- Good source of vitamins A, D, E and K
- But can gain weight
- Limit flexibility
- Limit stamina
- Cause health problems such as coronary heart disease/diabetes/high blood pressure

(p.136)

Give the exercise-related function of two vitamins.
- Protects cells and keeps them healthy.
- Has a role in the absorption of calcium, which keeps bones and teeth healthy.
- Works with other B group vitamins to help break down and release energy from food.
- Keeps the skin, eyes and nervous system healthy.
- Helps form haemoglobin.
- Helps the body to use and store energy from protein and carbohydrate in food.

- Makes red blood cells.
- Releases energy from food.

(p.137)

Eating a diet with sufficient calcium and iron would have physiological benefits for an athlete. State the importance of these two minerals for the athlete.

- Iron helps production of red blood cells/haemoglobin which helps transport oxygen and improves stamina
- Calcium for bones
- Calcium for muscle contraction/nerve transmission (important during exercise)

(p.138)

What are the possible physiological effects of a lack of water on a performer?

- Increased body temperature/overheating
- Reduced sweating/reduce blood flow to skin
- Increased blood viscosity/blood becomes thicker
- Increased heart rate/cardiovascular drift
- Lower blood pressure
- Lower cardiac output
- Transportation of oxygen/carbon dioxide less efficient
- Possible cramp
- Headaches/dizziness

Answers to Activities

(p.138)

Copy and complete Table 4 to summarise the exercise-related role and source for each of the food groups listed.

Food group	Exercise-related function	Source
Carbohydrates	Primary energy source. Used in both high-and low intensity exercise.	Bread potatoes, rice, pasta
Fats	Secondary energy source, used for low-intensity, long duration exercise. Good source of vitamins A, D, E and K.	Found in sweet, e.g. chocolate, and savoury foods, e.g. meat
Proteins	Important for muscle growth and repair and are a minor source of energy.	Meat, fish, eggs, dairy products
Vitamins	*Any of the following:* ● Protects cells and keeps them healthy. ● Has a role in the absorption of calcium, which keeps bones and teeth healthy. ● Works with other B group vitamins to help break down and release energy from food. ● Keeps the skin, eyes and nervous system healthy. ● Helps form haemoglobin. ● Helps the body to use and store energy from protein and carbohydrate in food. ● Makes red blood cells. ● Releases energy from food.	Meat, fish, eggs, dairy products, vegetables, fruit

Food group	Exercise-related function	Source
Minerals	● Necessary for efficient nerve and muscle function. ● This helps regulate fluid levels in the body. However, too much sodium is linked to an increase in blood pressure which can increase the risk of a stroke or heart attack. ● This helps in the formation of haemoglobin in red blood cells which helps transport oxygen. A lack of iron can lead to anaemia.	Meat, fish, eggs, dairy products, cereals, vegetables, fruit and nuts
Fibre	Slows down the time it takes the body to break down food, which results in a slower, more sustained release of energy.	Wholemeal bread and pasta, potatoes, nuts, seeds, fruit, vegetables and pulses
Water	Transports nutrients, hormones and waste products around the body. It is the main component of many cells and plays an important part in regulating body temperature.	

(p.140)

Create your own table and summarise the positive and negative effects of glycogen loading, creatine, bicarbonate of soda and caffeine consumption.

With a partner or in small groups, see if you can remember the positive and negative effects of glycogen loading, creatine, bicarbonate of soda and caffeine consumption.

Needs some of the following information:

Glycogen loading:

Positive: Increased glycogen storage, increased glycogen stores in the muscle, delays fatigue increases endurance capacity.

Negative: During the carbo-loading phase – water retention which results in bloating, heavy legs, affects digestion, weight increase. During the depletion phase – irritability, can alter the training programme through a lack of energy.

Creatine:

Positive: Helps improve recovery times, can perform at higher intensity for longer.

Negative: Dehydration, bloating, muscle cramps and slight liver damage.

Bicarbonate of soda:

Positive: Reduces acidity to delay fatigue.

Negative: Vomiting, pain, cramping, diarrhoea or a feeling of being bloated!

Caffeine:

Positive: Stimulant/increased mental alertness, reduces fatigue, allows fats to be used as energy source/delays use of glycogen stores, improves decision making/improves reaction time, may benefit aerobic performance/endurance athletes.

Negative: Loss of fine control, against rules of most sports in large quantities, dehydration, insomnia, muscle cramps, stomach cramps, vomiting, irregular heartbeat, diarrhoea.

Answers to Practice questions

(p.141)

1 Which of the following statements about Vitamin D is true?

    a) **Helps absorb calcium, which keeps bones and teeth healthy.**

b) Helps form haemoglobin.

c) Makes red blood cells and keeps the nervous system healthy.

d) Keeps the skin, eyes and nervous system healthy.

a) Helps absorb calcium, which keeps bones and teeth healthy.

2 **Footballers need stamina to play the game effectively. State two classes of food that are most suitable for players who require stamina and explain why they are needed in their diet.**

- Carbohydrates and fats
- Carbohydrates are the principal source of energy used for both high and low intensity exercise
- Fats are an energy source for long duration, low intensity exercise

3 **Which class of food is most important for a weightlifter? Give reasons for your answer.**

- Protein
- For muscle growth and repair which will be needed after a training session where the performer has worked at high intensity

4 **Discuss the potential benefits and harmful effects to an athlete in taking caffeine supplements.**

- Increases alertness
- Improves decision making/improves reaction time
- Can benefit aerobic performance
- Fats can be used as an energy source
- Side effects include dehydration/insomnia/muscle cramps/vomiting/irregular heartbeat/diarrhoea

Chapter 4.2 Preparation and training methods in relation to maintaining physical activity and performance

Answers to Check your understanding questions

(p.146)

What are the benefits of performing a cool-down?

- Keeps the skeletal muscle pump working
- Maintains venous return
- Prevents blood pooling in the veins
- Limits the effect of DOMS (delayed onset of muscle soreness)
- Removes lactic acid

(p.146)

Describe how a games player would apply the specificity principle to improve fitness.

- Use same energy system(s) as they use in a game
- Use same muscle fibre type they use in a game
- Use similar skills/movements they use in a game
- Use similar intensity that they use in a game
- Use similar duration to the game

(p.149)

Explain the different stages in periodisation.

- The macrocycle is a long-term performance goal such as a personal best in athletics. It involves dividing the year up into stages. The macrocycle includes:

- Preparation period: is similar to pre-season training where fitness is developed.
- Competition period: is the performance period where skills and techniques are refined.
- Transition period: is the end of the season where rest and recovery takes place.
- The mesocycle is a 4–12 week period of training with a particular focus such as power.
- The microcycle is a description of a week or a few days of training sessions.

(p.150)

What factors would you consider when delivering a circuit training programme to develop muscular endurance?

- Decide on the number of stations/exercises
- Ensure sport specific exercises are included/replication of movement or skill patterns
- Target the relevant muscle groups
- Take care with the order of exercise to alternate body areas
- Take into account the time available or frequency of sessions (of circuit training)
- Decide on the number of repetitions/sets and the intensity/time that is spent at each station
- Work out how many recovery/rest periods there are going to be
- Equipment/space available
- Take into account level of fitness/ability/age/gender/injuries/size of group/motivation

(p.151)

Which methods of training could be used to improve a) power and b) stamina?

a) Power = Interval, circuits and weights, where the intensity has to be high.

b) Stamina = Continuous, fartlek, interval, circuits, weights, where the intensity will be low.

Answers to Activities

(p.144)

Copy Table 2 and decide on the validity and reliability of the tests.

Test	Validity	Reliability
Multi-stage fitness test	Involves a running action so sport specific for a runner but not a cyclist or swimmer.	Only a prediction of VO₂ (max).
Vertical jump	Only valid for power in the legs.	It is quite hard to time the jump so that a mark can be made when the performer is at full height. Different techniques are used so a lack of consistency.
30-m sprint test	Only measures leg speed not arm speed. Not valid for a swimmer or cyclist as not sport specific. Also not sport specific in that there is no change in direction.	There can be human error with the timing. If performed outside, the surface could affect the result, especially during wet conditions.
Illinois agility run	Not sport specific with those sports that require bats, sticks and rackets since you perform the test empty handed.	Could be human error with timing. If performed outside, the surface could affect the result, especially during wet conditions.

(p.145)

Write about *what* you do for a warm-up and try to explain *why* you do it.

Any warm-up with the three stages: pulse raiser, specific stretches and specific movement patterns related to their sport/activity.

(p.149)

Table 6 is an example of a periodised year for a rugby player. Label the different periods of the macrocycle and explain what the rugby player is going to do in each of these periods.

	July	Aug	Sept	Oct	Nov	Dec	Jan	Feb	Mar	Apr	May	June
Activity	Preparation period Fitness work Conditioning		Competition phase Skill-based activities and maintenance of fitness								Transition phase Rest and recovery	

Pre-season starts   Competitive season starts   Season finishes

(p.150)

Consider a 100-metre and 400-metre sprinter. These are both anaerobic events but the needs are different. Discuss the different demand for these events with a partner.

- 100m = 10 seconds – energy needs to be provided quickly over a short period of time.
- 400m = 45 seconds as 400m much harder anaerobic event with a big build-up of lactic acid.

(p.150)

Plan an interval training session for a 100-metre and a 400-metre sprinter.

These need to take account of:

- Duration of the work interval is shorter for 100m
- Intensity or speed of the work interval is higher intensity for 100m but both high
- Duration of the recovery period – longer for 400m
- Number of work intervals and recovery periods. More work intervals for 100m as shorter distance so more recovery intervals.

(p.152)

Answers to Practice questions

1 Which of the following statements about data is true?
  a) Qualitative data can be written down or measured with numbers.
  b) Quantitative data is descriptive and looks at the way people think or feel.
  c) Reliability means the test can be repeated accurately.
  d) Subjective data is based upon facts and is measurable.

c) Reliability means the test can be repeated accurately.

2 Describe how you would apply the 'FITT' principles to improve fitness.
  - Frequency-train more often
  - Intensity-train harder
  - Time/duration-train for longer
  - Type-use different forms of exercise
  - Overload-work/train harder than normal

3 **What are the physiological benefits of performing a warm-up?**
- Reduces possibility of injury/ increase flexibility/elasticity of muscle tissue
- Release of synovial fluid
- Increases body/muscle temperature
- Better oxygen delivery/ blood flow
- Increased speed of nerve conduction/reaction time
- Allows for rehearsal of movement/ same skills as in activity
- Mental rehearsal/stress or anxiety reduction/psychological preparation
- Supplies adequate blood flow to heart so increasing its efficiency

4 **When planning a training programme for an elite athlete, tapering and peaking are crucial to the athlete's success. What do you understand by the terms 'tapering' and 'peaking'?**
- **Tapering:** reducing the volume and or intensity of training prior to competition
- **Peaking:** organising training so a performer is at their best both physically and mentally for a major competition

Chapter 5 Biomechanical principles and levers

Answers to Check your understanding questions

(p.155)

Using your knowledge of Newton's Three Laws of Motion, try to explain how a high jumper takes off from the ground.
- A description of the law of inertia – body remains in a constant state of motion unless acted upon by a force.
- Force is applied by the muscles on the ground at take-off.
- The change in the state of motion occurs at the take-off.
- A description of the law of acceleration – magnitude of force governs the acceleration at take-off.
- The direction of force also governs direction of acceleration.
- The more force that is applied, the more height is achieved.
- A description of the law of action/reaction – for every force there is an equal and opposite reaction force.
- In the take-off, the reaction force is a ground reaction force.

(p.158)

Give two factors that can increase stability.
- Low centre of mass.
- Line of gravity should be central over the base of support to increase stability.
- The more contact points, the larger the base of support becomes.
- The greater the mass the more stability there is because of increased inertia.

Name and sketch the lever system that operates during extension of the elbow.

First class lever

Answers to Activity questions

(p.154)

When Usain Bolt ran his world record 100 metres, his acceleration out of the blocks was 9.5 m/s. Work out the force at work on Bolt who has a mass of 94 kg. Your answer will be in newtons.

- Force = mass × acceleration (F = ma)
- Therefore: 94 × 9.5 = 893 newtons

(p.155)

Complete Table 2 below, giving an example of how each of Newton's laws can be applied to a sport of your choice.

Answers will depend on what sport you choose:

Newton's laws	Application
Law of inertia	Inertia: apply this to making something stop or start or change direction
Law of acceleration	Acceleration: something where the more force is used, the faster something will go
Law of reaction	Use of a ground reaction force: another jumping example (not football)

(p.157)

Calculate the average speed for the three components of a triathlon in Table 3.

Distance	Time	Average speed (m/s)
1.5-km swim	**30 mins 30 secs**	0.82m/s
40-km cycle	**90 mins**	7.41m/s
10-km run	**45 mins**	3.7m/s

(p.158)

Choose a sport and explain how one of the factors above can be used to increase stability.

A sport where one of the following have been considered:

- Low centre of mass.
- Line of gravity should be central over the base of support to increase stability.
- The more contact points, the larger the base of support becomes.
- The greater the mass, the more stability there is, because of increased inertia.

(p.160)

Label the fulcrum, effort and resistance for flexion of the elbow on Figure 11 then do the same for extension of the elbow.

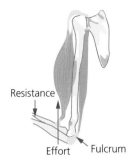

Resistance

Effort   Fulcrum

Answers to Practice questions

(p.161)

1 Which of the following statements is true?

   a) A first order lever has the resistance in the middle.

   b) A first order lever has the effort in the middle.

   c) A second order lever has the fulcrum in the middle.

   d) A third order lever has the effort in the middle.

d) A third order lever has the effort in the middle.

2 Name and sketch the lever system that operates during plantar-flexion of the ankle joint.

Second order lever

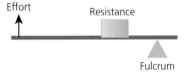

Effort   Resistance

Fulcrum

3 What do you understand by the terms mechanical advantage and mechanical disadvantage?

Drawing of either a lever which has a mechanical advantage or one that has a mechanical disadvantage:

Mechanical disadvantage:

● When the resistance arm is greater than the force arm.

● Cannot move as heavy a load but can do it faster/large range of movement.

Mechanical advantage:

● When the force arm is longer than the resistance arm.

● Can move a large load over a short distance and requires little force.

4 Using Newton's second law of motion, explain how an athlete is able to accelerate towards the finish line.

● Mass of runner is constant.

● Force = Mass × Acceleration.

● The greater the force exerted on the floor, the greater the acceleration of the athlete.

● Force governs direction so the athlete will accelerate in the direction of the applied force.

● Force is provided by muscular contraction of the gastrocnemius, quadriceps, gluteals (only need to name one of these but all are creditworthy).

● The reaction force comes from the ground.

5 If a sprinter runs at a speed of 8 metres per second for 30 seconds, calculate the distance covered.

● Distance = Speed × Time

● 8 × 30 = 240m

Chapter 6.1 Psychological influences on the individual

Answers to Check your understanding questions

(p.165)

1 Name the three parts of the Hollander model of an interactionist approach to sport.

- Core values
- Typical responses
- Role related behaviour

2 What is the formula associated with the interactionist approach to personality?

- $B = f(P \times E)$

3 What are the features of the trait theory of personality?

- Personality characteristics are innate, consistent and stable.

4 Why do some sports psychologists think that it is difficult to predict behaviour in sport?

Some are sceptical because there is no link between personality and performance, behaviour can change during the game and personality research can be invalid and unreliable.

(p.168)

1 Name three parts of an attitude.

Three of the following:
- Cognitive
- Affective
- Behavioural
- Timing

2 Name three things you should consider when using persuasion to change an attitude.

- Relevance
- Status
- Quality

3 Name three ways a player could show a positive attitude.

- Belief in their ability
- Enjoying taking part
- Training and playing regularly

4 How could a negative attitude be formed?

- Bad experience
- Injury
- Lack of ability or success
- No reinforcement
- Negative role models

(p.174)

1 When performing in sport, a player may suffer from an increase in activation known as arousal. Explain the effect of increased arousal on performance according to drive theory.

- The relationship between arousal and performance is explained by the formula: $P = f(D \times H)$.

- Increases in motivation cause increased drive/arousal.
- Increases in drive result in the increased of probability of good performance.
- A graph showing linear/straight line/proportional relationship between arousal/performance.
- This relationship is not realistic – cannot keep improving.
- An increase in arousal means an increase in likelihood of dominant response.
- If the dominant response is well learned or the performer is an expert, then performance is improved.
- If the dominant response is not learned, probability of poor performance increases.

2 **Use catastrophe theory to explain how over-arousal can affect performance.**
- Increased arousal improves performance to an optimum point at a moderate level of arousal.
- Increases in cognitive and somatic anxiety experienced as arousal increases, causes a dramatic drop in performance.
- The performer tries to recover but may not be able to do so, unless the initial anxiety is low and there is time.
- Any failure to recover may cause even more anxiety.

3 **Name three features of the peak flow experience.**
- Effortless movement
- Total control
- High confidence
- Low anxiety
- Extreme focus

4 **What would be the optimal level of arousal for an expert rugby player attempting a tackle?**

High: the skill is gross requiring less control and the expert might be able to deal with the pressure.

5 **What would be the optimal arousal level for a novice golfer attempting a putt?**

Low: The task requires control and the novice operates best at low arousal.

Answers to Activity questions

(p.165)

Some people support the idea that personality can predict behaviour: they are credulous; they trust the theories.

Some people think that personality does not accurately predict behaviour: they are sceptical; they have doubts about the link between personality and performance.

Give two reasons why you think people might be credulous and two reasons why you think people might be sceptical about the interactionist approach to personality. There are some pointers in the text above!

Answers might include:
- **Credulous**
- Behaviour changes as competition increases
- There are personality tests that predict behaviour and can be used as part of talent identification
- Personality types can be linked to elite sporting performance such as being calm under pressure.
- **Sceptical**
- There is no link between personality and choice of sport
- Behaviour and personality can change during the game

(p.168)

Copy and complete Table 1 to show which attitude component can be changed using the different methods of attitude change.

Attitude component	Method of change
Cognitive	Challenge a belief Point out the benefits of a new technique
Affective	Make it fun
Behavioural	Use role models Use reinforcement

(p.173)

Study the inverted-U theory and the zone of optimal functioning. Can you suggest some differences and similarities between the two theories?

Similarities:

● Both suggest that the optimal level of arousal varies with factors relating to the performer and the task.

● Both suggest that less than optimal arousal levels, too much or too little, could impair performance.

Differences:

● Inverted U suggests that arousal can be shown as a point on a graph; the Zone indicates that arousal is displayed in an area or band.

Answers to Practice questions

(p.175)

1 According to the inverted-U theory, low levels of arousal produce the best performance when:
   a) the performer is a novice and the skill is gross
   b) the performer is a novice and the skill is fine
   c) the performer is an expert and the skill is gross
   d) the performer is an expert and the skill is fine.

b) the performer is a novice and the skill is fine

2 **The performance and behaviour of sports performers may be affected by their personalities. Discuss this statement using suitable examples, with reference to the interactionist theory of personality.**
   ● $B = f(PE)$: behaviour is a function of personality and environment.
   ● Inherited trait amended by environment/situation.
   ● Leads to stable behaviour: in a certain situation allows behaviour to be predicted.
   ● Change environment/change behaviour.
   ● For example, normally calm, but becomes aggressive in sport, e.g. boxer.

3 **Name and explain one theoretical principle that a coach could use to change a negative attitude into a positive one.**

Cognitive dissonance:
   ● Challenge attitude component
   ● Causes unease
   ● Motivates performer to replace or change attitude
   ● Make activity fun
   ● Use role models of similar ability

Persuasive communication:
   ● High status, expert
   ● Quality, so performer can understand.

- Relevant
- Timing of communication

4 **When performing in sport, a player may suffer from an increase in activation known as arousal. Explain the effect of increased arousal on performance according to drive theory.**

- Formula: $P = f(D \times H)$
- Increases in motivation increase drive/arousal.
- Increases in drive result in increases of probability of good performance.
- Linear/ straight line/ proportional relationship.
- But, not realistic – cannot keep improving.
- Increase in arousal = increase in likelihood of dominant response.
- If dominant response is well learned/expert performer = improved performance.
- If dominant response is not learned, probability of poor performance increases.

Chapter 6.2 Further psychological effects on the individual

Answers to Check your understanding questions

(p.181)

1 **Name two features of cognitive anxiety.**

- Loss of concentration
- Irrational thinking – lack of belief in ability

2 **Name two features of somatic anxiety.**

- Increased heart rate
- Muscular tension

3 **Name three ways of measuring anxiety in sport.**

- Questionnaire
- Observation
- Physiological tests

4 **Using a table, give one advantage and one disadvantage of each method named in the answer to the question above.**

Measure	Advantages	Disadvantages
Questionnaire – favoured by Eysenck. Involves giving short, written answers that can then be standardised to scale to compare results.	Deals with lots of info Quick/efficient Cheap Objective	Questions misunderstood Too general: Yes/No only. Biased answers Weak validity/unreliable Depends on mood state
Observation – researcher watches players in action several times and notes aspects of their behaviour and personality.	Realistic True picture of athlete	Subjective – results vary Comments opinioned Time consuming Athletes behaviour may change Consistency of data collection?
Physiological methods Body measurement	Factual Easy to compare Realistic	Costly Needs training to learn method May restrict movement May cause additional stress

(p.186)

1 Name three features of aggression.
- Intent to harm
- Outside the rules
- Hostile

2 Name three features of assertion.
- Within the rules
- Motivated
- No intent to harm

3 What aspects of play can cause frustration in sport?
- Losing
- Being fouled
- Crowd
- Referee decision

4 What can a referee do to control aggression during a game?
- Be consistent and immediate in making decisions.
- Talk to players to calm them down.
- Punish foul play

(p.188)

1 What is motivation?
- The drive to succeed.

2 What is the difference between intrinsic motivation and extrinsic motivation?
- Extrinsic motivation comes from an outside source.
- Intrinsic motivation comes from within.

3 What is the difference between tangible and intangible rewards?
- Tangible rewards are physical and can be touched, e.g., a trophy.
- Intangible rewards can't be touched, e.g., praise.

4 Which type of motivation is more permanent?
- Intrinsic
- Extrinsic motivation is good in the early stages of learning.

5 How could a coach ensure that the motivation levels of experienced players in their team are maintained?
- Set challenging goals
- Correct errors via negative feedback
- Attribute success internally
- Make the performer feel responsible by giving praise for personal improvement

Answers to Activities questions

(p.180)

Some results of the SCAT test are given below. Study the results of the three different performers and then suggest how you would use the results in the situations described below if you were the team coach. The maximum score is 30 and the minimum is 10. The higher the score, the greater the level of competitive anxiety.

Player A: SCAT score 22, Player B: SCAT score 26, Player C: SCAT score 15

Which player(s) would you?

a) **Nominate to take penalties.**

Player C

b) **Pick as your captain.**

Players A or C

c) **Pick as a team mentor.**

Players A or B or C: high or low anxiety does not mean you will not make a good mentor

d) **Introduce to anxiety control techniques.**

Players A and B

e) **Substitute in a close and aggressive match.**

Player B

(p.186)

Look at all the methods used to reduce and prevent aggression in sport. Put them in a copy of Table 1, under the headings: Players, Coaches, Officials. (You can list each method more than once in each column.)

Players	Coaches	Officials
Walk away from the situation	Punish players with fines	Punish players by sending them off
Channel the aggression	Reinforce non aggressive acts	Apply the rules consistently
Use relaxation techniques	Encourage peer group pressure	Talk to players to calm them down
Apply peer group pressure	Substitute players	Give immediate sanctions
Set non-aggressive goals	Talk to players to calm them down	
	Set non aggressive goals	
	Point out responsibilities to the team	

(p.188)

Study the list of ways that a coach could use to motivate players in their charge. Suggest which of the methods listed could be used for a novice and which could be used for a more advanced performer.

To motivate a novice:

- Early rewards
- Break the skill into parts
- Make training fun
- Point out role models
- Use positive feedback to inspire

To motivate a more experienced player:

- Set challenging goals
- Correct errors via negative feedback
- Attribute success internally
- Make the performer feel responsible by giving praise.

Answers to Practice questions

(p.188)

1 Two players from opposing teams both challenge for the same ball during a game. One player gets injured during the clash. This is an example of:

a) aggression

b) instrumental aggression

c) foul play

d) assertion

d) assertion

2 Sport performers can experience anxiety during performance. Explain the different types of anxiety that can be experienced in sport and use examples to show how these types of anxiety can have a negative effect on performance.

- Competitive trait anxiety, worry and nerves before most games
- Competitive state anxiety, temporary and situation specific, anxiety when taking a penalty.
- Cognitive anxiety psychological feelings of worry and being unable to cope, loss of concentration when playing, mis-directed pass.
- Somatic anxiety – increased heart rate, muscular tension results in weak serve
- Equivalent examples accepted.

3 Aggression is an unwelcome aspect of team performance. Explain why aggression might occur during team games.

- *Instinct theory:* Evolution, protect pitch, instinctive, catharsis, sport as an aggressive outlet.
- *F/A hypothesis:* Goals blocked, build-up of frustration, catharsis
- *Learned cues:* Cue hypothesis, learned trigger causes aggression
- *Social learning:* Copy peers, Copy significant others, behaviour copied if reinforced, live behaviour copied.

4 To achieve good results, sports performers need to be motivated. Explain the different forms of motivation that may be available to help the sports performer succeed.

- Intrinsic from within.
- Extrinsic from outside source.
- Tangible, physical reward, e.g. trophy.
- Intangible, non-physical reward, e.g. praise

Chapter 6.3 Psychological influences on the team

Answers to Check your understanding questions

(p.193)

1 Using examples, identify the four types of others, according to Zajonc, who could be present at a sporting event.

- Audience
- Co-actors
- Competitive co-actors
- Social reinforcers

2 **What is evaluation apprehension?**
- The perceived fear of being judged

3 **What strategies could a coach use to limit the effects of evaluation apprehension?**
- Improve confidence
- Use cognitive and somatic relaxation techniques
- Introduce evaluation gradually
- Lower the importance of the event
- Use mental rehearsal, learned well to ensure the dominant response is correct

4 **How does drive theory help explain the effects of an audience on performance?**
- The audience increases arousal levels, which means the performer relies in the dominant response.
- If the dominant response is correct, more likely if the performer is an expert, then facilitation will occur.
- If the dominant response is incorrect, more likely if the performer is a novice, then inhibition will occur.

(p.202)

1 **What are the features of a team or group?**
- Interaction
- Communication
- Shared goals and values
- Collective identity

2 **Name and explain the four stages of group formation.**
- *Forming* – getting to know others
- *Storming* – conflict
- *Norming* – co-operation
- *Performing* – working together to achieve goals

3 **What do you understand by the term social loafing?**
- The loss of motivation of an individual team member

4 **What are the co-ordination problems that can affect team cohesion?**
- Lack of communication
- Poor tactics
- Strategies
- Unacceptance or misunderstanding of roles

5 **What might affect the potential productivity of a sports team?**
- Having the most experienced, skilful players and facilities and how these players interact.

(p.206)

1 **What are the benefits of goal setting?**
- Improved confidence
- Improved motivation
- Gives a target
- Provides task persistence
- Eliminates errors

2 Name three types of goals.

- Long-term
- Outcome
- Short-term
- Process
- Performance

3 Why could goals that are set just on winning have a negative impact on performance?

Because not every performer can win and this may cause loss of motivation and confidence if the goal is not reached. Performance and process goals can improve technique and be achieved by every competitor.

Answers to Activity questions

(p.193)

Think back to your early years of playing sport. How did you feel when someone you knew came to watch? Did that audience help or hinder your performance?

Answer: any relevant example.

(p.193)

Make a list of the ways a coach or player could reduce the effects of social inhibition. Check your list against the points above.

- Gradually introduce evaluation
- Peer pressure
- Familiarisation, train with distractions
- Lower the importance of the event

(p.202)

Complete Table 1 to suggest which strategies could be used to specifically reduce social loafing and co-ordination problems and promote cohesion. You can use the same strategies more than once.

Reduce social loafing	Reduce co-ordination problems	Promote cohesion
Individual goals Specific role Promote motivation Using statistics Reward exceptional contribution	Setting goals Involve all in goal setting Specific role Clear tactics Promote motivation Maintain communication Get fitter	Involve all in goal setting Establish group identity Team meetings to resolve conflict Individual goals Set more challenging goals

(p.206)

Imagine you are a swimmer with the long-term goal of trying to achieve a qualifying time for the Regional Finals. What short-term goals could you set to help achieve your aims?

Answer as appropriate but might include:

- Process goals, to improve technique when performing the start or turn.
- Performance goals, to lower the personal best time by 0.2 seconds.

(p.206)

Answers to Practice questions

1 According to Zajonc, the crowd cheering on their team during a match is best described in terms of the type of others present as:

   a) co-actors

   b) social reinforcers

   c) audience

   d) competitors

b) social reinforcers

2 What do you understand by the term 'evaluation apprehension'? Explain how the concept of evaluation apprehension can affect performance.

Three from:

- Perceived fear of being judged.
- Causes increased arousal.
- Inhibition effects on performance.
- Worse if being judged by perceived expert.
- Worse if being judged by people known to performer.

3 Steiner suggested that the relationship between the individual members of a team and their overall performance may be expressed as:

Actual productivity = Potential productivity – Losses due to faulty processes

Explain the terms 'actual productivity' and 'potential productivity' and the factors that might affect them.

Three from:

- Actual productivity – performance achieved.
- Potential productivity – team's best possible performance.
- Depends on resources.
- Ability/skills knowledge of players.
- How those players interact.

4 **Suggest potential causes of the losses due to faulty group processes.**

Four from:

- Co-ordination losses.
- Players skills/tactical failings lack of team work.
- More interactive sports more difficult to co-ordinate.
- Ringlemann effect.
- Motivational losses.
- Social loafing.

5 **Team leaders set goals to motivate their teams. What are the characteristics of effective goal setting?**

Any four from the SMARTER principle:

- Specific
- Measured
- Achievable

- Realistic
- Timed
- Evaluate
- Re-do
- Not just based on winning, should include process and performance.

Chapter 7 The role of technology in physical activity and sport

Answers to Check your understanding questions

(p.208)

Define what is meant by sports analytics.

The analysis of sports data using analytical tools and methods for data to be subjected to analytical procedures in order to try and improve results.

(p.211)

Identify three potential problems a sports coach might have if they choose not to use video analysis programmes, but rely instead on their own observation and analysis skills.

- Issues with memory retention of the performance observed.
- May lead to incorrect decisions during matches/competitions, e.g. when making substitutions.
- May lead to incorrect training programmes being implemented.

(p.212)

Imagine you are a basketball coach and you have the shooting data in Table 1 available on your main two offensive players.

1 Use the data in Table 1 to explain which player (i.e. Player 1 or Player 2) has been the most successful at shooting.

2 What other additional information would you need to consider when making your judgement on the relative shooting capabilities of Player 1 and Player 2?

3 How could you use the data to inform your offensive players shooting strategies in their next match?

1 Player 1 has been the most successful at shooting with lay ups (100 per cent success rate compared to 80 per cent for player 2), set shots in the key (75 per cent success rate compared to 60 per cent for player 2). But they were both the same at 25 per cent for 3 point shots.

2 Considerations would include the amount of pressure from opponents when executing the shot; the angle/actual relative distances of shots; the game situation when shots were attempted – did this add to the pressure when taking the shot?

3 Strategies would include trying to feed player 1 into the basket for lay ups and into the key way for set shots whenever possible; also try to avoid taking 3-point shots unless game context requires it and the team is a long way behind, as the relative success of 3-pointers was very low at 25 per cent for both players.

(p.213)

Identify different reasons for individual variations in an individual's REE over a period of time.

- Due to overall weight/obesity
- Due to height; height/weight ratio

- Due to chemistry of body in response to various drugs
- Due to illnesses

(p.214)

Identify four different ways in which GPS data can help improve player performance.

- It helps overall to monitor player performance (e.g. is it 'as expected'?).
- It can measure impact, e.g. G-forces.
- It can help make objective decisions about replacements.
- It can decrease injury risk by gauging levels of fatigue.
- It can help manage workload during rehabilitation, and ultimately get the through it successfully at a quicker rate.
- It can help make better use of training time and ensure training meets game demands.
- It improves tactical analysis.
- It enables player comparisons.

(p.215)

Identify three ways to ensure data integrity is maintained.

- Regularly backing-up data
- Controlling access to data and protecting against malicious intent via security mechanisms
- Designing interfaces which prevent the input of invalid data; taking care when entering data
- Using error detection and correction software when transmitting data
- Not switching on, logging on to and then leaving a computer unattended for anyone to access

Answers to Activity questions

(p.209)

A netball coach tries out two different players in the position of Centre in pre-season matches, with a view to selecting one of them to start the first competitive league game of the season. They both play two out of the four pre-season games against similar levels of opposition. Give examples of valid, objective data which is quantitative in nature that you would advise the netball coach to collect to help inform them when making their decision.

- Number of passes attempted; number of successful passes completed (i.e. ratio/percentage success rate).
- Number of successful Centre passes at game restarts.
- Number of passes to team mate in the circle; number of successful passes into the circle (i.e. ratio/percentage success rate).
- Number of pass interceptions achieved.
- Total distance covered (in km).

(p.209)

To help understand the basis of reliability of information received, think about standing on a set of weighing scales which should be well maintained to ensure meaningful data is obtained. When would the scales be considered:

a) reliable

b) unreliable?

a) *reliable* when the same/similar weight readings are received every time you step on the scales (when weight levels are stable!).

b) *unreliable* when very different weight readings are received every time the scales are used, regardless of whether or not weight has been gained/lost!

(p.211)

Visit one of the following links to find out more about PA and motion analysis software used in sport.
- **Dartfish:** www.dartfish.com
- **Upmygame:** www.upmygame.com
- **Prozone:** www.prozonesports.com

No solutions – visit sites to analysis software internet reference.

(p.211)

Choose an invasion game where opponents are in direct competition with one another (e.g. hockey, netball, rugby, football, basketball, etc.) and attempt to design and complete your own simple player analysis. Focus on one player involved in the match and gather data on one aspect of skill or technique (e.g. passing) used in the activity selected.

You can look at the number of passes made in a set time period. This can then be expressed as a ratio or percentage of successful passes during the time observed.

No solutions – own design/solutions.

(p.213)

Think about and write down three pieces of information a rugby coach might receive from a GPS tracking system during training and matches.
- Metres being covered (i.e. overall distances)
- Level of fatigue/amount of effort being made/ effort in attack and defence
- Technical success rates; monitor performance levels
- Force being applied into tackles (i.e. G-forces)
- Speed of performers/dynamic acceleration
- Player heart rate
- Recovery time of a player

Answers to Practice questions

(p.215)

1 **Which of the following statements best describes 'objective data' in relation to a netball performer?**
   a) **Her shooting technique looked poor at times.**
   b) **Her passing technique looked good in the match.**
   c) **Her shooting technique in the match was 80 per cent overall.**
   d) **Moving free was the weakest aspect of her performance.**
   c) Her shooting technique in the match was 80 per cent overall.

2 **Define and give examples of quantitative data research in relation to assessing an individual's physical fitness levels.**
   - Quantitative data research is formal, objective and provides factual information/numerical data.
   - Examples include the multi-stage fitness test, VO_2 max test, skinfold measurements, vertical jump test, agility run test, etc.

3 Technology can be used to optimise performance over a long-term timeframe (e.g. months). Identify possible benefits of using video technology to help refine technique towards 'the perfect model'.
- Decreases injury risk
- Develops more efficient movement patterns
- Improves performance overall via increased accuracy

4 Define the term 'indirect calorimetry'.

The measurement of the amount of heat generated in an oxidation reaction by determining the intake or consumption of oxygen or by measuring the amount of carbon dioxide released and translating these quantities into a heat equivalent.

Glossary

Adrenaline – A stress hormone that is released by the sympathetic nerves and cardiac nerve during exercise which causes an increase in heart rate.

Affective component of attitude – Relates to feelings and interpretation such as enjoyment.

Aggressive cue hypothesis – Aggression is caused by a learned trigger.

Agonist – The muscle that is responsible for the movement that is occurring.

Amateur – A person who plays sport for the love of it and receives no financial gain.

Angina – Chest pain that occurs when the blood supply through the coronary arteries to the muscles of the heart is restricted.

Antagonist – The muscle that works in opposition to the agonist to help produce a coordinated movement.

Area of support base – The larger the area the greater the stability.

Arousal – A level of activation, a degree of readiness to perform.

Arteriovenous difference – The difference between the oxygen content of the arterial blood arriving at the muscles and the venous blood leaving the muscles.

Articulating bones – Bones that meet and move at the joint.

Associative stage of learning – The second stage of learning as motor programmes are developed.

Atheroma – A fatty deposit found in the inner lining of an artery.

Atherosclerosis – This occurs when arteries harden and become clogged up by fatty deposits.

ATP-PC system – An energy system that provides quick bursts of energy and is used for high intensity exercise. It can only last for up to ten seconds.

Autonomous stage of learning – The final stage of learning used by an expert.

Balanced diet – A diet containing a variety of foods from each of the food groups so that there is an adequate intake of nutrients.

Ballistic stretching – Involves performing a stretch with swinging or bouncing movements to push a body part even further.

Behavioural component of attitude – The actions of the performer.

Behaviourist theory – Explains how actions are links to stimuli.

Bilateral transfer – When the learning of one skill is passed across the body from limb to limb.

Blood pressure – The force exerted by the blood against the blood vessel wall.

Bohr shift – When an increase in blood carbon dioxide and a decrease in pH results in a return of the affinity of haemoglobin for oxygen.

Bradycardia – A decrease in resting heart rate to below 60 beats a minute.

Buffering – The ability of the blood to compensate for the buildup of lactic acid or hydrogen ions to maintain the pH level.

Cardiac hypertrophy – The thickening of the muscular wall of the heart so it becomes bigger and stronger. It can also can mean a larger ventricular cavity.

Carron's antecedents – The factors that might influence cohesion.

Catharsis – Cleansing the emotions by using sport as an outlet for aggression.

Chaining – Linking the sub-routines or parts of a task when practising.

Channelling – The pushing of ethnic minorities into or away from certain sports or positions within a team.

Cilia – Microscopic, hair-like projections that help to sweep away fluids and particles.

Co-action – When others do the task at the same time but separately.

Cognitive anxiety – Psychological anxiety.

Cognitive component of attitude – A belief, such as the belief in the ability to win.

Cognitive dissonance – New information given to the performer to cause unease and motivate change.

Cognitive stage of learning – The first stage of learning used by a novice.

Cohesion – The tendency for individuals to work together to achieve their goals and the forces that keep the group members on task.

Commercialisation of sport – The process of trying to gain money from sporting activities.

Competition period – The performance period where skills and techniques are refined.

Competitive sport Anxiety Inventory (CSAI) – A questionnaire used by sports psychologists to measure anxiety.

Concentric contraction – When a muscle shortens under tension.

Constructivism – Building up learning in stages based on the current level of performance.

COPD – Chronic obstructive pulmonary disease is the name for a collection of diseasessuch as emphysema.

County sport partnerships (CSPs) – National networks of local agencies working together to increase numbers in sport and physical activity.

Creatine – A compound the body makes that supplies energy for muscular contraction. It can also be used as a supplement to increase athletic performance.

Credulous approach – When the link between personality and behaviour is accepted.

Diffusion – The movement of gas molecules from an area of high concentration or partial pressure to an area of low concentration or partial pressure.

Disability – Physical, sensory or mental impairment which adversely affects performance.

Discrete skill – A skill that has a clear beginning and end.

Discrimination – The unfair treatment of a person or a minority group.

Distributed practice – Involves rest intervals between practice sessions.

Dominant response – The stand-out response that the performer thinks is correct.

Dorsi-flexion – Pulling the toes up to the shin.

Drive reduction – An endoftask period when performance may get worse.

Eccentric contraction – When a muscle lengthens under tension or performs negative work and acts like a brake.

Effort – The force applied by the user of the lever system.

Equal opportunities – The right to access the same opportunities regardless of factors such as race, age, gender and ability.

Ethnic groups – People who have racial, religious or linguistic traits in common.

Evaluation apprehension – The perceived fear of being judged.

Externallypaced skill – When the performer has no control over the start and the speed of the skill.

Extension – Increasing the angel between the bones of a joint.

Extrovert – A person with a loud, bright personality.

Feedback – Information to assist error correction.

First class lever – The fulcrum lies between the effort and the resistance.

Flexion – Decreasing the angle between the bones of a joint.

Foot racing – Historically a form of competitive running/walking involving feats of endurance.

Frontal plane – Divides the body into front and back halves.

Fulcrum – The point about which the lever rotates.

Gender socialisation – The act of learning to conform to culturally defined gender roles through socialisation.

Glycaemic index – This ranks carbohydrates according to their effect on our blood glucose levels.

Glycogen – The stored form of glucose found in the muscles and the liver.

Gogli tendon organs – These are activated when there is a tension in a muscle.

Golden triangle – The relationship between sport, the media and business.

Haemoglobin – An ironcontaining pigment found in red blood cells which combines with oxygen to form oxyhaemoglobin.

Harvard step test – This involves stepping up and down on a bench to a set rhythm for five minutes. Recovery heart rates are then recorded.

Hyper-extension – Increasing the angle beyond 180° between the bones of a joint.

Infographics – A graphic visual representation of information, data or knowledge intended to represent information quickly and clearly.

Insight learning – Using experience and understanding to solve problems relating to the whole skill.

Instinct theory – When aggression is spontaneous and innate.

Interaction When a group works together to produce results.

Inter-psychological learning – Learning from others externally.

Internalisation – The learning of values and attitudes that are incorporated within yourself.

Intra-psychological learning – Learning from within after gaining external knowledge from others.

Isometric contraction – When a muscle is under tension but there is no visible movement.

Lewin's formula – Behaviour is a function of personality and environment.

Longitudinal axis – Runs from the top to the bottom of the body.

Macrocycle – A period of training involving a longterm performance goal.

Mental practice – Going over the skill in the mind without movement.

Mesocycle – Usually a 4 to 12week period of training with a particular focus such as power.

Metabolic cart – A device which works by attaching headgear to a subject while they breathe a specific amount of oxygen over a period of time.

Micocycle – The description of a week or a few days of training sessions.

Motor neurons – Nerve cells which transmit the brain's instructions as electrical impulses to the muscles.

Muscle spindles – These detect how far and how fast a muscle is being stretched and produce the stretch reflex.

Negative transfer – When the learning of one skill hinders the learning of another.

Operant conditioning – The use of reinforcement to ensure that correct responses are repeated.

Outcome goal – A goal set against the performance of others and based on a result.

Parasympathetic system – A part of the autonomic nervous system that decreases heart rate.

Peak flow experience – The ultimate intrinsic experience felt by athletes from a positive mental attitude, with supreme confidence, focus and efficiency.

Peaking – Planning and organising training so a performer is at their peak both physically and mentally, for a major competition.

Performance analysis (PA) – The provision of objective feedback to a performer who is trying to get a positive change in performance.

Periodisation – The division of the training year into specific sections for a specific purpose.

Plantar-flexion – Pointing the toes/pushing up on your toes.

Plateau – A period of no improvement in performance.

Positive transfer – When the learning of one skill helps the learning of another.

Professional – A person who plays sport for financial gain.

Progressive part practice – Practising the first part of a skill then adding parts gradually.

Purkinje fibres – Muscle fibres that conduct impulses in the walls of the ventricles.

Rating perceived exertion (RPE) – Giving an opinion as to how hard your body is working during exercise.

Rational recreation – The postindustrial development of sport.

Resistance – The weight to be moved by the lever system.

Retention – The ability to remember important information and recall it from the memory system.

Ringelmann effect – When group performance decreases with group size.

Sagittal axis – Runs from front to back of the body.

Sagittal plane – Divides the body into right and left halves.

Sceptical approach – When the link between personality and behaviour is doubted.

Second class lever – The resistance is between the fulcrum and the effort.

Social action theory – A way of viewing socialisation, emphasising social action.

Social development – Learning by association with others.

Social learning theory – Learning by associating with othersand copying behaviour.

Social loafing – Individual loss of motivation in a team player due to lack of performance identification when individual efforts are not recognised.

Somatic anxiety – Physiological anxiety.

Sponsorship – Companies paying for goods to be publicly displayed or advertised at sporting events.

Sports Competition Anxiety Test (SCAT) – A questionnaire used by sports psychologists to measure anxiety.

Stacking – The disproportionate concentration of ethnic minorities in a sports team.

Static stretching – When the muscle is held in a stationary position for 30 seconds or more.

Steady state – Where the athlete is able to meet the oxygen demand with the oxygen supply.

Stroke – A stroke occurs when the blood supply to the brain is cut off.

Stroke volume – The volume of blood pumped out by the heart ventricles in each contraction.

Sympathetic system – A part of the autonomic nervous system that speeds up heart rate.

Tapering – Reducing the volume and/or intensity of training prior to competition.

Tetanic contraction – A sustained muscle contraction caused by a series of fast repeating stimuli.

Third class lever – The effort is between the fulcrum and the resistance.

Tidal volume – Volume of air breathed in or out per breath.

Transverse axis – Runs from side to side across the body.

Transverse plane – Divides the body into upper and lower halves.

Triadic model – The three parts of an attitude: cognitive, affective, behavioural.

Vascular shunt mechanism – The redistribution of cardiac output.

Venous return – The return of blood back to the right side of the heart via the vena cava.

Video motion analysis – A technique used to get information about moving objects from video.

Whole practice – Performing a skill in its entirety without breaking it into subroutines.

Wholepartwhole practice – Assessing a skill, identifying a weakness to practise, then putting the skill back together.

Zero transfer – When the learning of one skill has no impact on the learning of another.

Index